Handbook of
Classical Mythology

TITLES IN ABC-CLIO'S
Handbooks of World Mythology

Handbook of Classical Mythology

William Hansen

A B C CLIO

Santa Barbara, California • Denver, Colorado • Oxford, England

Copyright 2004 by William Hansen

Library of Congress Cataloging-in-Publication Data

Hansen, William F., 1941-
 Handbook of classical mythology / William Hansen.
  p. cm. — (Handbooks of world mythology)
 Includes bibliographical references and index.
  ISBN 1-57607-226-6 (hardcover : alk. paper) — ISBN 1-85109-634-5 (eBook)
 1. Mythology, Classical.   I. Title.   II. Series.

BL723.H36   2004
292.1'3 — dc22

2004004434

08 07 06 05 04   10 9 8 7 6 5 4 3 2 1

This book is also available on the World Wide Web as an e-book.
Visit abc-clio.com for details.

ABC-CLIO, Inc.
130 Cremona Drive, P.O. Box 1911
Santa Barbara, California 93116–1911
This book is printed on acid-free paper.
Manufactured in the United States of America

for my daughter Inge

CONTENTS

PREFACE

Like *Star Wars* or *The Lord of the Rings* or the fictional Old West or feudal Japan in samurai films, classical mythology consists not only of a corpus of stories but also of a world, one with a geography and a history as well as relationships and rules and narrative conventions. Whereas most works on classical mythology focus their attention on the stories, neglecting the world in which they are situated, the present book explores both elements in an effort to give each its due. The result is a sort of ethnography of the imaginary.

Accordingly, I treat classical mythology as a largely self-contained system that can be enjoyed and appreciated as such, an approach that is possible because the ancient mythological narratives transpire in a fairly consistent world in terms of setting, characters, and conventions, even when the texts in which they are preserved are centuries apart in date, for despite an increase in geographical knowledge and a less earnest attitude toward the gods on the part of sophisticated persons, later mythographers retain the largely fabulous physical world of early Greek narrators and continue to retail essentially the same myths and legends. An acquaintance with other aspects of classical culture such as literature, art, religion, history, philosophy, science, and the Greek and Latin languages will deepen one's understanding of classical mythology, but an appreciation of its story-world should be the first step.

Although the present book stands by itself as an introduction to classical mythology, it can also serve as a supplement to other modern works on classical mythology or as a companion to accompany the reading of ancient authors of mythologically rich works such as Homer, Hesiod, the composers of the *Homeric Hymns*, the Greek tragedians, Apollodoros, and Ovid.

In writing this book I have benefited from the inspiration of many persons in the present and the past, of whom I wish to mention my wife, Mary Beth, and two friends with a passion for myth, Alexander (Luke) Russell and Gregory Schrempp.

William Hansen, 2004

A NOTE ON THE USE OF ANCIENT TEXTS

Citations of ancient Greek and Roman authors are of two basic types.

1. Most works are conventionally divided into books or chapters or verses or pages, much like the Bible, so that they are customarily cited by these conventional divisions. Accordingly a citation is the same whether one consults the original ancient text or a modern translation (for example, Genesis 2: 2–4, Homer *Iliad* 4.1–10, Apollodorus *Library* 2.5.9). Since the translation of Greek and Latin texts in the present work are my own, I cite these works in this way.

2. But in a few instances, such as in collections of fragments, the enumeration is not conventional but peculiar to a particular editor. In these cases, in order to refer to a particular passage of an ancient author, one mentions the editor whose edition one is using, for example, ancient author + fragment number + last name of editor. Thus Hesiod frag. 3 MW signifies the third fragment of Hesiod in the compilation edited by Merkelbach and West.

INTRODUCTION

The gods have devised a destiny for wretched mortals,
to live in misery, while they themselves are free of cares.

—HOMER *ILIAD* 24.525–526

On a hot day some twenty-five centuries ago, Socrates and one of his companions, Phaidros, were walking alongside the cool stream of the Ilissos outside the walls of Athens. "Tell me, Socrates," said Phaidros, "wasn't it from the Ilissos somewhere around here that Boreas is said to have carried off Oreithyia?" He was thinking of the myth according to which a daughter of the king of Athens was playing on the banks of the stream when suddenly the god of the north wind abducted her, carrying her off to his northerly kingdom. "Yes, that's what they say." "Was it from here, then?" "No," Socrates replied, "the spot is actually some distance downstream, at the place where you cross over to the precinct of Agra. There is an altar of Boreas somewhere around there." Phaidros asked if Socrates believed the story was true. Socrates replied that clever men might explain the story away by saying, for example, that the force of the north wind pushed the girl off the nearby rocks as she was playing and that after she had died in this way people said she had been taken away by Boreas. After all, he said, such men take pains to rationalize the centaurs, Chimaeras, Gorgons, and other strange creatures. As for himself, having no time to waste on such speculations, he was content to accept the usual beliefs about them.[1]

This passage offers a glimpse into an ancient society in which mythology was a part of everyday life. Phaidros and Socrates were familiar enough with the myth of Boreas and Oreithyia that a bare allusion was sufficient to bring the story to mind: "Tell me, Socrates, wasn't it from somewhere around here by the Ilissos that Boreas is said to have carried off Oreithyia?" We learn that Athenians generally accepted the myth as true, for Socrates says that he has no time to waste in explaining this or that myth away and is content to accept the customary beliefs about them. In fact, the exact spot where the abduction had taken place was not only remembered but even regarded as sacred, for an altar had been set up there. Nevertheless, a skeptical minority rejected elements of the old stories that were inconsistent with their own experience of the world, in this case the representation of the north wind as a living being who might take a human maiden for his bride. It appears that the question of the truth or falsity of the myth of Boreas and Oreithyia was a perfectly reasonable topic of discussion among intelligent adults, and an acceptance of the literal truth of the myth was possible for an independent thinker such as Socrates. Even the skeptical few did not discard the tradition in toto, only the parts that were counterexperiential, accepting the rest as historical.[2]

BASIC CONCEPTS

The Greeks conceived of the history of the universe as falling into three great eras according to the dominant players in each era: gods, heroes, and humans. The gods preceded the great men and women of old, and the heroes and heroines in their turn yielded the world stage to ordinary humans.[3] Generically speaking, narrative accounts of the events in the three periods of time correspond respectively to our terms *myth, heroic legend,* and *history.*

This book focuses upon the first two eras and therefore upon the first two genres, myth and heroic legend, which taken together can be called *mythology.* Since classical myths and heroic legends developed largely before the historical period and the events are set mostly in the prehistoric period, classical mythology could be called the traditional prehistory of the classical lands, Greece and Rome.

Greek and Roman myths and legends are essentially *stories.* Since they are anonymous narratives that were transmitted from one person to another and from one generation to the next, they can be further described as *traditional* stories. And since for the most part they developed at a time when writing was unknown or little used, they are mostly *oral* stories.

A traditional story ordinarily differs in several ways from literary fiction such as a short story. First, a traditional story has numerous composers, for each person who transmits it shapes it in some way. Originally all such stories were transmitted orally, but in literate societies traditional stories can be transmitted also in writing. Second, for the most part their composers are anonymous. Third, the text of a traditional story is not fixed but emergent, in that it is sensitive to an interplay of factors including the narrator, the narrator's competence, the genre, the situation, the audience, and the goals of the participants (Bauman 1984, 37–45). Characteristically, the texts of a traditional story show variation and geographical distribution, since different persons in different places relate the story, and no two of them do so in precisely the same way.

Since a traditional story possesses no fixed or proper form, its shape and content reflect the narrator's response to the particular occasion that calls forth the tale. The poet Hesiod twice describes the creation of the first woman.[4] In one poem he says that two deities (Hephaistos and Athena) fashion and dress her and that she is Zeus's gift of evil to men, whereas in another poem he recounts how she is fashioned and attired by many deities (Hephaistos, Athena, the Hours, the Graces, Aphroditê, and Hermes), is given the name Pandora, acquires a husband Epimetheus, and finally opens a fateful jar, from which terrible evils escape into the world. The two versions differ drastically in emphasis and content, reflecting the nature of the context in which each is employed. In his *Theogony*, Hesiod focuses primarily upon the constituents of the world, so that he is interested in the first woman primarily as a representative of mortal women. In the *Works and Days*, he is interested rather in the quality and conditions of human life, so that here he calls attention to the entry into human life of miseries such as toil and diseases. Since every narration is motivated, the myth of the first woman has no neutral or normal form. Hesiod slants each narration to its situational context.

Mythological narratives are generally represented by their narrators as accounts of events that actually happened, and for this reason their principal characters tend to be named persons with genealogical connections to other characters known from myth and legend, and the events are set at a definite point in space and time. So in the myth of the north wind's abduction of a maiden, the principal characters are Boreas (the north wind) and Oreithyia (an Athenian princess), the scene of the abduction is the bank of the Ilissos at the place where one crosses over to the precinct of Agra, and chronologically the events are set during the reign of the girl's father, Erechtheus, who according to tradition was an early king of Athens. These details of person, place, and time lent credibility to the story, which was reinforced by the fact that the exact spot of the abduction was known and physically marked by an altar, and most Athenians of Socrates's day, it appears, accepted the tradition as true. In short, it was a belief-story, a narrative that was told and received by most persons as essentially accurate. With regard to its classification as a mythological narrative, it makes no difference whether the narrative really preserves traces of an actual event or not, for just as no one in Socrates's day could have known if the story of Boreas and Oreithyia reflected an actual occurrence, no one in our day can either.

In contrast to myths and legends, folktales are presented as fictional accounts, and for this reason their characters are mostly unnamed (for example: a princess, a lion, an Athenian) or bear generic names, and their action takes place in generic settings (town, countryside, on a road) and in the indefinite past. For example, in an ancient Greek folktale, a man who was cutting wood beside a river dropped his axe. The stream carried it off, whereupon the man sat on the bank and wept. Taking pity on him, the god Hermes came and asked him why he was crying. After the woodcutter told him, the god went down into the water, brought up a gold axe, and asked the man if it was his. When the man said that it was not, the deity brought up a silver axe, asking if this was the one he had lost. After the man said that this was not his either, the god finally brought him his own axe. The man acknowledged it as his, and in recognition of his honesty the god let him have all three axes. The woodcutter joined his companions and recounted what had happened to him, after which one of them went to the same river, deliberately threw his axe into the current, and began to wail. Hermes appeared as before, fetched a gold axe, and asked him if it was his. When the man greedily said that it was, Hermes gave him neither the gold axe nor his original axe.[5]

The narrator of this tale does not name the honest and the dishonest wood-cutters or situate the events in a particular locality or at a particular time. It was unimportant to him to convince anyone that the events really occurred, for the point of the narration was to amuse or to illustrate a moral principle or both. The mythological genres of myth and heroic legend differ as a group from the nonmythological genre of folktale in their quality of *alleged historicity*, and this variable affects their form in several ways, such as in their being framed as specific or indefinite narratives.

Let us look more closely at the two temporal periods in which classical mythology is set. First is the era of the gods, the principal characters of narrative concern in the early cosmos. The category "gods" is a broad one, inasmuch as it includes not only the familiar gods of cult as well as many other major and minor deities but also physical parts of the cosmos such as the earth, the sky, and the luminaries, which in Greek mythology are divine beings. Stories dealing with this period tell how the world came into being and how cosmic order was established. They recount how the principal gods were born and acquired their individual prerogatives (how Zeus came to be ruler of the gods, how Apollon came to be in charge of prophecy, and so on) and how their cults were founded. The myths tell how the first humans came into being, what their relationship to the gods is, and why the quality of human life is such as it is. Traditional oral stories set in this period are termed *myths*, their principal characters are usually gods, their setting is the remote past, and their overt topics are mostly the establishment of the cosmos and the relationship of its constituent parts (Bascom 1965). Myths are primordial and foundational, and they are also totalizing in that, unlike modern science, they offer an explanation for everything, the whole universe and all that is in it.[6]

Second is the era of heroes and heroines, the memorable men and women of the past and their contemporaries, who lived before our time, which Herodotos calls the "human era." Those persons settled lands, established great families, overcame terrifying monsters, founded cities, engaged in memorable wars, and undertook difficult quests, including journeys to the realm of the dead. They were beings of great passion and ambition and talent, having in some cases divine blood in their veins, and they lived life in a big way. Traditional oral stories that tell of such persons and are set in this period can be called *heroic legends*. Typically the principal characters are members of prominent families, and temporally their setting is the more recent past. Legends can be foundational, like myths, but on a local level. When the god Zeus overcomes the monster Typhon and organizes the cosmos, we have myth; when the hero Kadmos overcomes a dragon and founds the city of Thebes, we have heroic legend.

The distinction between myth and heroic legend as discrete genres of traditional narrative is, however, an ideal one, for many stories do not fall neatly into one category or the other. The narrative of the Great Deluge is usually called a myth, and yet the characters of principal interest are human beings, the flood hero and his wife. In contrast, the story of Hades's abduction of Persephonê focuses principally upon gods, but the events transpire in a world of humans, as usually is the case in accounts of culture heroes. The alleged historicity of myths and legends as opposed to folktales is also an unreliable criterion, since the same legend can be accepted as essentially true by one person and rejected as ridiculous by another, and similarly the same myth can be widely believed in one century and disbelieved in another.

Since mythology consists of stories, it is not identical with religion, in which persons express in belief and action their reverence toward supernatural beings. But there is an obvious overlap between the two in that mythological characters include many of the gods and heroes of cult, and mythological narratives can be associated with particular cults in different ways. For example, a story may include an action that is treated as a precedent in cult. Demeter carried a torch and drank a particular beverage in the course of her search for her daughter, and so her worshippers also bear torches and drink this drink. A story may give an *aition*, or cause, for a cult. After the people of Corinth murdered the children of Jason and Medeia, an oracle instructed the Corinthians to institute regular rites in honor of the children, which they did. A story may gloss a commemorative rite or object. Apollon appeared in a dream to a man trapped in a cavern, instructing him to lacerate his body. He did so, and vultures, taking him for dead, flew down into the cavern and by means of their claws carried him out. In honor of his rescue, the man constructed an altar for Apollon of the Vultures.

HOW CLASSICAL MYTHOLOGY CAME INTO BEING

How did classical mythology come into being? Has all of it survived? How do we know about it today? Although we cannot discover in detail how classical mythology developed, we can sketch in broad lines an outline of its history and transmission.

A Mix of Traditions

When the proto-Greeks began entering the Balkan Peninsula around 2000 B.C., they carried religious and narrative traditions with them. Since they were speakers of an Indo-European language, some traditions were developments of their Indo-European inheritance, as we can infer from parallels in other Indo-European peoples. Certain features of Greek mythology, such as polytheism, anthropomorphic deities, and traditions about the past structured as narratives and transmitted orally, were characteristic of all ancient societies of which we have much knowledge and were not peculiarly Greek. In other respects the newcomers borrowed much from local and neighboring peoples, since the Greeks, like most other polytheistic peoples, displayed a nonexclusive attitude toward religious traditions, making the assumption that other societies worshipped many of the same deities as they themselves did and allowing that different nations called their deities by different names if for no other reason than that they spoke different languages. Because of this attitude, the Greeks readily identified their own deities with similar deities of other nations and sometimes took over associated mythological narratives. They also borrowed the cults and mythology of foreign deities with no Greek analogues, adapting them to their own religious and mythological system.

We can broadly distinguish three ingredients of Greek mythology, as of Greek culture generally: a substratum made up of borrowings from local, prehellenic peoples such as the Pelasgians and the inhabitants of Minoan Crete; a superstratum consisting of the Greek reworking of their own Indo-European inheritance; and an adstratal element made up of borrowings from the peoples of Asia Minor, the Near East, and elsewhere (Puhvel 1987, 126–143). An instance of a substratal feature is the myth underlying Zeus's birth and rearing in a cave on Crete. Superstratal elements include the name and province of the sky-god Zeus, corresponding to the Vedic sky-god Dyaus, and the Divine Twins, who in Greek tradition are known collectively as the Dioskouroi (Latinized form = Dioscuri), or "Sons of Zeus," corresponding to the Vedic Asvins. A few narratives appear to derive from the Indo-European repertory, such as the legend of the hero who commits three grave offenses, told in Greek tradition of Herakles and in Scandinavian tradition of Starkad.[7] Likely to be Indo-European are the notions that the gods speak a language of their own and that they imbibe a special beverage of undeath that renders them immortal and unaging. At the adstratal level are myths that the Greeks borrowed from their eastern neighbors, including the Succession Myth, the Combat Myth, and the Flood Myth, and some types of monsters such as the Sphinx that the Greeks adapted from Near Eastern prototypes.

The Archaic Period

The collapse of the prosperous and militant Mycenaean civilization of the Late Bronze Age around 1200 B.C. was followed by a period of political and material decline in Greece, during which many mainlanders emigrated to Asia Minor. In time they idealized the Mycenaean Age as a glorious period of heroes, closeness to the gods, material wealth, and grand military efforts such as the great campaign against Troy, crystallizing these qualities and events in story (Bowra 1964). Particular heroes of legend came to be associated with prominent and prosperous cities of the Late Bronze Age (Nilsson 1965).

In addition, the panhellenic movement that began around the eighth century B.C. and extended into the classical period led to the development of cultural institutions that fostered communication among the Greek city-states, emphasizing elements that were common to different Greek groups and de-emphasizing those that were regional and divisive (Nagy 1990, 52–115). Among these developments were the foundation of panhellenic shrines and cults at Delphi (the oracle of Apollon), Delos (the sanctuary of Delian Apollon), and Eleusis (the Eleusinian Mysteries) and the institution of panhellenic games at Olympia, which according to tradition were founded in 776 B.C. The same culturally centripetal force that played down local traditions fostered the formation of the panhellenic Olympian mythology that is found in the Homeric epics, the Hesiodic epics, and the Homeric Hymns.

The Homeric and Hesiodic poems, the oldest of which appear to date from the eighth century, did much to codify for the Greeks the way their gods looked and acted, just as the vase-painters and sculptors did much to codify how satyrs, centaurs, and other strange beings looked. Early Greek epic poetry, including also the cyclic epics, translated informal oral traditions into formal verse compositions. The myths and legends underlying these works gave accounts of the world from its beginning to the end of the heroic age. They established the basic characters, relationships, setting, events, and conventions of Greek mythology.

In later times this early Greek epic poetry, written down or in some cases composed in writing, served Greeks and Romans as great storehouses of mythological information. From the seventh century B.C. onward, written works were supplemented by a rich tradition of mythological art, especially vase-painting and statuary.[8]

The Classical Period

The myths and legends that made up traditional Greek prehistory were widely recognized as a distinct class of story. Prose compilations began appearing in the sixth century and continued to be made throughout the classical period, such as those by Pherekydes of Athens and Hellanikos of Lesbos.[9] The fifth-century historian Herodotos distinguishes traditions about men of distant times such as King Minos of Crete from those about men of more recent times such as Polykrates of Samos, who lived in what Herodotos calls the human age.[10] Pindar and other lyric poets drew upon this body of myths and heroic legends for their exempla, and the Athenian tragedians mined the legends of the heroic age for the plots of nearly every tragic drama they wrote. Thus in Pindar's *First Olympian Ode*, where he sings the praises of Hieron of Syracuse, winner of the single-horse race in the Olympic Games of 476 B.C., the poet recounts the story of the hero Pelops, who won his wife, Hippodameia, in a chariot race. Although mythology ostensibly focused upon the past, it often served as a means for speaking and thinking about the present.

The inherited stories were not without their critics and skeptics. Some persons were offended by the immoral behavior of the gods in mythological narratives, an objection that sprang from the feeling that the gods should behave, not with the license of a class of powerful beings, but as exemplars of moral behavior. If gods were the best of beings, their behavior should also be the best. Other critics objected to the pervasive element of the fabulous, which was inconsistent with their own empirical experience of the world. Fabulous elements seemed infantile.

Rationalist interpretations of mythological narratives appeared early and were widespread, as in the passage from Plato with which this chapter begins. When Phaidros asked if Socrates believed that the story of the abduction of the maiden Oreithyia by Boreas was true, Socrates answered that clever men might explain the story away by saying that the force of the north wind pushed the girl off a rock as she was playing and that after she had died in this way people said she had been taken away by Boreas, for such men take pains to rationalize the centaurs, Chimaeras, Gorgons, and other strange creatures. This approach was codified in Palaiphatos's *On Unbelievable Tales*, which probably dates from the late fourth century B.C., the earliest surviving treatise on the interpretation of mythology.[11] Palaiphatos codified the rationalistic approach to the fabulous elements in Greek myths and especially legends. He states as a principle that if something does not exist in his own day, it did not exist in the past either. He means that since centaurs, for example, were not seen in fourth-century Greece, they must not have been seen in earlier times either, for which reason one should conclude that they never existed at all. Holding that all fabulous elements of traditional prehistory arose through misunderstanding, he offers explanations for the incredible motifs found in many familiar stories, such as that the idea of Amazons arose from a misunderstanding of male warriors who, like certain peoples of his own day, wore long robes, bound their hair, and shaved their faces and thus might appear to be women. Since no army of women was attested in Palaiphatos's day, he asserts that none existed in earlier times either.

Skepticism regarding the gods and their myths is already attested in the sixth century B.C. The presocratic philosopher Xenophanes of Colophon rejected the anthropomorphism of the gods, saying that humans have merely projected their own qualities onto their deities by imagining that they were born, wear clothes, speak, and have humanlike bodies. He declared that if horses or lions could draw, they would portray their gods in the form of horses or lions. Xenophanes was not an atheist, for he asserted that there was one god, who was unlike mortals in body or in thought. The representation by Homer and Hesiod of the gods as thieves and adulterers and deceivers was also offensive to him.[12] Since Xenophanes denied the gods humanoid bodies and humanlike speech and other behavior, since indeed he denied a plurality of gods, he must also have rejected the traditional stories about the gods, for if the gods did not look and behave much like humans, then the myths of their mating and struggles and so on were impossibilities.

A different kind of interpreter of myth was Theagenes of Rhegion, who lived in the late sixth century. Theagenes's solution was to understand offensive mythological passages in Homer, not literally, but allegorically. Some critics were offended by Homer's representing the gods behaving in an unseemly way, such as in the battle of the gods in the twentieth book of the *Iliad*. But for Theagenes the passage is really about the strife of natural elements. Properly understood, the scene is not offensive at all, since it actually conveys in a veiled way a higher truth about the nature of the cosmos: dry wars with moist, heat with cold, and light with heavy, since water can extinguish fire, and fire can dry up water. For every element in the cosmos, Theagenes said, there is a contrary element, though the totality itself is constant and eternal. Homer expresses this natural strife poetically in the form of a divine battle, in which he can represent fire as Apollon, Helios, or Hephaistos and water as Poseidon or the Scamander River. Similarly, he can represent the moon metaphorically as Artemis, the air as Hera, understanding as Athena, desire as Aphroditê, reason as Hermes, and so on.[13]

So far as we know, Theagenes was the first person to interpret mythology as allegory, the notion that the true significance of a mythological text lies in the form of a secret, or at least unobvious, subtext that is accessible to those who know how to unlock it and understand it aright. The early allegorists defended Homer from critics who, like Xenophanes, were offended by Homer's representation of the gods' immorality, for the allegorists argued that such passages were deliberate allegories on the part of the poet, who wished to convey physical or ethical truths metaphorically.

The allegorism of Theagenes and the rationalism of Palaiphatos represent two basic approaches to the interpretation of mythology that in one form or another have enjoyed a continuous and vigorous life from antiquity to our own day. They represent a middle way between a literal acceptance of mythological tradition and a wholesale rejection of it, salvaging it by understanding it in a special way. The allegorists were the first to interpret mythology symbolically, holding that mythological things and events should be understood metaphorically, whereas the palaephatists codified the rationalist trend, deeming that mythology should be understood literally and that its unrealistic elements resulted from misunderstandings of historic events. For the allegorist mythology was a treasure of truth; for the rationalist, it was a junk heap of human error.

The Hellenistic and Imperial Periods

After the conquest of Greece by Alexander the Great, the Greek city-states lost their independence and along with it the institutions that belonged to free and relatively cohesive communities. Culture became more fragmented and specialized. Hellenistic high culture was characterized by antiquarianism, scholarship, intellectualism, and an interest in local and regional traditions, reversing the panhellenic trend that began in the eighth century. Some disused genres were revived, notably epic, but as a purely literary genre rather than as an oral form, as in Apollonios (Apollonius) of Rhodes's *Argonautika*, or *Voyage of the Argo*. The manner of retelling the old stories also changed. Whereas the early poets preferred to narrate myths and legends with an objective stance, poets of the Hellenistic and Imperial periods showed a subjective interest in the feelings of the characters. How did Medeia feel as she fell in love with Jason? What was it like to be metamorphosed into a tree?

The Hellenistic and Imperial periods were the heyday of prose mythography. Some authors wrote books that elucidated the myths and legends found in or alluded to by major poets such as Homer and Pindar. Other authors published collections of myths or legends focused upon a particular theme such as metamorphosis, romance, or catasterism. A number of these works survive to our day, including the *Metamorphoses* of Antoninus Liberalis, the *Pathemata* of Parthenios, the *Catasterisms* of Pseudo-Eratosthenes, and the *Narratives* of Konon. The *Metamorphoses* of the Roman poet Ovid, one of the most beloved and influential of all works of classical mythology, is a poetic elaboration of the genre of mythological compilation organized around a particular theme.

In addition to thematic collections, some authors produced handbooks that treated all of Greek mythology. The most important of these to survive is Apollodoros's (Latinized = Apollodorus) *Library*, a retelling of Greek mythology in the form of a continuous narrative from the beginning of the cosmos till the end of the heroic age. Also useful is Hyginus's *Fabulae*, or *Stories*, a Latin (or Latinized) handbook of mythology organized as a lexicon. These eclectic compilations drew upon the early Greek epics, the early prose mythographers, and the Greek tragedians, among other sources.

Interpretatio Romana

A momentous event in the history of Greek mythology was its gradual and wholesale adoption by the Romans, another Indo-European-speaking people, resulting in *classical* mythology.[14] We can distinguish three components in the process. First, the Romans adopted Greek narrative traditions about the prehistory of the cosmos from the beginning till the end of the heroic period, taking over Greek myths and heroic legends and making them their own. Their assimilation of Greek traditional prehistory was possible in part because native Roman traditions focused upon human events in Italy itself, so that there was little competition between Roman and Greek views of the early history of the world. The Greek historian Dionysios of Halikarnassos comments appreciatively upon a total absence of myths about Ouranos, Kronos, Zeus, Tartaros, and so on, among the Romans, for which he credits Romulus, who in the course of founding Rome and establishing its institutions wisely got rid of all the traditional stories that represented the gods behaving in a scandalous manner.[15]

These borrowings from the Greeks must have taken place both from the bottom up and the top down over a long period of time. Literate adults who had the leisure and resources for education and reading could get their mythology from books, whereas the children of families with Greek slaves might learn theirs orally from their Greek nannies and tutors, and soldiers heard foreign traditions while abroad doing military duty. It did not always come easily. In his *Satyrica,* the Roman novelist Petronius portrays a Roman nouveau riche who wishes to show off his knowledge of Greek literature and mythology but gets it only half-right: "Do you remember," Trimalchio asks a dinner guest, "the twelve labors of Hercules or the story about Ulysses and how the Cyclops broke off his thumb with pincers? When I was a boy, I used to read these stories in Homer."[16] Trimalchio would not have found an account of Hercules's labors in Homer, and though he could have found the story of Odysseus (Latinized form = Ulysses), the hero did not lose his thumb. Trimalchio's aspiration to appear learned in Greek culture indicates that such an accomplishment was prestigious for a Roman of his day.

Second, the Romans mostly retained their own deities but identified them with the Greek deities to whom they appeared most closely to correspond, deciding that Roman Jupiter was the same as Greek Zeus, Juno the same as Hera, Neptune the same as Poseidon, Venus the same as Aphroditê, Vulcan the same as Hephaistos, and so on. This process began as early as the sixth century B.C. In a few instances there was no good match, so that the Romans adopted the Greek god, assimilating the name to the Latin language. Thus Apollon became Apollo, Hades (via his byname Plouton, "Wealthy One") became Pluto, the healer Asklepios became Aesculapius, and similarly the hero Herakles became Hercules. So when the Roman poet Ovid retells the Greek myth of Aphroditê, Hephaistos, and Ares, the story is essentially Greek but the names of the characters are Roman: Venus, Vulcan, and Mars.

And, third, the Romans elaborated and codified their own connection to the system. As early as the fifth century B.C., Greek mythographers reported, or speculated, that the Trojan hero Aineias had not only escaped the destruction of Troy at the conclusion of the war but had sailed west with a band of refugees and founded a new settlement in Italy. There was even a tradition that Aineias had founded Rome itself, but since the traditional date of the foundation of Rome was centuries later than the supposed date of the fall of Troy, it made better sense if a descendant of Aineias served as the founder of Rome. By the fourth century B.C. there were Roman families who claimed Trojan descent. The possibility that Aineias settled in Italy was canonized by the Roman poet Virgil in his epic poem, *Aeneid,* which also reflected the claim of Julius Caesar, as a member of the Julian family, to be a descendant of Venus through Aineias and his son Iulus. The Roman self-identification as Italianized Trojans allowed them to view their current relationship with Greeks as a continuation of the ancient conflict of Trojans and Greeks, but more importantly it gave Romans a pedigree and a prominent niche in world history that befitted the importance that Rome came to have. On the principal that it is better to be wanted for murder than not to be wanted at all, it was better to have fought in the Trojan War and lost than not even to have been a player.

Classical Mythology after Antiquity

The esteem that educated persons accorded Greek traditional prehistory declined as time went on, but its deathblow was Christianity, which pitted it against Hebrew traditional prehistory. In a world of declining paganism and ascending Christianity, pagan religious and mythological traditions were doomed. Since Christians, like Jews, accepted the mythology preserved in the Hebrew scriptures as historical, they could not at the same time accept the corresponding Greek accounts. If one was true, the other had to be false or at least less true. A popular explanation was that Hebrew writings preserved an accurate account of early world history, whereas the Greeks had a distorted version of the same events. In this case the Great Deluge was a historical event, which the Hebrews had right, whereas the Greeks preserved a garbled account of it in the myth of Deukalion's flood. Similarly, the god of the Hebrews was the true god, and the gods of the Greeks and Romans were demons or euhemerized mortals. Another interpretive strategy was to give up claims of historicity on behalf of classical mythology and to understand the narratives instead as allegories. For some persons this approach had the advantage of acknowledging the value of the pre-Christian literature of Greece and Rome, justifying its appreciation and preservation, while taking it out of competition with Hebrew mythological literature in the realms of history and theology.

How Do We Know about Classical Mythology Today?

No longer taken seriously as history, classical mythology was eventually transmitted only through works of literature and art, principally via the ancient Greek and Latin authors that the scribes of late antiquity and the Middle Ages chose to copy and so to preserve.

In addition, new manuals of classical mythology were compiled, especially in Latin, such as Fulgentius's *Mitologiae* (*Mythologies*), the works by the anonymous authors known as the Vatican mythographers, and Boccaccio's fourteenth-century *De Genealogia Deorum* (*On the Genealogy of the Gods*).[17] The sixteenth century saw the first printed editions of important works of ancient mythography, such as Apollodoros's *Library* and Hyginus's *Tales*, upon which the Renaissance handbooks drew. The genre of the mythological reference work has persevered into our own times with the widespread publication of popular handbooks in different vernacular tongues, making the old stories accessible to ordinary readers. Notable for their popularity in the English-speaking world are Thomas Bulfinch's *The Age of Fable: Or, Stories of Gods and Heroes* (1855), often referred to as *Bulfinch's Mythology*, which made classical mythology available to a mass audience, and Edith Hamilton's *Mythology: Timeless Tales of Gods and Heroes* (1940), which enjoyed a successful career in the following century. In addition to compendiums belonging to popular scholarship, a learned tradition produced scholarly reference works such as the seven volumes of Wilhelm Roscher's *Lexikon der griechischen und römischen Mythologie* (1884–1937) and the eight volumes of Hans Christoph Ackermann's and Jean-Robert Gisler's equally monumental *Lexicon Iconographicum Mythologiae Classicae* (1981–1997).[18] In the latter half of the twentieth century, classical mythology became solidly institutionalized as a college course across the United States, and usually as a very popular one, stimulating a veritable industry to meet the demand for textbooks.

Retellings of classical mythology from antiquity to the present day influence readers' perception of classical mythology, inasmuch as both the selection of the stories and the manner of their narration depend upon the taste and times of the individual authors. There is, for example, a world of difference between the journalistic presentation of Apollodoros in the first or second century A.D., the allegorism of Fulgentius in the fifth century, the Victorian sweetness of Nathaniel Hawthorne's *Wonder-Book for Girls and Boys* or the nature mythology of George Cox in the nineteenth century, and the faithfulness to ancient sources found in Edward Tripp's twentieth-century *Meridian Handbook of Classical Mythology*.[19] What is true of the handbook tradition is of course equally true of the iconographic tradition.

Has all of classical mythology survived? It has not and could not, since not every narration of every myth and legend has been preserved. Mythological narratives vary according to narrator, audience, and situational context, and no particular narration can claim special validity over the others. Can we say at least that a text of every Greco-Roman myth and legend has survived? We cannot say that either, for we encounter ancient allusions to stories that are otherwise unfamiliar to us and therefore are lost. Nevertheless, the information that we do possess in works of literature and visual art from the earliest attestations of Greek mythology until classical mythology ceased to be a living system a thousand years later is extremely rich and abundant.

THE MYTHOLOGICAL WORLD: PLACES

The physical world of Greek mythology reflects early Greek views concerning the earth, sky, dwelling place of the gods, and abode of the dead, that is to say, early cosmological and geographical speculation and knowledge. Since it rests more upon speculation than upon knowledge, most of it is imaginary, but it established itself as the conventional stage for Greek mythology and, following the Roman adoption of Greek mythology, for Greco-Roman mythology as well. Although seven hundred years separate the Greek poet Homer from the Roman poet Ovid, the world in which Ovid sets his myths and legends is recognizably the same as Homer's. As geographical knowledge increased, Greek and Roman narrators updated the mythological world in one respect or another, but never radically.

The universe was viewed sometimes as a three-story, sometimes as a four-story, structure.[20] The top story is the sky, the roof of the cosmos and also the home of the celestial gods. Below the sky is the earth, the home of humans, minor deities, and scattered monsters. Beneath the earth, in the four-story cosmos, is the realm of the human dead and, at the very bottom, Tartaros, a vast world for the storage of defeated gods and monsters. In the tripartite universe, the abode of the dead is located within Tartaros instead of occupying a level of its own.

sky	sky
earth	earth
death realm	Tartaros (including death realm)
Tartaros	

Figure 1.1. Scheme of the Four-Story Cosmos and of the Three-Story Cosmos

Describing the three-story cosmos, the poet Hesiod declares that if a bronze anvil should fall from the sky, it would travel for nine days and nights and land on the earth on the tenth day, and if it should fall from the earth, it would similarly travel for nine days and nights and reach Tartaros on the tenth.[21] In the tripartite cosmos, then, these realms must be poised evenly apart. The poet Homer, speaking of the four-story universe, says that Tartaros is as far beneath Hades' realm as the sky is from the earth.[22] From top to bottom, then, Homer's four-layered cosmos is composed of sky, earth, death realm, and Tartaros, which also seem to be arranged at equal intervals from one another.[23] The subterranean realm of the dead is permanently dark, the lofty realm of the Olympian gods is always bright, and in between them the human realm is one of alternating light and darkness. The conception is anthropocentric: humans in the middle, the gods above, and the dead and quasi-dead below. Imaginary universes, unconstrained by the messiness of reality, tend toward geometric regularity and symmetry.

Let us now consider these cosmic realms more closely.

Earth

The earth consists of three great land masses, which the Greeks called Europe, Asia, and Libya, bordering upon a shared central sea, the Mediterranean. The Romans took over the Greek terms for Europe and Asia but called the southern continent Africa. The body of water known to the Greeks as the Euxine Sea (and to us as the Black Sea) divides Europe from Asia, the Nile River divides Asia from Libya (Africa), and Libya is separated from Europe by the Pillars of Herakles (the Strait of Gibraltar).

The surface of the earth is essentially flat and circular, and a river runs around it, flowing back into itself.[24] When the divine smith Hephaistos fashioned a shield for the hero Achilleus on which he depicted the earth as it might appear from above, he made the world stream flow around the shield's rim.[25] This river is Okeanos, a word that we have borrowed as *ocean* with a somewhat different meaning, since for the early Greeks Okeanos is a freshwater stream rather than a body of salt water, and he is also a living god.

Homer says that the central sea and all rivers, springs, and wells issue from Okeanos.[26] In other words, all the earth's waters are part of a single, connected system, whose source is Okeanos. Although the terrestrial waters appear to be conceived as a circulatory system, on the analogy of human blood circulating in arteries and veins, it is not likely that it was so conceived. Neither the Greeks nor anyone else understood that blood actually circulates, being pumped from and returning back to the heart, until William Harvey discovered the human circulatory system in the seventeenth century of our era. The idea that the heart sends blood through the veins (that is, that blood is distributed from a single source) is, however, found in the ancient Greek medical writers, and this idea probably furnished the model for the early notion of the relationship of the earth's waters to one another. The unidirectional relationship is expressed genealogically by Hesiod when he says that Okeanos's wife Tethys bore to him 3,000 sons, who are the rivers of the earth, and 3,000 daughters, who are nymphs of springs and ponds.[27] Physically speaking, the waters of Okeanos are the source of the earth's streams and springs, just as biologically speaking he is their sire.

Figure 1.2. View of the Earth from Above.

The center of the earth's surface lies precisely in Apollon's holy sanctuary at Delphi, where a conical stone called the "navel" (*omphalos*) marked the spot. Its location was ascertained by Zeus. Wishing to learn where the exact center of the earth lay, he once arranged for two birds to fly due inland, one from the eastern end of the earth and another from the western. The two birds met over Delphi, in commemoration of which the navel stone as well as the figures of two birds were set up.[28] So the center of the earth lies in Greece. Just as the Greeks' conception of the three- or four-tiered universe is anthropocentric, their conception of the surface of the earth is Hellenocentric. Humans live on the middle floor of the cosmic house, and Greeks live in the center of the middle floor.

Not surprisingly, most events in classical mythology take place in Greece, which consists in story as it did in reality of small, independent communities situated amid stretches of uncultivated land. The geography of myths and leg-

ends is much like that of European folktales: if you set out in any direction, you
will pass through a sort of no-man's-land and presently find yourself in a neighboring kingdom, where happily the local language is the same as your own.
Each community is a little cosmos surrounded by a wilderness, just as each
household is a still smaller cosmos within the town, each cosmos being a place
of relative safety and order and predictability surrounded by a region of uncer-
tainty—but also of excitement.

The excitement that awaits in the wilderness offers opportunity and also
danger. For one thing, the wilderness is a sexually charged place, the countryside and mountains being home to nubile nymphs of different sorts, divinities
who, as their name implies (nymph = "maiden of marriageable age"), are sexually ripe, and many nymphs do indulge in sexual activity with abandon, dancing
and frolicking with satyrs and rural gods. The maiden huntress Artemis roams
the mountains, sometimes in the company of like-minded nymphs, a band of
athletic, man-avoiding females. On one occasion the god Zeus was attracted to
one of the chaste nymphs in Artemis's band, Kallisto; taking the form of
Artemis herself, he embraced her, reassumed his male form, and ravished her.[29]
On another occasion, the youth Aktaion, hunting in the countryside with his
dogs, came by chance upon Artemis and her nymphs as they bathed. The indignant goddess transformed him into a stag, whereupon his own hounds tore him
apart. So the lands outside of human settlements amount to an extensive play-
ground of unregulated sexual opportunity and adventure (Forbes Irving 1990,
82–86). Sexuality is free but also potentially dangerous.

At the same time, the wilderness is home to highwaymen and monsters. A
traveler may encounter robbers lying in wait for persons who are making their
way to a particular city or shrine. Different badmen, for example, prey upon
gods and pilgrims who journey to Delphi (Fontenrose 1959, 22–45). Sometimes
they are not so much robbers as bizarrely evil characters, each with a special
trick, who challenge passersby for their lives. The youthful Theseus met several
predators of this sort as he traveled from Troizen to Athens. One was Sinis the
Pine-Tree Bender, who lived at the Isthmus of Corinth. He forced travelers to
bend pine trees down to the ground and hold them there; persons who were too
weak to hold them down were thrown into the air and perished. Theseus, of
course, treated Sinis to his own medicine.

Other sites are the dwelling places of individual monsters. A god wishing to
establish his cult or a hero wishing to found a city often encounters danger at
the site in the form of a hostile creature, whom he must slay before he can construct his sanctuary or city. The god Apollon must overcome the dragon Python
before he can establish a temple for himself at Delphi, and the hero Kadmos is
similarly obliged to slay a resident dragon before he can found the city of

Thebes.[30] Such beings incarnate the dangerous disorder of unregulated nature, which gods and heroes render safe and orderly, replacing wildness with an emblem of civilization: a splendid temple or town, a little cosmos where once there was found only the dangerous chaos of wilderness. A combat between god or hero and monster leading to the establishment of a new order is a cosmogony on a larger or smaller scale.

The farther one moves away from the center of the earth, the more extraordinary the places and inhabitants are. To the east of the Greeks dwell the Amazons, a nation of female warriors.[31] Some distant communities are so lovely that they appear to be survivors of the Golden Age, preserving the paradisal conditions of life that the world has otherwise lost. In the far north dwell the Hyperboreans, the people "beyond Boreas," which is to say beyond the north wind, beyond the cold in a wondrous northerly place where the climate is springlike. Beloved of the gods, the Hyperboreans spend their time feasting and dancing.[32] In the far west the Hesperides, or Daughters of Evening, live in a garden where they pass their time dancing and singing while also guarding the precious golden apples, a wedding gift from Earth to Zeus on the occasion of his marriage to Hera. The poet Hesiod says that the Hesperides live beyond Okeanos, at the edge of the world, near Night, where the monstrous Gorgons dwell.[33] At the edges of the world the monstrous and the lovely can be neighbors.

Another fabulous group is the Ethiopians (*Aithiopes*, "Burnt People"). They live beside the River Ocean in two groups, half of them in the east where the sun rises and half in the west where it sets. They are dear to the gods, who visit them often and feast with them.[34] This tradition implies that white is the default skin color for humans and that dark skin is a consequence of proximity to the sun. The same notion underlies the myth of Phaethon, who once drove the chariot of the Sun so close to the earth that Ethiopians acquired a dark complexion.[35] In contrast to the sunny Ethiopians, the Kimmerians live on the banks of Okeanos in misty darkness, eternal night, since Helios never shines there.[36] In the extreme west, on the banks of Okeanos, lies another dark place, Erebos, the realm of the dead. It is thither that the hero Odysseus once sailed in order to consult with the ghost of the seer Teiresias.[37]

Greek tradition tells of the existence of black dwarves less than two feet tall, Pygmies, who dwell beside the streams of the River Ocean.[38] Whether the tradition was inspired by actual knowledge of the Congolese people of small stature known to us as Pygmies and to themselves as BaMbuti is not known, but Europeans applied the Greek name to the BaMbuti in the belief that they were the Pygmies of ancient lore.

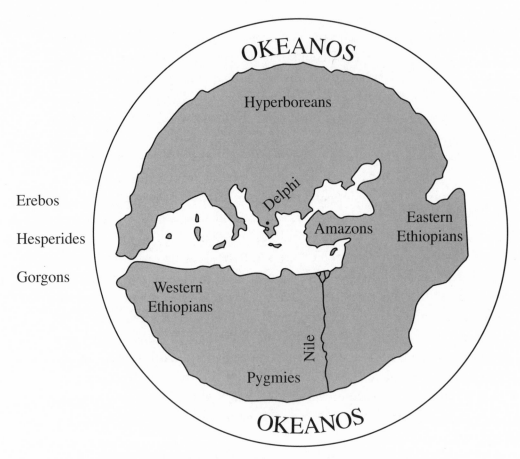

Figure 1.3. Map of the Earth with Select Peoples and Sites.

Sky

The early Greeks thought of the visible world as being much like a big house in which the earth serves as the floor and the sky as the ceiling or roof. Homer and other narrators describe the sky as made of bronze or iron, because these metals are strong and bright.[39] In shape the sky is a vaulted dome. This cosmic house is basically the kind of structure called by the Greeks a *tholos*, a round building with a conical roof (Brown 1968, 45).

Like any other roof, the sky requires support. In Greek cosmology the god Atlas, or Bearer, holds it up with his head or shoulders and tireless hands or, alternatively, holds pillars that keep the earth and the sky apart.[40] The image of Atlas as the supporter of the sky was so familiar that the Greeks called architectural columns in the form of male figures atlases (*atlantes*), like the columns in the form of females known as caryatids.[41] Atlas stands at the ends of the earth somewhere, in the extreme west near the Hesperides, on land or in the sea, as a consequence of which the great body of water in the west, the Atlantic Ocean, takes its name from him.[42] In northern Africa there is also found a mountain named Atlas, which was called "the column of the sky" by the folk who lived in its vicinity.[43] So the roof of the Greek cosmic tholos-style house is supported by a god or by pillars or by a mountain or by a combination of these. Whoever or whatever it is, it stands at an edge rather than in the center of the earth, where one might expect to find the support of a roof that is held at only one point.

The sky is home to a number of beings, among them the Olympian gods and the celestial luminaries—the sun, moon, and the other planets and stars. The Greek word *planet* signifies "wanderer," for unlike a "fixed star," a "wandering star" did not move around the pole in a regular daily circle, and for this reason the ancients classified the sun and moon along with Mercury, Venus, Mars, Jupiter, and Saturn as planets.[44] Very attentive to the lights in the sky, the ancients employed the luminaries as a natural calendar, the sun marking the passing of the day, the moon marking the passing of the month, and the constellations marking the passing of the seasons, indicating to farmer and pastoralist and sailor the times to begin or cease different tasks.[45]

Most often mentioned are Helios (Sun), Selenê (Moon), and Eos (Dawn). The goddess Eos arises each morning from her bed beside her lover Tithonos in order to bring light to mortals and immortals, after which the god Helios ascends from the River Ocean, crosses the sky from east to west in his chariot, and sails back east in a golden cup on the River Ocean during the night in order to be in place for his next day's journey.[46] At night the goddess Selenê rides across the sky in her celestial chariot or wagon. Ancient narrators also speak of Day and Night as goddesses who travel across the sky in their own chariots, so that the phenomena sun, dawn, and day can be independent of one another.

In early Greek tradition the constellations are called the "wonders" that ornament the sky. Among those mentioned by the early poets are the Pleiades, the Hyades, Orion, and the Great Bear, which is also called the Wain, or Wagon, the easily recognized constellation Ursa Major known to us familiarly as the Big Dipper.[47] Each constellation is the result of a catasterism in the mythological past, that is, the gods' translation of someone or something earthly to a station among the stars. As the celestial wonders move across the vault of the sky, they may chase each other or conclude their descent along the vault of the sky with a dip into the waters of the River Ocean. For example, Zeus transformed the nymph Kallisto into a bear and placed her in the sky as the Bear, where now the hunter Orion, who also was placed there by a god, pursues her but never catches her.[48]

The other notable dwellers in the sky are of course the Olympian gods, the principal deities of classical mythology. They get their name from Mount Olympos, a mountain range in northern Greece that rises 10,000 feet into the sky, on the top of which they live their largely carefree lives in perfect weather. At other times the divine dwelling place Olympos is identified with the sky. Precisely how and where in the sky the ancient gods dwell was no clearer to the Greeks and Romans than how and where in the sky Jehovah and his angels dwell are to Jews, Christians, and Muslims today. They just do. In addition to their fine palaces on Olympos, whether it is imagined as a mountaintop or as the sky, the gods possess individual shrines here and there on earth which they visit.

Zeus's splendid Olympian court consists almost entirely of his own siblings and children. It is a minisociety unto itself, featuring a king (Zeus) and his royal consort (Hera), complemented by officials in charge of the different operations of civilized life: a musician (Apollon), a cupbearer (Ganymedes), heralds (Hermes, Iris), a craftsman/builder (Hephaistos), a superintendent of the hearth (Hestia), and for extra-Olympian matters a superintendent of waters (Poseidon), superintendents of agriculture (Demeter) and viticulture (Dionysos), a war department (Athena, Ares), and so on. The gods pass their time in the pleasures of feasting, drinking, conversation, song, and sex, delighting in beautiful and valuable objects, and following with amused interest the theater provided by the activities of earthlings. The divine lifestyle and morality are essentially those of rich, powerful, and privileged humans. Since the deities themselves need not concern themselves with work, their few cares have to do with matters such as the welfare of their favorites upon earth, in particular their own mortal progeny, who unlike the gods are weak, vulnerable, and subject to death. Despite their splendid conditions of life, the gods are quick to anger when a mortal neglects a sacrifice, breaks an oath, competes with a deity, or offends in some other way, and they readily punish the impious individual or even the entire community to which he or she belongs.

Death Realm

The place where humans go to when they die, the world of the dead, is usually said to be located somewhere beneath the surface of the earth, although in Homer's *Odyssey* it is found on the far side of the River Ocean in the distant west.[49] Since the world of the dead is situated sometimes below and sometimes beyond the horizon, it is preferable to refer to it generically as a "death realm" rather than as an "underworld."

Ordinarily the final stop in a mortal's cosmic career, the death realm is reached in one of several ways. Some persons simply reappear there following their death as if the transferal of a self from this world to that is somehow automatic. So Odysseus's companion Elpenor, who drunkenly falls from Kirkê's house and breaks his neck, seems to reach the death realm almost instantly and in any case is already there when Odysseus arrives, prompting Odysseus to remark on the speed of his travel, which Elpenor does not explain.[50] Alternatively, some dead persons are led to the realm of the dead by Hermes in his role of Escorter of Souls (*psychopompos*). According to Homer, after Odysseus slew the arrogant suitors in his house, Hermes summoned their souls with his caduceus, and the suitors' souls followed him from Ithaca; traveled along the streams of Okeanos; passed the White Rock, the Gates of Hades, and the Community of Dreams; and came to the Meadow of Asphodel, where souls dwelled.[51] Hermes enchanted the souls of the slain men by means of his wand, and the souls fluttered after him like so many birds. In later sources we hear of the ferryman Charon, who for a fee transports the newly dead across the stream that separates the realm of the living from that of the dead. In order that the deceased person have the necessary fare, kinfolk placed a coin in the mouth of the corpse. In the absence of purses and pockets, the mouth was one of the places that Greeks carried coins in daily life, so that it was natural to equip a body with Charon's fare.

On rare occasions a living person managed to visit the death realm and to return, which is one of the ways that humans may be thought to have acquired some knowledge of that distant place. An Orpheus or a Theseus journeyed down through a cave into the bowels of the earth, or an Odysseus sailed to the western end of the earth. After the age of heroes, however, living humans no longer ventured to visit the world of the dead, or if they did, they did not succeed. In the human era it sometimes happened that the *soul* of a person who died went to the death realm and was allowed presently to return to its earthly body, whereupon the corpse revived, and the person described to the living his privileged glimpse of the afterlife.[52]

The world of the dead is situated in a distant place that is nearly impossible for a living person to reach. After all, it must not be allowed to be a destination for the casual tourist. What is the place like? As a land it is known as Erebos, or Darkness, a misty place devoid of light, for Helios never shines there. Indeed the Sun's ultimate cosmic threat is to cease shining for gods and humans and to go down instead to the death realm and shine for the dead.[53] When Erebos lies in the extreme west, as it does in Homer's *Odyssey*, the River Ocean separates it from the land of the living. When it lies beneath the earth, as it does in most sources, it is set off from the land of the living by some other river. The idea of a river separating the realms of the living and the dead is a constant, whatever it happens to be called. In addition, there are different streams and lakes in Erebos itself, the names of which suggest sheer misery: Acheron (Grief), Kokytos (Wailing), Styx (Shuddering), and Phlegethon or Pyriphlegethon (Burning). The newly arrived dead may be obliged to drink from the waters of Lethê (Forgetfulness), thereby losing all memory of their previous existence, doubtless a boon.

The place of the dead is also a house, the House of Hades. This image implies that the dead dwell in a structure, a kind of terminal inn operated by the Lord and Lady of Death, Hades and Persephonê.[54] Within their gated yard the voracious, multiheaded hound Kerberos (Latinized form = Cerberus) stands guard, a watchdog in reverse, since he welcomes persons coming to the place, wagging his tail and fawning, but he devours anyone he catches outside the gates. Whether an ancient author calls the death realm Erebos or the House of Hades makes little difference, since in practice the terms are interchangeable. In early sources, Hades is regularly the name of the god and not of his realm, but presently this name too is applied to the site. Some Greek phrases involving the name Hades are ambiguous, such as "send someone to Hades," in which case Hades could be understood as the god or as his domain.

Erebos is a repository for the dead in general, the good as well as the bad, so that its function is not to make life's balance sheet come out right by rewarding the inadequately rewarded or punishing the inadequately punished. Not a heaven or a hell, it is just the place one goes when one dies. Souls carry on an existence there in a minimal way, for although they preserve the external appearance they had when they died, their bodies are no more substantial than smoke, and their cognitive powers are nearly nonexistent, though they are not thereby greatly deprived since in this vast cosmic cellar there is no light to illuminate anything anyway, nor are there coherent sounds to hear or solid bodies to touch.

Nevertheless, a few interesting exceptions are found. The deceased Sisyphos is obliged to roll a stone up a hill, and as soon as it approaches the top, it rolls down again, forcing him to begin anew, which he does endlessly, like a person trapped in a world of autistic repetition. Tantalos stands in water beneath fruit-bearing trees, but whenever he tries to quench his thirst, the water level drops, and whenever he reaches for a piece of fruit, the wind wafts the branch away. Sisyphos, Tantalos, and several other unfortunates—Tityos, the Danaides, Ixion, Oknos—are fixtures of the Greek mythological death realm. Certain souls fare better than the average. Minos judges disputes among the dead just as he must have done in life when he was a Cretan king, and the great hunter Orion continues to pursue game.[55] They engage in the same enjoyable activities in Erebos as they did in life. Unlike the souls of the ordinary dead, certain persons must retain bodies and minds much like those that they enjoyed when they were alive, for if, for example, Tantalos could not think or feel or suffer from thirst, his torture would have no point. Some persons do not end their days in the House of Hades at all but spend eternity in an entirely delightful place such as the Isles of the Blessed. The fortunate hero Menelaos is informed that when his time comes, he will not die but will be translated to the Elysion Field, a paradise located in the distant west.[56]

So although most human souls proceed to the same cosmic basement where they endure the same sensory deprivation, a gloomy but not a tortuous existence, a few are singled out for special treatment, good or bad. The seeds of heaven and hell are here, but only the seeds.

Tartaros

Tartaros is spatially the lowest of the worlds that make up Greek mythic cosmology. It is primarily a prison for supernatural beings who are not subject to death and so cannot be killed, only stored.[57] Since they are huge, Tartaros also must be huge, and since they are strong, it also must be strong if it is to confine them. It is here that the Olympians imprisoned the Titans after they vanquished them in the battle for cosmic supremacy, it is here that Zeus confined the monster Typhon after he overcame him in single combat, and it is here that Zeus threatened to cast any Olympian god who disobeyed him: "I will grab him and cast him into misty Tartaros, far away, beneath the earth where the very deep pit is, with iron gates and a bronze threshold, as far beneath the House of Hades as the sky is from the earth."[58]

The strange place is described in detail by Hesiod.[59] Tartaros is enclosed by a bronze wall, above which is a neck, as though the place were an immense jar, and above the neck are the roots (that is, the bottom) of the earth and the springs of the sea. The neck is surrounded by three layers of Night. This is a way of saying that it is thrice invisible and gloomy, inasmuch as it is three times darker than ordinary darkness. Tartaros is so vast inside that if one should enter through its gate, one would fall for more than a year, buffeted by the terrible winds inside, before reaching its bottom. It is in this darkness that Zeus keeps hidden the defeated Titans, who cannot hope to escape, for Poseidon has installed a bronze door, and the Hundred-Handers, serving presumably as guards, live nearby. Many other dark beings have their home here as well, notably (since for Hesiod it includes Erebos) the rulers of the dead, Hades and Persephonê, and their horrible hound. Also the waters of Styx are found here, a branch of the River Ocean.

Physical Model versus Biological Model

The foregoing describes mostly what one could call a *physical model* of the universe, in which the cosmos consists of three or four physical realms, layered one upon another much like the stories of a building: the earth, functioning as the foundation or floor, the home of mortals; the sky above, a vaulted roof, serving as the home of the Olympian gods and the luminaries; and Erebos and Tartaros below, cellars to confine those who have died and those who cannot die. The physical model of the universe represents cosmic parts as functional things—a ceiling, a floor, a cellar, a prison.

But the parts of the mythological universe are also alive, and when this aspect is emphasized we can speak of a *biological model.* In the biological model the principal elements of the cosmos such as the earth and the sky are first and foremost living creatures who are capable of cognition, affect, and sexual reproduction. In this case the earth is not so much a floor as a huge, anthropomorphic female named Gaia, mother of gods and humans—mother of gods because she is the biological mother of the family of gods known as the Titans, and mother of humans because she furnished the soil from which the first human beings were fashioned and because she continues to nurture human beings by sending up the plants that sustain them. The sky, Ouranos, is an equally vast anthropomorphic male. In the earliest period of the cosmos Ouranos and Gaia mate and produce offspring.

The idea that the earth, Gaia, is a living female being is a common one throughout antiquity and, in addition to mythology, finds frequent expression in ritual, poetry, and philosophy.[60] Indeed, the idea that Earth and Sky are cosmic mates is never far from mind. As the tragedian Aeschylus says,

> Sacred Sky longs passionately to pierce Earth, and
> passion takes hold also of Earth to join in marriage.
> Showers fallen from the bridegroom, Sky,
> make Earth pregnant, and she in turn gives birth
> to flocks of sheep and to grains, the gift of Demeter,
> and the dew of their marriage brings to completion
> the fruitfulness of the trees.[61]

The rain that falls from sky to earth, impregnating her, is represented here as being analogous to a man's impregnating a woman with semen. Similarly, in one of the rites of the Eleusinian Mysteries, the mystics looked to the sky, saying "Rain!" and then to the earth, saying "Conceive!" Indeed, features of the earth's surface are sometimes spoken of as though they were parts of a female body: caves are wombs, stones are bones, and the center of the earth is a navel, not to mention the terrestrial waters that interconnect and move through the earth like blood in a mammalian body. Many ancients believed not only that the earth is a living female but also that she passes through the same stages of life as human females do. In her youthful, fertile years, which are now past, she produced major life forms such as large animals, whereas in her present senescence she is capable only of producing small and simple creatures.[62]

This sexual view of the cosmos is found in the Greek language as well. Greek has three genders, each noun being masculine or feminine or neuter. When a concept or thing is personified, it inherits the gender of the corresponding noun in the Greek language. For example, *helios* (sun) is a grammatically masculine noun so that the personified sun, Helios, is male, whereas *selenê* (moon) is a feminine noun so that Selenê is female. The Greek word for "river" is masculine, and in Greek mythology rivers are deities, which accordingly are male. The names for most trees, on the other hand, are grammatically feminine, so that tree spirits are female. Fruits are grammatically neuter, neither male nor female (Thomson 1972, 17–18). Grammatically speaking, then, the Greek landscape is one of males and females operating in the sexually interactive roles of fructifier and fructified. Sky is to earth as rivers are to trees and as males are to females. Male rivers fertilize the female trees, which bear offspring in the form of fruit, infants whose sexual selves are not yet realized.

The surface of the earth, herself female, is also gendered in a metaphorical way. Scattered over the earth are towns and sanctuaries, each a little cosmos founded by a man or a god, and most of them managed by men. Outside these orderly places is the wilderness, untamed but perhaps tamable, full of mysteries and hidden places, forbidding access or inviting adventure, concealing dangers. The earth's surface has the feel of a largely female realm dotted with small places staked out by men for human habitation or worship.

Whether the physical or the biological model prevails on a particular narrative occasion depends upon the context. If a cosmic element is to play an active role, it is personified, but if it is merely to be the setting for the action of another, it is treated as a thing.

THE MYTHOLOGICAL WORLD: CHARACTERS

The Principal Gods

The major gods of ancient Greece in myth and cult are the twelve Olympians. They are a family consisting of Zeus; his brother Poseidon; his sisters Hera,

Demeter, and Hestia; his sons Hermes, Hephaistos, Ares, Apollon, and Dionysos; and his daughters Athena, Aphroditê, and Artemis. Zeus's other brother, Hades, the ruler of the dead, resides among his subjects and so is not strictly an Olympian.

But the matter is not so simple as that. For one thing, the ancient sources sometimes disagree about the parentage of deities. According to one tradition, Aphroditê is a daughter of Zeus and Dionê, and therefore is a daughter of Zeus, but according to another she emerged from the semen of the god Ouranos, in which case she is not. For another thing, the Greeks were in agreement about the number of the Olympian gods—twelve—but they did not agree exactly which were the twelve, and if you tally the Olympian gods I have just listed, you will find that they add up to thirteen. The reason why the Greeks insisted upon the number twelve is that it is a *pattern number*, a culturally favored number, being a multiple of the extremely popular Indo-European pattern number three.[63] To the Greeks, as to us, twelve is a comfortable number, just right, whereas its neighbors on each side, eleven and thirteen, seem awkward, and for us thirteen is even taboo, a number to be avoided. In lists or visual representations of the twelve gods, sometimes Dionysos is absent, perhaps because he was deemed to be the most recent Olympian; at times Hestia is omitted, perhaps because she was rather colorless; and sometimes other deities are present or missing.

Zeus is the ruler of the family, a privilege that he wins during the conflict of the Olympian gods against the Titan family of gods. In this respect the Olympian hierarchy differs from actual Greek families, which were not organized into descent groups ruled by the best warrior; other than that, Zeus is a married male and presides over the other Olympians somewhat like the parent of a large brood, wherein his situation is typical of that of a Greek family, which was headed by a senior male (*kyrios*). The gods and goddesses marry, set up households, and have children or in some cases remain unmarried. Some of them have affairs or, taking advantage of their relatively high social position and considerable power, mate with beings who are hierarchically lower in the cosmic order. Like their human counterparts perhaps, the male deities are more likely than the females to engage in extramarital sex, their encounters being mostly heterosexual but also sometimes (for the males) homosexual. Several goddesses remain virginal by choice.

The historian Herodotos declares in a famous observation that Homer and Hesiod defined the gods for the Greeks, saying that the two poets distinguished their names, provinces, skills, and forms.[64] It appears, then, that the name and appearance of a deity together with his or her powers and cosmic assignment constitute a basic divine dossier, although one could add several other kinds of useful information such as the deity's genealogy and his or her personality.

Since the Olympians are the most important gods in classical mythology, let us consider them individually, touching upon some of these qualities. I begin with the five brothers and sisters who make up the elder generation of Olympians and proceed to the younger generation.

The patriarch of the clan is Zeus (Roman name = Jupiter). The other Olympians are his siblings or children. His principal province is the sky, and his weapon is the thunderbolt, by means of which he maintains his position as king of gods and humans. As ruler of the Olympians, he presides over a celestial court, frequently consulting but not necessarily respecting the opinions of his fellow gods. Beyond his job as ruler of the gods, his principal roles in mythology are warrior and lover. He is far and away the most promiscuous of the gods, not to mention the most inventive in his promiscuity.

Hera (Juno) is Zeus's sister and, in the mythic present, his wife. Several of the younger Olympians are their children. Hera is hostile to the other females with whom her husband, Zeus, has had sexual relations, whether the females were willing partners or not, as well as to the children produced by her husband's affairs, and her major activity in myth is the persecution of these women and their children, a negative and reactive role, which tends to make her unattractive as a character. She plays a positive role, however, as the divine protector of the hero Jason.

Poseidon (Neptune) is a brother of Zeus. He is lord of the seas and all other waters, as an emblem of which he wields a trident. His wife is Amphitritê.

Demeter (Ceres) is a sister of Zeus. Her province is agriculture, especially grains, the cultivation of which she taught to mankind. She has no husband, but she has a daughter, Persephonê, by Zeus. As a maiden, Persephonê was abducted by Hades, with whom she now rules in the land of the dead.

Hestia (Vesta), the other sister of Zeus, is the maiden goddess of the hearth. She has little role in myth, her importance residing rather in cult.

Zeus, Hera, Poseidon, Demeter, and Hestia comprise the elder Olympians. Now we consider the younger generation of Olympians.

Aphroditê (Venus) is a daughter of Zeus and Dionê, although according to another tradition she is not immediately related by blood to the other Olympians. The lovely goddess of sexual love, she is wed to Ares (in Homer's *Iliad*) or to Hephaistos (in Homer's *Odyssey*) but in any case is promiscuous, as befits a love goddess. She owns a wondrous belt or band, the cestus, that makes its wearer sexually irresistible. Aphroditê is often attended by Eros (Love), who is sometimes represented as her son, and Himeros (Longing), or by one of the divine sisterhoods, the Graces or the Hours, who personify different aspects of her and her sphere of influence.

Apollon (Apollo) and Artemis (Diana), brother and sister, are children of Zeus and Leto. Both are archers. Apollon's provinces include music, prophecy, and healing. Artemis is the protectress of the young but also a virgin huntress, roaming the countryside alone or in the company of maiden nymphs. She frequently plays the role of the readily offended deity, taking revenge on a mortal for having slighted her in one way or another.

Athena (Minerva) is the maiden daughter of Zeus and Metis. She emerged fully grown and fully armed from the head of her father, Zeus, sometime after he had swallowed her pregnant mother, Metis. Athena's roles in myth have mostly to do with war, women's crafts (principally weaving), and the city of Athens, her major provinces of concern. She has a special fondness for the hero Odysseus and his family, acting as their divine champion and protector, as Hera does for the hero Jason.

Ares (Mars) is a son of Zeus and Hera. Like Athena he is a god of war, but unlike her he is associated with the extremes of warrior behavior, battle frenzy on the one hand and cowardice on the other. Ares is the husband or lover of Aphroditê, who bore him Phobos (Fear) and Deimos (Terror), personifying aspects of his powers as a god of battle, and these two deities sometimes accompany him.

Hephaistos (Vulcan), a son of Zeus and Hera, or of Hera alone, is the hunchbacked or crippled smith of the gods. He plays the role of the marvelous craftsman, building palaces and fashioning wondrous objects for the gods. According to Homer's *Odyssey,* he is wed to Aphroditê, who is unfaithful to him.

Hermes (Mercury) is an unmarried son of Zeus and Maia. Bearing a special wand with wondrous powers, the caduceus, and wearing winged sandals, he is a cosmic intermediary, carrying messages from Olympos to earth or escorting the souls of the newly dead from earth to Erebos. At other times he plays the role of the sly and amoral trickster.

Dionysos (Bacchus) is a son of Zeus and a mortal woman, Semelê. When Semelê perished, Zeus sewed into his thigh the fetus she was carrying, and in time Dionysos was born from his thigh, as Athena had been from his head. Dionysos taught humans viticulture, including the making of wine, and traveled around the world attended by satyrs and maenads introducing his cult to different human communities. His mate is Ariadnê.

There are other denizens of Olympos who are not numbered among the Olympian deities as such. The hero Herakles (Hercules) is son of Zeus and a mortal woman, Alkmenê. A man of extraordinary strength, he accomplished twelve great labors, or tasks, in addition to many other deeds, and after death he

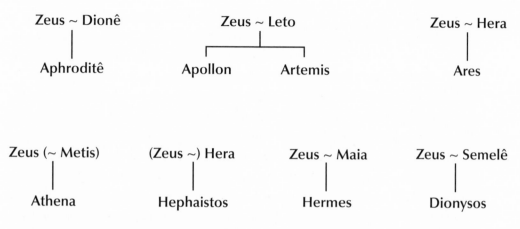

Figure 1.4. The Younger Olympians

was accepted as a god among the Olympians, where he has a wife Hebê (Youth). Ganymedes is also found on Olympos, serving as cupbearer to the gods, and the Hours and at times other celestial nymphs such as the Graces can be found there.

Tradition wavers between representing a god's individual powers as internal or external. Is Aphroditê powerfully seductive because she is a beautiful and sensuous female or because she possesses a wondrous garment, the cestus, which has the property of making its bearer sexually irresistible? Is Zeus supreme because he is the strongest of the gods or because he wields the most powerful weapon in the universe, the thunderbolt, while also retaining inside him the ultimate consultant, the goddess Metis (Cleverness), whom he once swallowed?[65] Now intrinsic and now extrinsic, a deity's peculiar power may be represented as being inherent, or it may be externalized in the form of a tool such as Hermes's caduceus, Aphroditê's cestus, and Zeus's thunderbolt.

The gods are officials in a cosmic bureaucracy that covers all imaginable territory. Each deity has his or her own province, or focused sphere of influence, in the cosmic order, Zeus being in charge of the sky, Demeter in charge of grains, Aphroditê in charge of erotic love, and so on. Many gods have multiple provinces. Poseidon is responsible not only for the waters but also for horses and earthquakes, for which reason a common epithet for him is Earthshaker. When the other Olympians acclaimed Zeus as king of the gods, he assigned or confirmed their different offices.[66] The usual Greek word for a deity's area of responsibility in the cosmic order is *honor* (*timê*), a term that in the corresponding human context refers to an office held by a civic official. A popular theme of Greek myths is how a particular deity acquires his or her peculiar provinces of concern.

Since the significance and number of honors are an index of a deity's importance, the individual gods place great value upon the personal validation that the possession by them of one or more provinces signifies. By the same token, they resent any slight to their honors by human beings as well as any challenge within their allotted spheres of influence, as when the talented but hubristic mortal weaver Arachnê refuses to acknowledge the superior ability of Minerva, whose cosmic provinces include women's domestic crafts.[67]

The individual occupations of the male deities are mostly divine versions of the occupations of men, and the occupations of the goddesses similarly correspond to those of women, with a few exceptions. Greek and Roman women did not engage in hunting as a sport, an activity that was proper to males, yet the goddess Artemis roams the wilderness as a huntress. Real Greek and Roman women did not act as soldiers, yet Athena is a goddess of war.[68] Although women did not serve as heralds, the goddess Iris is one of the gods' messengers. In these cases female deities specialize in activities in which human females did not participate.

Sometimes a deity and his or her province are identical, most obviously in the case of personified abstractions such as Eros or Persuasion or Longing. Helios can be the god who drives the chariot that conveys the sun through the sky, in which case the sun is a physical object independent of the god, or he can be the sun itself. A dryad, or tree-nymph, is an anthropomorphic being who is able to come and go at will, but she is also a particular tree, just as each river god is an anthropomorphic being who can roam as he may wish but at the same time is identical with the stream itself. The Greeks treated Aphroditê and Dionysos as anthropomorphic deities, but sometimes "Aphroditê" meant simply "sexual intercourse" and "Dionysos" signified simply "wine." Midway between the extremes of same and different are cases in which a kind of sympathy exists between a deity and a province. While a god is absent or incapacitated, for example, the god's cosmic province may cease to function or exist. Demeter, grieving for her missing daughter, once left Olympos and angrily caused all agriculture to come to a halt; on another occasion, Thanatos (Death) was captured and bound to a chair by the trickster Sisyphos, after which death ceased to function as a force in the world: humans and animals stopped dying.[69]

The Nature of Gods and Humans

Gods and humans act essentially alike, displaying the same sorts of feelings and holding essentially the same values (Burkert 1985, 182–189). They even look much alike. A Greek myth recounts how Prometheus fashioned the first human beings from clay in the image of the gods. Strictly speaking, then, gods are not anthropomorphic; humans are theomorphic. Nevertheless, gods and humans are not physically identical. For one thing, gods are of greater stature than humans and indeed in their natural state are really huge. According to Homer, Ares was once laid out on the battlefield at Troy after he had been hit by a stone cast by Athena. His body extended seven *pelethra,* around 700 feet.[70] An ancient hymn mentions a necklace for the goddess Eileithyia as being nine cubits in length, or over thirteen feet long.[71] The Greeks also believed that the heroes of old were much taller than persons of their own day.[72]

For another thing. the gods are better-looking than humans. That impressive stature and beauty are core qualities of divinities is illustrated in a legend recounted by Herodotos. The deposed tyrant Peisistratos and his supporters devised a trick in order for Peisistratos to regain his position. They dressed up in armor a good-looking and unusually tall girl, placed her in a chariot, and escorted her into Athens, having sent ahead a number of persons to announce that the goddess Athena was personally conducting Peisistratos to her own acropolis. The Athenians, naively believing that the woman was the goddess herself, received Peisistratos back.[73] The special qualities of the maiden that induced people to take her for a goddess were her height and her comeliness. In size and beauty, then, gods are superior to humans.

The gods, moreover, know a lot more than humans do. Humans have very limited knowledge of the present and past because they see little of the world, for which reason most human knowledge is little more than hearsay, and because they live for so short a time (Clay 1983, 148–157). But the gods are knowledgeable because they travel great distances easily, because they see much, having in the case of celestial deities also the advantage of being able to look down and survey the whole world (the sky-god Zeus and the sun-god Helios are therefore especially knowledgeable), and because they are more perceptive.[74] Gods can recognize other gods who are disguised or invisible to human beings, whereby they understand factors of causality that are hidden from humans. And of course, having lived long, they have witnessed many things firsthand.

Whereas their vast knowledge of the past and present differs in degree from that of humans, the difference in their knowledge of the future is absolute, for humans have no certain knowledge of what lies ahead, but gods are privy to fate (*moira*), the broad outline of future events. Each human being has a personal fate, an individual allotment in life, the general course that his or her life will inevitably take, as do the grander events of the universe, and as does the universe itself. So the gods are far more knowledgeable than humans are, but they are by no means omniscient, although human beings, because of their own limited understanding, sometimes mistakenly credit the gods with knowing everything.

There are other absolute differences between gods and humans. Gods, for example, are physically radiant. When Demeter, disguised as an old woman, stepped over the threshold into the palace of Alkinoos in the town of Eleusis, her head brushed the ceiling and a divine light filled the doorway.[75] During epiphanies the gods sometimes give hints that things are not as they appear, and humans may respond to these cues with awe or fear, perceiving that things are not normal, and they often surmise that they are in the presence of a divinity. Jupiter and Mercury in the guise of mortals visited the humble cottage of Philemon and Baucis, who offered them such hospitality as their modest resources permitted. When the hosts noticed that however much wine they drained from the bowl, the wine kept refilling itself, with fear and amazement they raised their hands in prayer to their guests, whom they correctly supposed to be disguised divinities.[76] The goddess Athena in the form of the mortal man Mentor accompanied young Telemachos on a voyage to the palace of King Nestor of Pylos. When Nestor invited the company to spend the night in his palace, Athena/Mentor turned herself into a vulture and flew away. Everyone was astonished, but Nestor correctly interpreted the event, informing Telemachos that that was none other than Athena, who had similarly watched over Telemachos's father, Odysseus.[77] Aphroditê took the form of a beautiful and radiant maiden when she had in mind to seduce the Trojan shepherd Anchises. Despite her disguise he took her straightaway for a goddess, but when she assured him she was not, they lay together. Afterward she acknowledged her divinity to him.[78] And when Apollon wanted to recruit priests for his new sanctuary in Delphi, he took the form of a dolphin and leaped aboard a ship of Cretan men. Whenever the men had in mind to approach the dolphin, it shook so greatly that the ship rattled, terrifying the men. After the vessel neared Delphi, the god leaped from the ship in the likeness of a star, sending off sparks as high as the sky, and entered his sanctuary, where he kindled a fearful light. Then in the form of a youth he leaped back to the ship and addressed the crew, who naturally enough perceived that their passenger had to be one of the immortal gods.[79]

The gods have their own peculiar language, with which they presumably converse among themselves.[80] The ancient poets record some of its vocabulary but nothing of its grammar. For example, there is a kind of bird that the gods call *chalkis* but men call *kymindis,* and there is a river known to the gods as Xanthos and to men as Skamander.[81] When ancient narrators represent the gods speaking with one another or with anyone else, they always have the gods speak in the language of the narration, Greek or Latin, so that the curious fact that the gods possess a special language plays no role in mythological narrative.

Unlike human beings, who experience a life cycle that moves inevitably from infancy to maturity to senescence and death, individual gods reach a particular developmental stage and remain there, immortal and unaging. Once deities reach their ideal age, which they do very quickly, their development freezes, much like characters in present-day serial fiction or comic strips. Baby Zeus matured from infant to adult in a single year.[82] As soon as baby Apollon was swaddled and nourished with nectar and ambrosia, he declared to the goddesses in attendance that his divine spheres of influence would be music, archery, and prophecy, after which he got up and strode away, leaving the goddesses in a state of wonderment.[83] Athena emerged from Zeus's head fully grown and clothed in armor.[84] When Demeter in the guise of an old woman nursed a mortal infant in Eleusis, giving him nectar and ambrosia and burning away his mortal parts in the hearth, the child grew with unnatural speed (that is, closer to the pace of a young god than of a young human).[85] Zeus and his siblings will always be senior adults, just as Athena and the other younger Olympians will always remain junior adults. Sometimes the ancients changed their minds about the developmental age of a particular deity. Dionysos was revised by Greek artists from being a mature adult to a young adult, and Eros went from being an adolescent to a little boy.

A key difference between gods and humans, according to the poet Homer, lies in their respective diets.[86] Since the gods do not, like mortals, consume bread and wine, they are bloodless, producing instead a kind of immortal fluid, a thin substance called ichor. As a consequence they do not die.[87] When they feast, they consume nectar and ambrosia, which preserve the gods in their present state, keeping them from aging (Clay 1983, 144–148).

The Olympian gods nevertheless own herds of cattle, which graze in Pieria to the north of Mount Olympos, and individual deities also keep cattle and sheep in different locations.[88] The sun-god keeps seven herds of cattle and as many herds of sheep on an island belonging to him, Thrinakia. They are shepherded by two nymphs, daughters of Helios by Neaira. He takes pleasure in looking down on his herds on his daily journeys across the sky. Since these special animals are fixed in number, neither dying nor giving birth, it was disastrous when Odysseus's starving companions slaughtered several of them for food, although they had been warned not to harm the Sun's sacred cattle. Helios was outraged, and Zeus punished the men on his behalf, destroying their ship and drowning the impious feasters.[89] Apollon, also a cattle owner, was distressed when he discovered that fifty head of his cattle had been rustled by his baby brother Hermes.[90] The lord of the dead, Hades, also possesses cattle. They are in the care of a herdsman, Menoites, who pastures them sometimes in the upper world and sometimes in Erebos.[91]

Although the celestial gods provision themselves with their special foods, nectar and ambrosia, they are also represented as depending for their nourishment upon sacrificial meals made for their benefit by human beings on earth. Such meals are shared, the god consuming the smaller part and the humans consuming the larger part. The deity may be silently and invisibly present, enjoying the god's share, or may be in the celestial regions, enjoying the savor of the smoke that issues from the roasting meat and makes its way upward to the heavens. Just how much the gods depend upon sacrificial meals is unclear, and Greek poets exploited the ambiguity. When in the *Homeric Hymn to Demeter* the angry Demeter shut down the cycle of plant life on earth, the human race would have died out and consequently the gods would have been deprived of their sacrifices, had not Zeus intervened.[92] Aristophanes in his comedy *The Birds* represents the birds building their own city in the sky as a rival to Olympos. Among other things their plan was to induce humans to sacrifice to the birds, letting the gods starve to death.

The mechanism that transforms meat from human food into divine food is fire, which performs the function of transforming the worldly into the divine in other instances as well. Demeter, wishing to make a mortal infant immortal and ageless, anointed him with ambrosia, breathed upon him, and held him over the fire of a hearth in order to burn away his mortal parts.[93] Comic narratives relate how a widowed husband burned items of clothing, transmitting them thereby to his deceased wife in the death realm in order that she might dress more fashionably in the otherworld.[94] Transforming fire may also come down from above. When the mortal Herakles was dying, he placed himself on a pyre, where the fire burned away his mortal parts and Zeus's lightning transported him to Olympos, where he joined the gods as one of the immortals.[95] For the Greeks, a person or place struck by lightning became sacred, marked out by Zeus the hurler of thunderbolts. In such instances, Zeus and his lightning were virtually indistinguishable, for the god (known in this case by his epithet *Kataibates,* "the Descender") was thought actually to descend in the form of lightning. By means of such an epiphany, as lightning from the heavens, Zeus once came down to his human lover Semelê in the city of Thebes, destroying her mortal flesh but simultaneously rendering her immortal and conveying her via fire up to Olympos.[96]

The immortality of supernatural beings poses a problem in battles between supernaturals. What are the victors to do with the vanquished? When the Olympians overcame the Titans in their ten-year struggle, the vanquishers could not slay their opponents, since they were immortal. All they could do was to store them away in a place from which they could not escape. So they placed them under guard in Tartaros, a cosmic holding tank for beings that cannot die.

The gods have many other powers that human beings can only marvel at. Compared to humans, the gods are masterful shape-changers (Clay 1983, 160). They readily take the form of humans or animals in order to pass unrecognized or unnoticed in the world of mortals, for in general they prefer not to appear to humans in their true form; for one thing, it can be hard for a mortal to face an immortal who appears openly.[97] The wedding feast of the mortal Peleus and the Nereid Thetis, an event attended by both mortals and immortals, marked a turning point in this respect, for since that time gods have ceased mingling with humans or feasting with them openly. Because human beings for their part are aware that gods prefer not to appear to humans in their true guise, they face the problem of having to decide whether a being they are dealing with is really a human or a disguised god. When one of Penelopê's suitors, Antinoos, mistreated a beggar (who was really the disguised Odysseus), the other suitors were indignant, reminding him that the stranger might be a god, inasmuch as gods had the habit of assuming human shape and visiting the cities of men in order to observe behavior good and bad.[98] For the warrior on the battlefield, it was always a possibility that his opponent might be a deity in mortal guise. When Diomedes confronted Glaukos on the battlefield at Troy, he asked him if he was an immortal come down from the heavens, declaring that he would not do battle with the heavenly gods.[99] There was a tradition that Zeus and Hermes commonly traveled the earth together in disguise, the prototype of today's paladin and sidekick. Once when the apostles Paul and Barnabas were journeying together and working miracles, the local people took them for Zeus and Hermes walking the earth in human guise.[100]

The gods choose to treat a few mortal groups exceptionally, appearing to them as they are rather than in disguise. To the Phaeacians, for example, who are "close to the gods," they show themselves clearly and openly, and when the Phaeacians sacrifice hecatombs, the gods dine with them openly.[101] Similarly, the Olympians feast for days on end with the Ethopians beside the River Ocean.[102] This open feasting of gods and men is reminiscent of the state of things for early mankind, before the gods withdrew from the community of humans.[103] An odd case on the individual level is found in a passage in Homer's *Odyssey* in which the goddess Athena joins Odysseus and Telemachos: Odysseus perceives her in the guise of a woman, but Telemachos does not see her at all.[104]

Although the gods often adopt the form of human beings for the purpose of interaction with mortals, they can turn themselves into almost anything. Athena consorted with a group of humans in the form of a human but surprised everyone by departing in the form of a bird. Apollon took the form of a dolphin when he wished to board a ship. Zeus became a bull when he wanted to gain access to the maiden Europê and assumed the form of the goddess Artemis when he wished to take sexual advantage of the nymph Kallisto. Zeus's repertory of transformations for sexual purposes is so impressive and varied that the ancients made lists of them.[105] But the champion shape-shifters are the sea deities, who can undergo multiple metamorphoses in rapid succession, which they routinely do in order to avoid capture. They can even become nonliving things such as fire. When the hero Menelaos grabbed hold of Proteus, the Old Man of the Sea, he transformed himself successively into a lion, a snake, a panther, a boar, water, and a tree before finally yielding to his captor.[106] The mortal Peleus similarly ambushed the Nereid Thetis, wishing to marry her. She turned herself into fire, water, and a wild animal before resuming her original shape.[107]

A deity can also change someone or something else into a different form. Zeus metamorphosed the nymph Io into a cow in order to conceal from his wife, Hera, the fact that he was consorting with Io.[108] Often the transformation of a human into an animal is a punishment for misbehavior, as when the hunter Aktaion came upon Artemis bathing and was changed by her into a stag.[109] Less drastically, a god may enhance or worsen the physical appearance of a person for a particular purpose. Before Odysseus went to the palace of Alkinoos, Athena made him taller and sturdier, improved the looks of his hair, and in general "poured grace" upon his head and shoulders to improve his chances of a good reception. Later, to make Odysseus unrecognizable to the Ithacans, she did the opposite, giving him the appearance of a beggar by aging his skin, hair, and eyes and by dressing him in rags.[110] Deities can even disguise something complex and nonliving such as a landscape, making it unrecognizable. Athena once made the paths, bays, rocks, and trees of Ithaca so unfamiliar to Odysseus that he believed he was in another land.[111] Sometimes the gods deceive humans by replacing someone with a look-alike substitute made of cloud matter. When Ixion fell in love with Hera and was trying to force himself upon her, Hera told Zeus, who wanted to learn if this was really the case. So he placed beside Ixion a likeness of Hera made of cloud, with which Ixion had sexual intercourse, subsequently boasting that he had slept with Hera. Zeus punished him by binding him to a wheel that whirls through the air. Meanwhile the cloud, having been impregnated by Ixion, gave birth to a son Kentauros (that is, Centaur).[112] There was a tradition that Helen did not actually go to Troy with Paris at all; rather, Zeus fashioned a phantom of Helen out of clouds, which Paris unwittingly took with him to Troy, whereas Hermes conveyed the real Helen to Egypt for safekeeping.[113]

A different strategy for avoiding recognition is invisibility.[114] When a god wishes to be invisible, or to make someone else invisible, he or she does so by surrounding the being with thick air or mist or night. Night can serve as well as mist for this purpose, since it too is a substance, something material, as in the three layers of night that surround the neck of Tartaros.[115] Neither gods nor humans become simply invisible, their material selves somehow dematerializing or evaporating into space. Since classical mythology has a wholly materialistic view of reality, invisibility is accomplished by clouding the view of potential perceivers. When Odysseus was making his way as a suppliant to the palace of Alkinoos, his guardian goddess Athena took care to pour a large amount of mist around him in order that he not be seen by any of the locals before he reached the palace.[116] Odysseus's material self was still fully there, but the cloudy air that surrounded him blocked anyone else from seeing him. Even under normal circumstances, the eyes of human beings are clouded by an amount of mist that prevents them from fully appreciating the reality around them. Athena once lifted this fog from the eyes of Diomedes, permitting him to distinguish disguised and invisible gods from humans on the battlefield at Troy, just as gods do.[117] A similar notion of blocked perception is found in ancient legends in which a serpent licks a person's ears as he or she sleeps, cleansing them, after which the person becomes a seer or prophet. This happened to Melampous, who thereby acquired the ability to understand the language of animals. Humans are therefore capable of seeing and hearing much more than they do, but their sight and hearing is clouded, limiting its range of use, whereas the gods' perception is not blocked.[118] Since gods cannot escape their materiality, when a god wishes to enter a closed room, he or she cannot pass through the walls as though they were not there. Accordingly, Hermes once passed like a breeze through the keyhole of a bedroom door.[119] Early Greek bedrooms had no windows, so that when the doors were shut, the only opening was the keyhole.

Unlike humans, gods can quickly move from one place to another by flying through the air. They owe this ability to their wings or to their winged sandals or to their winged chariots or chariots drawn by winged horses.[120] Otherwise they simply run or leap through the air, or their sky-chariots travel through the air thanks to an unexplained principle, like Santa Claus's sleigh.[121] The chariots of some goddesses are drawn by birds—Hera's chariot uses peacocks, and Aphroditê employs sparrows—but these creatures are chosen less as a means of explaining the flight of the divine chariots than because of their appropriateness to the particular deity.[122] Thus Artemis's chariot is drawn not by birds at all but by stags.

A subtle power of the immortals is their ability to implant thoughts and feelings in human beings, frightening them or encouraging them or giving them an idea or an impulse for good or bad. Apollon sent fear into the womenfolk of Krisa and later placed courage into the chests of a crew of Cretan mariners.[123] When Helen left her husband and children to run off with Paris, it was a result of Aphroditê's influence upon her. The question of responsibility thereby becomes unclear. Whose fault is Agamemnon's bad judgment? Who should be blamed for Helen's adultery?[124] Beyond this, the gods can intervene in human affairs by causing or influencing natural events of the sort that are beyond human control, bringing about sunshine or rain, drought or sterility or epidemic (Dover 1994, 133–138). A benevolent god may send a favorable wind to propel a ship or may even guide it himself. In so complex a human event as a battle, the gods may choose to be the unseen, decisive factor.

A curious constraint on the power of the gods is that a god is not permitted to undo what another god has done. For example, Zeus and Hera once argued about whether males or females derive the greater enjoyment from sexual intercourse, Zeus claiming that females enjoy it more and Hera saying the opposite. So they asked Teiresias, a man with the unique qualification of having spent seven years as a woman. When Teiresias confirmed Zeus's position, Hera angrily blinded him. Since a god might not cancel the actions of another god, Zeus compensated Teiresias with the gift of prophecy.[125] The same rule can be found in modern folktales. In Perrault's *Sleeping Beauty*, a king and queen invited fairies to the christening of their newborn daughter, or rather all but one fairy. As each fairy was naming her gift to the child, the fairy who had been overlooked showed up and angrily declared that someday the princess would pierce her hand with a spindle and die. The last fairy to speak, explaining that she did not have the power to undo entirely what the elder fairy had done, only to modify it, declared that instead of dying the princess would fall into a sleep lasting a hundred years.[126] Is there, then, a universal rule among supernaturals according to which one supernatural is not allowed to invalidate the actions of another? Yes and no. The regulation is a narrative necessity that has been transformed into a mysterious rule of the supernatural world, for without such a rule some stories would come to an abrupt halt. If Hera blinded Teiresias and Zeus straightway gave him back his sight, or if one fairy declared that the princess would die and the next fairy neutralized the curse, the story would be immobilized, having nowhere to go.

Nature Spirits

In addition to the major gods, the countryside, mountains, and sea are replete with minor supernatural beings and other fabulous creatures. The most important are the nymphs, female spirits of the wild. In the sphere of ordinary Greek life the word *nymph* (*nymphê*) signifies a nubile female, that is, a girl who is marriageable or newly married, but in the sphere of mythology and popular belief the term denotes a youthful and lovely female supernatural being of lower rank who lives away from human habitation in one of the uncultivated places of the earth or in the sea.

There are different kinds of nymphs, distinguished mostly by their habitats. Among terrestrial nymphs the most commonly mentioned are dryads or hamadryads (nymphs of trees), naiads (nymphs of springs), and oreads (nymphs of mountains). This classification is somewhat casual in that the terms are not mutually exclusive (thus, a dryad can be a type of oread), and ancient authors often refer to this or that nymph without specifying which kind she is. Terrestrial nymphs are said rather sweepingly to be daughters of Zeus or of other gods such as particular rivers. But nymphs of the sea, Nereids and Oceanids, are the daughters respectively of the sea deity Nereus and his Oceanid wife Doris, whence the patronymic Nereid, and of the world-river Okeanos and his wife Tethys, whence the patronymic Oceanid. They are the mermaids of classical tradition, although like other nymphs they are portrayed as being clothed and human in appearance.

Some nymphs are immortal and others merely long-lived. Thus part of the pathos of the marriage of the hero Peleus and the Nereid Thetis was that he was a mortal man and she was an immortal goddess. Their son, the great warrior Achilleus, was like his father a mortal, despite his mother's desperate efforts to render him immortal. And her eventual grief at Achilleus's death was all the greater for the fact that it was unending.[127] But in a poem by Hesiod a naiad declares that a crow lives for nine human generations, a stag lives four times as long as a crow, a raven three times as long as a stag, a phoenix nine times as long as a raven, and a nymph ten times as long as a phoenix.[128] If a human generation is calculated at twenty years, then a nymph can expect to live 194,400 years. Otherwise it is said that a dryad lives only so long as does the tree whose spirit she is, and a naiad similarly coexists with her spring; that is, there is an identity or sympathy between dryads and trees on the one hand and naiads and springs on the other, such that they come into existence together and depart together. So nymphs are sometimes represented as minor gods and at other times as a distinct class of beings who are inferior to ordinary gods but superior to human beings.

Nymphs live mostly carefree lives, enjoying their youth, beauty, and freedom unconstrained by responsibilities to husbands or children. By the standard of ancient Greek females, their sexuality often tends to the extremes of overindulgence or underindulgence. Some nymphs dance and enjoy sex promiscuously with satyrs and the rural gods Hermes and Pan, and naiads in particular can be sexually aggressive. Other nymphs, such as the chaste oreads who accompany the virgin huntress Artemis, entirely avoid the company of males.

Males, however, do not always shun them, sometimes finding them all the more alluring. In between these extremes we hear of individual nymphs who mate with gods or men and bear them children. Thus the river god Okeanos and the Oceanid Doris are parents of many daughters, the Oceanids, and the mortal man Peleus and the Nereid Thetis are parents of the hero Achilleus. And sometimes nymphs play the role of supernatural nursemaids, like kindly fairies. When the goddess Aphroditê was impregnated by the mortal Anchises, she entrusted her baby to the dryads to rear.[129]

Unlike the nymphs, who are physically indistinguishable from human females, male spirits of nature are partly anthropomorphic and partly theriomorphic, emblematizing their mix of human and bestial natures, and they are unclothed. In form a satyr, or silen, is a man with horse features, a two-legged being with equine ears, mane, tail, and hooves, whereas a centaur is a horse with human features, a four-legged being having the entire torso of a horse to which the upper body of a man is attached instead of a horse's head and neck. Ancient artists frequently depict satyrs frolicking with nymphs, dancing and engaging in sexual play, and satyrs are among the attendants of the god Dionysos, sharing his love of drink and revelry. Centaurs have their own society, perhaps in the way that horses belong to a herd. They can be dangerous, especially when they drink excessively, which occurs whenever they get access to wine. The question of their status as mortals or immortals appears to have been open. The Greek traveler Pausanias came upon a grave of a silen, from which he inferred that silens must be born mortal.[130] On the other hand, ill circumstances induced the centaur Cheiron to trade his immortality for mortal status, so that he at least must have been born immortal.

The rural god Pan can also be mentioned here. He is a composite deity, a mix of man and goat according to the same recipe as that for satyrs, except that his bestial parts are goatish: hooves, goat's horns, goat's ears, and of course a goatee.

Satyrs and centaurs are given to immoderate drink, excessive eroticism (the satyrs may be portrayed in art with erect, oversized phalluses), and aggressive behavior and have little social organization. In their self-indulgence and lack of self-control, including their lack of civilized skill in handling alcoholic drinks, they are negative examples of maleness according to Greek values regarding appropriate behavior for free, adult, civilized males. Similarly, many nymphs are given to one of two behavioral extremes, lust or chastity, being in either case unconcerned with the normal responsibilities and cares appropriate to human females, so that in the end both lustful and virginal nymphs are alike in their rejection of the domestic life that was normal for Greek women. Opting for self-indulgence, they differ only in whether they express it as abandonment to sexuality or as avoidance of it. Just as satyrs and centaurs display typically male behaviors to excess, lusty and chaste nymphs model extremes of inappropriate behavior for human females.

The Relationship of Gods and Humans

The Olympian gods are immortal though they can be wounded, unaging once they have reached their final developmental stage, knowledgeable but not omniscient, and powerful but not omnipotent. They dwell on lofty Olympos, where they dine on nectar and ambrosia and live a more or less carefree existence. In contrast, humans are mortal, subject to aging, poorly informed, and frail. They dwell on earth, where they consume grain and wine, living brief lives beset by pain and cares. As the Greeks put it, gods are blessed and humans are wretched. One might expect that these two species, gods and humans, so dissimilar in nature, would each live an existence apart from the other, having little reason to interact. But the fact is that they need each other.

On the one side, it is in the interest of humans to win and maintain the goodwill of the gods toward them because the gods have immense influence over human beings and the natural world. For their own reasons the gods are pleased by certain human behaviors and offended by others. According to Hesiod, fish and birds and wild animals eat one another, but to humans Zeus gives the blessing of Dikê, or Justice. Zeus grants a blessed and prosperous life to the person who respects Justice, and a gloomy life to him who harms her. If a human community honors sworn oaths, eschews bribery, interprets the law honestly, treats fairly the stranger as well as the native, it is a just community, and if so, it flourishes, its people prospering and increasing. They enjoy peace because Zeus does not send them war. They experience no famine, for the earth produces grain for them, their trees bear nuts, their bees make honey, their sheep produce wool, and their women bear healthy children. But if a city is unjust and hubristic, if even only one inhabitant is evil, Zeus sends it terrible sufferings: famine, plague, human infertility, military defeats, the loss of ships at sea, and so on.[131] Thus the gods plagued the Thebans with sterility of plant and animal life because they harbored the patricide Oedipus, even though they did so unwittingly.[132] In short, many things in the world that are beyond human control lie within the control of the gods, and if the gods are so disposed, they can influence the world in the direction of human wishes, making life enjoyable, or at least endurable, or they can make it miserable.

But the relationship of gods and humans is not one-way only, for the gods also depend upon human beings for things that are important to them, such as their share of sacrificial meals, especially the savor of roasted meat. Beyond that, they are pleased by the celebration of their rites and by the establishment of new cult sites. When the priest Chryses prayed to Apollon to ask a favor of him, he reminded the god of the temples he had roofed for him. When Athena wanted Zeus to facilitate Odysseus's return home, she asked whether he was not pleased by the sacrifices that Odysseus had performed at Troy.[133] Like human beings, the gods enjoy being acknowledged and resent being neglected. So the two populations are bound together by a relationship of exchange. Mortals provide immortals with housing, sustenance, praise, prayer, entertainment, and so on while the gods create or maintain favorable conditions for mortals to carry on their lives and their work.[134]

Not only do gods and humans need each other generally, sometimes they also desire each other in the particular. Indeed, much sexual activity has transpired between the two groups. Aphroditê used to amuse herself by causing the immortal gods to mate with mortal women and the immortal goddesses to mate with mortal men. These matings produced the demigods, offspring who were half human and half divine, often excelling in one respect or another but subject to aging and death like their mortal parent, to the grief of their immortal parent. The demigods, or heroes, typified the denizens of the heroic age. Eventually Zeus put an end to this mating of immortals and mortals because of the pain it caused the otherwise carefree gods. After he made Aphroditê herself feel an irresistible attraction to a mortal man, so that she mated with him and bore him a child, she ceased to instill longing in the immortals for mortals, and in time the demigods died out and with them the extraordinary age they characterized.[135]

Among the gods themselves there is an ambivalence about mating with mortals. On the one hand, the relatively lower status of mortals means that such a match is humiliating for an immortal, especially for a goddess. After Aphroditê slept with Anchises, she forbade him ever to boast of it, lest Zeus slay him with a thunderbolt.[136] The nymph Kalypso complained that the gods became jealous whenever a goddess slept openly with a man, as Eos did with Orion and as Demeter did with Iasion.[137] On the other hand, the gods are like members of a privileged upper class who can take sexual liberties with persons of less power and lower status. The serial lover Zeus once cited a partial catalog of his partners: Dia, Danaê, Europê, Semelê, Alkmenê, Demeter, Leto, and his wife Hera—five mortal women and three immortals.[138] Deities are the initiators, and the human subjects of divine interest are willing or unwilling participants, as the case may be. In the case of nymphs, being lesser divinities, the relationship can be initiated by the humans, as when the mortal Peleus won over the Nereid Thetis as his wife. Since the status of nymphs lies between that of gods and humans, they frequently engage in sexual encounters or marriages with gods and with men.[139] For a human, sexual dealings with a divine being can have its dangers. Mortal men fear that they may become impotent after sleeping with a divinity, which the goddess or nymph evidently has the power to bring about.[140] The mortal woman Semelê, who wished for Zeus to appear to her in his full divine majesty, as he does for his celestial spouse Hera, was consumed in divine fire.

In addition the gods display considerable disinterested affection for mankind. They possess a vast store of knowledge and skills, which they share because of their love for individual human beings or for humanity. Different deities impart different arts because deities themselves specialize in the many responsibilities of the cosmos. For example, Harmonides owed his notable skill as a woodworker to Pallas Athena, who loved him exceedingly, and Antilochos owed his knowledge of horsemanship to Zeus and Poseidon, who loved him and taught him everything about the subject.[141] The women of Phaiakia owed their considerable skill at the loom to Athena, and individual bards learned their art from Apollon or the Muses, who love singers.[142] Humans as a whole owe their knowledge of agriculture to Demeter and their knowledge of viticulture to Dionysos, who taught these arts of civilization to human beings at a particular time in the past, just as Athena and Hephaistos taught different craft skills to humankind.[143] Apollon and Artemis invented the art of hunting, which they taught to the centaur Cheiron, who in turn passed it on to many heroes, from whom the rest of humanity has learned it.[144] Even the thieves' art is divine. The master thief Autolykos acquired his art from Hermes, who was pleased by Autolykos's many sacrifices.[145]

How do mortals and immortals communicate with each other? In the mythological past when gods and humans dwelled together like neighbors, they spoke to each other directly, but except for a few privileged human groups, these conditions are now gone, and in the mythological present the Olympians dwell unreachably far away. The two species can communicate directly when a deity pays a visit to a human community, but more often they communicate indirectly, or at least at a distance. Humans make their wishes known to the gods by means of prayer, and they express their goodwill by honoring the gods in verbal and nonverbal ways such as the performance of hymns, sacrifices, and spectacles. For their part the gods send omens, dreams, and oracles, and they express their goodwill by sending success in an enterprise or prosperity in general and their anger by means of thunderbolts, plagues, floods, storms at sea, military losses, and other miseries and disasters.

A god may impart information about the present, or reveal the will of the gods about a contemplated matter, or advise a person what to do, as the disguised Athena does at the beginning of Homer's *Odyssey* when she came in disguise to Odysseus's young son Telemachos and suggested a course of action. Among human beings a knowledge of the past and the future belongs in particular to the community's information specialists, the poets and the seers. The Muses and Apollon give poets the ability to sing, inspiring them with a knowledge of past events in human and divine history, so that they are able to narrate matters that human beings otherwise could not know, such as the origin of the cosmos, the doings of the gods, and the exploits of the heroes of the past. Mythological seers such as Teiresias and Kalchas discern what is fated to happen, what the will of the gods is, and what events of the past have crucially conditioned the present, and important persons consult them in order to interpret a problem, learn of the future, or gain guidance for their actions.

PECULIARITIES OF MYTHOLOGICAL NARRATIVE

In a number of ways the myths and heroic legends of classical mythology differ from narratives of other genres, both oral forms such as folktales and literary forms such as fiction.

Supernaturalism

First, there is the pervasive supernaturalism of mythological narrative. Creatures are divided into two great groups, one consisting of supernatural beings and the other of natural beings. Both appear in myths and heroic legends, although supernatural beings dominate the former and natural beings dominate the latter. In Greek myth, especially in cosmogonic myth, nearly everything is divine: the major parts of the physical cosmos (Earth, Sky, Sun, Moon, Tartaros, and so on), much of the furniture of the earth's surface (rivers, springs, certain trees, and so on), forces and states (Love, Strife, Day, Night, Fear, Sleep, Death, Diseases, Hope, and so on), the familiar gods (the Olympians, the Titans, and so on), the divine sisterhoods (Muses, Hours, Graces, and so on) and brotherhoods (Cyclopes, Hundred-Handers), and the monsters (Typhon, Kerberos, and so on). Most of them are also immortal, which means that once they come into being, they can never be gotten rid of but must be either integrated into the system or stored away somewhere.

Different conditions pertain to each group. Supernatural beings are generally immortal, powerful, and knowledgeable, whereas natural beings are mortal, frail, and ignorant. Supernatural beings have an understanding of both the natural and the supernatural realms, whereas natural beings perceive only natural processes and must resort to conjecture regarding the effects of the supernatural upon their lives, never being entirely certain how much they understand.

In mythic narratives set early in time, the supernatural is treated as unremarkable because everything is divine and supernatural. Although characters respond to one another in various ways (for example, a god responds hostilely to the aggression of another god), no response depends upon the status of another character specifically as a supernatural. Indeed, the supernatural as a category has meaning only when beings come into existence who are not supernaturals. Even so, in the primordial days of mankind, when men and gods live as neighbors and speak face to face, supernatural beings as such provoke no special reaction from natural beings, just as in Hebrew tradition Adam and Eve respond to Yahweh in the Garden of Eden no differently from the way they might respond to a man of some importance. It is only after the principal gods leave the community of humans and withdraw to distant and inaccessible homes, either upon the crest of a lofty mountain or in the heavens, that the supernatural calls forth a special response, and then only from natural characters. When now a deity manifests himself or herself in an epiphany, or when a deity interferes somehow with nature, or when humans merely suspect that a deity may be responsible for some unusual phenomenon, the response of the human characters is awe (Clay 1983, 167–168). For the supernatural has become unseen, its workings are mysterious, and humans, constrained by their limited knowledge and perception, can do no more than guess when it is affecting them.

Personification and Reification

Greek myth differs from ordinary fiction by the large role that personification and reification play in it. Personification is the attribution of human properties such as intellection, emotions, speech, and physical capabilities to a nonhuman entity or idea and often involves anthropomorphism, the attribution of human form to something nonhuman. Since classical religion and myth are polytheistic and every god is in effect a personification, the phenomenon of personification is pervasive. Examples of personified entities are the different parts of the physical cosmos ranging from Earth and Sky to individual rivers and trees, familiar gods of cult such as Zeus and Hera, and intangible abstractions such as Eros (Love) and Hemera (Day).

Reification is the treatment of a nonphysical thing, such as an abstraction, as a material object. When the god Zeus once became angry at mankind, he removed the "life" (*bios*) from the soil. When life was present in the soil, the earth was productive and easy to cultivate, but when it was absent, human beings had to toil in order to wrest food from the earth. The abstract notion of life is treated here as if it were a material object that a god might add or remove from the ground at will. On another occasion, Zeus angrily withheld fire from men, but Prometheus stole it and gave it to humans. In this myth fire is a material object that can be hidden, stolen, or given away. A myth about the centaur Cheiron recounts how the centaur received an incurable wound but, being immortal, could not die. Zeus transferred Cheiron's immortality to Herakles, and Cheiron died.[146] The property of deathlessness is handled as a thing that a god can simply withdraw from one creature and implant in another. In the myth of the love of Eos (Dawn) for the mortal Tithonos, Zeus granted Tithonos immortality at the request of Eos, but she forgot to ask him also to grant her lover eternal youth, so that he acquired one but not the other, and as he grew older, he shrank till he was nothing more than a voice. In this case immortality and youth are two separate qualities that can be implanted, and immortality does not automatically imply concomitant agelessness. Further, in the mythologized folktale of Cupid and Psychê, the goddess Venus dispatched the maiden Psychê to Proserpina to fetch a small amount of beauty and bring it back to Venus. As Psychê returned, she opened the box, but the contents proved to be not beauty but sleep, which promptly overcame her.[147] In this tale the abstract notions of beauty and sleep are hypostasized such that they are material substances that one can transport in a box.

Since narratives cannot be stories without characters who possess human-like minds, whether the characters themselves are represented as human beings, gods, machines, animals, plants, geometric figures, abstractions, or something else, the immense benefit that personification offers the storyteller is that anything whatsoever can be made to be a character. It matters not whether the entity manifestly exists in the physical world (in the sense that the earth is palpably there) or exists only as a noun in the language, representing a common idea or abstraction (such as "love" or "day"), or is a wholly imaginary creation (such as an Olympian god). Reification offers the corresponding possibilities in the case of nonmaterial referents, since it turns any idea or abstraction into a thing.

In short, if something can be thought or imagined, it can be given a part in a mythological story as a character via personification or as an object via reification. Once that happens, the narrator is free to make predications about it precisely as though it were a person or thing. Personified beings can be placed into relationships, as happens when the earth and the sky, personified as Earth and Sky, are represented as being sexual mates who produce children, and such beings can be made to have any other sort of experience that an actual person might be imagined to have. In the case of abstractions there is no sharp line between personification and reification. For Hesiod, Sleep is a living being, a son of Night and a brother of Death, whereas for Apuleius sleep is something that can be carried around in a little box.

A special advantage of reification for myth in particular is that something reified not only has material existence, allowing it to be treated as any other object, but also can be elevated to the level of principle. When Zeus withheld fire from mankind and Prometheus stole it, the contested object was not merely an instance of fire but all fire, the principle of fire. If you possess it, you have fire; if you do not, you lack fire. In contrast, the sleep that Psychê carried in a box was not the principle of sleep, the possession of which determined whether humans had the power to sleep or were condemned to continuous awakeness, but only an amount of the substance, with no cosmic implications.

In some stories a god and the god's province of influence are so closely identified that the deity is essentially a personification of an idea, which is then subject to the same range of narrative treatment that any other personified or reified notion is. When the cunning Sisyphos physically bound the god Thanatos (Death), no one could die, for death as a principle ceased to operate in the world. It was as though Zeus had withdrawn "death" from the cosmos and hidden it away somewhere. When the grain-goddess Demeter was angry at the gods because of the abduction of her daughter, she caused the cycle of plant life to shut down and cease to operate. An idea can be reified and treated like any other object, or it can be personified and treated like any other human or human-like being, or it can be regarded as a force or activity closely tied to a divine supervisor and treated like any other process whose proper operation depends upon the full and willing attention of the organization's manager. In the last instance, the activity may cease to function if the supervisor is restrained, angry, absent, and so on, as when in her grief and anger Demeter cared only for her kidnapped daughter.

Binatural Beings versus Composite Beings

When a feature of the world, whether physical (such as the earth) or conceptual (such as love), is personified, the being that results is binatural, possessing two natures. Gaia is both the physical earth upon which humans tread and plant crops and also a living, anthropomorphic female creature capable of thoughts, emotions, and sexual reproduction. In any narrative scene featuring a personified part of the cosmos, one aspect of the being is always foregrounded and the other deemphasized or forgotten, as if the two natures alternated, for even though both natures are somehow fully there, it is narratively awkward for both to be fully present to mind. Thus when Gaia is active as a female being, her aspect as earth is difficult to imagine, and when she is the earth, it is hard to picture her as a mother with children. Although one can accept her two aspects logically, as simple facts (that is, she is this but also that), it is not easy to combine them (for example, the earth talks with her children). When the classical scholar Walter Burkert speaks of "logic disregarding reality" as a characteristic of mythological narrative, he nicely captures the strangeness of cosmic binaturalism.[148]

The binaturalism of a Gaia, a combination of two complete natures, must be distinguished from the two natures of a satyr or centaur, who is composed of particular elements of two different, naturally occurring beings. In a satyr the upper body of a man is joined to the rear legs and tail of a horse. Thus a satyr is an incomplete man complemented by an incomplete horse, whereas Gaia is a complete earth and at the same time a complete, fully anthropomorphic and anthropopathic being. The recipe for these two kinds of creature is different and so is the relationship of form to behavior. Gaia is fully the earth and also fully a humanoid wife and mother with children, even if in any particular scene one aspect is foregrounded at the expense of the other. But a satyr is a composite being, a compromise between human and equine nature. Never fully human nor fully equine, he is something in between, a bestial man, a human beast.

Reversible and Irreversible Changes

Since change in traditional narrative is abrupt rather than gradual, mythological accounts of cultural change usually feature two temporal stages: before and after, then and now. The basic arts of civilized life are viewed as having been discovered or invented complete by someone on a particular occasion or taught or brought complete to humans by a god. Prometheus gave men fire. Demeter taught humans agriculture. Dionysos taught them viticulture. Athena taught women weaving. Kingship came from Zeus. Hermes invented the tortoise-shell lyre. Prometheus (or Hermes or Palamedes or Kadmos) introduced the alphabet. The idea of the *protos heuretes*, or first inventor or discoverer of a particular thing, was so well established that lists of them were made.[149]

An event involving a change is sometimes raised to the level of principle by its being represented not as a local event but as an unalterable cosmic precedent, no explanation being offered for its irreversibility. For example, once the gods induced Epimetheus (a divine member of the primordial community of men) to accept Pandora (the first woman), women became an inextricable part of the community of men. A principle had been established that was somehow irreversible, so that Epimetheus, once he perceived that he had been duped by the gods, was not allowed simply to return their gift to them, undoing what had been done, and as a consequence the human community from then on consisted irrevocably of both females and males. For the want of an established term, I call this principle *semel ac semper*, or *once-and-always*, the phenomenon according to which a particular action on a particular occasion in a myth implicitly establishes a principle that cannot be changed or a precedent that cannot be undone.

Several factors contribute to the once-and-always principle. The most important is narrative necessity, as in the case of the rule that a god is not permitted to undo what another god has done. If Epimetheus could simply send Pandora back to the gods, the myth would immediately reach a dead end. In the myth of the primordial division of meat between gods and men, if Zeus, having discovered that he had been tricked, had been permitted to disown his choice and insist on choosing again, or if the gods had been allowed simply to say that they are gods and they will have things the way they want them, the myth would fall apart. It cannot be allowed to happen, so that certain changes must be treated as irreversible even though there is no clear justification for it within the story itself.

To put the matter into perspective, the once-and-always principle is an instance of the device of the special, or arbitrary, rule, which is found in all genres of traditional narrative.[150] For example, success in a particular matter may be said to depend upon the satisfaction of a precondition that has no rhyme or reason other than to justify additional activity and so prolong the story enjoyably. Thus it was said that Troy could not be captured so long as the Trojans had in their possession a particular object, the Palladion. There is no obvious reason within the narrative why such a rule should exist, its true raison d'être being only to motivate an episode in which the Greeks steal the Palladion. The rule makes only backstage sense, on the level of story composition. But the device of the arbitrary rule contributes a pleasant element of mystery to a story, especially when the rule is attributed to the supernatural world, whose unseen workings endlessly fascinate the natural world.

NOTES

1. Plato *Phaedrus* 229a–230b.

2. See further Veyne (1988).

3. Cf. *Homeric Hymn to Apollon* 158–161; Herodotos 3.122; Clay (1989, 49); Vidal-Naquet (1986, 45).

4. *Theogony* 570–616, *Works and Days* 47–105.

5. The story, which is an international folktale (Hansen 2002, 42–44), is found in Greece as an Aesopic fable (Perry 173).

6. For myth as primordial, foundational, and counterfactual, see McDowell (1998, 80). For myth as totalizing, see Lévi-Strauss (1979, 17).

7. Littleton (1973, 123–127); Puhvel (1987, 241–255).

8. See, for example, Woodford (2003).

9. The Greek texts are collected by Fowler (2000). For the recognition of myths and legends as a distinct class of story, see Fowler (2000, xxviii). The works of the early Greek mythographers are not available in translation.

10. Herodotos 3.122.

11. See Palaephatus [Palaiphatos] (1996).

12. See, for example, Kirk and Raven (1962, 168–170).

13. Scholiast on Homer *Iliad* 20.67.

14. On the Indo-European element in Roman tradition, see Puhvel (1987, 144–165). On Roman myth and legend more generally, see Grant (1971); Bremmer and Horsfall (1987); Graf (1993); Wiseman (1994, 23–36; 1995); and Feeney (1998, 47–75).

15. *Roman Antiquities* 2.18–20.

16. Petronius *Satyrica* 48.7.

17. See Chance (2000); Seznec (1961).

18. See Gruppe (1921); de Vries (1961); Feldman and Richardson (1972); Bremmer (1988); Edmunds (1990); Sebeok (1965); Von Hendy (2002); and Schrempp and Hansen (2002).

19. For Hawthorne, see Panofsky (1965, 110–111); Cox (1883).

20. See West (1966, 356–379) for Hesiod's three-story cosmos; Kirk (1990, 2:296–298) for Homer's four-story cosmos; and, for a general discussion, Berger (1904) and Havelok (1987).

21. Hesiod *Theogony* 722–725. Hesiod makes his point with an anvil because he thinks that heavy objects fall faster than light ones.

22. Homer *Iliad* 8.13–16.

23. Nevertheless, in the *Odyssey* Odysseus reaches Erebos by sailing west. Horizontally distant and vertically distant are sometimes treated as being identical in early Greek cosmology.

24. On Okeanos, or the River Ocean, see Homer *Iliad* 14.200–210, 18.607–608, 21.195–197; Richard Janko, in Kirk (1992, 4:180–183); Mark Edwards, in Kirk (1991,

5:231–232); Hesiod *Theogony* 337–370, 786–791, *Shield of Herakles* 314–317; and Herodotos 2.23, 4.8, 4.36.

25. Homer *Iliad* 18.607–608; similarly, Herakles's shield in Hesiod's *Shield of Herakles* 314–317.

26. *Iliad* 21.195–7.

27. Hesiod *Theogony* 337–370.

28. For the literary and archaeological evidence, see Frazer (1898, 5:314–320).

29. See Ovid *Metamorphoses* 2.409–530; Richlin (1992).

30. On Apollon's combat with Python and on Kadmos's combat with the dragon of Ares, see Fontenrose (1959, 13–27, 306–320).

31. On the Amazons, see Tyrrell (1984); duBois (1982).

32. See Herodotos 4.32–36; Romm (1992, 60–67).

33. Hesiod *Theogony* 270–276.

34. Homer *Iliad* 1.423–424, 23.205–207; *Odyssey* 1.22–26; Romm (1992, 49–60). On traditions about blacks in classical antiquity, see further Snowden (1970; 1983).

35. Ovid *Metamorphoses* 2.235–236; cf. Pliny *Natural History* 2.80.189. The aetiology is Lamarckian, not Darwinian, in that a creature's experience becomes a physical trait that by an unexplained mechanism is transmitted to descendants.

36. Homer *Odyssey* 11.14–19; Heubeck (1989, 2:77–79).

37. Homer *Odyssey* 11.

38. On ancient traditions concerning the Pygmies, see Hansen (2002, 45–49). For the rediscovery of Pygmies or of Pygmy-like peoples in Africa, see Turnbull (1961, 15–20).

39. For bronze, see, for example, *Iliad* 17.425; for iron, see, for example, *Odyssey* 15.329. On Greek notions of the sky and its support, see Brown (1968).

40. Hesiod *Theogony* 517–520, 746–748; Homer *Odyssey* 1.52–54. See further West (1966, 311, 366). Notice that Atlas supports the sky, not the earth. There is no clear evidence for an earth-supporter in Greek tradition. The common misconception of Atlas as the supporter of the spherical earth (for example, "A842, *Atlas*. A man supports the earth on his shoulders," in Thompson's *Motif-Index of Folk-Literature*) was encouraged by notions of the sky as a sphere and by artistic representations of Atlas carrying the sky in the form of a sphere, as does the Farnese Atlas in Naples; see Dilke (1998, 145–146). The image of Atlas holding up the heavens, said to be common in sixteenth-century books of maps, led to books of maps being called atlases.

41. Vitruvius 6.7.6; Brown (1968, 46).

42. Herodotos (1.202) calls it "the so-called Atlantic Sea, beyond the Pillars of Herakles." Atlas lends his name as well to Atlantis, that is, "(island) of Atlas," the imaginary civilization described by Plato in his *Timaeus* and *Critias*.

43. Herodotos 4.184.3. According to Ovid (*Metamorphoses* 4.625–662), the god and the mountain are one and the same, the god having been transformed into the mountain.

44. Tester (1987, 3–4). The Greeks and Romans adopted the Eastern institution of the seven-day week, each day being named for one of the seven planets acknowledged by the ancients. The planet that in astrological thought governed the first hour of a particular day lent its name to the entire day (Zerubavel 1985). English preserves these names in Germanic translation (Strutynski 1975). For example, Thursday < Thor's Day < Jove's Day < Zeus's Day.

45. West (1978, 376–381); Edwards, in Kirk (1991, 5:211).

46. For Eos, see Homer *Odyssey* 5.1–2. For the rising of Helios, see *Odyssey* 3.1–2. For Helios's return, see Athenaios 11.469d–470d. The corresponding Roman names are Aurora (dawn), Sol (sun), and Luna (moon).

47. Homer *Iliad* 18.483–489; Edwards, in Kirk (1991, 5:211–213); Homer *Odyssey* 5.271–275; Hainsworth, in Heubeck et al. (1988, 1:276–278); Hesiod *Works and Days* 614–621; West (1978, 252–256, 314).

48. See further Fontenrose (1981).

49. See, in general, Gruppe, in Roscher (1924–1937, 6:35–95); Laurence Kahn-Lyotard and Nicole Loraux, in Bonnefoy (1991, 1:412–414).

50. Homer *Odyssey* 11.51–80.

51. Ibid. 24.1–14.

52. At the conclusion of his *Republic* (614b–621b), Plato describes the experience of Er, a soldier who perished on the battlefield but returned to life twelve days later, whereupon he gave an account of his soul's traveling to the realm of the dead. For medieval and modern accounts of near-death experiences, see Zaleski (1987) and Kellehear (1996).

53. Homer *Odyssey* 12.377–388.

54. On Hades, see Thieme (1968).

55. Homer *Odyssey* 11.568–629. See further Christiane Sourvinou-Inwood, "Crime and Punishment: Tityos, Tantalos and Sisyphos in Odyssey 11," *Bulletin of the Institute for Classical Studies* 33 (1986, 37–38), and Hansen (2002, 69–75).

56. On the Elysion Field and Menelaos, see Homer *Odyssey* 4.561–569.

57. The ancients sometimes refer to the realm of the human dead as Tartaros and the realm of imprisoned immortals as Erebos. Imaginary geography accommodates considerable variation.

58. Homer *Iliad* 8.13–16; Kirk, in Kirk (1990, 2:296–298).

59. Hesiod *Theogony* 722–819.

60. For example, Plato *Menexenus* 238a: "The earth does not imitate a woman in conception and birth, but a woman imitates the earth." See, in general, Guthrie (1957, 11–45). Into the seventeenth century of our era scientists held that minerals grew within the earth like plants by virtue of the plastic powers of the earth (Allen 1963, 92–112). The belief that the earth is a living female organism survives today among certain scientists in the form of the so-called Gaia Hypothesis.

61. *Danaides* frag. 44 Radt.

62. On cosmic senescence, see Lovejoy and Boas (1997, 98–102); Guthrie (1957); Hansen (1996, 144–145).

63. See Weinreich, "Zwölfgötter," in Roscher (1924–1937, 6:764–848); Guthrie (1950, 110–112). On pattern numbers generally, see Dundes (1980).

64. 2.53.

65. Zeus claims to be the strongest of the gods, able to take hold of any deity and cast him or her down into Tartaros, able even to win a cosmic game of tug-of-war against all the other gods together (Homer *Iliad* 8.1–27). There is no talk here of relying upon special weapons such as his thunderbolts.

66. Hesiod *Theogony* 389–396, 881–885. But according to Homer (*Iliad* 15.187–193) and other authorities, the three brothers Zeus, Poseidon, and Hades drew lots to determine their respective honors. As his province and residence Poseidon got the sea, Hades got gloomy Erebos, Zeus got the sky, and they were to share the earth and Olympos.

67. Ovid *Metamorphoses* 6.5–147.

68. Cf. Graf (1984).

69. *Homeric Hymn to Demeter* 302–313; Pherekydes (*FGH* 3 F 119).

70. *Iliad* 21.407.

71. *Homeric Hymn to Apollon* 102–104.

72. Aristotle *Politics* 7.13.3; Hansen (1996, 137–139).

73. Herodotos 1.60.

74. Helios sees and hears everything (Homer *Iliad* 3.277). Zeus sees and perceives everything (Hesiod *Works and Days* 267–269).

75. *Homeric Hymn to Demeter* 188–190.

76. Ovid *Metamorphoses* 8.679–683.

77. Homer *Odyssey* 3.371–379.

78. *Homeric Hymn to Aphrodite* 45–190.

79. *Homeric Hymn to Apollon* 388–501.

80. See West (1966, 387–388); Watkins (1970); Kirk, in Kirk (1985, 1:94–95); Janko, in Kirk (1992, 4:196–197); Sissa and Detienne (2000, 42).

81. Homer *Iliad* 14.290–291; 20.74.

82. Hesiod *Theogony* 492–493. See further West (1966, 302).

83. *Homeric Hymn to Apollon* 115–135.

84. Apollodoros (*Library* 1.3.6) describes her as fully armed; artwork shows her fully grown.

85. *Homeric Hymn to Demeter* 233–241.

86. *Iliad* 5.337–342.

87. Ibid. When, however, a god temporarily takes the disguise of human form in order to mix with humans, he or she consumes the same food and drink as humans do. So the goddess Athena, having assumed the form of a mortal man Mentes, dines on bread, meat, and wine when she pays a visit to Telemachos at his palace in Ithaca (Homer *Odyssey* 1.139–143).

88. On Olympian gods as cattle-owners, see *Homeric Hymn to Hermes* 70–72.

89. Homer *Odyssey* 12.127–142, 260–419. Helios also has sheep on the Greek mainland (*Homeric Hymn to Apollon* 410–411).

90. *Homeric Hymn to Hermes.*

91. Apollodoros *Library* 2.5.10, 2.5.12.

92. *Homeric Hymn to Demeter* 305–313.

93. Ibid. 233–262.

94. Herodotos 5.92; Lucian *Lover of Lies* 27.

95. Diodoros of Sicily 4.38.4–5. See further Edsman (1949).

96. See Rohde (1925, 581–582); Burkert (1960–1961).

97. Homer *Iliad* 20.131.

98. Homer *Odyssey* 17.481–487.

99. Homer *Iliad* 6.128–143.

100. *Acts* 14.

101. Homer *Odyssey* 7.199–206.

102. Homer *Iliad* 1.423–424.

103. Hesiod frag. 1.6–7 MW; Thalmann (1984, 99–102).

104. *Odyssey* 16.157–166.

105. On one occasion Zeus himself lists many of his sexual conquests for his wife Hera, though without specifying the particular transformations involved (Homer *Iliad* 14.312–328).

106. Homer *Odyssey* 4.414–423, 455–463.

107. Apollodoros *Library* 3.13.5.

108. Ovid *Metamorphoses* 1.610–611.

109. Ibid 3.173–205.

110. Homer *Odyssey* 6.229–235; 13.397–403. See Clay (1983, 161–165).

111. Homer *Odyssey* 13.187–216.

112. Apollodoros *Epitome* 1.20.

113. Ibid 3.5.

114. Clay (1983, 15–16, 166–167).

115. Hesiod *Theogony* 727.

116. Homer *Odyssey* 7.14–17.

117. Homer *Iliad* 5.127–128. Another device that renders one unseeable is the mysterious Cap of Invisibility (*aidos kyneê*) employed by Athena, Hermes, and the hero Perseus.

118. See further Kirk, in Kirk (1990, 2:69); Hansen (2002, 464–465).

119. *Homeric Hymn to Hermes* 145–147. For other examples, see Homer's *Odyssey* 4.802, 838–839; 6.20.

120. For winged deities, see Aristophanes *Birds* 573–576. For winged sandals, see Homer *Odyssey* 1.96–98. For a chariot with winged horses, see Pindar *Olympian* 1.86–87.

121. Iris runs through the air; Apollon leaps like thought (*Homeric Hymn to Apollon* 107–108, 114, 448). Apollon descends like night (Homer *Iliad* 1.47).

122. For a chariot drawn by peacocks, see Ovid *Metamorphoses* 2.531–533; by sparrows, see Sappho frag. 1 L-P.

123. *Homeric Hymn to Apollon* 447, 462.

124. For example, Priam tells Helen: "I don't hold you responsible; I hold the gods responsible" (Homer *Iliad* 3.164–165).

125. Ovid *Metamorphoses* 3.336–337.

126. Charles Perrault, "La Belle au bois dormant," first published in 1697. The fairies in this tale play the role that in antiquity the Fates play.

127. See Homer *Iliad* 18.78–93. On Thetis's efforts to render the infant Achilleus immortal, see Hansen (2002, 483–485). In Homer's *Odyssey*, Kalypso is referred to indifferently as a goddess or a nymph; she is immortal and offers to render Odysseus immortal if he will remain with her as her mate.

128. Hesiod frag. 304 MW.

129. *Homeric Hymn to Aphrodite* 273–275.

130. Pausanias *Guide to Greece* 6.24.8.

131. Hesiod *Works and Days* 213–285.

132. Sophocles *Oedipus the King*, ad init.

133. For Chryses, see Homer *Iliad* 1.39–41. For Athena, see Homer *Odyssey* 1.60–62.

134. Mortals offer entertainment for the gods' pleasure both intentionally, as when mortals perform a song, dance, or drama for the gods, and unintentionally, as when they go about their business while the gods act as spectators, like mortals at a spectacle. On the latter, see Griffin (1980, 179–204).

135. *Homeric Hymn to Aphrodite.*

136. Ibid. 281–290.

137. Homer *Odyssey* 5.118–129.

138. Homer *Iliad* 14.312–328.

139. Relationships of men and nymphs continue to be reported in the present day; see Larson (2001, 60–90).

140. On Odysseus, see Homer *Odyssey* 10.336–345. On Anchises, see *Homeric Hymn to Aphrodite* 187–190.

141. Homer *Iliad* 5.60–61, 23:306–8; Clay (1983, 168n).

142. Homer *Odyssey* 7.109–111; 8.477–481. We have Hesiod's own account of his transformative encounter with the Muses (*Theogony* 22–34) and a third-person account of the poet Archilochos's encounter with the Muses (Gerber 1999, 16–25).

143. *Homeric Hymn* 20.

144. Xenophon *On Hunting* 1.

145. Homer *Odyssey* 19.394–398.

146. Apollodoros *Library* 2.5.4; Robertson (1951).

147. Apuleius *Metamorphoses* 6.16.4, 6.21.1.

148. Burkert (1979, 20); cf. Olrik (1992, 46). Additional examples of the primacy of logic over reality are, for example, Kronos's swallowing (not eating) his children, who live inside him for years before being vomited out again, just as Zeus subsequently swallows Metis, who dwells inside him permanently; and Typhon's removing Zeus's sinews and storing them away until Kadmos gets hold of them by a trick and returns them to Zeus, who reinserts them into his body, permitting it to function physically again. The same rule operates in Greek Old Comedy: Lysistrata's sex strike, in which Athenian and Spartan women refuse to engage in sexual intercourse with their husbands until they should cease warring, is a happy idea but in a world of many sexual options for men (slaves, prostitutes, and other males) not a realistic one; the play simply ignores these options.

149. For example, Pliny (*Natural History* 7.56.191–7.60.214) and Hyginus *Fabulae* (274 and 277). See further Kleingünther (1933).

150. See further the entry "Special Rules and Properties" in Chapter 3.

2

TIME
What Happens in Classical Mythology

Like the generation of leaves, so also is the generation of men.
The wind pours the leaves onto the ground,
but when the season of spring comes
the woods blossom and produce other leaves.
Like the generation of men,
some are produced and some pass away.
—HOMER *ILIAD* 6.146–149

Time begins when the first thing happens, and in Hesiod's cosmogony the first thing that happened was the appearance of Chaos. Since the two great families of gods, the Titans and the Olympians, came into being later, time preceded the gods and was not something created by them. So the gods are not masters of time, except in small ways as when Athena prolonged a particular night in order to allow Odysseus and Penelopê to become reacquainted with each other after a long separation.

There are foreboding hints of an end-time. Hesiod sees himself as a member of the Race of Iron, who live in a degenerate era of misery and crime that will get worse and worse until finally Zeus will destroy it. He would rather have been born before it or after it.[1] From this we can infer that he expects something better to follow the present age, but it will be not so much an end of time as a transition, the conclusion of one age and the beginning of another.

DIVINE TIME AND HUMAN TIME

After the first cosmic beings—Chaos and Gaia—come on the scene, the world experiences a succession of divine sovereigns. They are Ouranos (Sky), Kronos, and Zeus, the last of whom establishes himself as the final and permanent ruler of the cosmos. Time unfolds for these beings as a succession of irreversible experiences, one event following another. For Ouranos and Kronos, the onset and conclusion of their own brief rules were the temporal markers of personal significance; for Zeus and his fellow Olympians, the important landmark was the Titanomachy, or battle against the Titans, in which the Olympian family of gods overcame the Titan family of gods and established itself securely as dominant in the universe. These were powerful events in the world of the gods, but they were sorted out early in the history of the universe, and once they were resolved, little of political weight has pressed upon the world of the Olympians. Hereafter what has been important to them is personal and family matters such as feasting, mating, and begetting children, but even the pace of producing offspring slows down, so that the Olympian gods presently settle into a comfortably steady state of relative stability. Outside of their own immediate world, their primary entertainment is viewing the constantly changing spectacle of human events on the earth's surface, which they choose sometimes to influence or participate in. For the gods, time remains a succession of unique events, or geometrically speaking, a linear experience, greatly compressed with mountains and valleys at the beginning and thereafter stretching out with small ripples into infinity.

Human beings, having been crafted by the gods, came on the scene later. Initially their experience of time was similarly linear, one unique event succeeding another, for gods and men made up two interacting communities, enjoying a carefree life that did not know sickness, pain, or toil. But after men gravely offended the gods, the latter avenged themselves by introducing into the human community not only the ambivalent element of women but also the unequivocal evils of hard work, illness, and death. The community of men became a community of both men and women as well as one that had to toil in order to survive. Since the earth no longer produced food automatically and abundantly as a gift for humans to gather at their pleasure, they had now to work the soil, plant seed, harvest crops, and store food against lean times, and similarly they had to tend animals, pasturing them, shearing them, milking them, slaughtering them, and so on, for food and clothing. Human beings became bound to the seasons, each time of year having its particular obligation and opportunity for the farmer and the pastoralist, so that time became a series of repetitions, an annual rotation of activities.[2] For mortals, the original linearity of time became entangled with cyclicity, so that the human experience of time emerged as a mix of repetition and irreversible succession.

What is true of gods and humans as groups is also true of them individually. Just as the divine struggles for supremacy in the early cosmos were quickly sorted out, after which the reign of Zeus has continued forever with no essential change, so also after a god was born, he or she quickly reached a particular developmental age, generally junior or senior adult, and has remained frozen there forever after, unaging. A time chart for the gods both collectively and individually would show a compressed beginning with mountains and valleys close together, followed by an infinite line with an occasional wave.[3] The case is quite different for humans. Just as the necessity of work binds most humans to the cycle of the year's seasons, so also each individual life rotates from birth through infancy, adolescence, adulthood, and senescence and ends inevitably in death. In mythological narrative, however, human mortality is emphasized more than human toil. Although the population consists largely of agriculturalists and pastoralists, the foregrounded characters are members of ruling families, and their concerns are grander—glory, power—or at least more dramatic—love, personal conflict—than utilitarian.

The experience of time conditions knowledge. The gods are knowledgeable, not because divine beings are omniscient but because they are creatures of leisure who have lived for a long time and therefore have seen and heard much, because they travel easily, because they are able to observe processes that are invisible to human eyes, and because they have some acquaintance with what is fated to happen. In contrast, humans live brief lives devoted largely to toil, can only guess at the hidden workings of the universe, experience little of the earth, and are not privy to destiny. For immortals, with their greater knowledge of the past and the future, time is more permeable and flowing, whereas mortals are relatively more confined to the present moment. For their knowledge of prehistory, distant events, and the future, humans depend upon traditional reports passed from person to person and information passed from gods to particular human beings. For information of divine origin, the important intermediaries for the human community are the seers and the bards. "Tell me now, Muses, you who have Olympian homes," sings Homer when he wishes to describe detailed human events that took place long before his own time. "For you are goddesses, you are there, and you know everything, whereas we ourselves only hear the report and do not actually know anything."[4]

WHAT HAPPENS IN CLASSICAL MYTHOLOGY

What classical mythology is depends upon whether one looks from the inside or the outside. From inside the system it is a body of natural and historical knowledge about the world before the human era, deriving from human reports of experiences passed down from person to person as well as information of divine origin shared by the gods with human beings. To the scholar peering into the system from without, it is a corpus of narratives about the imaginary activities of imaginary beings, and its truths are social and psychological. From either viewpoint the information is inconsistent, lacunate, and overlapping. There is no single, authoritative account of classical mythology, nor can there be, for it is in the nature of traditional story that every narration is merely a version. Here I offer mine, a synthesis of Greek and Roman traditions about the world from the origins of the cosmos to the end of the heroic era.

From Chaos to Cosmos

First to come into being was Chaos, followed by Gaia, Tartaros, and Eros. Of the four primordial beings, Chaos was space, not infinite space but bounded space, a chasm, a vast opening that was defined in some way (the Greek word *chaos* did not originally signify a state of utter disorder). Once space was there, Gaia (Earth) came into being, the solid foundation of the universe, and then Tartaros, the great prison for defeated gods and monsters. The fourth being on the scene, Eros (Love), was the force of attraction and mating, that is, sexuality.

The first generation of beings who somehow emerged into existence were binatural beings, at once things (space, earth, prison, love) and living creatures who were capable of thoughts, feelings, and action. Most of the elements of the eventual cosmos issued from them and their descendants as a result of sexual mating; or rather most of the constituents of the universe derived from two of them, Chaos and Gaia, since Tartaros for the present played no role, and Eros (Love) functioned only as the principle of sexuality that allowed reproductive activity to occur.

No reason is offered why the four primordial beings come into existence, nor why they come into being when they do rather than earlier or later, nor is any attention given to the preceding state of affairs, since space, matter, and time begin only when the first event occurs, which is the appearance of Chaos.

Two Cosmic Families

Chaos produced Erebos (Darkness) and Night, and these two mingled in love, producing in their turn Aither (Brightness) and Day. Gaia (Earth) gave birth to Ouranos (Sky) as a covering for herself and as a base for the gods, and she bore also the Mountains and Sea.

Before the arrival of Eros on the scene, sexuality did not exist, so that the first generation of beings, the Primordial Four, had no parents whatsoever and are said simply to come into being. From then on most beings issued from the bodies of other beings. The members of the second generation, the children of Chaos and the children of Gaia, had one parent, either Chaos or Gaia, who produced them parthenogenically, without sexual intercourse. But for the third and succeeding generations, heterosexual reproduction was the norm, although at first the mates were siblings (the brother and sister pair, Erebos and Night) or mother and son (Gaia and Ouranos), because the choice of sexual partners was limited and because the present order had not yet been established. The entire universe now came into being step by step, the result of offspring who mated, producing more offspring who mated, and so on until the elements of the familiar world were present. The different offspring were physical elements of the cosmos such as Sky and Sea, anthropomorphic deities such as Zeus and nymphs, and personified forces, states, times, and the like such as Erebos and Night, which we ourselves would classify as nonmaterial abstractions. All these entities were alive and capable of cognition, feeling, and action.

Since Chaos and Gaia did not mate with each other and their descendants did not mix, each was the head of a great family of world elements, for every new thing was born into one or the other of these two families, or descent groups, and the particular family to which it belonged was largely a function of its nature as a tangible or intangible.[5] The descendants of Gaia were visible and solid—anthropomorphic gods and parts of the physical world—whereas for the most part the descendants of Chaos were, like Chaos itself, things that we should classify as dark or intangible such as Night, Thanatos (Death), Hypnos (Sleep), and Eris (Discord).

How could abstract ideas and parts of the universe, which were neither male nor female, be thought of as heterosexual couples? Every Greek (and Latin) noun has a gender, most being masculine or feminine, although there are also neuters, and the gender of a personified being such as Night was determined by the grammatical gender of the corresponding noun. Since the grammatical gender of *night* in Greek is feminine, night was treated as a female being when it was personified as Night. Of the two beings to whom Chaos gave birth, one (Night) is feminine and the other (Erebos "darkness, murkiness") is masculine. So Chaos gave birth in effect to female and male darkness. And Night and Erebos in turn mated and had two offspring, Aither (Brightness), which is masculine, and Day, which is feminine. So male and female darkness begot male and female brightness. The primordial beings Chaos and Gaia, founders of the two great descent groups, could not mate with each other, Chaos being neuter and Gaia being feminine, so that they produced offspring asexually. What was inside of them simply emerged.

The Cosmic House

The cosmos was constructed much like a vast house. Gaia's first offspring was Ouranos (Sky), conceived as being not an expanse of air and space above the earth but as a concave ceiling, as solid a structure above as earth was below. Thus once the floor (Gaia) was established, the domed ceiling or roof (Ouranos) was produced and the interior was furnished with detail and texture (Mountains, Sea). Now that the cosmic house had been constructed, it was ready to serve as a theater for ambitious gods and monsters who would strive with one another for control of it, for dominion over the world.

The Succession of World Rulers

Gaia mated with Ouranos, bearing him the twelve children Okeanos, Koios, Krios, Hyperion, Iapetos, Theia, Rhea, Themis, Mnemosynê, Phoibê, Tethys, and Kronos, who were collectively called the Titans. She also gave birth to three mighty sons called Cyclopes, each having only one eye, set in his forehead, and to three other powerful beings, the Hundred-Handers, each with fifty heads and a hundred arms.

But Ouranos, who understood only sexuality, hated his children, and as each child was born he pushed it back into Gaia, causing her to groan in pain. Taking countermeasures, she created an adamantine sickle and displayed it to her children inside her, declaring that they should avenge their father's evil treatment of them. Only the youngest Titan, wily Kronos, had the courage to respond, volunteering to avenge their father's doings. Gaia concealed him in ambush and placed the sickle in his hands. In the evening when the guileless Ouranos came and lay upon Gaia, desiring and embracing her, Kronos reached out and with the sickle cut off his father's genitals and flung them away. Drops of blood fell upon Gaia, impregnating her, so that in time she gave birth to three sets of offspring who were connected in one way or another with blood and violence: the Erinyes (Furies), who take vengeance upon persons who shed the blood of their own kinsmen, as in the present case Kronos shed the blood of his own father; the Giants, who were born fully armed and ready for battle; and the Meliai, ash trees and the nymphs of such trees, the wood from which spear shafts would be made. The severed genitals ended up in the sea, where the ejaculate became sea foam, and within the foam a maiden Aphroditê, goddess of love, was formed. Ouranos's sovereignty passed to his son, Kronos, youngest of the Titans. So the first ruler of the cosmos was a tyrant who suppressed all growth. Such a world could develop no further.

Kronos mated with his sister Rhea, who bore him three daughters, Hestia, Demeter, and Hera, and three sons, Hades, Poseidon, and Zeus. Keeping constant watch, Kronos swallowed each child as it was born, for he had learned that he was destined to be overcome by one of his own sons, and he did not want anyone else to be king among the gods. Rhea was seized with grief and asked her parents, Gaia and Ouranos, how she might bear her next child in secret and punish Kronos. When she was about to bear her last child, Zeus, Gaia and Ouranos told her to bring him to the island of Crete. There Rhea hid her baby in a cave, and she wrapped a stone in swaddling clothes and gave it to Kronos, who swallowed it in the belief that it was his son.

When Zeus grew up, he gave Kronos an emetic, causing him to spew up the children he had swallowed. Then the young god released the Cyclopes, who had remained imprisoned within the earth, and they returned the favor by giving Zeus the thunderbolt. The older gods and the younger gods now engaged each other in battle, the Titans ranged on Mount Othrys, the Olympians on Mount Olympos some seventy miles distant. The fight raged without resolution for ten years. Finally Zeus released the Hundred-Handers, gave them nectar and ambrosia, and asked them to engage in the battle on the side of the Olympians in return for their release. Acknowledging the superior intelligence of Zeus and their debt to him, the Hundred-Handers agreed. In the final encounter each side attacked the other, causing the earth to roar and the sky to groan. Zeus charged down from Olympos, letting loose with his thunderbolts. Forests burned, the sea and the River Ocean boiled, and the Earth cried. Hurling 300 rocks at a time, the Hundred-Handers drove the Titans into the earth. There they fettered them, putting them in Tartaros, which is as far beneath the earth as the sky is above the earth.

Strangely, Gaia now mated with Tartaros and bore the monster Typhon, a dragon with a hundred serpentine heads, each spitting fire and emitting strange sounds. Typhon would have become ruler of mortals and immortals alike if Zeus had not perceived the threat. Another battle of cosmic proportions ensued as the two immortals engaged in battle, but Zeus finally overcame him with his thunderbolts and hurled him also into Tartaros. From Typhon come destructive winds, storms that scatter ships and ruin crops.

On the advice of Gaia, the other Olympian gods now urged Zeus to rule. So Zeus succeeded Kronos as king of the gods, and as the new head of the cosmic bureaucracy he distributed honors, or offices, to the individual members of his team, like a victorious general distributing spoils to his troops after a battle. Kronos had done the same when he had become king, for before the Titanomachy Zeus had summoned the gods to Olympos and promised that any god who should join him in the war against the Titans would retain the honor that he or she had held previously, and any god who had failed to acquire an honor from Kronos would obtain one from Zeus. So Zeus now put Poseidon in charge of the waters, Hades in charge of Erebos, Demeter in charge of agricultural grains, Styx in charge of divine oaths, and so on, making new assignments and confirming old ones. Zeus himself had already assumed the honor of kingship over the gods, having succeeded his father Kronos. The younger Olympians such as Hermes, who were not yet born, would acquire their allotments later.

Zeus consolidated his rule by means of a series of marriages. First he took the Oceanid Metis (Cleverness) to wife, the most knowledgeable of the gods. Gaia and Ouranos, however, revealed to him that Metis would bear him two children, a daughter, Athena, who would be Zeus's equal in strength and intelligence, and an invincible son who would become king of gods and men. So when Metis was about to give birth to Athena, Zeus tricked her and placed her in his belly. Precisely how he tricked her is no longer known, but since Metis had the ability to change shapes, a characteristic power of sea deities, he likely induced her to take the form of something edible or potable, and then swallowed her. She was not destroyed but took up residence inside him and thereafter helped him in counsel. So Zeus was not only physically powerful, as he had proved in overcoming Typhon, but also mentally powerful, since Metis herself resided in him. He thereby brought the succession of cosmic rulers to an end, having forestalled the birth of the son who would have overthrown him.

Zeus then took to wife Themis, who bore him the three Hours and the three Fates. Next he mated with the Oceanid Eurynomê, begetting the three lovely Graces. His fourth wife was Demeter, who bore him Persephonê, whom Hades subsequently seized to be his wife. Zeus then mated with Mnemosynê (Memory), and she gave birth to the nine Muses, goddesses who delight in feasts and song. After that Zeus mated with Leto, who bore him the beautiful children Apollon and Artemis, both of them archers. Finally he wed Hera, and she gave birth to Hebê (Youth), Ares, and Eileithyia. Afterward Zeus himself gave birth to the war-goddess Athena, who emerged from his head fully grown and attired in armor, whereupon Hera in anger and rivalry produced on her own and without sexual intercourse the smith-god Hephaistos.

Zeus had other children from affairs with other females, and two of his sons were received into the ranks of the Olympian gods. One was Hermes, whom the nymph Maia bore in a cave on Mount Kyllenê. Another was Dionysos, fruit of an affair with Semelê, a mortal woman from the city of Thebes. These affairs took place after the advent of human beings. With the birth of the younger Olympians—Apollon, Artemis, Athena, Hephaistos, Hermes, Dionysos (and in one tradition also Aphroditê)—the number of the Olympians, now twelve, ceased to grow. Zeus's brother Poseidon wed the

Oceanid Amphitritê, who bore him a son Triton, and Aphroditê wed Ares or Hephaistos.

So the young universe experienced a series of divine rulers. The first two were tyrants who felt threatened by their children, Ouranos preventing their birth and keeping them inside their mother, and Kronos swallowing them as soon as they were born. Their ideal was a static universe with no change or growth. In contrast, the would-be ruler Typhon was all wildness and disorder. Zeus represented a compromise between these unlivable extremes. Emblematic of the god and his administration was the series of marriages that he undertook and the offspring he begat—the Hours, the Fates, the Graces, the Muses, and so on, deities of prosperity and order and civilization. Zeus was moreover strong, as his triumph over Typhon showed, and intelligent, as his possession of Metis attests. Having prevented the conception of the son who was to overthrow him, Zeus promised cosmic stability. This was to be the nature of the world under the rulership of Zeus.

The First Humans

Prometheus created human beings from earth and water, molding them in the likeness of the gods. The creator of the first humans was thus a craftsman, a transformer, whose human counterparts were the potters who fashioned clay figures for religious and secular purposes; but Prometheus's prototypical human beings possessed the stature of present-day human beings and, unlike figurines formed by human craftsmen, were endowed with life. So humans have the same relationship to the gods that clay figurines do to mortal potters. The event took place in Panopeus, where the local clay had the odor of human skin.

As with the first stirrings of the cosmos, the genesis of human beings had no special significance or divine purpose. One day it just took place. If it is unclear why the first human beings were created, it is also unclear when they came into being. According to some sources, humans made their appearance during the reign of Kronos. In any case it was well before Zeus's relationship with Demeter and the birth of their daughter Persephonê, for the myth of Demeter and Persephonê presupposes the existence of normal human communities at Eleusis and elsewhere.

The Athenians, however, boasted that they were autochthonous, having been born like plants from the soil of Attica, and so represented a different line of humans from that created by Prometheus. And many other Greeks likewise claimed descent from a particular human being who had emerged from the earth in their territory, an earthborn person whom they regarded as the first man. The Greek people known as Myrmidons traced their own origin back to ants that Zeus had transformed into human beings on the island of Aegina, and indeed there is a similarity of sound between the ethnic name Myrmidons and the Greek word for "ants" (*myrmekes*), as though one derived from the other. So human beings had more than one origin.

The Division of Meat

According to yet a different myth of human origins, men and women were not created at the same time; rather, men were created first, for the original intention of the gods was to create only males, despite the fact that among the gods themselves and in the animal world both males and females were found.

One day the gods and these first men were settling the question of how meat would be divided between them. The event took place at Mekonê, later called Sikyon, in the northeastern Peloponnese. Zeus represented the gods, and Prometheus was also there, perhaps as an arbiter, for as a descendant of the Titan family of gods he belonged neither to the community of men nor to the family of Olympians. A great ox was slaughtered, which Prometheus divided into two portions. Zeus commented upon how unfairly Prometheus distributed the portions, but Prometheus merely invited Zeus to select the pile he preferred, which would define the gods' portion ever afterward, just as the other portion would forever be mankind's share. Although one of the portions apparently consisted of delicious fat and the other merely of the hide of the ox, Prometheus had actually concealed the meat inside the hide and the bones inside the fat. Zeus straightway chose the portion topped with fat, which is why still today men burn bones and fat on the altars of the gods. When Zeus saw that his pile consisted mostly of bones, he was enraged at Prometheus's deception.

Fixing the allotment of meat continued the fixing of honors among the gods that followed the Titanomachy. The present incident established how meat should be distributed between gods and men, introducing a further distinction between the two groups. Little by little privileges and relationships were being fixed in the young cosmos. At the same time this incident was the first in a string of events in which the relationship of gods and men progressively deteriorated. Prometheus's deceit introduced a sour note into the initially harmonious relationship of the Olympian gods and human men, in which the two groups had mixed freely and conversed directly, like the inhabitants of any two neighboring communities might do. Men got meat, but as a trade-off they also incurred the hostility of the gods, leading eventually to a separation of the communities of gods and humans.

The Theft of Fire

In their anger at Prometheus's trick, the gods hid away men's *bios*, or "life," keeping it concealed. If they had not done so, a man could have gotten by with working merely one day a year, and he would have had no need for either draft animals or ships in order to support himself. In the primordial paradise when harmony reigned between men and gods, the earth produced food so plentifully that sowing and plowing were unnecessary, and the only task was the delightful work of harvesting the bountiful produce, which could be done in a single day each year. But after the gods withdrew nature's vital energy from the soil and hid it away someplace on Olympos, beyond the reach of men, humans have had to struggle throughout the year for their sustenance.

As if that were not enough, Zeus also withheld fire from mankind, hiding it away as well, for fire too was something that could be transported and concealed. The immediate consequence of this act was to render useless the abundance of meat that men acquired through Prometheus's deceit, for without fire men could not convert the flesh into food suitable for human beings. Indeed, without fire men were deprived even of the ability to manufacture utensils and tools, for they could neither fire clay pots nor smelt metals, nor could they employ fire for warmth and light. In short, humans would live no better than animals.

At this crisis Prometheus once more acted on behalf of mankind, stealing fire from the gods, concealing it in a fennel stalk. The practice of carrying fire in a stalk of giant fennel was an old one in Greece and Italy and served a practical purpose in an age when it was easier to transport fire than to start a new one. The dry pith inside a fennel stalk, when lit, burns slowly, allowing a person to carry it from one place to another without its going out. Prometheus adapted this method of transporting fire to thievish purposes, to which it was well suited, since the fire smoldering inside the fennel stalk could not be seen. The Titan made the divine element of fire permanently available to men by placing it in trees, for once fire was stored in wood, men could extract it by friction whenever it suited them. Human beings now possessed fire for cooking, heat, light, and technology. Their life would be above that of the animals, but of course below that of the gods.

The Loss of Paradise

When Zeus saw that men had fire, he became angrier still and decided to give men an evil gift in exchange for the theft of fire. On his orders Hephaistos fashioned a lovely maiden from clay and water, Athena dressed her attractively in wondrous clothes and taught her weaving, the Graces placed golden necklaces around her neck, the Hours put a garland of spring flowers upon her head, and Aphroditê poured grace and charm upon her, exciting love and desire, after which Hermes put in her mind the shamelessness of a dog and the deceit of a thief, and gave her a voice. Hermes announced that her name was Pandora, or All-Gift, since the Olympian gods had all contributed to her creation. When Hephaistos brought this beautiful evil to gods and men, they were struck with amazement. Zeus then had Hermes bring her as a gift to Epimetheus, the slow-witted brother of Prometheus, and he accepted her despite Prometheus's having warned him not to accept anything from Zeus. Devising miseries for men, Pandora lifted the lid off of a *pithos*, or large storage jar, and scattered its contents. Before this, men had lived free of hard work, diseases, and death, but now these painful miseries became part of men's lives, for the spirits that had been contained in the great jar began now silently to stalk the earth and the sea by the thousands, bringing misery to men. Only Hope remained within the jar, for Zeus decreed that Pandora should replace the lid before it could escape.

From Pandora are descended all women, who are painful for men to live with but also painful to live without. As for Prometheus, Zeus's wrath also fell upon the Titan for matching wits with him. Zeus had him bound to a column, where each day an eagle came and fed on his liver, which each night grew back again.

This sequence of three linked myths (meat > fire > woman) envisions a primordial world without women, although it was not a world without females, since on the divine level there were goddesses as well as gods, and on the bestial level there must have been females as well as males, for one would not slaughter an animal for food if animals could not reproduce themselves. Had not Prometheus, acting as man's champion, offended Zeus, humans would have remained a community of males living in harmony with the gods in a cosmos without the disheartening miseries of hard work, sickness, and death. Until the advent of death-bringing diseases, the community of men had no need to replenish itself and so no need of procreation, or, more accurately, until the advent of woman and procreation the male community had no need of mortality. Women and death entail each other, for reproduction must be balanced by death just as death must be balanced by reproduction. Since Prometheus did offend Zeus, men have been confronted with the confusing ambivalence of women. All in all, a great trade-off occurred, in which men acquired amenities that belonged to the gods, but they also acquired, along with divine hostility, a number of miseries including a gendered community.

Now the primordial community of gods and men was no more. In place of a carefree life of ease, of convivial meals shared with the gods in their presence, the human condition now meant scarcity and hard work, and communion with the gods now took the form of a sacrificial meal in which humans enjoyed the better portion of the animal but were obliged to dine alone, or with guests unseen.

The Great Deluge

Unfortunately, human behavior got even worse in the eyes of the gods, degenerating to such an extent that Zeus decided to destroy the human race by means of a great flood. But Prometheus privately tipped off his own son, Deukalion, who built a boat, filled it with provisions, and embarked on it with his wife, Pyrrha, daughter of Epimetheus and Pandora. Zeus covered much of the earth with water, destroying nearly all life. Deukalion and Pyrrha, however, sailed safely on the waters of the deluge for nine days and nights, coming to land eventually on a peak of lofty Mount Parnassos. After disembarking, they performed a sacrifice to Zeus of Escape, whereupon Zeus sent Hermes to grant them any wish they should choose. They wished for humans, and Zeus instructed them to throw stones behind them, which they did, and those cast by Deukalion became men and those cast by Pyrrha became women. From these "pebbles" (Greek *laas*) has come the word *people* (*laos*).

The great deluge was the latest installment of divine hostility toward humans. The gods exceeded their earlier hostile acts of withdrawing nature's vital energy, concealing fire, creating woman, and releasing baneful diseases into the world, for in the present case they attempted to destroy the human race by drowning. As in the concealment of fire, their plan was thwarted by Prometheus. The gods did not again attempt a large-scale extermination of human beings for several generations, when Zeus engineered a great war at Troy in order to reduce the human population.

The deluge is much like a return to chaos, requiring a new cosmogony and anthropogony. The world is a watery waste, and then the waters recede, allowing water and land their own separate domains, and finally human beings are created.

The Origin of Nations

The children of Deukalion and Pyrrha were Hellen, Amphiktyon, and Protogeneia. Hellen was the eponym of the Hellenes (Greeks). With the nymph Orseis he had three sons, Doros, Xouthos, and Aiolos (Latinized forms = Dorus, Xuthus, and Aeolus), and he divided the country among them. Doros got the region beyond the Peloponnese, calling the inhabitants Dorians after himself. Aiolos reigned in Thessaly, naming the inhabitants Aeolians. And Xouthos received the Peloponnese as his lot. He had two sons Achaios (Latinized form = Achaeus) and Ion, from whom the Greeks known as Achaeans and Ionians have come. The descendants of Deukalion and Pyrrha settled in different places, and many of them gave their names to their regions or to their descendants.

The Gods Establish Their Cults

Around this point in the chronology, Greek mythology is so rich in stories that I must be content to exemplify. Many myths recount how individual deities acquired their spheres of influence and established their major cults on earth, and other myths tell of the mating of gods and human beings. The relative sequence of these myths relative can be difficult to decide, since they may be self-contained narratives.

The Eleusinian Mysteries

Zeus had wed his sister Hera, and Poseidon had wed the Nereid Amphitritê, but their brother Hades had no mate. Zeus allowed him to abduct Persephonê, Zeus's daughter by Demeter, though Zeus said nothing of this arrangement to Demeter, who would have regarded the match as undesirable, or to his daughter, whose intention at that time was to remain a maiden. So one day as the girl gathered flowers in a meadow, the earth gaped open and Hades burst forth on his chariot, seized her, and carried her down to Erebos, his subterranean kingdom. In the guise of an old woman, Demeter searched the earth for her missing daughter. Although her quest was unsuccessful, she encountered kindly persons, including the Eleusinians, whom she rewarded with the extraordinary gift of wheat and its cultivation. They in turn shared the seeds of this grain with others until the entire inhabited world abounded in it. The goddess also established her special rites at Eleusis, the Eleusinian Mysteries. After she learned that Persephonê had been abducted by Hades, Zeus dispatched Hermes to the realm of the dead to bring Persephonê back, and mother and daughter were joyously reunited, but when Demeter discovered that Persephonê had eaten food in Erebos, a mere pomegranate seed, she understood that Persephonê would belong partly to the death realm forever. Thereafter Persephonê lived half of the year with her spouse in Erebos and half with her mother and the other immortals in the upper world. Persons who have been initiated into the Mysteries confront death more optimistically.

The Delphic Oracle

Shortly after his birth on the little isle of Delos, Apollon declared that his provinces of interest would be the lyre, the bow, and prophecy. With the last of these in mind he set out in search of a place to build an oracular temple where humans might offer sacrifice to him and he might prophesy. Deciding upon a site on Mount Parnassos, he laid out its foundations and human craftsmen completed the work. But the project was threatened by a monstrous dragon that dwelled at a nearby spring and wrought much destruction in the land, killing the inhabitants and their sheep. Apollon shot the monster with an arrow, and she perished and rotted (Greek *pytho* = rot) on the spot, for which reason the place was named Pytho and the god himself called Pythian Apollon. After that it was safe for men to sacrifice there. Now the god needed priests for his new sanctuary. Spotting a ship bearing Cretans from Knossos, Apollon took the form of a dolphin and leaped onto the vessel, and the ship no longer obeyed its rudder but made its way to Krisa, the port of Pytho. Taking the form of a youth, Apollon revealed his identity to the seafarers, informing them that they had been selected to manage his temple. He bade them sacrifice to him as Apollon Delphinios (Apollon of the Dolphin), after which he led them singing up the slope of Parnassos to his temple. Later the city of Pytho was renamed Delphi.

Who Will Possess Athens?

Just as according to one tradition the brothers Zeus, Poseidon, and Hades drew lots for possession of the three principal domains of the cosmos (the sky, the sea, and the death realm), so also the gods once decided to take individual possession of different cities where they would receive worship. Athena and Poseidon both went to Attica to compete for possession of that region. As evidence of his claim to the place, Poseidon struck a rock on the Acropolis with his trident, and the sea poured forth. For her part Athena planted an olive tree. Sitting as judges, the gods awarded the country to Athena, who named the city Athens after herself. In anger Poseidon flooded the nearby Thriasian plain. In historical times Poseidon's miracles—a well of sea water and the imprint of his trident upon a rock—could be seen on the Athenian acropolis, along with Athena's olive tree.

Bacchic Rites

The youngest of the Olympians, Dionysos, went to different cities, introducing his rites accompanied by a virtual army of bacchae, or female celebrants, whom he equipped with wands called thyrsi. In most communities the population welcomed him, but at other times an impious person denied his divinity, as happened, for example, at Thebes. When Dionysos arrived there, he induced the women to leave their homes and revel on Mount Cithaeron, but the local monarch, Pentheus, was indignant at these proceedings and went to the mountain to spy on the revelry. He was discovered by the bacchantes, and in a state of madness his mother, Agauê, who was among the god's celebrants, tore him apart limb from limb in the belief that he was a wild animal. The Thebans learned firsthand the terrible consequences of denying the power of Dionysos.

The Arts of Civilization

Just as wheat and its cultivation came from Demeter and viticulture and winemaking from Dionysos, so also most of the other important elements of culture and civilization were introduced by individual gods. Thus the art of the smithy came from Hephaistos, war from Ares, hunting from Artemis and Apollon, the institution of kingship from Zeus, and so on. Or, as a Greek poet put it, smiths belonged to Hephaistos, warriors to Ares, hunters to Artemis, lyre-players to Apollon, and kings to Zeus. The deity in each case was the inventor or discoverer or owner of the art, and humans were their pupils. If a man was a king, it was because Zeus made him one, and it was Zeus who watched how the man behaved and who rewarded him accordingly, so that a monarch's prosperity or lack of it was an index of divine judgment on him.

In some instances a god instructed humans once and for all in an art, as Demeter did. In other instances gods worked through an intermediary. After Artemis and Apollon invented hunting, they gave it as a gift to the good centaur Cheiron, who taught it to his fosterlings and pupils, some twenty-one heroes including Nestor, Hippolytos, Achilleus, Meleager, Odysseus, and Palamedes, and from them the knowledge of hunting spread to other men. Or sometimes a deity taught his or her craft repeatedly and unseen. So Athena has placed a knowledge of weaving into the minds of individual maidens at different times.

The Mating of Gods and Humans

Much mating took place between mortals and immortals. The underlying cause of this activity was Aphroditê, who made individual immortals feel erotic desire for individual mortals, resulting in the birth of the demigods, or heroes, who were partly divine but ultimately mortal. After a time Zeus wished this sexual mixing to stop, so that he caused Aphroditê herself to feel sexual longing for a mortal man, after which the humiliated goddess ceased bringing about the mating of immortals and mortals. The cessation of this sexual activity heralded the eventual disappearance of the demigods, for as the divine element in the human population became more diluted with each new generation, the heroic age wound down and came naturally to an end.

Eos

The goddess of dawn, Eos, carried many mortal men away for her erotic purposes and bore them a number of children. Since she had once lain with Aphroditê's lover Ares, Aphroditê caused Eos to be in love continually. Eos loved Tithonos and conveyed him to Ethiopia, where they slept together, and she bore him several children, including Memnon, who fought and perished at Troy. She also carried off Kephalos (Latinized form = Cephalus), bearing him a son Phaethon. Another of her lovers was the great hunter Orion, whom she bore away to the island of Delos, but Artemis killed Orion because the gods were jealous of Eos falling in love with a mortal.

Zeus

Like Eos, Zeus was a serial lover, having erotic dealings with partner after partner. When King Akrisios of Argos learned from an oracle that his daughter Danaê would give birth to a son who would kill him, he kept her secluded in an underground chamber. Zeus poured through the roof in the form of a stream of gold, however, and had sexual intercourse with Danaê, who bore a son, Perseus. Zeus had an affair with a Theban woman, Semelê, who perished (or became immortal) when the god appeared to her in his full divine majesty; their son was Dionysos. On another occasion Zeus snatched up the handsome Trojan youth Ganymedes and translated him to Olympos to serve as his cupbearer and erotic companion.

Thetis

Although both Zeus and Poseidon were erotically interested in the Nereid Thetis, a prophecy foretold that a son born to her would be more powerful than his father, so that neither god cared to pursue the attraction. But the hero Peleus was also drawn to her and, advised by the centaur Cheiron, lay in wait, seized her, and held on while she changed from one shape to another—fire, water, and different animals—until she resumed her original form. They were married on Mount Pelion with a grand wedding ceremony attended by immortals and mortals, the last social event in which immortals and mortals intermingled. Thetis bore Peleus a son, Achilleus, whom she tried secretly to make immortal like herself by burning away his mortal parts, but Peleus came upon her secret rites and, misunderstanding them, shouted out in dismay, whereupon Thetis, frustrated in her attempt to give her son immortal life, deserted both father and son, returning to her fellow mermaids in the sea. Their son Achilleus became the greatest warrior at Troy, a more powerful man than his father.

Aphroditê

After Aphroditê caused many gods to mate with mortals, Zeus implanted longing in her for the Trojan prince Anchises, in order to prevent her from boasting among the gods that she had mated gods to mortal women, who bore them mortal offspring, as well as goddesses to mortal men. Taking the form of a beautiful maiden, Aphroditê approached Anchises on Mount Ida, where he was herding sheep. After they made love in his shepherd's hut, she resumed her divine form and revealed her true identity to him, declaring that she would bear him a son, Aineias (Latinized form = Aeneas). The local nymphs would rear the child and eventually turn him over to Anchises. Ashamed to have conceived a child with a mortal man, however, she instructed him on pain of death never to reveal the child's true mother to anyone; rather, he was to say that the boy's mother was a mountain nymph.

The Heroic Age

After the establishment of cosmic order under the sovereignty of Zeus, mythological interest shifts to events concerning the ever-spreading and ever-multiplying human population, focusing upon a half-dozen or so great families with many branches, whose descendants are traced generation after generation until the heroic age fades out and the historical period begins. They are the Deukalionids, or descendants of Deukalion, who spread out over much of Greece, including Aetolia and Thessaly; the Inachids, who descended in a separate line from Inachos, son of the Titans Okeanos and Tethys, and settled in Argos, Crete, and Thebes; the Atlantids, or descendants of the Titan Atlas, who occupied parts of the Peloponnese and also Troy; the Asopids, descendants of the River Asopos, who were found in places such as Aigina, Salamis, and Phthia; the kings of Athens, some of whom were autochthonous; and the Pelopids, descendants of Pelops, son of Tantalos, whose father was Zeus, and who settled in different parts of the Peloponnese such as Elis, Mycenae, and Sparta. The mythology is so multistranded that it is impossible to relate it as a single continuous narrative, for many events happen at the same time. The culminating engagement of the heroic age, the Trojan War, is itself an unusually complex event in that it brought together many members of many families into a single place at the same time. The other great conflict of the heroic era, the war at Thebes, belonging to the history of the Inachids, is also complex but much smaller in scale.

A Family of the Heroic Age: The Pelopids

Let us consider one of these great families, the Pelopids, which eventually plays a major role in the Trojan War.

Pelops was one of several children of Tantalos, who was in turn a son of Zeus and Plouto. Favored by the gods, Tantalos was allowed to share their feasts, but he once slaughtered and boiled his own son Pelops, serving him to the gods. The gods detected the cannibalistic fare and did not eat it, except for Demeter, who consumed a shoulder of Pelops. The gods brought Pelops back to life again, substituting an ivory shoulder for the one that Demeter had eaten. The resuscitated youth was so handsome and attractive that Poseidon became enamored of him and carried him to Olympos, where they were lovers.

Tantalos abused the gods' hospitality by passing on to his friends certain secrets of the gods, which he had learned from their table conversation. Or he shared divine food, ambrosia, with his friends. The gods created a special punishment for him in Erebos. He stood in water with fruit trees on either side of him, and whenever he wanted to drink, the water dried up, and whenever he wanted to eat, winds wafted up the branches of the trees, taking the fruit beyond his reach. After Tantalos once again offended the gods, Poseidon returned Pelops to earth.

Pelops and Hippodameia

When Pelops was of marriageable age, he wished to compete for the hand of Hippodameia, whose father, King Oinomaos of Pisa, offered her to the man who could beat him in a chariot race. Oinomaos instituted this contest because he did not wish to give his daughter to another man to marry, having a passion for her himself. A suitor was obliged to take Hippodameia in his own chariot and set out at full speed for the Isthmus of Corinth, whereupon Oinomaos, fully armed, would set out after them in his chariot. If a suitor should manage to reach the Isthmus alive, he would win Hippodameia as wife, but if Oinomaos caught up with them, he killed the suitor. The king had the advantage of possessing horses that had been given to him by his father, Ares. Twelve youths had lost their lives in this way, and Oinomaos had cut off their heads and nailed them to his house. In order to have a chance in the race, Pelops needed extraordinary equipment. So he prayed to Poseidon, reminding the god of their love affair and asking him now to lend him his chariot and horses for the race. The god gave him his winged chariot and horses.

Pelops traveled from Anatolia to Oinomaos's kingdom in western Greece. When Hippodameia saw how handsome he was, she fell in love with him and asked Oinomaos's charioteer Myrtilos to sabotage her father's chariot. Myrtilos, who was himself in love with Hippodameia and wanted to please her, agreed to do so. So he did not insert the linchpins into the wheel hubs of the chariot. On the day of the race, Pelops set out with Hippodameia in his chariot, and Oinomaos pursued them, but presently the wheels came off, and he became entangled in the reins and perished. Recognizing Myrtilos's treachery, Oinomaos cursed him, praying that Myrtilos himself should perish at Pelops's hands. After the race Myrtilos tried to rape Hippodameia, and when she told Pelops of his behavior, he cast Myrtilos from the flying chariot. Myrtilos drowned in the waters below, which were thereafter called the Myrtoan Sea, but before he died he cursed the family of Pelops. After Pelops was purified of the killing, he returned to Pisa and took over Oinomaos's kingdom. Having subjugated much of the surrounding regions, he named the peninsula Peloponnese (Pelops's Island) after himself.

Atreus and Thyestes

Pelops and Hippodameia had several sons, including Atreus and Thyestes. Atreus once made a vow to sacrifice to Artemis the most beautiful lamb that should be born in his flock, but when a golden lamb was born, he strangled it and kept it in a chest. Now, Atreus's wife, Aeropê, was in love with her brother-in-law Thyestes, who seduced her, after which she gave the lamb to Thyestes.

When the Mycenaeans received an oracle telling them to choose a Pelopid as their king, they sent for Atreus and Thyestes as sons of Pelops. The Mycenaeans were discussing who should be their king, when Thyestes proposed that they give the throne to the man who possessed a golden lamb. Atreus of course agreed to this, but since Thyestes produced the lamb, Thyestes became king of Mycenae. Zeus intervened, sending Hermes to Atreus with instructions that Atreus should propose a second contest for the kingship, namely, that Atreus should become king if the sun should travel backward. Thyestes agreed. The sun set in the east as a divine indication of Thyestes's usurpation. So Atreus became king of Mycenae and banished his brother.

When subsequently Atreus learned of the adultery of Aeropê and Thyestes, he sent a herald to his brother with a message in which he proposed a reconciliation. Upon Thyestes's arrival, Atreus slaughtered three children sired by Thyestes with a naiad, dismembered them, boiled them, and served them without their extremities. After his brother had dined, Atreus displayed to him the extremities of his children and banished him once again.

Now Thyestes in turn burned for vengeance. An oracle informed him that he would get his revenge if he should father a son by his own daughter. Sometime later Thyestes and his daughter Pelopia had sexual intercourse without

The judgment of Paris: Hera, Athena, and Aphroditê stand before Paris, with Hermes looking on.

knowing the identity of their partner, and she bore a son Aigisthos (Latinized form = Aegisthus). When he grew up and learned who his father was, he killed Atreus and gave the kingdom back to Thyestes.

Agamemnon and Menelaos

At the murder of Atreus, his two sons, Agamemnon and Menelaos, were spirited away to safety but subsequently returned with Tyndareus and expelled Thyestes, granting him his life on the condition that he swear to live elsewhere, which he did. Thereupon Agamemnon became king of Mycenae and married a daughter of Tyndareus, Klytaimnestra. They had several children, including Orestes, Elektra (Latinized form = Electra), and Iphigeneia. Agamemnon's younger brother, Menelaos, wed Helen, another daughter of Tyndareus, after which Tyndareus turned over to Menelaos the kingdom of Sparta.

Antecedents to the Trojan War

Humans spread out over the earth, becoming so numerous that the earth was oppressed by their weight. Zeus decided to bring about a great war at Troy in order to empty the earth of humans by means of death and thereby lighten earth's load, as he had done earlier when he had sent a great flood. He had already put a stop to the mating of gods and humans. The aim of these two plans, the initia-

Eris (Strife).

tion of a great war and the cessation of mating between mortals and immortals, was to reduce the number of humans on the surface of the earth and more specifically to extirpate the heroes and their kin, the mixed offspring of mortals and immortals who because of their frailty and finite lives caused the gods to feel so much grief. The community of gods and the community of humans would then become entirely separate. Freed of ties to human mates and human progeny, the gods could resume the carefree lives that they had enjoyed before the advent of human beings.

So the goddess Eris (Strife) tossed before Hera, Athena, and Aphroditê a golden apple as a prize for the most beautiful of them. Since each goddess claimed the prize, Zeus had Hermes take them to a certain Trojan shepherd, Alexander, or Paris, on Mount Ida to act as judge. Each goddess offered to give the youth a particular gift if he should chose her. Hera said she would make him a powerful ruler, Athena said she would make him a victorious warrior, and Aphroditê said she would make him an irresistible lover, promising him the hand of Helen. Paris awarded the apple to Aphroditê. He then sailed to Sparta, where for ten days he was entertained by Menelaos. When Menelaos had to sail to Crete to take care of a certain matter, Aphroditê brought Helen and Paris together in bed, after which he persuaded her to leave with him. She abandoned her daughter, Hermionê, put much of her husband's property onboard Paris's ship, and sailed to Troy.

Learning of Helen's departure, Menelaos went to his brother, Agamemnon, in Mycenae, asking him to collect men to campaign against Troy, and Agamemnon dispatched a herald to the different kings who had been suitors of Helen, reminding them of their oath. For before Helen's father had given her to Menelaos, he had exacted an oath from all her suitors that they would come to the aid of Helen's husband if he should suffer a wrong with respect to his marriage, which now had happened. Some were eager to join the proposed expedition, whereas others were not. When the envoys came for Odysseus, he pretended to be a fool, yoking a horse and a donkey to his plough, and sowing his fields with salt. But one of the envoys, the clever Palamedes, placed Odysseus's infant son Telemachos before the plough, and Odysseus betrayed his rationality by stopping his plow.

The army mustered at Aulis, on the east coast of Boeotia, many men and over a thousand ships from all over Greece, under the leadership of Agamemnon. While they were performing a sacrifice to the gods, a serpent darted from the altar to a bird's nest in a nearby tree, where it consumed nine sparrows and then turned to stone. The seer Kalchas interpreted the sign to signify Zeus's will regarding Troy: they would fight a war for nine years and take the city in the tenth. The army set sail, but not knowing the route to Troy they put in at Mysia and, supposing it to be Troy, began to ravage the countryside. Telephos, king of the Mysians, sallied out with his men in defense of his land and engaged the Greeks. He was wounded in the thigh by Achilleus. Accomplishing nothing, the Greeks returned home.

Helen and Alexander (Paris) brought together by Aphroditê and Eros, with Peitho (Persuasion) looking on.

Eight years later they mustered again at Aulis, having in the meantime learned the way to Troy. Telephos's wound had not healed since the time that Achilleus had inflicted it, and Apollon had informed him that he would be cured only by the person who had wounded him. So Telephos sought out Achilleus and offered to show him the course in return for the treatment of his wound. Achilleus healed him with rust from the spear that had injured him, and the Mysian king revealed how to reach Troy. But a new obstacle arose, for the expedition was unable to sail for lack of wind, and the seer Kalchas revealed that the army could not sail until Agamemnon should sacrifice to Artemis the most beautiful of his daughters. Agamemnon had offended Artemis when he felled a deer with an arrow and boasted, "Not even Artemis could have shot better," and, a generation earlier, Atreus did not sacrifice the golden lamb that he had vowed to her. So now Agamemnon sent messengers to Klytaimnestra, asking her to send their daughter Iphigeneia, saying that he was giving her in marriage to Achilleus. But when his daughter arrived, Agamemnon laid her on an altar to sacrifice her. Artemis snatched her and carried her away to the barbarous Taurians, substituting a deer on the altar.

On the way to Troy the Greeks put in at the island of Tenedos, where Philoktetes was bitten by a water snake. Since the agonizing sore did not heal and gave off an unbearable stench, Odysseus conveyed Philoktetes to the island of Lemnos, where the Greeks abandoned him, leaving him only his bow so that he might subsist by shooting birds.

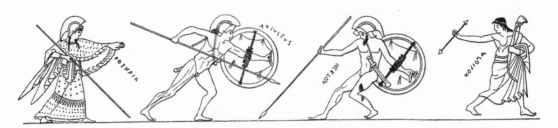

Duel of Achilleus and Hektor, with Athena and Apollon looking on.

Odysseus and Menelaos went ahead to Troy to demand the return of Helen and Menelaos's property, but the Trojans, meeting in assembly, not only refused to do so but even threatened to kill the envoys, who were saved by the intercession of a Trojan, Antenor. His favor would one day be repaid.

The Trojan War

Exasperated at this insolence, the Greeks sailed against Troy, and the Trojans, learning that the fleet was coming, rushed to the sea and tried to prevent the Greeks from disembarking. Achilleus had been warned by his mother, Thetis, not to be the first to disembark, for the first man to land would also be the first to die. This man chanced to be Protesilaos, who slew many men before he himself was killed by Hektor. Protesilaos's wife, Laodameia, loved him so much that after his death she fashioned an image of him that she treated in all respects as though it were alive. The gods took such pity on her that Hermes brought her husband up from Hades' realm for a brief visit, and she rejoiced when she saw him, thinking that her man had come home from Troy, but after he returned to Hades's realm she killed herself.

Achilleus and his Myrmidons landed. Straightaway Achilleus killed Kyknos, a son of Poseidon, by throwing a stone at his head, for he was invulnerable everywhere except there. After this the Trojans fled in fear to the safety of their city, where the Greeks pursued them with much slaughter and began a siege of the city. As time went on, Achilleus slew or captured other men who were unwary enough to be caught, including the youth Troilos, who was exercising his horses in a sanctuary of Apollon, and Lykaon, one of the sons of Priam, king of Troy. The other chieftains also conducted raids in the countryside and on the nearby islands, capturing cities, taking men and women captive, and seizing cattle and other booty. In this way eight years passed. Different gods favored one side or the other. Not surprisingly Aphroditê, to whom Paris had awarded the prize of the golden apple, supported the Trojan cause, whereas Hera and Athena were pro-Greek. Zeus made an effort to remain neutral.

In the ninth year of the war, Agamemnon gravely offended Achilleus. Since Agamemnon was obliged to return a captive woman who had been allotted to him, he intended to take Briseis, a woman who had been given to Achilleus. Furious, Achilleus retired to his hut, refusing to fight any longer and pointing out that it was not he who had a grievance against the Trojans. In addition, he persuaded his mother, Thetis, to intercede with Zeus to make the fighting go poorly for the Greeks in order that they might all the more appreciate the consequences of Achilleus's absence from the battlefield. Once the Trojans perceived that Achilleus was no longer doing battle, they sallied out of the city and fought more confidently. Although the Greeks constructed a defensive wall around their ships, the fighting reached the Greek wall, and presently the Trojan champion Hektor broke through it and set fire to several ships. At this crisis Achilleus, still refusing to rejoin the fighting, agreed to lend his armor to his companion Patroklos, who planned to put in an appearance on the battlefield in the guise of Achilleus in the hope of disheartening the enemy and checking their advance. Seeing Patroklos and taking him for Achilleus, the Trojans did indeed turn and flee, and Patroklos, exhilarated by his success, chased them, killing among others Sarpedon, a son of Zeus, but Patroklos himself fell in combat to Hektor. In grief and anger Achilleus now burned to rejoin the fighting. Equipped with new armor forged for him by the divine smith Hephaistos, Achilleus drove the Trojans back, slaughtering many men, including Patroklos's slayer, Hektor.

The Trojans were aided by different exotic peoples including the Amazons, who were led by their beautiful queen, Penthesileia, a daughter of Ares. She slew many Greeks in battle but was herself slain by Achilleus, who became enamored of her after her death. Achilleus's countryman Thersites mocked him for this passion and even gouged out the eyes of the dead Amazon with his spear, whereupon Achilleus killed him. The Ethiopians, led by Memnon, son of Eos (Dawn) and Tithonos, also lent support to the Trojans. Eventually the two sons of divine mothers, Memnon and Achilleus, faced each other in combat. Memnon fell, but Eos got permission from Zeus to grant immortality to her son and conveyed him from the battlefield.

Presently Achilleus met his end as well. Routing the Trojans in battle and pursuing them into the city, he was felled by an arrow shot by Paris that struck him in the ankle or heel, for although Achilleus was for the most part invulnerable, having been dipped by his mother into the waters of Styx when he was an infant, the liquid did not come into contact with the part of him that she held, which remained vulnerable. When a great fight ensued over the body of

Eos with the corpse of Memnon.

Achilleus, Aias (Latinized form = Ajax) and Odysseus distinguished themselves by their successful efforts to retrieve the body and its armor. Thetis and other nymphs came and bewailed the death of Achilleus. The Greeks cremated him and buried his bones with those of his companion Patroklos. When the arms of Achilleus were offered as a prize to the bravest man, Aias and Odysseus contended for them, with Trojan captives acting as judges. The prize was awarded to Odysseus on the grounds that he had done the Trojans more harm. Aias became so disturbed with the pain of his loss that he plotted to attack against his own army at night, but Athena caused his mind to be deranged so that he slaughtered cattle and herdsmen in the belief that they were Greeks. After regaining his senses he killed himself.

Since the war had dragged on into its tenth year, the Greeks were becoming despondent. The seer Kalchas prophesied that Troy could not be taken unless the Greeks had the bow and arrows of Herakles. These were in the possession of Philoktetes, whom the Greeks had abandoned on the island of Lemnos before the war. So Odysseus and Diomedes were dispatched to Lemnos, and having obtained Herakles' bow and arrows by deceit, they persuaded Philoktetes to sail with them to Troy. Once he was cured of his wound by Machaon, Philoktetes fought Paris in single combat and killed him. Menelaos angrily mutilated Paris's body, which the Trojans managed to retrieve and bury.

Memnon.

At the death of Helen's husband, Paris, the Trojans Deiphobos and Helenos competed for her hand. Since Deiphobos was preferred, the seer Helenos left Troy and settled on Mount Ida, where Odysseus ambushed him and took him captive, for according to the Greek seer Kalchas, Helenos knew the oracles that protected Troy. Brought to the Greek camp, Helenos was forced to reveal to the Greeks how Troy might be taken, saying that, first, the bones of Pelops had to be fetched; second, Achilleus's son Neoptolemos had to fight; and, third, the Palladion (Latinized form = Palladium), a wooden image that had fallen from heaven, had to be stolen from the Trojans, for so long as it remained inside Troy, the city could not be captured. So the Greeks brought the bones of Pelops to the Greek camp. And Odysseus and Phoinix went as envoys to King Lykomedes on the island of Skyros, persuading him to let Neoptolemos accompany them back to Troy. Neoptolemos, earlier called Pyrrhos, was the love child of Achilleus and a daughter of Lykomedes. Upon their return Odysseus gave him the arms of his father, Achilleus, and with them the youth slew many Trojans, including King Eurypylos of Mysia, son of Telephos, who had come with a large force of Mysians to help the Trojans. And, finally, to get hold of the Palladion, Odysseus and Diomedes made their way by night to Troy, where they succeeded in stealing the image and bringing it to the Greek camp.

The architect Epeios now set about constructing a hollow wooden horse, with openings on each side, a stratagem suggested to him by Athena or Odysseus. When it was completed, Odysseus persuaded the fifty bravest Greeks to conceal themselves inside, having carved on the outside of the horse this inscription: "The Greeks dedicate this thank-offering to Athena for their return home." That night the remaining Greeks set fire to their tents and sailed away as though they were giving up the campaign, but in fact they sailed only to nearby Tenedos, where they secretly waited. At daybreak the Trojans discovered that the Greeks' camp was deserted and concluded that they had fled. Joyfully

Greeks exiting from the Wooden Horse.

the Trojans dragged the wooden horse inside the city and deliberated what to do with it. Since both the prophetess Kassandra (Latinized form = Cassandra) and the seer Laokoon (Latinized form = Laocoon) declared that there was an armed force inside the horse, some Trojans wanted to burn it or push it over a cliff, but most were in favor of sparing it inasmuch as it was a votive offering. After performing a sacrifice, the Trojans celebrated with a feast. Apollon moreover sent them a sign that seemed to confirm this choice: two serpents swam from the sea and devoured the sons of Laokoon.

That night as the Trojans slept, the Greeks sailed back from Tenedos, guided by a beacon lit by Sinon, who had been left behind for that purpose. When the men in the horse deemed the enemy to be asleep, they exited the sides of the horse and opened the gates for their comrades. Then they proceeded fully armed into the individual houses of the city and slew the inhabitants as they slept. Achilleus's son Neoptolemos killed King Priam, who had fled to the altar of Zeus of the Courtyard. As he raced to his house, Antenor's son Glaukos was rescued by Odysseus and Menelaos in gratitude for the fact that they themselves had once been saved by Antenor; indeed, the Greeks hung a leopard's skin before Antenor's house as sign that the entire household was to be respected. The Trojan Aineias carried his father, Anchises, out of the city, which the Greeks permitted on account of Aineias's piety. In contrast, Menelaos made his way to the house of Deiphobos, who had married Helen upon the death of Paris, and killed him, leading Helen away to the Greek ships. He had intended to kill Helen as well, but after glimpsing her lovely breasts he put his sword away. Locrian Aias raped Kassandra as she clung to a wooden image of Athena. Neoptolemos threw Hektor and Andromache's son Astyanax from the wall of the city. In short, the Greeks slew or took captive all the inhabitants of Troy except for a few who escaped.

After they set fire to the city, they sacrificed to the gods and set about dividing the spoils. Agamemnon acquired Priam's daughter Kassandra, Odysseus got Priam's widow, Hekabê (Latinized form = Hecuba), and Neoptolemos chose Hektor's widow, Andromachê. Another daughter of Priam, Polyxenê (Latinized form = Polyxena), was slaughtered on the grave of Achilleus.

The Returns

As the Greeks were about to sail away, the seer Kalchas detained them, saying that Athena was angry at them on account of the impious behavior of Locrian Aias. In response, the enraged Greeks wished to kill Aias, but when he fled to an altar of Athena they let him be. They now conferred in assembly about what to do. Menelaos held that they should embark, whereas Agamemnon argued that they should stay and sacrifice to Athena in the hope of appeasing her wrath. Thereupon several leaders set out for home. Diomedes and Nestor had a good voyage, whereas storms prevented the return of Menelaos

Kassandra raped by Aias at the image of Athena, with priestess fleeing.

and his companions. Others set out for home on foot, not trusting in the sea. But Agamemnon and the remainder first sacrificed to Athena and then set sail. Nevertheless, at the request of the angry goddess, Zeus sent a storm against the fleet, and Athena personally cast a thunderbolt at the ship of Locrian Aias, shattering it, although Aias himself managed to scramble onto a rock. When he boasted that he had reached safety despite the intentions of the goddess, Poseidon struck the rock with his trident, splitting it, so that the vaunter fell into the sea and drowned.

Some ships were driven to Euboea during the night, where a certain Nauplios kindled a beacon that induced some of the Greeks to make for the shore, where their ships were wrecked on the rocks with great loss of life. Nauplios was motivated by his wish to avenge the death of his son Palamedes, who had been stoned to death at Troy because of the machinations of Odysseus. For it had been Palamedes who, before the war, had demonstrated that Odysseus was attempting to avoid conscription by playing the fool. When Nauplios learned of his son's death and sought satisfaction for it without success, his thoughts turned to revenge. He sailed around Greece and contrived that the wives of the Greeks should commit adultery in the absence of their husbands, as Klytaimnestra did with Aigisthos. Later, when he learned that the Greeks were sailing home, he lit this false beacon fire, and the Greeks—taking it for a harbor—wrecked their ships upon the rocks.

Odysseus arrived at Ithaca in the tenth year following the Trojan War after experiencing extraordinary adventures. There he and his son Telemachos, now grown, slew the arrogant suitors who passed their days riotously in Odysseus's palace while pressing the king's wife, Penelopê, to remarry. But many Greeks never reached home at all and instead settled down in other lands. Similarly, the few Trojans who managed to escape the destruction of their city settled in various places, among them Aineias and his company, who resettled in Italy.

What happened to the Pelopids Menelaos and Agamemnon? When Agamemnon, commander of the combined Greek forces, reached his kingdom of Mycenae along with his Trojan concubine Kassandra, his wife, Klytaimnestra, and her lover, Aigisthos, murdered them both, and Aigisthos took over the rulership of Mycenae. Klytaimnestra thereby got her revenge for the deceitful way in which, prior to the war, Agamemnon had persuaded her to send their daughter Iphigeneia to the Greek camp, where he wished to sacrifice her. Another daughter, Elektra, secretly took her baby brother, Orestes, away from the palace, turning him over to a certain Strophios in Phocis, who raised him with his own son, Pylades. After Orestes grew up, he asked the oracle at Delphi whether he should go after his father's murderers, and the god gave him permission to do so. So Orestes and his companion Pylades went unrecognized to Mycenae, where Orestes killed his mother and her lover. Having done so, Orestes was pursued by the Furies and driven mad. He went to Athens and was tried at the court of the Areopagus, where he was acquitted, but since he still suffered from madness he consulted the god again, and Apollon told him he would be free of his sickness if he should fetch a particular wooden image that was in the possession of the Taurians. Orestes and Pylades sailed to the land of the Taurians, but they were captured and brought before the local king, Thoas, who sent them to his priestess, for it was the custom of the Taurians to sacrifice all strangers who came their way. But when the priestess Iphigeneia recognized the intended victim as her brother Orestes, the three of them took the wooden image and departed with it. Having reached Mycenae, Orestes married Pylades to his sister Elektra, and he himself wed Hermionê.

As for Menelaos, he was driven by winds to different lands, including Egypt. According to one tradition he discovered the real Helen there at the court of King Proteus, for the Helen who had accompanied Paris to Troy was merely a phantom fashioned out of clouds by the gods. After eight years of wandering Menelaos and Helen returned finally to Sparta. Eventually both were transported by the gods to the Elysion Field.

The End of the Heroic Age

Some heroes of the Trojan War had memorable offspring. Achilleus's son Neoptolemos actually fought in the war. Agamemnon's daughter Elektra saved her brother Orestes's life and helped him avenge their father's death. Odysseus's son Telemachos manfully helped his father overcome the dangerous suitors in their home.

But more often their offspring were not notable, and in any case there is little that is remarkable to relate about the generation that followed this younger generation, which therefore may be deemed the last generation of the heroic era. The extraordinary era of the heroes did not end with a bang but faded into ordinariness, becoming the familiar world in which the divine blood running in human veins was too diluted to be significant (Odysseus declared that he was the second-best archer of his generation, after Philoktetes, who was inferior in archery to men of earlier generations, and Nestor often spoke of the superiority of earlier heroes to those of the generation of the Trojan War), in which the gods have become less concerned to intervene and earthly events are on the whole less striking and grand than when the world was younger. The era of the demigods, or heroes, became the human era, our age. Zeus's plan was fulfilled, according to which the divine and human communities should be separate so that the gods might be free from the cares and grief of intimate involvement in human affairs.

WHAT DOES CLASSICAL MYTHOLOGY SAY?

It is not possible to declare that classical mythology means one thing and not another, since it is not a fixed entity, and even if it were, it would inevitably mean different things to different persons. But I offer a possible, if also partial, reading.

The Nature of the Physical World

The physical world was not created by the gods, so that it is greater than the gods. It was not created for us, for humans. We are just part of it.

It had a beginning, so that it will probably have an end. Indeed, it is declining right now, all the time, slowly, in the way a person ages. The earth was once more youthful and more vibrant and more creative than she is now. But she is all we have: a piece of wonderful and beautiful order, surrounded by chaos and darkness and meaninglessness.

The apparent orderliness of the cosmos is intentional. The stars and planets, including the sun and moon, with their regular cycles were intended to mark the days and the seasons and the years as a cosmic calendar. Probably everything in the cosmos has significance and purpose.

The earth is alive, and so are most other cosmic elements of the universe, and they are divine beings.

The Nature of the Gods

The gods are powerful but not all-powerful. They have not always existed but, like the cosmos itself, came into being at a certain time for reasons that are not clear. The major gods are immortal. There are also countless lower gods such as nymphs, who are long-lived but perhaps ultimately mortal like human beings. The gods are a privileged but mostly positive force in the universe, forming an orderly and reasonable family of rulers, who are committed to positive change and growth, unlike their divine predecessors, who either fostered inertia and the status quo or were violent and tyrannical.

We used to live in one community consisting of gods and men, but in our greed to get a better portion of food than the gods should have, we gravely offended them. For this and other reasons they withdrew to their own dwelling place far away, so that now our interaction is distant and indirect: we discern their will through oracles, seers, omens, dreams, and other similar means. And we dine without them.

The Nature of Humans

We were formed by the gods as physical copies of them, and like them we are male and female. Or perhaps we emerged from the earth in different places, like plants. In any case we were made from the soil of the earth, and when we die our physical selves become soil again, rejoining the mother and nurturer of us all. We owe reverence and worship to the gods, including the earth, because they are our parents and because they are powerful.

Our own powers are very limited and finite, especially when compared with those of divine beings. On the other hand, we share one feature with the gods that sets us apart from the animals, our reason, a spark of the divine fire.

We are subject to death, and from a cosmic perspective we live only a short while. Once we lived like the gods and even with the gods, but our present lot includes hard work, pain, and illness. The responsibility for this may lie with women in particular or with humans generally, or it may just be in the nature of things, but the important fact is that it is irreversible. Suffering must be accepted as an inescapable part of human existence.

We keep trying anyway because we have hope, the hope of better times, better conditions, the pleasures of a mate to share our days, perhaps loving children, good friends. We should win and maintain the goodwill of the gods and strive to win their blessings, for to anger the gods would make things worse.

Most of the arts and elements of civilization we owe to the gods: from Zeus and Hera we have the idea of kings and queens, from Athena we have weaving, from Prometheus we have fire, from Demeter we have grains, from Dionysos we have wine, from Artemis we have archery, from Apollon and the Muses we have song, and so on. Without these, life would be much harder, much less rich.

All human groups are ultimately descendants of the primordial humans who were formed by the gods or grew from the soil of the earth; or perhaps we are descendants of the pious couple who survived the great flood or of the stones they cast behind them. Although we have spread out over the earth, we are ultimately members of a single family. Differences in languages and customs have arisen naturally as a result of the separation of human groups; differences in skin color result from our nearness to or distance from the sun.

When we die, as eventually we must, our soul survives us. We go to a gloomy place beneath the earth or in the west, a desolate land of human souls, where conditions are essentially the same for everyone, good or bad, rich or poor. A few of us, however, receive special treatment, such as persons who have gravely offended the gods or are close relatives of the gods. For reasons that cannot be revealed, persons who have been initiated into the Eleusinian Mysteries and other mysteries will face death with more optimism than will others.

The Heroes, or Demigods

In some cases gods and goddesses mated with human beings, producing offspring who were exceptional in one way or another. Such persons were common in earlier times, when the gods spent more time on earth and were closer to us. These persons and their peers, heroes, went on great expeditions, engaged in seemingly impossible quests, fought in great wars like those at Thebes and Troy, established important cities, begot noble children, founded prominent families. They rid the world of many monstrous beings, making it safe and habitable. They benefited the rest of us by civilizing deeds.

Behavior Options

Traditions about earlier times tell of persons of every imaginable kind, including those who have offended or pleased in various ways, such as humans who did not observe the rules of justice that Zeus gave us, breaking oaths, giving crooked judgments, mistreating strangers, or allowing crimes to go unpunished; persons who neglected to give the gods their due, omitting to sacrifice to them at the appropriate time or to give proper acknowledgment of their divinity; persons who boasted they were equal or superior to the gods or even engaged in actual contests of superiority with the gods. In some instances, such as that of Narcissus, the folly was the result of simple naïveté, but doubtless in most it was the result of *atê*, or mental blindness, which prevents a human from seeing matters clearly and so from acting in his or her own best interests. Such was the case with Helen, whom Aphroditê caused to desert her family in order to accompany Paris to Troy, and later the case also with Agamemnon, who in his pride alienated his best warrior, Achilleus, causing so much unnecessary grief and loss of life at Troy. On the other hand, other persons were renowned for their clarity of vision and understanding—their wisdom, their fair judgments of disputes, their leadership in difficult matters, their courage in times of danger, their sacrifice on behalf of others, their piety toward the gods.

Similarly, our traditions tell of different figures who engaged in every variety of love and erotic relationship, not only heterosexual and homosexual loves but also loves with gods, with humans, with nymphs, in the form of marriages, affairs, rapes, incestuous relationships, and so on—not to mention mortals and immortals who were entirely averse to love.

These figures are not so much models of behavior as they are illustrations of the range of options. All these persons of the past are good to keep in mind. We think through the narratives of their experiences, since they crystallize human life and human possibilities in striking and memorable ways.

NOTES

1. Hesiod *Works and Days* 174–201.

2. Vidal-Naquet (1986, 42). For the farmer's year, see Hesiod Works and Days 381–617.

3. Cf. Zerubavel (2003, 25–34).

4. Homer *Iliad* 2.484–487.

5. Philippson (1936, 8–9); West (1966, 35).

3

DEITIES, THEMES, AND CONCEPTS

ABSENT DEITY

When a deity is away (or distracted or incapacitated or angry), his or her cosmic province ceases to function.

Since it was time for Sisyphos to die, Thanatos (Death) came to fetch him, but the wily Sisyphos managed to bind Thanatos to a chair, whereupon humans and animals ceased to die. Only when Thanatos was freed did death once again become a feature of the world (scholiast Homer *Iliad* 6.153). In this story death occurs when the god Thanatos comes and fetches a person; accordingly, if the god is prevented from carrying persons away, no one dies.

The theme of the incapacitated deity also appears in a myth in which the monster Typhon wrestled with Zeus and managed to remove the god's sinews, leaving Zeus unable even to walk until his allies stole the sinews back (Apollodoros [Apollodorus] *Library* 1.6.3). In a different version, Typhon stole Zeus's thunderbolts, and Zeus could not function as weather god until he had regained them.

The weakest form of incapacitation is distraction. On one occasion the childbirth-goddess Eileithyia, by keeping her legs closed together, was attempting to delay Alcmena's delivery of Hercules, but a perceptive servant of Alcmena distracted the goddess. In surprise she opened her legs, allowing the laboring mother to do the same, and the child was born (Ovid *Metamorphoses* 9.280–323).

The myth of Demeter and Persephonê has the best known instance of the absent deity. At the disappearance of her daughter Persephonê, Demeter departed from Olympos in grief and anger. Presently she brought it about that no seed sprouted on earth, so that all agriculture came to a halt. If Zeus had not intervened, humans would have perished from famine, and the gods would have been deprived of their sacrifices (*Homeric Hymn to Demeter*). Somewhat similarly, Hephaistos worked in a cave near the River Ocean for nine years, making wondrous objects, his whereabouts unknown to gods and mortals except for the Okeanid and the Nereid who had saved him (Homer *Iliad* 18.394–405).

At its mildest, the theme takes the form of a mere threat. Helios (Sun), angry that Odysseus's companions slaughtered several of his beloved cattle, once threatened to leave the sky and shine instead among the dead if Zeus did not avenge his loss. Faced with the possibility of such a cosmic inversion, Zeus promptly promised action (Homer *Odyssey* 12.376–388).

These myths and legends treat deities like foremen or managers. When the manager is absent or incapacitated or when the shop's tools are missing, work stops.

> ***See also*** Demeter
> ***Suggested reading:***
> William Hansen. *Ariadne's Thread: A Guide to International Tales Found in Classical Literature.* Ithaca, NY: Cornell University Press, 2002, 305–314, 443–444.

ADAMANT

Fabulous metal of extreme hardness used by gods and heroes.

Adamant was created by Gaia, who made from it the sickle with which Kronos castrated his father, Ouranos (Hesiod *Theogony* 161–182). The sickle with which Zeus battled the monster Typhon was likewise made of adamant, and the hero Perseus decapitated the Gorgon Medusa with an adamantine sickle given to him by Hermes (Apollodoros *Library* 1.6.3, 2.4.2). The helmet of the hero Herakles was made of adamant (Hesiod *Shield of Herakles* 137). When Zeus had Prometheus bound, his bonds were adamantine (Aeschylus *Prometheus Bound* 148).

Etymologically adamant signifies "unconquerable."

> ***See also*** Wondrous Objects
> ***Suggested reading:***
> Martin L. West, ed. and comm. *Hesiod: Theogony.* Oxford: Clarendon Press, 1966, 215.

AEOLUS (GREEK AIOLOS)

Name of two different characters.

One Aeolus is steward of the winds, and the other is the eponymous ancestor of the Aeolians.

On his way home from Troy, Odysseus came to Aiolia (Latinized form = Aeolia), a floating island that was home to Aeolus and his family. He entertained Odysseus and his companions hospitably, and when it was time for Aeolus's guests to depart, he bound the winds in a leather bag, tied it securely, and presented it to Odysseus, even sending a zephyr to propel Odysseus's ships. For Zeus had made Aeolus steward of the winds, and he was dear to the gods. The journey went well for the Achaeans, and their homeland was in sight, but while

Odysseus slept, his mistrustful companions opened the leather bag, thinking that it must contain gold or silver. The winds rushed out, a storm wind snatching the mariners and carrying them out to sea again. Returning to Aiolia, Odysseus asked once again for help, but Aeolus ordered him away, saying that it would not be right for him to give aid to someone who obviously was hateful to the blessed gods (Homer *Odyssey* 10.1–79).

The other Aeolus was one of the three sons of Hellen and Orseis: Doros, Xouthos, and Aeolus. Hellen is the eponymous ancestor of the Hellenes, or Greeks, and Doros and Aeolus are the eponymous ancestor of the Dorians and the Aeolians, branches of the Greek people. When Hellen divided the country among his sons, he gave the area around Thessaly to Aeolus, who named the inhabitants Aeolians (Apollodoros *Library* 1.7.3).

    See also Eponymy; Winds

    Suggested reading:

Filippo Giudice. "Aiolos," in *LIMC* 1:398–399.

William Hansen. "Homer and the Folktale," in *A New Companion to Homer,* edited by Ian Morris and Barry Powell. Leiden: Brill, 1997, 442–462, at 454–455.

R. Strömberg. "The Aeolus Episode and Greek Wind Magic." *Acta Universitatis Gotoburgensis* 56 (1950): 73–84.

AETIOLOGY (ALSO ETIOLOGY)

Assignment of a cause (Greek *aition*) or origin for something.

Mythological aetiologies trace the origin of a feature of the landscape, a trait of plants or animals, an element of culture, or the like to a discrete event that took place in the past.

For example, Daedalus and his son Icarus were imprisoned in the Labyrinth, but the inventive Daedalus constructed wings from feathers and glue for himself and his son, so that they might escape by flying away. Daedalus warned his son not to soar too high lest the sun melt the glue nor too low lest the damp air loosen it. But Icarus, ignoring his father's instructions, flew so high that the glue melted, his wings disintegrated, and he fell to his death in the sea below, which was thereafter called the Icarian Sea (Apollodoros *Epitome* 1.12–13). In Greek tradition a river or a body of water is often said to have acquired its name from a person who drowned in it.

Aurora (or Eos, goddess of the dawn) weeps tears of sorrow for her slain son Memnon, and her tears appear all over the earth as dew (Ovid *Metamorphoses* 13.621–622). Thus dew is the tears of the dawn goddess. In this mythologem the aetiology of dew is presented as an ongoing process rather than as a single event in the past.

Helios's son Phaethon once got permission from his father to drive the sun chariot across the sky. But the youth was unable to control the chariot, which at times came close to the surface of the earth, scorching it and turning the skin of Ethiopians dark (Ovid *Metamorphoses* 2.235–236). The story offers an account of the origin of black persons, implying that white is the default skin color of human beings, although it assigns no positive or negative value to light or dark color.

Arachnê (Spider) was the name of a maiden who boasted of her skill in weaving. She even engaged in a contest with the goddess of weaving, Minerva. In anger, the goddess pummeled Arachnê, who thereupon hanged herself. Minerva turned Arachnê into a spider (Ovid *Metamorphoses* 6.5–145). Arachnê was thus the first spider, and it is because she hanged herself that spiders hang, and similarly it is because Arachnê was a furious and skilled weaver that spiders are persistent and astonishing weavers.

Aetiologies for rites and other customs often take the form of a precedent. When the grieving Demeter was searching for her daughter Persephonê and came to the palace of the ruler of the Eleusinians, several women invited her to join them, and in particular an old woman named Iambê joked with her, making her smile. For this reason women make jokes at the festival known as the Thesmophoria (Apollodoros *Library* 1.5.1). Once when King Minos of Crete was performing a sacrifice to the Charites (Graces) on the island of Paros, he received the sad news of his son's death. Accordingly, he threw down the garland from his head and bade the flute player be silent, but he completed the sacrifice anyway. That is why even now the Parians sacrifice to the Charites without garlands or flutes (*Library* 3.15.7).

Aetiological motifs frequently come at the conclusion of a narrative, lending closure, as in the story of the weaver Arachnê's transformation to a spider. But it is not necessary that they do so. The aetiology of black skin is just one detail among others in the middle of the narrative about Phaethon, which ends with his death.

See also Transformation; Waters

AINEIAS (LATINIZED FORM AENEAS)

Trojan hero at the time of the Trojan War.

Aineias was the son of a goddess and a mortal. As related in the *Homeric Hymn to Aphroditê*, Zeus arranged for Aphroditê to feel a sexual longing for the mortal Anchises, in order that, having been thus humiliated, she would in turn cease causing the other gods to mate with mortals, producing offspring who were half human and half divine. The plan succeeded, so that Aineias was among the last of the demigods, heralding the end of the era of heroes. After

Aphroditê seduced Anchises and bore Aineias on Mount Ida, she turned him over to local nymphs to rear, and later the child was given to his father.

Aineias was a member of a noble Trojan line, one that paralleled and rivaled the line to which King Priam of Troy belonged (Homer *Iliad* 13.459–461, 20.178–186). Both lines descended ultimately from Tros, the eponym of Troy. Tros had three sons: Ilos, Assarakos, and Ganymedes. After Ganymedes was translated to Olympos to be cupbearer of the gods, the lines of Ilos and Assarakos remained. Ilos founded the city of Ilios (or Ilion, Latinized form = Ilium) on the Trojan plain, which was ruled first by himself and then in succession by his son Laomedon and his grandson Priam. Assarakos's line stayed on Mount Ida, the original base of the Trojans, overlooking the plain.

A principal theme of Aineias's life is close escape from danger. As Aineias herded cattle on Mount Ida, Achilleus attacked him, but he got away to the town of Lynessos. Achilleus then destroyed that town, but once again Aineias eluded him. In Homer's *Iliad* he escaped death in battle at the hands of Diomedes when he was rescued by Apollon and Athena (Book 5) and later at the hands of Achilleus after Poseidon saved him (Book 20). According to one of the cyclic epics *Iliou Persis* (*Destruction of Troy*), Aineias and his followers secretly withdrew from Ilios to Mount Ida just before the destruction of Troy, for Aineias apparently interpreted the killing of Laokoon by sea serpents as a sign of what was about to happen more generally.

A secondary theme of Aineias's life is piety. Although this trait is occasionally mentioned in Greek narrators, it becomes important only in Roman sources. Aineias's notable act of piety was his carrying, or leading, his father out of Troy at its fall.

Accounts of the fate of Aineias at the time of the fall of Troy differ considerably. His escape before the city's destruction to his family's base on nearby Mount Ida, according to the *Iliou Persis*, was probably connected with the old tradition that he was destined to rule the Trojans after the fall of Troy and the annihilation of the Trojan royal family (Homer *Iliad* 20.307–308; *Homeric Hymn to Aphroditê* 196–197). Although the original meaning was doubtless that Aineias would rule the remnants of the Trojans in the Troad, the prophecy could be taken to mean that he would rule over Trojans in a new settlement elsewhere. According to a different tradition, Aineias fled during the sack of the city, carrying his father Anchises on his back, and was allowed to pass by the Greeks on account of his piety (Apollodoros *Epitome* 5.21). He is then said to have sailed to the west, founding this or that city, including even Rome. Roman tradition developed him as a pious survivor of the fall of Troy who escaped with a small band of refugees, sailed off in search of a new home, and settled eventually in Italy, where he and his company mixed with the local population of

Latins, and his descendants founded Rome. But according to the cyclic epic *Little Iliad*, Aineias survived the destruction of Troy but did not escape, for Achilleus's son Neoptolemos sailed for home with Aineias as his captive.

In mythological illustration Aineias may be depicted as a warrior carrying his aged father upon his shoulders.

See also Hero; Trojan War

Suggested reading:

Michael J. Anderson. *The Fall of Troy in Early Greek Poetry and Art*. Oxford: Clarendon Press, 1997, 62–74.

Elias Bickerman. "*Origines Gentium*." *Classical Philology* 47 (1952): 65–81.

Fulvio Canciani. "Aineias," in *LIMC* 1:381–396.

Timothy Gantz. *Early Greek Myth: A Guide to Literary and Artistic Sources*. Baltimore: The Johns Hopkins University Press, 1993, 713–717.

N. M. Horsfall. "The Aineias-Legend from Homer to Virgil," in Jan N. Bremmer and N. M. Horsfall, *Roman Myth and Mythography*, Bulletin Supplement 52. London: Institute of Classical Studies, University of London, 1987, 12–24.

T. P. Wiseman. *Remus: A Roman Myth*. Cambridge: Cambridge University Press, 1995, 50–54.

ALOADS (GREEK ALOADAI OR ALOEIDAI)

Two mortal brothers, Otos and Ephialtes, who challenged the gods.

Aloeus wed Iphimedeia, but she fell in love with Poseidon and would often visit the sea, pouring seawater onto her lap with her hands. Poseidon lay with her, begetting two sons, Otos and Ephialtes, known as the Aloads (sons of Aloeus). Each year they grew a cubit in breadth and a fathom in height, so that when they were nine years old they were nine cubits broad and nine fathoms high, whereupon they decided to do battle with the gods. So they piled Mount Ossa on top of Mount Olympos, and Pelion on top of Ossa, and threatened thereby to ascend to the sky, saying that they would fill the sea with mountains and the land with seawater. Desiring goddesses for their wives, Ephialtes wooed Hera, and Otos wooed Artemis. They also bound Ares, although Hermes managed to liberate him by stealth. Finally Artemis did away with the Aloads on the island of Naxos by means of a trick, changing herself into a deer and leaping between them, and the brothers, trying to hit the animal with their javelins, struck each other (Apollodoros *Library* 1.7.4; cf. Homer *Odyssey* 11.305–320).

A cubit is about eighteen inches and a fathom about six feet, so that the Aloads each measured around thirteen feet in breadth and fifty-four feet in height when they reached their ninth year. Since their ambition was to reach the celestial Olympos, overcome the gods, and marry goddesses, they belong to the mythological tradition of hubristic characters, like the monster Typhon, who challenge the gods, desiring to be gods or to possess what gods possess. But being also simple-minded, the Aloads were easily overcome by a ruse.

The Aloads' mischievous exploit of imprisoning the god Ares is related more fully in Homer's *Iliad* (5.385–391), where the goddess Dionê cites the incident in a catalog of painful experiences inflicted by mortals on immortals, saying that powerful Otos and Ephialtes once bound Ares in bonds, and he lay imprisoned for thirteen months in a bronze cauldron until the boys' stepmother informed Hermes, who stole away the confined god, who had grown faint from his bondage.

See also Combat Myth and Legend; Giants; Triads
Suggested reading:
Joseph Fontenrose. *Orion: The Myth of the Hunter and the Huntress.* University of California Publications: Classical Studies, 23. Berkeley: University of California Press, 1981, 112–120.
Timothy Gantz. *Early Greek Myth: A Guide to Literary and Artistic Sources.* Baltimore: The Johns Hopkins University Press, 1993, 170–171.
Erika Simon. "Aloadai," in *LIMC* 1:570–572.

AMBROSIA
Wondrous food and salve of the gods.

Ambrosia is a food for divine beings (Homer *Odyssey* 5.93; Hesiod *Theogony* 640) or for their horses (Homer *Iliad* 5.777) or for their mortal favorites (*Iliad* 19.347–348), usually but not always represented as a solid. Etymologically it signifies "undeath." Ambrosia and nectar together sustain the Olympian gods, like the wheat and wine consumed by mortals. The poets also call the night "ambrosial," perhaps because it refreshes the sleeper.

At other times ambrosia functions as a perfume or salve (*Odyssey* 4.445–446; *Homeric Hymn to Demeter* 237), and its effect can be that of a preservative, as when the nymph Thetis pours nectar and ambrosia into the nostrils of the slain Patroklos (*Iliad* 19.38–39) and Aphroditê anoints the corpse of Hektor with ambrosial oil (*Iliad* 23.186–187). Just as ambrosia prevents a mortal man's corpse from decaying, so also should it keep the living gods from aging, although for many Greek authors ambrosia rather maintains the gods' immortality, that is, keeps them from dying, which is not quite the same thing.

Ambrosia is brought to Zeus from beyond the Clashing Rocks by certain doves (*Odyssey* 12.61–65), but it can also exude from the earth (*Iliad* 5.777).

See also Nectar
Suggested reading:
Jenny Strauss Clay. *The Wrath of Athena: Gods and Men in the* Odyssey. Princeton, NJ: Princeton University Press, 1983, 145–148.

J. G. Frazer, trans. and comm. *Apollodorus: The Library*. London: Heinemann, 1921, 2:355–358.

R. B. Onians. *The Origins of European Thought about the Body, the Mind, the Soul, the World, Time, and Fate*. Cambridge: Cambridge University Press, 1951, 292–299

Giulia Sissa and Marcel Detienne. *The Daily Life of the Greek Gods*, trans. by Janet Lloyd. Stanford: Stanford University Press, 2000, 77–80.

Paul Thieme. "Ambrosia," in *Indogermanische Dichtersprache*, edited by Rüdiger Schmitt. Darmstadt, Germany: Wissenschaftliche Buchgesellschaft, 1968, 113–132.

ANTHROPOGONY

Coming into being of a human or of humans.

An anthropogonic myth recounts the origin of a human (or humans) on earth or in a particular region.

As a synthesis of regional traditions, Greek mythology has multiple accounts of the origin of human beings. Most draw upon one of three models, each with its own imagery: artisanal, agricultural, or transformative. For example, humans were fashioned by a god or grew out of the earth or were transformed from stones.

Artisanal imagery underlies the myth according to which Prometheus formed the first humans from earth and water in the likeness of the gods (Apollodoros *Library* 1.7.1; Ovid *Metamorphoses* 1.76–88). Just as human potters fashioned figurines from clay, so also a god once fashioned human beings from clay. The site of this event was Panopeus, which claimed to possess clay that was left over from Prometheus's handiwork. The local clay had the peculiarity of smelling like human skin (Pausanias *Guide to Greece* 10.4.4). According to a different tradition, mortal men were created first (we are not told how), and sometime later the first woman was created by the gods in committee, different deities contributing according to their different spheres of influence: Hephaistos fashioned her from earth and water in the image of the goddesses, Athena taught her to weave, Aphroditê poured charm over her, various goddesses clothed and ornamented her, and finally Hermes made her deceitful and gave her a voice, dubbing her Pandora (All-Gift), since all the Olympians gave her gifts (Hesiod *Theogony* 570–616, *Works and Days* 53–105). When the creator of humans is a potter, he takes the gods as his models, fashioning the new beings in their image.

Alternatively the first human beings grew from the earth like plants. According to Attic tradition, the Athenians were unique among the Greeks in being autochthonous, having sprung from the soil of Attica rather than having immigrated there from elsewhere (Isokrates *Panathenaikos* 124–125). Being literally native to the region, they could claim an inalienable relationship to it. The Athenian royal family was itself autochthonous. Homer says that the plowland gave birth to Erechtheus, an early king of Athens (*Iliad* 2.546–549). A similar claim was made by the Arcadians, for the earth sent up their first king, Pelasgos, in order that there might be a race of mortals (Pausanias 8.1.4); accordingly, Aeschylus calls Pelasgos "earthborn" (*Suppliants* 250–251). According to Herodotos, the Athenians themselves were originally Pelasgians (1.56–58). Myths of other first men, ancestors sprung from the earth, are found in the mythic traditions of different Greek regions. One of the strangest of these concerns a crop of men known as the Spartoi, or Sown Men, who were born from

Prometheus fashioning a human being, with Athena looking on.

the earth at the future site of Thebes. After Kadmos had slain the Dragon of Ares, he plowed the soil and on the advice of Athena sowed it with the monster's teeth, after which a crop of armed men emerged from the ground. Although they fought one another, five of the earthborn men survived, namely, Echion, Oudaios, Chthonios, Hyperenor, and Peloros, and joined Kadmos in founding Thebes (Apollodoros *Library* 3.4.1; Ovid *Metamorphoses* 3.95–130). Offspring of the dragon-fertilized earth, the Spartoi were claimed as ancestors by particular Theban families in classical times. There are also accounts of humans originating specifically from trees. In Virgil's *Aeneid*, Evander informs Aeneas about a woods in which people were born from the trunks of oak trees (8.313–318).

Or human beings are really metamorphosed stones or animals. After most persons perished in the great deluge, the pious survivors Deukalion and Pyrrha were instructed by an oracle to throw stones behind them. Those thrown by Deukalion turned into men, and those thrown by Pyrrha turned into women. Humans are therefore called "people" (Greek *laos*) because they came from "pebbles" (*laas*) (Apollodoros *Library* 1.7.2).

According to a regional tradition, Zeus once abducted the nymph Aigina, taking her to an island then called Oinonê but subsequently known as Aigina (Latinized form = Aegina). She bore him a son, Aiakos (Latinized form = Aeacus). Aiakos grew up, and since the island was otherwise uninhabited, Zeus

transformed the ants (Greek *myrmekes*) into people, who were known as Myrmidons (Hesiod frag. 205 MW; Apollodoros *Library* 3.12.6). The myth rests
upon the observation that communities of humans at work resemble industrious societies of ants and also that the word *Myrmidons*, name of a Greek
people, resembles the Greek word for ants. These transformational myths conclude with a folk etymology linking humans with the thing from which they
were transformed: people (*laos*) from pebbles (*laas*), or Myrmidons from ants
(*myrmekes*).

In the mythic manner the creation or emergence of humans, as of any other
creature or object or cultural practice, is ordinarily represented as a discrete
event, not as a gradual process. But sometimes a line of gods seems inexplicably
to degenerate into a line of humans, so that the mortals come into being as the
result of an unexplained and unremarked devolution. Thus the line of Titans
represented by the brothers Prometheus and Epimetheus fades from immortal
to mortal. When the gods fashion the first mortal woman, they give her to the
Titan Epimetheus. Apart from the fact that he is a fool, why should Epimetheus
be deemed a more appropriate mate for Pandora than an ordinary human male?
We should expect the offspring of Prometheus and a nymph, the flood-hero
Deukalion, to enjoy divine status, but when he weds Pyrrha, daughter of
Epimetheus and Pandora, the two appear to become the first human couple, and
the offspring of Deukalion and Pyrrha are entirely human. The boundary be-
tween gods and humans is often fuzzy, especially in early times.

In all Greek anthropogonic myths, the gods come into existence before human beings do. In the technological model, in which god is a potter, and in the
agricultural model, in which (in a sense) god is a farmer, mythic imagery derives
from everyday production, the former emphasizing the derivative status of humans relative to the gods, the latter the intimate relationship of humans to the
local soil. In the transformative model the emphasis is rather upon particular
qualities—industriousness, community, hardness, and the like—that humans
are perceived to share with something else. Ultimately, however, all anthropogonic myths rely upon a transformation, whether it is from clay, seeds, animals, stones, gods, or something else.

In most cases no reason is given for the creation or emergence of humans,
but there are exceptions. In the Pandora myth, in which the gods intended originally to create only men, the first woman was fashioned as a punishment for
mortal men. And Zeus transformed ants into Myrmidons for Aiakos, who otherwise would have ruled an uninhabited island. A similar reason, if only implicit, probably underlies the Spartoi (Sown Men) at Thebes, since they join
Kadmos and his few companions in founding a new city.

See also Cosmogony

Suggested reading:

Sue Blundell. *The Origins of Civilization in Greek and Roman Thought.* London: Croom Helm 1986, 3–23.

Murray Fowler. "The Myth of Erichthonios." *Classical Philology* 38 (1949): 28–32.

Margherita Guarducci. "Leggende dell'antica Grecia relative all'origine dell'umanità e analoghe tradizioni di altri paesi." *Atti della Reale Accademia Nazionale dei Lincei,* 6th series, Memorie della classe di scienze morali, storiche e filologiche (1926): 2:379–459.

W. K. C. Guthrie. *In the Beginning: Some Greek Views on the Origins of Life and the Early State of Man.* Ithaca, NY: Cornell University Press, 1957.

Lutz Röhrich. "Anthropogonie," in *Enzyklopädie des Märchens,* edited by Kurt Ranke et al. Berlin: Walter de Gruyter, 1977, 1:579–586.

Francis Vian. *Les origines de Thèbes: Cadmos et les Spartes.* Paris: Librairie C. Klincksieck, 1963.

APHRODITÊ (ROMAN VENUS)

Goddess of sexuality.

Aphroditê's sphere of influence is sexual love among deities, humans, and animals. The Romans identified her with their goddess Venus.

Two quite different traditions concerning her origin were in circulation. According to Hesiod, while Ouranos (Sky) was having sexual intercourse with his mate Gaia (Earth), he was ambushed

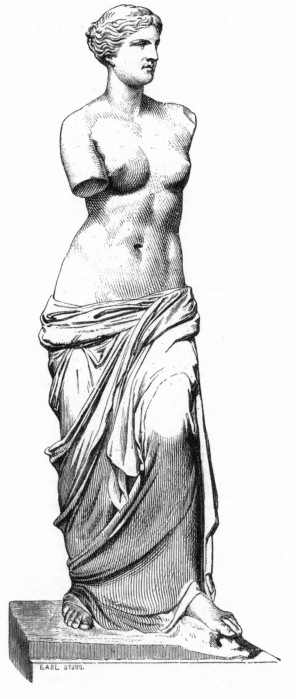

Aphroditê of Melos (Venus di Milo).

and castrated by his son Kronos, who cast his father's genitals into the sea. Foam issued from them, and within the foam a maiden grew. The genitals came eventually to land at Cypress, where Aphroditê stepped ashore. She acquired

Aphroditê.

her honor, or divine province, of sexuality straight-away—girls' smiles, whispers, and deceptions and the pleasures of sexual love (*Theogony* 176–206). In this violent and sexually charged myth, Aphroditê was one of the oldest gods, born from the semen that issued from the severed genitals of Ouranos. Folk etymology perceived in her name the Greek word for foam (*aphros*) and accounted for it by representing her as foam-born, which became one of her stock epithets (*aphrogenes*). According to Homer, however, she was the daughter of Zeus and Dionê (*Iliad* 5.370–430) and so belongs to the younger generation of gods. In either case, she is one of the twelve Olympians.

Aphroditê has the power to implant longing in one being for another or to render a being sexually irresistible to another. For Greeks, the basic dynamic of love was attraction, just as the basic dynamic of its opposite, strife, was repulsion. In this respect her province overlaps with that of Eros (Sexual Love), who like Aphroditê herself was sometimes represented as a primeval deity and sometimes as one of the younger gods. Thus for the poet Hesiod, the god Eros was one of the primordial four, the first beings to appear in the nascent cosmos (*Theogony* 116–122), since in Hesiod's cosmogony the constituents of the world come into being mostly by means of birth from earlier constituents, who mate with one another, and the principle of erotic attraction must be there from the beginning in order for mating to be possible. But popular tradition held that Eros was simply a son of Aphroditê (Pausanias 9.27.2), and so in effect an aspect of her. Eros is often represented in literature and art as accompanying Aphroditê, as also does Himeros (Hesiod *Theogony* 201), each companion being a personified abstraction that externalizes one of her characteristic qualities, Erotic Love or Longing. The Graces and the Hours also appear at different times as her attendants.

The goddess's power of instilling sexual longing or attraction has few limits, but among them are the three virginal goddesses Athena, Artemis, and Hestia, who are not moved by her. Otherwise, according to the *Homeric Hymn to Aphrodite,* she amused herself in the mythological past by making gods and goddesses mate with mortals. The offspring of these unions were demigods, the heroes of the heroic age. Zeus put an end to Aphroditê's boasting about these successes, causing her in turn to feel an irresistible longing for a particular mortal man, Anchises, whose child she subsequently bore. She reined in her erotic mischief, and the age of heroes came to an end shortly thereafter.

Just as Zeus has his thunderbolts and Poseidon his trident, Aphroditê has her own special weapon, the cestus (Greek *kestos himas*), or embroidered strap worn around her breasts that renders her sexually irresistible. When an intrinsic quality of a being is thus externalized, it can be transferred to another being, and indeed Aphroditê once loaned her cestus to Hera to guarantee the success of an intended seduction (Homer *Iliad* 14.187–223). But as the deity in charge of erotic activity, Aphroditê can simply grant another being the quality of erotic irresistibility, implanting it as an attribute, as she does for Paris in the episode of the Judgment of Paris. The goddess Eris, or Strife, tossed a golden apple into the midst of a wedding party, indicating that it was for the most beautiful female. Since Hera, Athena, and Aphroditê each claimed it, Zeus had a certain Trojan prince, Paris, act as judge. Each goddess offered the youth a particular bribe if he should chose her. Hera promised to make him a powerful ruler; Athena, to make him a victorious warrior; and Aphroditê, to make him an irresistible lover, so that he could have even Helen. Paris awarded the apple to Aphroditê and then sailed to Sparta, where Helen lived with her husband. Abandoning husband and daughter, Helen went to Troy with Paris.

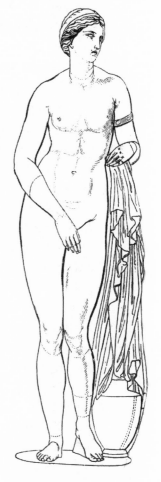

Aphroditê.

Sometimes Aphroditê facilitates love in other ways. The beautiful maiden Atalantê obliged each of her suitors to race her, although she herself ran fully armed and gave her competitor a head start. If she caught up with him, she executed him on the spot, but if a man could outrun her, he might marry her. All her suitors perished, until Melanion tried. As they raced, Melanion threw aside several golden apples that Aphroditê had given him, and since Atalantê paused to gather them up, the youth outran her, winning her as wife (Apollodoros *Library* 3.9.2). When the sculptor Pygmalion fell in love with the ivory statue of a maiden carved by himself, Venus in answer to his prayers turned the statue into a living maiden, who became his wife (Ovid *Metamorphoses* 10.243–297).

Just as Aphroditê can make love work well, she can also do the opposite. When the women of the island of Lemnos failed to honor the goddess, she caused them to have such a foul smell (presumably in the genital region) that their husbands deserted them for other women (Apollodoros *Library* 1.9.17). Similarly, when the maiden Smyrna did not give Aphroditê due honor, the goddess angrily made her conceive a passion for her own father (*Library* 3.14.4). After the daughters of Kinyras somehow offended Aphroditê, she caused them to sleep with foreigners (*Library* 3.14.3), and in the same way when the Propoetides denied the goddess's divinity, Venus in her wrath made them the first women ever to prostitute themselves (Ovid *Metamorphoses* 10.238–242).

In Homer's *Odyssey*, Aphroditê is wed to Hephaistos, an unlikely match of beauty queen and lame blacksmith that virtually guarantees marital instability. In any case, she is promiscuous. While married to Hephaistos, she carried on an affair with Ares, who came to her house when Hephaistos was away. But Hephaistos, informed by Helios of his wife's adultery, forged an invisible net in his smithy, placed it above his bed, and pretended to depart upon a trip. Ares presently paid Aphroditê a visit, but as soon as they lay in Hephaistos's bed, the web fell upon them and trapped them in place. Hephaistos returned and indignantly summoned the other gods to witness the trapped lovers (Homer *Odyssey* 8.266–366). Aphroditê also had a love affair with the handsome youth Adonis (Apollodoros *Library* 3.14.4). Her seduction of the mortal Anchises was caused by Zeus, who placed in Aphroditê a longing for the Trojan prince. Adopting the form of a mortal maiden, she seduced Anchises on Mount Ida, where he was tending his herds. After they lay together, she revealed her true identity, informing him that she would bear a son Aineias, whom she would turn over to the local nymphs to rear for his first years. She forbade Anchises to reveal to anyone that he had slept with Aphroditê. Her humiliation in mating with Anchises and bearing his child brought to an end Aphroditê's causing other gods and goddesses to mate with mortals, producing mixed offspring, and so signaled the forthcoming end of the heroic age (*Homeric Hymn to Aphrodite*).

Among her numerous epithets are Golden, Kypris (Cypriote, because of her cult on Cypress), Paphian (referring to the city of Paphos on Cypress), Kythereia (Cytheran, referring to the island of Kythera, another cult site), Laughter Loving (*philommeides*), and the nearly homonymous Genital Loving (*philommedes*).

In mythological illustration ancient and modern, Aphroditê is characteristically represented as a lovely mature female, partially clad or nude. Often she is accompanied by a bird such as a dove or swan or by her son Eros (Roman = Cupid or Amor). She may bear a scepter. In poetry her chariot can be drawn by sparrows, doves, or swans.

See also Honor

Suggested reading:

Jenny Strauss Clay. *The Politics of Olympus: Form and Meaning in the Major Homeric Hymns.* Princeton, NJ: Princeton University Press, 1989, 152–201.

Angelos Delivorrias. "Aphrodite," in *LIMC* 2:2–151.

Timothy Gantz. *Early Greek Myth: A Guide to Literary and Artistic Sources.* Baltimore: The Johns Hopkins University Press, 1993, 99–105.

Geoffrey Grigson. *The Goddess of Love: The Birth, Triumph, Death and Return of Aphrodite.* London: Constable, 1976.

Evamaria Schmidt. "Venus," in *LIMC* 8:192–230.

APOLLON (LATINIZED FORM APOLLO)

God of music, archery, prophecy, and illness/healing.

Apollon.

Apollon and his twin sister, Artemis, are children of the elder Olympians Zeus and Leto, Zeus's sixth wife and immediate predecessor to his spouse in the mythological present, Hera (Hesiod *Theogony* 918–920). According to the *Homeric Hymn to Apollon*, Leto experienced two difficulties when she was in labor with Apollon: the reluctance of different places to serve as the home of the future god and the hostility of Hera to Leto and her son. When Leto was in labor, she approached many different lands in search of a home for her son, but all except the little island of Delos declined. Although Delos initially feared that after his birth Apollon would be scornful of the modest island, Leto swore an oath that he would build a temple there and honor Delos above all other places, whereupon the island joyfully consented to be the god's birthplace. But Leto's problems were not over, for she continued in labor for nine days and nights, unable to give birth because Hera was jealously keeping Eileithyia (goddess of childbirth) distracted. Finally the goddesses attending Leto dispatched Iris to Eileithyia, and as soon as Eileithyia set foot upon Delos, Leto gave birth to Phoibos Apollon (*Homeric Hymn to Apollon* 1–119). Since the poet of the hymn represents Hera as resenting Leto's pregnancy, he presumably regards Zeus's relationship with Leto as an affair that took place during his marriage to Hera.

As soon as the infant Apollon was given nectar and ambrosia, he exuberantly declared that his honors, or divine provinces, would be the lyre, the bow,

Apollon with lyre.

and prophesying the will of Zeus (*Homeric Hymn to Apollon* 120–132). Here the god simply declared what his divine powers would be, but a different myth represents Hermes as inventing the lyre, which he gave as a gift to his older half-brother Apollon, or he effected a trade such that Apollon gained charge of the lyre and Hermes acquired cattle of one of his honors (*Homeric Hymn to Hermes* 467–495). In any case, Apollon became god of music, principally of stringed instruments, and on Olympos Apollon plays his lyre for the other immortals while the Muses sing and different deities dance (*Homeric Hymn to Apollon* 182–206). The satyr Marsyas once challenged the god to a musical contest, and it was agreed that the winner might do what he wished with the loser. Apollon played his lyre, and Marsyas played his flute, but when Apollon played his instrument upside-down and bade Marsyas do the same, the satyr could not and so lost the contest. The god hung him from a tree and flayed him alive (Apollodoros *Library* 1.4.2).

The second honor that Apollon claimed for himself was the bow. In fact, he shares the province of archery with his sister Artemis, for both are renowned archers and indeed invented hunting, which they taught to the centaur Cheiron, who in turn instructed different heroes in the art (Xenophon *On Hunting* 1.1–2). Apollon or Artemis can shoot a mortal with an unseen arrow, causing the person mysteriously to die, as in the case of a certain Phrontis, helmsman of Menelaos's ship, who was slain by the "gentle arrows" of Phoibos Apollon one day as he steered his vessel near Cape Sounion (Homer *Odyssey* 3.278–283); that is, Phrontis died suddenly and unaccountably. A particularly dramatic instance appears in the legend of the proud and fertile Niobê, who compared herself favorably to Leto, saying that the goddess had borne only two children whereas she herself had borne many. Then Leto's children, though a mere two, slew Niobê's many, Apollon cutting down her six sons and Artemis her six daughters (Homer *Iliad* 24.602–609).

Apollon's third honor is prophecy, a province that he exercises primarily at oracular temples, where mortals can ask a question of the god and receive an answer. Searching the earth for an appropriate place to establish his oracle, Apollon eventually selected Krisa. He laid out the foundations of the temple, and mortal craftsmen finished it. But danger loomed, for at a nearby spring there dwelled a dragon that killed whomever she encountered. So Apollon slew her with an arrow, and she rotted in the sun, for which reason the place acquired the name Pytho and Apollon was called Pythian. Once the dragon was slain, the god completed the establishment of his sanctuary (*Homeric Hymn to Apollon* 214–544). In this narrative the place-name Pytho and the divine epithet Pythian, which resemble the Greek word for "rot," are explained by folk etymology as deriving from the rotting of a monstrous serpent slain by the god. Alternatively, in some sources the monster herself, nameless here, is called Python. Pytho was an earlier name for the community later known as Delphi.

Apollon's connection with prophecy is expressed in other ways as well. As the inventor of prophecy, Apollon is ultimately the teacher of all mortal soothsayers, instructing, for example, the famous diviner Melampous (Apollodoros *Library* 1.9.11). And Apollon fathered a seer, Mopsos, who once bested the great seer Kalchas in a contest in divination (Apollodoros *Epitome* 6.2–4).

Apollon's power over sickness and healing is important in mythological narrative (Ovid *Metamorphoses* 1.521–522). When, for example, Agamemnon insulted an aged priest of Apollon at Troy, the old man prayed to his god, asking him to make the Greeks pay for his ill treatment. Granting his prayer, Apollon came down from Olympos and for nine days shot arrow after arrow at the mules, hounds, and men in the Greek camp, causing a mysterious pestilence in which beasts and men died (Homer *Iliad* 1). Here the god's supernatural arrows cause, not sudden death, but mortal sickness. Among Apollon's offspring was the healer Asklepios, who became the greatest of physicians, able even to raise the dead (Apollodoros *Library* 3.10.3–4).

Overall, Apollon is unfortunate in love. Enamored of the nymph Daphnê (Greek *daphnê* = laurel, bay) he pursued her, but she ran from him, begging her father, a river god, to transform her beauty. In answer to her prayer she was changed into a bay tree, whereupon the god declared that laurel would be his special tree (Ovid *Metamorphoses* 1.452–567). Sometimes Apollon proposed to grant a special boon in exchange for sexual favors. Wishing to sleep with the Trojan princess Kassandra, Apollon offered to teach her how to foretell the future. And he did so, but when she still refused to sleep with him, he brought it about that everyone would disbelieve her prophecies (Apollodoros *Library* 3.12.5). He propositioned Sibyl of Cumae in a similarly businesslike fashion, offering to grant her any wish. She asked to live as many years as there were grains in a particular heap of sand. Since she neglected to ask also not to age, the god offered to grant her this also; she still rejected his love, and as a result she lived century after century, aging but unable to die (*Metamorphoses* 14.130–153). At other times Apollon found himself losing to a mortal competitor. Marpessa was courted by Apollon and the human youth Idas. When Zeus permitted the maiden to choose which of the suitors she preferred, she selected Idas, for she feared that Apollon would leave her when she grew old (Apollodoros *Library* 1.7.8). Apollon had sexual intercourse with Koronis (Latinized form = Coronis), but she preferred to live with a mortal lover, Ischys. When a raven brought Apollon word of her cohabitation, he cursed the bird, changing its color from white to black, and killed Koronis (Apollodoros *Library* 3.10.3). He had an affair with a Spartan youth, Hyacinth (Greek *Hyakinthos*), but once when they were throwing the discus, he made a cast, Hyacinth rushed forth to retrieve the discus, and it bounced up and struck him, killing him. The grieving god declared that the dead boy should be transformed into a flower whose petals would display the letters AI AI, representing the lament that people utter at funerals (Ovid *Metamorphoses* 10.162–219).

Among Apollon's epithets is Phoibos (Latinized form = Phoebus), signifying perhaps "radiant," which can be used either in conjunction with the god's name (thus, Phoibos Apollon) or by itself. It is used also of Helios and so is not a distinctive epithet. Although Apollon and Helios are not identical, their shared epithet has encouraged the mistaken notion that Apollon is essentially a sun god. Other Apolline epithets are Far-Shooting, Lycian, Oblique (*Loxias*), Pythian, and Silver-bow.

In mythological art Apollon is represented as a handsome youth, beardless or bearded. He may wear a garland of laurel or carry bow and arrows or be associated with a tripod. His chariot is pulled by swans (Alcaeus frag. 307 Lobel-Page).

See also Artemis; Combat Myth and Legend; Oracles

Suggested reading:

Jenny Strauss Clay. *The Politics of Olympus: Form and Meaning in the Major Homeric Hymns.* Princeton, NJ: Princeton University Press, 1989, 17–94.

Joseph Fontenrose. "Apollo and Sol in the Latin Poets of the First Century B.C." *Transactions of the American Philological Association* 70 (1939): 439–455.

———. "Apollo and the Sun-God in Ovid." *American Journal of Philology* 61 (1940): 429–444.

———. *Python: A Study of Delphic Myth and its Origins.* Berkeley: University of California Press, 1959.

Timothy Gantz. *Early Greek Myth: A Guide to Literary and Artistic Sources.* Baltimore: The Johns Hopkins University Press, 1993, 87–96.

Wassilis Lambrinudakis. "Apollon," in *LIMC* 2:183–327.

Erika Simon and Gerhard Bauchhenss. "Apollo," in *LIMC* 2:363–464.

Ares.

ARES (ROMAN MARS)

God of war.

Ares is a war deity with an insatiable taste for violence and slaughter. Accordingly, he is not an attractive deity to either mortals or immortals. Doubtless Zeus spoke for many when he told him (Homer *Iliad* 5.890–891):

> You are the most hateful to me of the gods who dwell on Olympos,
>> For strife is always dear to you, and wars and battles.

Although Ares and Athena are both war deities, they reflect different aspects of the phenomenon, Ares embodying that which is distasteful in battle and Athena representing its splendor and nobility.

Ares was one of three children born to the elder Olympians Zeus and Hera, the other two being Hebê (Youth) and Eileithyia, goddess of childbirth (Hesiod *Theogony* 921–923). Although all three siblings dwell on Olympos, where in the mythological present Hebê is the spouse of the deified Herakles (Homer *Odyssey* 11.601–604), only Ares is accounted one of the Olympians. According to a different tradition, Juno (Hera) bore Mars (Ares) without sexual intercourse after Jupiter had borne Minerva (Athena) on his own (Ovid *Fasti* 5.229–258). According to other authors, however, it was Hephaistos, not Ares, whom Hera bore on her own.

In the few myths in which Ares plays an actual narrative role, he suffers humiliation. The strong youths Otos and Ephialtes once tied Ares up and imprisoned him in a bronze jar, where he remained for thirteen months, until Hermes learned of his plight and rescued him (Homer *Iliad* 5.385–391). According to Homer's *Odyssey*, Aphroditê was wed to the divine smith Hephaistos but once carried on a furtive affair with Ares. When the all-seeing Helios (Sun) informed Hephaistos that he was being cuckolded, Hephaistos created a snare for

Ares.

the lovers, covering his bed with netting so fine that it was invisible. Then he pretended to depart on a trip. Ares promptly made his way to Hephaistos's house, the lovers went to bed, and the web fell upon them, trapping them like fish in a net. Hephaistos immediately returned and opened up his house to display to the other Olympians the lovers trapped flagrante delicto. Eventually the smith released the two lovers, who scurried away in different directions (8.266–366).

Nevertheless, Ares has many loves and begets many offspring. Although some of his mates and children have no obviously fierce quality, others suggest by their name or behavior the ferocious or militant nature of their father. For example, Aphroditê bore him two sons, Phobos (Fear) and Deimos (Terror), as well as a daughter, Harmonia (Hesiod *Theogony* 933–937). The sons personify aspects of Ares as a god of battle and accompany him on the battlefield, whereas the daughter incarnates the union of opposites represented by the relationship of Ares and Aphroditê. The Dragon of Ares, a huge serpent that guarded a spring at the future site of Thebes, was a son of Ares. Kadmos slew it and sowed its teeth in the soil, and from these seeds a crop of armed warriors sprang up (Apollodoros *Library* 3.4.1). The god had a fierce son in Oenomaus (Greek Oinomaos), who obliged his daughter's suitors to compete with him in a chariot race. For the suitors the penalty for losing was death, after which Oenomaus nailed their heads above the door of his palace (Hyginus *Fabulae* 84). Another fierce son was Diomedes the Thracian, owner of a herd of man-eating mares (Apollodoros *Library* 2.5.8), and among his daughters was Penthesileia, leader of the Amazon contingent at Troy (Apollodoros *Epitome* 5.1). The barbarous nature of Ares is also implied by his close connection with Thrace (Homer *Iliad* 13.301, *Odyssey* 8.361).

The mythological tradition sometimes imputes qualities such as savagery or danger or militancy to objects and places by associating them with Ares's name. Hippolytê, queen of the Amazons, owned the Belt of Ares as a sign of her being foremost among the Amazons (Apollodoros *Library* 2.5.9), a nation of warriors. The belt appears to possess no special virtue other than its name. In barbarous Colchis there is a Grove of Ares, where a dragon used to watch over the Golden Fleece (Apollodoros *Library* 1.9.1, 1.9.23), just as at the site of Thebes there is a Spring of Ares, which the Dragon of Ares guarded before Kadmos slew it (*Library* 3.4.1).

Ares was identified by the Romans with their god Mars, whom they treated more respectfully than the Greeks did Ares. The founders of Rome, Romulus and Remus, were sons of Mars and the Vestal priestess Silvia (Ovid *Fasti* 3.1–166).

See also Athena

Suggested reading:

Philippe Bruneau. "Ares," in *LIMC* 2:479–492.

Timothy Gantz. *Early Greek Myth: A Guide to Literary and Artistic Sources.* Baltimore: The Johns Hopkins University Press, 1993, 78–81.

Erika Simon and Gerhard Bauchhenss. "Mars," in *LIMC* 2:505–580.

ARGONAUTS (GREEK ARGONAUTAI)

Youths who sailed on the ship *Argo* in quest of the Golden Fleece.

The story of the Argonauts, or sailors on the ship *Argo*, is part of the legend of Jason and the Golden Fleece. It is one of several narratives of collective enterprises in which most of the prominent heroes of a particular generation participate. Others are the hunt for the Calydonian Boar and the Achaean campaign against Troy.

According to the mythographer Apollodoros, Jason summoned the best men in Greece to sail with him on the ship *Argo* in quest of the Golden Fleece, which was found in distant Kolchis. Among the Argonauts were the singer Orpheus, the winged Zetes and Kalais (sons of the north-wind, Boreas), Kastor and the boxer Polydeukes (the Dioscuri, or sons of Zeus), Telamon and Peleus, Herakles, Theseus, Idas and the sharp-sighted Lynkeus, Kaineus, the trickster Autolykos, the maiden Atalantê, Admetos, Meleager, the runner Euphemos, the transformer Periklymenos, and Augeas. With these and other companions, Jason set out from Iolkos in Greece. Among their many adventures are the following.

They first put in at the island of Lemnos, ruled by Queen Hypsipylê. The Lemnian women once failed to honor Aphroditê, who thereupon gave them a foul smell, causing their husbands to sleep with other women. In revenge, the Lemnian women slew all their fathers and husbands, but Hypsipylê spared her father, ruler of the island, after which she herself became queen. The Argonauts slept with the Lemnian women.

They stopped then at Mysia. When Hylas went after water, nymphs of the pond seized him because of his beauty, and he disappeared. While his lover Herakles searched for him, the *Argo* departed, leaving them behind. According to another tradition, Herakles was left at Aphetai after the *Argo* declared that the ship was unable to bear his weight.

The ship put in at the land of the Bebrykes, which was ruled by Amykos, who compelled all strangers to box with him, killing them. When he challenged the best boxer on the *Argo* to box against him, Polydeukes accepted and killed the challenger with a blow.

Their next stop was Thrace, home of the blind seer Phineus. The gods had sent the Harpies against him, so that whenever he sat at table the Harpies would fly down from the sky, snatch some of the food, and befoul the rest. The Argonauts wanted to consult with Phineus about their route, and he offered to help them if they got rid of the Harpies. So they placed food on a table, the Harpies came, and the winged sons of Boreas, Zetes and Kalais, drew their swords and pursued the Harpies, chasing them permanently away. Phineus then advised the Argonauts about their route and also how to pass safely through the Symplegades, or Clashing Rocks.

When they reached the Symplegades, they released a dove, which managed to fly through the two rocks, except that as they clashed together they snipped off the tip of the bird's tail. Phineus had advised them to attempt to pass through only if the bird passed safely through. So they made the attempt, passing through, except that the rocks sheared off the rear tip of the ship.

They came to Kolchis, and Jason stole the Golden Fleece with the help of Aietes's daughter Medeia, who had fallen in love with him. Then they set out for the return trip to Greece.

They encountered other difficulties on the way. Among them were the Sirens with their seductive song, against whom Orpheus sang a counter-song. When they passed Crete, the brazen monster Talos prevented them from coming ashore, pelting the *Argo* with stones. But Medeia overcame him by a trick. A single vein ran from Talos's neck to his ankles, with a bronze nail driven into it at the end. Medeia promised to make him immortal, but instead she pulled out the nail so that his ichor flowed out, and he perished.

Presently Jason and the Argonauts reached Iolkos, and Jason presented the fleece to his uncle, King Pelias, who had dispatched him to bring it. Then they sailed to the Isthmus of Corinth and dedicated the *Argo* to Poseidon (*Library* 1.9.16–27).

The legend of the Argonauts is a Greek development of an international folktale, *The Extraordinary Companions*, which recounts how men with different amazing abilities help a protagonist accomplish a task. In Greek tradition the tale has been integrated into the narrative of Jason and his quest for the Golden Fleece, but somewhat loosely, for although the Argonauts aid Jason in the course of the voyage, they do not really help him to secure the quest-object itself.

See also Jason; Tasks

Suggested reading:

Antti Aarne and Stith Thompson. *The Types of the Folktale: A Classification and Bibliography.* FF Communications, 184. 2nd revision. Helsinki: Academia Scientiarum Fennica, 1961, Type 513: *The Extraordinary Companions.*

Janet Ruth Bacon. *The Voyage of the Argonauts.* London: Methuen, 1925.

Rolf Blatter. "Argonautai," in *LIMC* 2:591–599.

Wolfgang Fauth. "Argonauten," in *Enzyklopädie des Märchens.* Berlin: Walter de Gruyter, 1977, 1:767–773.

Timothy Gantz. *Early Greek Myth: A Guide to Literary and Artistic Sources.* Baltimore and London: The Johns Hopkins University Press, 1993, 341–373.

Artemis.

ARTEMIS (ROMAN DIANA)

Goddess of the hunt.

Artemis and her twin brother, Apollon, were born to the elder Olympians Zeus and Leto, who was Zeus's wife before his marriage to Hera (Hesiod *Theogony* 918–920), or perhaps Zeus fathered the twins on Leto while he was wed to Hera, since Hera reacted hostilely to the prospect of Leto's giving birth (*Homeric Hymn to Apollon* 89–119). Leto delivered Apollon on Delos and Artemis on nearby Ortygia (*Homeric Hymn to Apollon* 14–18; Pindar *Nemean* 1.1–4 in *The Odes*), or Quail Island.

Artemis belongs to the younger generation of Olympians. Like Hestia and Athena, she remains a virgin by choice, rejecting erotic dealing with males. Aphroditê has no influence over Artemis. She finds pleasure rather in wild boar and deer, whom she slays with her bow and arrows, and in roaming the mountains in the company of nymphs, among whom she is conspicuous for her height and beauty; and she loves the dance (Homer *Odyssey* 6.102–109; *Homeric Hymn to Aphrodite* 16–20). Indeed, Artemis and her brother, both archers, invented the art of hunting, which they passed on to the centaur Cheiron, who in turn instructed many prominent youths during the heroic era (Xenophon *On Hunting* 1.1–2), whence it has become general knowledge among mortals. She is the goddess of wild things, of wild creatures and places, of the undomesticated

Artemis.

feminine, the adolescent girl as adult. In the world of ancient Greece, hunting and roaming freely outdoors were characteristic of males, not females.

Like Apollon, Artemis often turns her gentle, unseen arrows on a mortal, who then dies a sudden death, as when for no apparent reason Artemis shot a particular woman on a ship, and she dropped dead into the hold (Homer *Odyssey* 15.477–479). An arrow sent by Artemis can also be a desirable form of death. Odysseus, surprised to encounter his mother in the death realm, asked her how she had died: "Was it a lingering illness, or did arrow-pouring Artemis visit you and slay you with her gentle arrows?" (*Odyssey* 11.172–173). The swineherd Eumaios said that he used to live on the island of Syria, a paradisal place where famine and diseases are unknown. When the men and women grow old there, Apollon and Artemis visit them and slay them with their gentle arrows (*Odyssey* 15.403–411). But Artemis can serve as divine executioner, as when Eos (Dawn) carried off the mortal Orion to be her lover, provoking the jealousy of the gods, so that Artemis slew him (Homer *Odyssey* 5.121–124). Similarly, Theseus was bringing Ariadnê with him from Crete to Athens, but Dionysos informed Artemis, who killed her (*Odyssey* 11.321–325). Most dramatically, after the fertile matron Niobê boastfully compared herself to Leto, saying that the goddess had borne only two children whereas she herself had borne many, Leto's two children slew Niobê's many, Apollon cutting down her six sons and Artemis her six daughters (Homer *Iliad* 24.602–609). Usually, but not always, Artemis's victims are female and Apollon's are male.

Easily offended, Artemis reacts swiftly and terribly. She is sensitive to cultic neglect, as when Oineus, king of Kalydon (Latinized form = Calydon), made an offering of first-fruits to all the gods but forgot Artemis. In her wrath the goddess sent against Kalydon a boar of extraordinary size and strength that destroyed people and cattle and prevented the land from being sown (Apollodoros *Library* 1.8.2), leading to the famed Calydonian boar hunt. Here, as often, a story is set in action by mortal error and divine response. When Admetos was celebrating his marriage to Alkestis (Latinized form = Alcestis), he performed a sacrifice but forgot to sacrifice to Artemis, and as a result, when he opened the door to his bedroom, he found that it was full of snakes (*Library* 1.9.14). Like any other deity, Artemis dislikes mortal hubris, particularly if it slights her in any way, as when Agamemnon killed a deer and boasted that not even Artemis could have shot so well. The angry goddess thereupon prevented the Greek fleet from sailing against Troy until Agamemnon should sacrifice the most beautiful of his daughters to her (Apollodoros *Epitome* 3.21). Finally, inviolable herself, Artemis demands sexual purity of her followers, in particular of the oreads who sometimes roam the wilds with her, forbidding them erotic contact with males. But males tend to find Artemis sensuous and her chaste nymphs attractive. Kallisto (Latinized form = Callisto), for example, was a nymph or human companion of Artemis in the hunt who had sworn to remain a virgin, but Zeus fell in love with her and, taking the form of Artemis, lay with her against her will. Subsequently Artemis shot her because she had not preserved her virginity (Apollodoros *Library* 3.8.2). The goddess is unforgiving, executing Kallisto as if she had given up her virginity willingly. Similarly, when the hunter Aktaion (Latinized form = Actaeon) inadvertently came upon Artemis bathing, she instantly transformed him into a deer and caused his frenzied hounds to devour him (*Library* 3.4.4). But for all her erotic

Artemis.

aversion to males, Artemis herself does sometimes enjoy the companionship of male hunters such as Orion (Hesiod frag. 148a MW) or Aktaion (Kallimachos *Hymn* 5.110–116) in the hunt. And her followers include males, such as the chaste hunter Hippolytos (Euripides *Hippolytos*).

Among her epithets are Arrow-Pourer, Mistress of the Animals, and Wild.

In statuary, Artemis is often represented as a youthful huntress armed with a bow and quiver of arrows and clothed in a chiton, a short or highly girded garment suitable for active pursuits, and accompanied by a wild animal such as a deer. As mistress of wild animals, she may stand between two or more wild animals, who pose in bilateral symmetry.

See also Apollon; Hunters; Nymphs
Suggested reading:
Timothy Gantz. *Early Greek Myth: A Guide to Literary and Artistic Sources.* Baltimore: The Johns Hopkins University Press, 1993, 97–99.

Lilly Kahill. "Artemis," in *LIMC* 2:618–753.

Erika Simon and Gerhard Bauchhenss. "Diana," in *LIMC* 2:792–855.

Jean-Pierre Vernant. *Mortals and Immortals: Collected Essays,* edited by Froma Zeitlin. Princeton, NJ: Princeton University Press, 1991, 195–257.

Asklepios.

ASKLEPIOS (LATINIZED FORM AESCULAPIUS)

Mortal healer who was able to raise the dead.

According to the mythographer Apollodoros, Apollon had sexual intercourse with Koronis (Latinized form = Coronis), daughter of Phlegyas in Thessaly, but she herself preferred to live with a certain mortal man, Ischys. When a raven brought Apollon word of her cohabitation, he cursed the bird, changing its color from white to black, and he killed Koronis, though as she lay on her funeral pyre he removed from her womb the infant Asklepios and entrusted him to the centaur Cheiron. The centaur reared him, instructing him in the arts of healing and hunting, and in time Asklepios became a great surgeon, able not only to prevent persons from dying but also to revive those who had already died. Athena had given him blood from the vein of the Gorgon, and he used the blood flowing on the left for destruction and that on the right for salvation, thereby raising the dead. Zeus, fearing that other persons might learn this treatment from Asklepios, killed him with a thunderbolt, and Apollon, angered at this, slew the Cyclopes, fashioners of Zeus's thunderbolts. Zeus was about to cast Apollon into Tartaros when Apollon's mother, Leto, intervened, so that Zeus instead ordered Apollon to work as a laborer for a mortal man, Admetos, for the period of a year (*Library* 3.10.3–4; cf. Pindar *Pythian* 3 in *The Odes*).

Tradition connects Asklepios with two great healers of Greek tradition, the god Apollon, from whom he inherits perhaps a predisposition to healing, and the centaur Cheiron, from whom in any case he receives practical training, which Athena enhances by providing him with wondrous blood from the slain Gorgon Medusa. According to Diodorus of Sicily, moreover, Asklepios did not revive merely an occasional corpse but rather brought back the dead on so large a scale that Hades lodged a complaint with Zeus, charging that the number of the dead was steadily decreasing (*Diodorus of Sicily* 4.71.2). The hero's success threatened the distinction between immortals and mortals as well as the cosmic balance between the living and the dead.

When Zeus angrily smote Asklepios with a thunderbolt, Apollon smote the beings who forged Zeus's thunder-weapon, the Cyclopes. Should this not result in the supply of thunderbolts being now finite? It should, and for this reason, perhaps, some ancient authors report that Apollon slew, not the Cyclopes, but their sons (Pherekydes frag. 35 Fowler).

There is a tension between the Asklepios of mythological narrative and the Asklepios of Greek and subsequently also Roman cult. In story, Asklepios is a mortal human, or more properly a hero (Pindar *Pythian* 3.7 in *The Odes*), inasmuch as he has one divine and one human parent and lives in the heroic period; his two sons, both physicians, take part in the campaign against Troy (Homer *Iliad* 2.729–733). Or he is an immortal in the sense that he has been catasterized, having been placed in the sky as a constellation (Hyginus *Poetic Astronomy* 2.14). For Greeks and Romans he was a great god of healing, but his ongoing influence on human health does not agree with his role in mythology.

In statuary, Asklepios is typically portrayed holding a staff with a snake coiled around it.

Suggested reading:

Emma J. Edelstein and Ludwig Edelstein. *Asclepius: Collection and Interpretation of the Testimonies.* 2 vols. in 1. Baltimore: The Johns Hopkins University Press, 1998.

Timothy Gantz. *Early Greek Myth: A Guide to Literary and Artistic Sources.* Baltimore: The Johns Hopkins University Press, 1993, 91–92

Bernard Holtzmann. "Asklepios," in *LIMC* 2:863–897.

ATHENA (ALSO ATHENÊ AND ATHENAIA) (ROMAN MINERVA)

Goddess of war and crafts.

Zeus's first wife was the Okeanid Metis (Cleverness). When she was about to give birth, Gaia (Earth) and Ouranos (Sky) informed Zeus that Metis was fated to bear first a daughter, Athena, who would be Zeus's equal in strength and counsel, and then a son, who would be king of gods and men, and that, in order to forestall the birth of a son who would supplant him, he should swallow Metis. So he tricked her, swallowing her and keeping her in his belly, where she gives him counsel. Zeus engaged in more marriages, and after he married his seventh and present spouse Hera, he gave birth to Athena from his head, whereupon Hera in anger gave birth without sexual union to a son Hephaistos (Hesiod *Theogony* 886–929). It is unclear why Zeus must swallow Metis in order not to beget a second child, and in particular it is unclear why he swallows her while

Zeus giving birth to Athena, with Poseidon and Hephaistos looking on.

she is pregnant with their daughter Athena, and why Athena exits from his head. But he does swallow Metis, and the result is that it is he who actually gives birth to Athena. It is ambiguous, then, whether Athena's parents are Metis and Zeus or, since Zeus both begets her and gives birth to her, Zeus alone. Hera takes the latter view, since she attempts to match Zeus's achievement by producing a child entirely on her own.

According to a different account, Metis was not so much a wife of Zeus as an unwilling sexual partner, who transformed herself into many different forms in the hope of escaping him (Apollodoros *Library* 1.3.6), for Metis, like other sea deities, was capable of rapid metamorphosis. Zeus nevertheless succeeded in mating with her and later in swallowing her as well. Prometheus or Hephaistos smote the head of the parturient god with an axe, and Athena leaped out fully armed (*Library* 1.3.6). Entering the world mature and armed is characteristic of warriors, for the Giants and the Spartoi (Sown Men), two sets of aggressive warriors, also are born armed and physically mature.

Athena is a maiden goddess. Her virginity, like that of Hestia, is asexual, lacking the eroticism and allure that characterize the huntress Artemis. A Greek hymn describes her as not caring for the doings of Aphroditê but instead liking warfare and fine workmanship, for it is Athena who taught craftsmen to make carriages and chariots, and it is Athena who taught maidens in their homes to do female crafts, putting this knowledge into their minds (*Homeric Hymn to Aphrodite* 7–15). So Athena has two principal honors, or divine spheres of interest: war and craftsmanship.

As a goddess of battle, Athena shares an interest in war with Ares, but the two deities are dissimilar in character, Athena representing the positive aspects of war such as its nobility, Ares representing negative aspects such as bloodthirst and violence, despite the fact, or perhaps because of it, that among mortal Greeks men alone served as soldiers. The high esteem in which Athena was held relative to Ares was acted out in encounters between Athena and

Athena.

Ares on the battlefield at Troy, as recounted in Homer's *Iliad*. On one occasion, Ares was stripping the armor from a fallen warrior when he spotted Diomedes, eagerly made for him, and lunged at the man with his spear. But Athena, who in the meantime had donned the Cap of Invisibility, pushed Ares's spear aside, and when Diomedes now drove forward with his spear, Athena leaned upon it, driving it into Ares's belly. The wounded god uttered a terrifying cry and retreated to Olympos (5.846–906). On a subsequent occasion, Ares, seeing Athena in battle, attacked her with his spear but was unable to pierce her aegis. She in turn struck him in the neck with a boulder, laying him out flat on the battlefield (21.391–415). In each case intelligent strategy wins out over simple, impulsive force, Athena emerging triumphant and Ares losing both battle and dignity. The aegis that Ares is unable to pierce is an object made of goatskin, as its name implies (Greek *aigis*, from *aix*, "goat"). Ancient artists represent Athena's aegis as a cloak fringed with snakes and bearing the head of the Gorgon Medusa, which the goddess placed there after Medusa was decapitated by the hero Perseus (Herodotos 4.189; Apollodoros *Library* 2.4.3). It was fashioned for her by her mother, Metis (Hesiod frag. 343 MW). She can hold it up in order to terrify her human opponents, causing them to scatter like stampeding cattle (Homer *Odyssey* 22.297–299).

While Athena was aiding Diomedes on the battlefield, she took the place of his charioteer, joining Diomedes on his chariot, after which the axle groaned mightily with the weight of the goddess and the hero (Homer *Iliad* 5.838–839). Great weight is a characteristic of supernatural beings generally. Pliny mentions a Triton who used to climb up onto the side of ships at night and sit there, weighing down one side of the vessel such that it would tip or even submerge (*Natural History* 9.4.10).

Perhaps related to the goddess's interest in warriors is her love for various heroes—Perseus, Herakles, Diomedes, and in particular Odysseus and his family. She vigorously championed Odysseus's welfare on Olympos and on earth, perhaps because she felt that she and Odysseus were so much alike, relying as they did on intelligence (Homer *Odyssey* 13.299–302).

As a goddess of craftmanship, Athena is the divine source of human knowledge concerning traditional male industries such as the construction of ships and wagons and traditional female domestic industries, particularly spinning and weaving. Thus she advised Argos, the builder of the great ship *Argo* on which the Argonauts sailed, and even participated in its construction (Apollodoros *Library* 1.9.16), and it was on Athena's initiative and with her advice that Epeios constructed the Wooden Horse that led to the fall of Troy (Homer *Odyssey* 8.492–495, *Little Iliad*). Athena and Hephaistos share the honor of craftsmanship (*Homeric Hymn* 20), the goddess being associated mostly with softer crafts such as woodworking, the god being linked to harder crafts such as metalworking. Athena's role as the inventor of woolworking underlies the story of Minerva (the Roman name for Athena) and the hubristic maiden Arachnê (Spider). Renowned for her skill in weaving, Arachnê arrogantly challenged the goddess of weaving herself to a contest. In the end, Minerva pummeled Arachnê in anger, the girl hanged herself, and Minerva turned her into a spider, in which form she continues to hang and weave (Ovid *Metamorphoses* 6.5–145).

A third honor of Athena's is her sovereignty over the city of Athens. The gods once decided to take individual possession of different cities where they would receive worship, and Athena and Poseidon both went to Attica to compete for its possession. As evidence of his claim to the place, Poseidon struck a rock on the Acropolis with his trident, and the sea poured forth. For her part Athena planted an olive tree. Sitting as judges, the twelve gods awarded the region to Athena, who named the city Athens after herself (Apollodoros *Library* 3.14.1).

A strange myth recounts how Athena once came to the lame smith Hephaistos, wishing him to fashion weapons for her. Hephaistos, however, conceived a passion for Athena and tried to have sexual intercourse with her, but the virgin Athena would not allow it. The god ejaculated onto her leg, and in disgust the goddess wiped off his semen with a piece of wool and threw it to the ground. From the semen that came into contact with the earth there was born a son, Erichthonios. Athena reared him, and he became a king of Athens in early times (*Library* 3.14.6). So Athena is both maiden and mother.

Athena and a favorite companion, the nymph Chariklo, were once bathing in a spring on Mount Helikon at midday. Chariklo's son Teiresias happened to be hunting on the mountain at that time, and in his thirst for water he came to the spring and saw what he should not see. Athena immediately took away his sight. When Chariklo exclaimed at her son's fate, Athena declared she could not change his punishment but she could grant him the honor of becoming a great seer despite his blindness, and she did so (Kallimachos *Hymn* 5).

Athena plays a role in the Judgment of Paris. A cyclic epic relates how the gods were feasting at the wedding party of Peleus and Thetis when the goddess Eris (Strife) appeared and started a quarrel about beauty among Athena, Hera, and Aphroditê. Zeus told Hermes to conduct the goddesses to the Trojan youth Alexander, or Paris, on Mount Ida for his judgment. The goddesses offered bribes to Paris, Hera promising him kingship, Athena offering victory in war, and Aphroditê holding out marriage with Helen. Because of the prospect of marriage with Helen, Paris chose Aphroditê (*Kypria*). The Judgment of Paris led to the seduction or abduction of Helen and so finally to the Achaean campaign against Troy to retrieve her, or Trojan War. Paris's choice endeared him to Aphroditê, who favored Paris and the Trojans throughout the war, but it earned him the undying hostility of Athena and Hera, who accordingly sided with the Achaeans, or Greeks.

Among the many names and epithets of Athena are Pallas, which is used with the goddess's name (Pallas Athena) or independently (Pallas); Tritogeneia, a word of uncertain significance; Atrytonê, of uncertain meaning; *glaukopis*, usually rendered "gray-eyed" or "owl-eyed," like Hera's epithet "ox-eyed"; and Polias or Poliouchos (Guardian of the City).

In mythological art Athena is represented as a youthful female outfitted with the trappings of a male soldier such as helmet, armor, spear, and shield. Other attributes are her aegis and her bird, the owl. Her birth from the head of Zeus is a popular scene in ancient illustration.

See also Ares; Hephaistos

Suggested reading:

Fulvio Canciani. "Menerva," in *LIMC* 2:1050–1109.

Pierre Demargne. "Athena," in *LIMC* 2:955–1044.

Timothy Gantz. *Early Greek Myth: A Guide to Literary and Artistic Sources.* Baltimore: The Johns Hopkins University Press, 1993, 83–87.

Joseph Russo. "Athena and Hermes in Early Greek Poetry: Doubling and Complementarity," in *Poesia e religione in Grecia: Studi in onore di G. Aurelio Privitera,* edited by Maria Cannata Sera and Simonetta Grandolini. Naples: Edizioni Scientifiche Italiane, 2000, 595–603.

ATLAS

Strong god who supports the sky.

Atlas bearing the sky represented as a sphere.

Hesiod relates that the Titan Iapetos married the Okeanid Klymenê, and she bore him four sons: Atlas, Menoitios, Prometheus, and Epimetheus. Zeus struck arrogant Menoitios with a thunderbolt, sending him down to Erebos, and he made Atlas stand at the boundaries of the earth, near the Hesperides, and hold up the sky with his head and arms. Zeus bound devious Prometheus to a column, where each day an eagle ate his liver, which grew back again during the night. And Zeus gave Epimetheus the maiden whom Hephaistos had molded (*Theogony* 507–534, 746–757). So Atlas is one of four brothers who experience the hostility of Zeus, and his task of holding up the sky is a punishment, not an honor. According to Homer, rather than supporting the sky with his own body, Atlas stands in the sea and holds the long columns that keep earth and sky apart (*Odyssey* 1.52–54). The Atlantic Sea (later Atlantic Ocean) acquired its name in antiquity from the presumed location of Atlas, as also did the fictional island of Atlantis.

The sky is a solid object that, like the roof of a house, needs support, and Atlas by virtue of his name (Atlas = Bearer) seems destined to do so. Hesiod envisions him as a powerful being who stands at the western edge of the world where, like a living column, he holds up the roof of the world. (It is unclear why, as the sole support of the sky, Atlas stands at the edge of the world, resulting in a cantilevered roof, rather than at its center.) Since the poet does not explain why the sky did not fall before it was supported, he does not acknowledge the interval of time between the castration of Ouranos (Sky), when the sky presumably assumed its current position, and its present support by Atlas. The Succession Myth and the myth of the sons of Iapetos are somewhat independent stories that are not fully integrated with each other.

In a divergent tradition the sky is supported by Mount Atlas, a lofty mountain in Africa that the locals called "the pillar of the sky" (Herodotos 4.184.3). Ovid links the Titan and the mountain by reporting that Perseus turned the god into a rocky mountain by displaying the Gorgon's head to Atlas, petrifying him (*Metamorphoses* 4.621–662).

Atlas once nearly managed to pass his task on to another strongman. The eleventh labor of Herakles was to obtain some of the Golden Apples of the Hesperides. On the advice of Prometheus, the hero did not himself go after the apples but relieved Atlas of his cosmic burden and sent him. But when Atlas returned from the Hesperides with three apples, he declared he did not want to support the sky any longer, telling Herakles to hold it up in his place. Advised by Prometheus once again, Herakles promised he would do so but told Atlas to hold the sky while he placed a pad on his head. When, however, Atlas put down the apples and took the sky back, Herakles gathered up the apples and departed (Apollodoros *Library* 2.5.11). In this version of an international tale known as *Holding Up the Rock*, Atlas plays the role of the slow-witted strongman.

Ancient sources are nearly unanimous in making Atlas the supporter of the sky, not of the earth, nor of the earth and sky. Today's common but mistaken belief that Atlas holds up the earth probably derives from representations, found first in Hellenistic and Roman art, in which the sky that the Titan holds up is depicted as a sphere (see *LIMC* 3:16). From the practice of using such illustrations on the cover or first page of books of maps, such books came to be known as atlases.

Atlas fathered many daughters, including the nymph Kalypso (Latinized form = Calypso), who kept Odysseus in erotic captivity in the course of his return from Troy to Ithaca (Homer *Odyssey* 5), and seven sisters known as the Pleiades who were borne to him by the Okeanid Pleionê. The Pleiades eventually were placed among the stars, becoming a constellation (Apollodoros *Library* 3.10.1–3; Hyginus *Fabulae* 192).

See also Titans

Suggested reading:

Antti Aarne and Stith Thompson. *The Types of the Folktale: A Classification and Bibliography.* FF Communications, 184. 2nd revision. Helsinki: Academia Scientiarum Fennica, 1961, Type 1530: *Holding Up the Rock.*

Beatriz de Griño et al. "Atlas," in *LIMC* 3:2–16.

William Hansen. *Ariadne's Thread: A Guide to International Tales Found in Classical Literature.* Ithaca, NY: Cornell University Press, 2002, 197–201.

H. W. Stoll and A. Furtwängler. "Atlas," in Roscher 1:704–711.

Bellerophon slaying the Chimaera.

BELLEROPHON (ALSO BELLEROPHONTES)

Youth who slew the monstrous Chimaera.

After the Corinthian youth Bellerophontes, grandson of the wily Sisyphos, accidentally killed his brother, he went to the court of Proitos to be purified of the blood-crime. There Proitos's wife, Stheneboia, fell in love with the youth and propositioned him, but when he rejected her advances, she told her husband that Bellerophontes had propositioned her. Believing her, Proitos angrily sent Bellerophontes to his father-in-law, the Lykian monarch Iobates, with a letter in which he instructed Iobates to kill its bearer.

Instead of killing the youth outright, however, Iobates ordered him to slay the Chimaera, thinking that the youth would perish in the attempt. The monster had a lion's head in front, a dragon's head at the end of its tail, and a fire-breathing goat's head in the middle. Though a single creature, it had the power of three, and it ravaged the countryside and cattle. Bellerophontes mounted the winged horse Pegasos (Latinized form = Pegasus) and, flying in the air, killed the Chimaera from above. Since the youth had survived the task, Iobates ordered him to do battle against the Solymoi, and when he succeeded at this also, Iobates told him to fight the Amazons. When Bellerophontes killed them, Iobates arranged for a select band of Lycians to ambush him, but Bellerophontes killed all of them. Marveling at the youth's prowess, Iobates finally showed Bellerophontes the letter, asked him to stay in Lykia, offered him his daughter Philonoê as wife, and gave him half the kingdom (Homer *Iliad* 6.152–211; Apollodoros *Library* 2.3.1–2). According to Pindar, the hero obtained the wonderhorse Pegasos, offspring of Poseidon and Medusa, with the help of Pallas Athena and used it to his advantage also in his battles against the Solymoi and the Amazons (*Olympian* 13.60–92).

Although Bellerophontes's heroic career began well, it eventually turned sour. He attempted to fly Pegasos up to Olympos in order to join the company of the gods, but the horse threw him (Pindar *Isthmian* 7.44–47 in *The Odes*). Becoming hateful to all the gods, Bellerophontes wandered alone on the plain of Aleios, eating his heart out and avoiding other humans (Homer *Iliad* 6.200–202).

Bellerophontes is the earlier form of the hero's name; the spelling Bellerophon is found in later Greek authors and in Latin authors. The name signifies Slayer of Belleros, and there was a tradition according to which he did slay a certain Belleros, but the incident plays a minor role in the legend as we have it.

In mythological illustration Bellerophon can be shown riding the winged horse Pegasos and slaying with his spear the monstrous Chimaera.

> **See also** Biographical Pattern; Hero; Monsters
>
> **Suggested reading:**
> Timothy Gantz. *Early Greek Myth: A Guide to Literary and Artistic Sources.*
>   Baltimore: The Johns Hopkins University Press, 1993, 313–316.
> Anne Jacquemin. "Chimaira," in *LIMC* 3:249–259.
> Catherine Lochin. "Pegasos," in *LIMC* 7:214–230.
> Stith Thompson. *A Motif-Index of Folk-Literature.* Bloomington: Indiana
>   University Press, 1955–1958, K978: *Uriah letter;* K2111: *Potiphar's Wife.*

BIOGRAPHICAL PATTERN

Recurrent elements in traditional accounts of the lives of male heroes and, to a lesser extent, of gods.

Many biographical narratives of legendary persons show considerable resemblance to one another in their sequence of action. From the mid-nineteenth century onward, scholars have published lists of recurrent motifs in the traditional biographies of gods and especially heroes, offering different explanations for the similarities. A central dynamic of some biographical legends is the presence of two male figures (father, uncle, grandfather, and so on), one displaying a benevolent or passive attitude toward the hero and the other showing hostility. We might call these two the benevolent-passive father-figure and the hostile father-figure. For example, Oedipus has hostile Laios (biological father) and benevolent Polybos (foster father); Theseus has passive Poseidon (biological father) and passively hostile Aigeus (putative father); Perseus has passive Zeus (biological father) and hostile Akrisios (grandfather), followed by a second set, benevolent Diktys (foster father) and hostile Polydektes (would-be stepfather); and Jason has benevolent Aison (biological father) and hostile Peleus (uncle).

On one level, at least, such stories appear to portray the typical development of males with a focus upon the difficulties experienced by fathers and sons, each of whom perceives the other as threatening, the father fearing displacement and the son fearing exclusion. Ordinary reality is transformed into narrative via simplification, acting out, and exaggeration. The narrative simplifies the complexity of a real-life father in his relationship to his son by selecting two aspects out of many, supportiveness (or passivity) and hostility, each of which appears in the story as a simple character (benevolent, passive, or hostile). The characters may then act out their peculiar attitude, which in real life might not be clearly externalized. The hostility of the father can be expressed as an attempt by the hostile father figure to do away with the hero, and the hero's dealing with the threatening aspect of his father may similarly be expressed by the hero's acting in such a way that, intentionally or not, the hostile father figure comes to harm. Overall, the stages and actions of ordinary male development are exaggerated so that they appear as colorful extremes. A young man's leaving home appears as travel in an exotic land. His establishing himself as a capable adult appears as the accomplishment of a great task. His marriage to a female outside of his familiar world appears as marriage to a foreign bride. And his coming to terms with the resentful side of his father appears as displacement of the hostile father figure.

> *See also* Jason, Oedipus, Perseus, Theseus
>
> *Suggested reading:*
>
> Clyde Kluckhohn. "Recurrent Themes in Myths and Mythmaking." *Daedalus* 88 (1959): 268–279.
>
> Lord Raglan. "The Hero of Tradition." *Folklore* 45 (1934): 212–231; reprinted in *The Study of Folklore*, edited by Alan Dundes. Englewood Cliffs, NJ: Prentice-Hall, 1965, 142–157, with headnote by the editor.
>
> Robert A. Segal, ed. *In Quest of the Hero.* Princeton, NJ: Princeton University Press, 1990.
>
> Archer Taylor. "The Biographical Pattern in Traditional Narrative." *Journal of the Folklore Institute* 1 (1964): 114–129.

CATASTERISM (GREEK KATASTERISMOS)

The translation of a being or object from earth to a station among the stars, so that the being or object becomes a star or, more usually, a star cluster.

Every star cluster is the result of a catasterism in the mythological past. Since the heavenly lights are (as Homer says) celestial wonders that crown the sky, translation to the heavens is an honor. Ancient mythological narrators treat vaguely whether a catasterism is simply a translation to the heavens in which the subject becomes immortal and ageless but remains materially the same or is also a transformation into something else, for they speak indifferently of asterisms as actual living entities inhabiting the sky and also as groupings of luminaries. Thus in his description of the making of Achilleus's shield, the poet Homer says (*Iliad* 18.483–489),

> He [= Hephaistos] represented the earth on it, and the sky, and the sea,
> the tireless sun and the full moon,
> and all the wonders with which the sky is crowned:
> the Pleiades, the Hyades, strong Orion,
> and the Bear, which is also called the Wagon.
> She turns around in one place and keeps a wary eye on Orion,
> and she alone never bathes in the River Ocean.

The Bear is female because the word *bear* in Greek is grammatically feminine and perhaps also because the constellation Ursa Major (Greek *Arktos Megalê*), or Great Bear, came into being as the result of the catasterism of a female being. In any case, she watches Orion warily since she is a bear and he is a hunter, and in her caution never ventures to enter the River Ocean (that is, never dips below the horizon). So the Bear is a living being fully capable of perception and emotion and at the same time she is a cluster of lights lending beauty to the sky. In short, she is a binatural being, a living creature and at the same time an element of the physical cosmos affixed to the celestial dome or sphere.

According to Hesiod, the maiden Kallisto had lived as a huntress in the mountains, keeping company with Artemis. But Zeus ravished her, and when Artemis discovered Kallisto's pregnancy, the goddess angrily changed her into a bear, and as such Kallisto gave birth to a son, Arkas. Sometime later she entered a sanctuary of Zeus, unaware that it was unlawful to do so, and was pursued by the Arcadians and her own son, who were on the point of putting the creature to death, but Zeus, mindful of their earlier relationship, took her and placed her among the stars, calling her Bear (frag. 163 MW). A catasterism normally occurs at the conclusion of the myth or legend, as here, lending closure to a narrative by freezing a character into a new state and by serving as an aetiology for a familiar astral phenomenon.

As for Orion, he too had been a hunter. At one period in his life, he was hunting on the island of Crete along with the goddesses Artemis and Leto. When, however, he boasted that he would slay every animal that existed on the earth, Gaia (Earth) angrily sent up a huge scorpion, which stung him, causing his death. On account of his courage, Artemis and Leto asked Zeus to place Orion among the stars, and he did so. Zeus also placed the scorpion there as a reminder of the event (Hesiod frag. 148a MW). This scorpion is of course Scorpio.

Orion had also been lustful. According to Hyginus Astronomus, the Pliades (Greek Pleiades) are seven sisters, daughters of Plionê (Greek Pleionê) and Atlas. Only six of them are discernible in the sky because six sisters had consorted with gods and the seventh with a mortal, Sisyphos, for which reason her star is faint. Now once Plionê and her daughters were traveling through Boeotia when Orion noticed them and desired Plionê, whereupon the females fled and he pursued. After seven years of flight and pursuit, Jupiter took pity on Plionê's daughters and placed them among the stars, and even now they seem to flee Orion and he seems to follow them as they set. The Pliades enjoy more honor than the other stars because the rising of their sign signifies summer and the setting of their sign indicates winter (2.21). Zeus intervenes here, not to resolve the relationship of pursuit and flight but to freeze it forever in a different form, as he does when a fox that was fated never to be caught was being pursued by a dog that was fated always to catch its prey; Zeus turned both animals into stone (Antoninus Liberalis *Metamorphoses* 41).

Like other mythological narratives, the many myths and legends featuring a catasterism show considerable variation in detail. For example, once she is an asterism, the Bear does not bathe. Is it because she fears the hunter Orion, as Homer implies, or because Juno persuaded the sea deities Oceanus and Tethys not to allow her to enter their waters, as Ovid says (*Metamorphoses* 2.508–531)?

See also Transformation; Translation

Suggested reading:

Fr. Boll and W. Gundel. "Sternbilder, Sternglaube und Sternsymbolik bei Griechen und Römern," in Roscher 6:867–1071.

Theony Condos. *Star Myths of the Greeks and Romans: A Sourcebook.* Grand Rapids, MI: Phanes Press, 1997.

Joseph Fontenrose. *Orion: The Myth of the Hunter and the Huntress.* University of California Publications: Classical Studies, 23. Berkeley: University of California Press, 1981.

CENTAURS AND HIPPOCENTAURS
(GREEK KENTAUROI AND HIPPOKENTAUROI)

Composite male beings, part human and part equine.

Ancient art represents centaurs as having the upper part of a man (head and trunk) connected to the lower part of a horse (body and four legs). They are therefore more horse than man. But in early Greek art the proportions are reversed, the rear half of a horse being grafted onto the backside of an entire man.

Ancient authors often employ the compound "hippocentaur" (horse-centaur) instead of "centaur." This usage agrees with the myth in which Kentauros (that is, Centaur) is properly the name of the father of the centaurs, and hippocentaurs are his composite offspring (Diodorus of Sicily 4.69.5–70.1). Early poets also refer to them simply as "wild beasts."

Centaurs dwell in the mountains, the wild habitat also of satyrs and nymphs, not in cultivated areas. They are hypermasculine, showing a weakness for wine and women and being given to violent behavior. According to Homer,

Battle of the Centaurs and the Lapiths.

the centaur Eurytion was a guest at the house of the Lapith Peirithoos, became drunk, and did evil things (which Homer does not specify), as a result of which the Lapith heroes angrily dragged him outside and cut off his ears and nostrils. This incident was the beginning of the trouble between centaurs and men (*Odyssey* 21.287–304), the Lapiths being a human group who were kinsmen of the centaurs. Later sources tell of one or more conflicts, the initial trouble taking place at the wedding celebration of Peirithoos and Hippodameia when the centaurs, smelling the wine, rejected the milk they had been served, got drunk, lost their senses, and tried to make off with the Lapith women, including the bride. The Lapiths overcame them in the ensuing battle, the humans employing conventional weapons, their opponents using tree trunks. This initial skirmish may have been followed by a more protracted war in which the Lapiths succeeded in driving away the centaurs from the region of Mount Pelion (Pindar frag. 166; Ovid *Metamorphoses* 12.189–535). The Centauromachy (Battle with the Centaurs) was a popular subject with artists, and its portrayal on the west pediment of the Temple of Zeus at Olympia ranks among the most striking works of ancient art.

On a later occasion, Herakles visited the centaur Pholos, who served a meal of meat, Herakles's portion being roasted, his own being raw. Desiring wine, Herakles opened a jar of wine that was the common property of the centaurs, but they smelled the wine and came to Pholos's cave, armed with trees and rocks. Herakles drove them away by means of firebrands and arrows, and they took refuge with Cheiron, who chanced to be struck in the knee by one of Her-

Centaurs hunting.

akles's arrows. Although Herakles withdrew the shaft and treated the wound with medicine given him by Cheiron, the wound proved to be incurable. Cheiron wished to die but, being immortal, could not; so he gave up his immortality to another, and then died. Taking an arrow from the corpse of a centaur, Pholos accidentally dropped it on his foot and died also (Apollodoros *Library* 2.5.4). Sometime later Herakles and his wife Deianeira, wishing to cross the River Euenos, encountered the centaur Nessos, who ferried persons across the stream for a fare. Herakles entrusted his wife to the centaur, but he made sexual advances as he carried her across. The enraged Herakles slew the lecherous centaur (*Library* 2.7.6).

That centaurs might be dangerous to undefended humans generally is shown by an incident in the legend of Peleus. Akastos and Peleus went hunting, but while Peleus was napping, Akastos hid Peleus's sword and deserted him in the expectation that he would be overcome by the centaurs that lived in the mountains. And indeed after Peleus awoke and began searching for his sword, he was captured by centaurs and would have perished if he had not been saved by the intervention of the good centaur Cheiron, who also returned his sword to him (Hesiod frag. 209 MW; Apollodoros *Library* 3.13.3). The hunt took place on Mount Pelion, birthplace of the centaurs.

Quite different myths of the origin of centaurs are found. When Ixion became enamored of the goddess Hera and attempted to force himself upon her, she told her husband Zeus, who made a cloud in the likeness of Hera and placed it beside Ixion, who taking it for Hera had sexual intercourse with it. The cloud bore a son, Kentauros (that is, Centaur), who proved to be arrogant and overbearing, respecting neither humans nor gods. He mated with certain mares in the area of Mount Pelion, and their offspring were human above and horse below (Pindar *Pythian* 2.25–48 in *The Odes*; Apollodoros *Epitome* 1.20). The strange trick of fashioning a female double out of a cloud is not unique to this myth but is found also in the legend of Troy, in which, according to some authors, the gods conveyed the real Helen to Egypt while Paris unwittingly took with him to Troy a phantom Helen made by the gods from clouds (Apollodoros *Epitome* 3.5).

Other myths of origin account for individual centaurs rather than centaurs as a group. In one, the god Kronos transformed himself into a horse and had sexual intercourse with the Oceanid Phillyra, who gave birth to the centaur Cheiron (scholiast Apollonios of Rhodes *Voyage of the Argo* 2.1231–1241), a myth that once again presents the composite nature of centaurs as being a consequence of the mating of a horse and an anthropomorphic being. But a third myth makes the centaur Pholos the son of Silenos and a melian nymph (Apollodoros *Library* 2.5.4). Inasmuch as Silenos is a satyr, this tradition represents one composite equine being begetting another. Since all centaurs, like all satyrs, are male, they cannot constitute a self-reproducing community, or if they do, a centaur (or satyr) father must be sufficient to beget a son of like nature.

Their sexual behavior is that of half-bestial males having little experience with, or access to, females, or perhaps no self-control. In contrast, the centaur Cheiron had a wife, Chariklo, about whom nothing further is known, and daughters, although Cheiron, sometimes called the good (or wise) centaur, is obviously not typical of the species. Female centaurs are missing from mythological narrative, but they are found in ancient art. Lucian mentions a painting by Zeuxis, whom he characterizes as a painter who favored nontraditional subjects. Among his novelties was a painting that portrayed a female hippocentaur nursing twin infant centaurs, one at her breast in the manner of humans and the other in the manner of horses, while her mate stood nearby (*Zeuxis* 3–6).

Cheiron himself was born immortal, but after he was wounded by Herakles and could not be cured of his pain, he voluntarily gave up his immortality so that he could die (Apollodoros *Library* 2.5.4, 2.5.11). He was a half-brother of Zeus, for both had been fathered by Kronos. Since Cheiron's parentage was unique, his condition of immortality was not the rule (if there was one) for centaurs, and Nessos, Pholos, and many other centaurs were as subject to death as any mortal, although they were possibly long-lived.

Cheiron was unique among centaurs not only in his gentle domesticity but also in his wisdom and knowledge and in his fondness for humans. He was the tutor of many heroes, whom he reared in his home. Jason lived for twenty years with Cheiron's family in his cave, where he was raised by the centaur's daughters (Pindar *Pythian* 4.101–116, *Nemean* 3.43–63 in *The Odes*), and fragments are extant of an early work entitled *Precepts of Cheiron* in which the wise centaur is represented as advising the young Achilleus. Cheiron was the discoverer of botanical medicine as well as veterinary medicine and taught the healer Asklepios the medicinal arts. According to Xenophon (*On Hunting* 1.1–17), hunting was the invention of Apollon and Artemis, who gave knowledge of it as a gift to Cheiron on account of his justice, and he in turn taught it to his young heroic pupils, among them Nestor, Hippolytos, Achilleus, Meleager, Odysseus, and Palamedes, all of them proving to be excellent hunters.

> *See also* Pan; Satyrs and Silens
>
> *Suggested reading:*
>
> Page duBois. *Centaurs and Amazons: Women and the Pre-History of the Great Chain of Being.* Ann Arbor: University of Michigan Press, 1982.
>
> Timothy Gantz. *Early Greek Myth: A Guide to Literary and Artistic Sources.* Baltimore: The Johns Hopkins University Press, 1993, 143–147, 277–281.
>
> Madeleine Gisler-Huwiler. "Cheiron," in *LIMC* 3:237–248.
>
> William Hansen. *Phlegon of Tralles' Book of Marvels.* Exeter: University of Exeter Press, 1996, 170–174.
>
> D. S. Robertson. "Prometheus and Chiron." *Journal of Hellenic Studies* 71 (1951): 150–155.
>
> Thomas Sengelin et al. "Kentauroi et Kentaurides," in *LIMC* 8:671–721.

CHARON

Ferryman of the dead.

Charon is a bearded, unkempt old boatman who ferries newly deceased mortals across the lake or stream that separates the land of the living from the land of the dead (Pausanias 19.28.1–2). The watery boundary is Acheron (Euripides *Alkestis* 444; Plato *Phaedo* 113d). As his fare, Charon himself takes from the mouth of his passengers the coin, usually an obol, that kinsmen customarily place there, after which he ferries his passengers across the waters and returns alone to the opposite shore. In the same way mortals might bring a honey-cake as a sop for Hades's hound Kerberos (Latinized form = Cerberus), who similarly allows dead persons to enter the death realm but not to leave again (Apuleius *Metamorphoses* 6.19).

Although Charon seems to lack a divine genealogy, he is treated as a divine being. In modern Greek folktales and ballads, Charos (or Charontas) is Death himself, like Thanatos in ancient tradition.

Passage on Charon's ferryboat is one of several ways for mortals to reach Erebos. In Homer's *Odyssey* the realm of the dead lies in the far west rather than beneath the earth, though one must nevertheless traverse the River Ocean to get there, which Odysseus did in his own ship. But Odysseus visited Erebos while he was a living man, and the dead accomplished the journey differently. After Penelopê's arrogant suitors lost their lives, the god Hermes, carrying his golden caduceus, escorted their souls through the air to the land of the dead (*Odyssey* 24).

Among Charon's attributes is the *pilos*, or workman's cap.

See also Hermes

Suggested reading:

Margaret Alexiou. "Modern Greek Folklore and Its Relation to the Past: The Evolution of Charos in Greek Tradition," in *The 'Past' in Medieval and Modern Greek Culture*, edited by Speros Vryonis, Jr. Malibu, CA: Undena Publications, 1978, 221–236.

Joachim Kühn. "Fährmann," in *Enzyklopädie des Märchens*, edited by Kurt Ranke et al. Berlin: Walter de Gruyter, 1984, 4:785–793.

Christiane Sourvinou-Inwood. "Charon I," in *LIMC* 3:210–225.

Otto Waser. "Charon." *Archiv für Religionswissenschaft* 1 (1898): 152–182.

COMBAT MYTH AND LEGEND

Story recounting how a god or hero overcomes a monster in battle. The combat of a hero and a monster is an international, migratory story that is found in many forms in classical mythology.

As a myth, the story tells of the victory of a god over a monstrous opponent (Zeus versus Typhon, Apollon versus Python, and so on), and as a legend it tells of the victory of a mortal hero over a monster (Kadmos versus the Serpent of Ares, Perseus versus Ketos, Herakles versus various monsters, and so on). The combat of the god Zeus and the monster Typhon can exemplify the mythic form of the type here, and the combat of the hero Kadmos (Latinized form = Cadmus) and the Serpent of Ares can exemplify the story as a legend.

According to the mythographer Apollodoros, Gaia (Earth) had sexual intercourse with Tartaros and gave birth to Typhon, a hybrid of man and beast, his upper body being humanoid and his lower body consisting of huge coils of hissing vipers. Immensely strong, he was so great in size that his head often touched the stars while one hand reached the west and the other the east. A hundred dragon heads projected from his arms, fire came from his eyes and mouth, and he was winged. When he made a rush at heaven, the Olympian gods fled, except for Zeus, who cast thunderbolts at Typhon from a distance and struck him with an adamantine sickle at close range, wounding the monster. But as they grappled, Typhon entwined Zeus with his coils, wrested the sickle from him, severed the sinews of his hands and feet, and deposited the helpless god in a cave. Typhon put the sinews in the care of the dragoness Delphynê, who like him was partly humanoid and partly bestial. But Zeus's allies stole back his sinews and fitted them to the god. Mounting a chariot with winged horses, Zeus pursued Typhon to Mount Nysa, pelting him with thunderbolts. There the Moirai (Fates) tricked him into tasting the "ephemeral fruits," persuading him that he would be strengthened thereby. Finally Zeus piled Mount Aetna in Sicily upon Typhon, and to this day fire from the god's thunderbolts issues from the mountain (*Library* 1.6.3).

According to the Roman poet Ovid, Cadmus consulted the Delphic oracle in order to learn what land he should settle in, and Phoebus Apollo responded that Cadmus would encounter a heifer in the wilderness and should follow the cow till she knelt down to rest; there he should build a city and call the land Boeotia (Cow Land). Presently Cadmus did indeed meet a heifer, followed her until she lay down, and, intending to sacrifice her to Jove, sent some of his men to a spring in an ancient, untouched forest. But a serpent sacred to Mars dwelled in a cave from which the spring flowed. Fire flashed from its eyes, it had a triple tongue and three sets of teeth, and it was so huge that it could rear itself above the trees of the forest. After the serpent killed Cadmus's companions, Cadmus struck it with his spear, and following a great struggle, the monster perished. At the advice of Minerva, Cadmus planted the dragon's teeth, producing a crop of men who fought one another. Five of these men survived, and with them Cadmus founded the city of Thebes (*Metamorphoses* 3.6–137).

These stories are best understood as being different realizations of a migratory type, or plot. Typical features of the type in its mythic form are: (1) The enemy is of divine origin and (2) has a distinctive habitation. (3) He possesses an extraordinary appearance and extraordinary properties and (4) is vicious and greedy. (5) He conspires against heaven. (6) A divine champion appears to face him. (7) The champion fights the enemy. (8) The champion nearly loses the battle, but (9) the enemy is finally destroyed after being outwitted, deceived, or bewitched. (10) The champion disposes of the enemy and celebrates his victory (Fontenrose 1959).

The hero's monstrous opponent, incarnating danger and disorder, is often described as being a dragon (Greek *drakon*, "serpent") or as being dragonlike, and its destruction may allow the protagonist to establish a new instance of order such as a cosmos (Zeus institutes cosmic order after he vanquishes Typhon), a sanctuary (Apollon completes his new temple at Delphi once he kills Python), or a city (Kadmos founds Thebes after he slays the Serpent of Ares).

See also Apollon; Herakles; Perseus; Zeus
Suggested reading:
Joseph Fontenrose. *Python: A Study in Delphic Myth and Its Origins.* Berkeley: University of California Press, 1959.
William Hansen. *Ariadne's Thread: A Guide to International Tales Found in Classical Literature.* Ithaca, NY: Cornell University Press, 2002, 119–130.

COSMOGONY (GREEK KOSMOGONIA)

Birth or coming into being of the cosmos, or world.

A cosmogonic myth is a traditional, narrative account of the origin of the world. Since *cosmos* implies not only a world of matter but also a world of order, the cosmogonic process can stretch from the first state or event to the organization of the constituent parts as a system.

The richest and best-known mythic cosmogony in classical antiquity is that narrated by Hesiod in his *Theogony,* according to which the world began with the appearance of four primordial beings, who were born or otherwise came into being in the following order: Chaos (Chasm, or Bounded Space), Gaia (Earth), Tartaros (Gloomy Realm), and Eros (Erotic Love). Genealogically speaking, the first two were the more important, for the cosmogonic process consisted primarily of the successive production of generations of offspring by Chaos and Gaia and their descendants. The descendants of Chaos were mostly intangible elements such as Nyx (Night), Hemera (Day), Thanatos (Death), Hypnos (Sleep), Eris (Strife), Machai (Battles), and Horkos (Oath), whereas the descendants of Gaia were all tangible elements such as Ourea (Mountains), Pontos (Sea), the Olympians gods, and a variety of monsters. Of the other two primordial beings, Tartaros later mated with Gaia, and Eros did not mate at all, though his existence was necessary since it was a precondition to the possibility of erotic activity in the world.

The Hesiodic cosmos is dualistic, consisting essentially of two great descent groups, one founded by Chaos and the other by Gaia, the former made up for the most part of states and forces and the latter of palpable beings, all of them alive, cognizant, and capable of sexual activity. The founders produce their initial offspring by parthenogenesis (that is, without sexual intercourse with another being), but once sexual partners become available, reproduction takes place by means of the mating of males and females, gradually bringing the constituents of the familiar world into being.

Nonetheless, one or two important steps were accomplished by agency other than mating. One was the separation of Gaia (Earth) and Ouranos (Sky), whose mating kept their offspring confined within Gaia, discomfiting her and stalling the cosmic process of constant separation and differentiation. So Kronos, incited by Gaia, lopped off the genitals of his father, Ouranos, with a sickle, causing the unmanned Ouranos to give up his position upon Gaia and to retreat to his present location far above her. Perhaps another step was the creation of the first human beings, though we cannot be sure, since Hesiod does not report how the primordial humans came into existence, only that men were on the scene initially and the first woman, fashioned from clay by Hephaistos, was introduced later. Possibly the first men were fashioned from clay by Prometheus. However they came into being, humans derive proximally or ultimately from the earth, so that they belong to the great family headed by Gaia.

Hesiod does not speculate about what, if anything, preceded the appearance of Chaos or precisely how the primordial four came into being, and as in other Greek cosmogonic myths, no explanation is offered for why the first thing happened when it did, or why it happened at all. There was no purpose in it or plan to it, and indeed there hardly could have been, since the principal gods did not come into existence until later and were merely a part of the process. One day, as it were, the cosmos just started happening. The movement overall was one of differentiation, as beings came out of or came loose from other beings, as though all the eventual constituents of the cosmos had already been there from the beginning but concealed within one another or tangled together. As in a kit, the parts were present but not yet arranged usefully.

The physical universe eventually acquired a houselike structure, with a floor (Gaia), roof (Ouranos), and a cellar (Tartaros). Divine struggles for control of the nascent world, including the Titanomachy, in which the Olympian gods overcame the Titan gods, and the combat of Zeus and the dragon Typhon, in which Zeus triumphed, led to the eventual victory of Zeus and his fellow Olympians and to the sovereignty of Zeus, whereupon Zeus as ruler of the world distributed honors, or cosmic responsibilities, to the different gods. With the establishment of cosmic order under Zeus, Hesiod's cosmogony is complete.

Since no Greek or Roman cosmogony enjoyed canonical status, variant and competing accounts coexisted. In his *Library*, the mythographer Apollodoros draws his cosmogony largely from Hesiod, although he begins his account, not with Chaos, but with the mating of Ouranos and Gaia. In a different cosmogonic myth, known from allusions in Homer (*Iliad* 14.200–210, 246) and later authors, the primordial chaos is watery. In this tradition, Okeanos (River Ocean) and his spouse Tethys were the parents of the gods and perhaps of all things. Since Okeanos was the freshwater river that encircled the earth, his spouse Tethys must be the salt waters, so that together they made up all the waters of the cosmos. Theirs was the first marriage in the world, but they had a quarrel such that they no longer slept together. Okeanos and Tethys, it appears, were much like Ouranos and Gaia in that they were the primordial married couple, the progenitors of the principal gods, and finally the victims of marital strife that led to a cessation of their sexual relationship. We can only guess at the process of the cosmogony. Probably, as in Hesiod, the primeval parents produced offspring by mating, and their offspring in turn produced offspring. Possibly the land emerged from the primeval waters, becoming an orb of dry land surrounded by and resting upon the original watery chaos. Watery cosmogonies are familiar from the mythologies of ancient Near Eastern peoples including the Egyptians, the Babylonians (*Enuma Elish*), and the Hebrews (*Genesis* 1).

> ***See also*** Anthropogony; Combat Myth and Legend; Succession Myth
>
> ***Suggested reading:***
>
> Joseph Fontenrose. *Python: A Study of Delphic Myth and Its Origins.* Berkeley: University of California Press, 1959, 217–273.
>
> G. S. Kirk and J. E. Raven. *The Presocratic Philosophers.* Cambridge: Cambridge University Press, 1957, 8–72.
>
> Jean Rudhardt. *Le thème de l'eau primordiale dans la mythologie grecque.* Bern: Éditions Francke, 1971.
>
> Martin L. West, ed. and comm. *Hesiod: Theogony.* Oxford: Clarendon Press, 1966.

CULTURE HERO

Character in myth or legend who enables or facilitates human civilization by such actions as overcoming monsters that obstruct the establishment of cultural order, acquiring elements such as fire or water that are necessary for civilization, or imparting important cultural information.

Broadly speaking, culture heroes are of two kinds, those who remove obstacles and those who contribute something new. Each helps to make human culture possible. Whereas some mythologies feature a single culture hero whose activities take place at the beginning of time, classical mythology has numerous culture heroes, both divine and human, who were active at different times in the early history of the world.

Most dramatically a divine or mortal champion, regularly male, overcomes a dangerous, hostile monster that obstructs the establishment of order. Thus, Zeus vanquished Typhon, permitting the god to establish cosmic order. Apollon slew Python, allowing him to establish his sanctuary and rites at Delphi. Kadmos (Latinized form = Cadmus) killed the Serpent of Ares, enabling him to found the city of Thebes. The new form of order ranges from the cosmos itself to the microcosm of a sanctuary or a city. Many heroes rid the world of monsters whose activities threaten the safety and order of ongoing civilized life, as when Oedipus overcame the Sphinx, who preyed upon the Thebans. Herakles devoted virtually his entire life to destroying monsters and ogres.

Rather than being removers of bad things, other culture heroes are givers of good things, facilitating civilized life by providing humans with something useful. They may be male or female. According to a mythologically inspired passage in Plato, humans did not at first have to provide for themselves, since the earth produced all food on its own. But with the passing of the Golden Age the spontaneous crops ceased, and humans were faced with the problem of survival. The difficulty was that they lacked the arts of civilization, which they had not previously needed. But the gods intervened, giving humans different gifts and imparting the knowledge that was necessary for their use: Prometheus gave them fire, Hephaistos and Athena gave them crafts, and other deities gave them seeds and plants (*Politics* 274c-d). More particularly, Demeter gave the gift of wheat to the Athenians and taught them how to prepare it for food, and the Athenians shared the seeds and the knowledge with their neighbors, until agriculture spread throughout the inhabited world. She also gave laws to human beings so that they could live in justice (Diodorus Siculus 5.4.3–6.3). Similarly Dionysos traveled the world teaching humans viticulture and winemaking (Diodorus Siculus 3.63.4). All in all, civilization is owed ultimately to the upper gods. The lower gods have their own riches—fertility, minerals—but not cultural ideas.

Outstanding among culture heroes is Prometheus. Not only did he give fire to humans but, according to Aeschylus, he was also responsible for a host of other cultural benefits. He taught mankind to build houses, to distinguish the seasons and understand the signs of the stars, to use numerals and letters, to yoke oxen, to tame horses, to sail on ships, to manufacture medicines, to foresee the future, and to interpret dreams and other warnings. Humans, previously as helpless as children, were taught by Prometheus to think and see (*Prometheus Bound* 442–506).

In classical mythology, as also in other traditions, the roles of culture hero and trickster can be combined in a single character, doubtless because cleverness and inventiveness are common to both roles. So mankind's great champion, Prometheus, is not only a culture hero par excellence but also a cunning deceiver, tricking the Olympian gods out of the better portion of sacrificial meat and stealing fire from them in order to give it to men. The other trickster among the Greek gods, Hermes, is at the same time a creator of culturally useful knowledge, discovering the use of fire-sticks and inventing the lyre. The two gods differ entirely in their personalities and styles. The selfless Prometheus deceives the gods in his role as champion of human beings and imparts culturally useful information to humans in order to better their lives, whereas the amoral Hermes acts for his own benefit, trading away his lyre to his older brother Apollon only in order to acquire cattle as one of his divine spheres of influence.

Certain mortals are similarly credited with making basic contributions to human civilization. For example, in Arcadian tradition the first human being was Pelasgos, who grew out of the earth. After his fellows chose him as king, he invented the idea of huts as shelter from the rain and as buffer from the extremes of temperature and the idea of using sheepskins as cloaks. Likewise he introduced the eating of acorns, for up to that time people's diet had consisted only of leaves, grasses, and roots (Pausanias 8.1.4–6). Indeed, the ancients were fascinated with the notion that every cultural idea had its *protos heuretes* (first discoverer or inventor), and lists of such inventors were drawn up (for example, Hyginus *Fabulae* 274, 277).

Overall the activity of culture heroes implies an evolutionary view of human history in that human life is represented as having improved over time. The contrary view is crystallized in the Myth of the Ages, which rests upon a devolutionary model.

See also Myth of the Ages; Trickster

Suggested reading:

Sue Blundell. *The Origins of Civilization in Greek and Roman Thought.* London: Croom Helm, 1986, 168–175.

Adolf Kleingünther. *Protos Heuretes: Untersuchungen zur Geschichte einer Fragestellung.* Philologus suppl. 26. Leipzig: Dieterich'sche Verlagsbuchhandlung, 1933.

Arthur O. Lovejoy and George Boas. *Primitivism and Related Ideas in Antiquity.* Baltimore: The Johns Hopkins University Press, 1997 [1935].

Stith Thompson. *A Motif-Index of Folk-Literature.* Bloomington: Indiana University Press, 1955–1958, 1:122–123: A531 *Culture hero (demigod) overcomes monsters;* A541 *Culture hero teaches arts and crafts.*

Jean-Pierre Vernant. "The Myth of Prometheus in Hesiod" and "Sacrificial and Alimentary Codes in Hesiod's Myth of Prometheus," in *Myth, Religion, and Society: Structuralist Essays by M. Detienne, L. Gernet, J.-P. Vernant, and P. Vidal-Naquet,* edited by R. L. Gordon Cambridge: Cambridge University Press, 1981, 43–79.

CYCLOPES (GREEK KYKLOPES)

Race or family of huge, one-eyed beings.

Greek mythology knows two groups of Cyclopes who have nothing in common beyond their appearance.

According to one tradition, the Cyclopes were three brothers, offspring along with the Titans and the Hundred-Handers of the primordial parents Gaia (Earth) and Ouranos (Sky). Prevented by their father from being born, the Cyclopes were eventually released from within their mother by the younger god Zeus, whereupon they furnished him with his characteristic weapon, the thunderbolt (Hesiod *Theogony* 139–146, 501–506). These Cyclopes are essentially blacksmiths, forgers of thunderbolts, and their names reflect their function: Brontes (Thunderer), Steropes (Lightner), and Arges (Flasher). But there is a myth according to which Zeus killed the healer Asklepios, a son of Apollon, with a thunderbolt after he brought dead persons back to life, whereupon Apollon in retaliation slew the Cyclopes, manufacturers of Zeus's thunderbolts (Apollodoros *Library* 3.10.4), which leaves unexplained how Zeus has acquired his thunderbolts thereafter.

A different tradition (Homer *Odyssey* 6.4–6, 9.105–555) represents the Cyclopes not as a particular set of brothers but as a society of one-eyed giants who dwell in an unspecified, out-of-the-way place in the world. They are arrogant, brutish shepherds whose society lacks laws and assemblies, each man ruling his own wife and children and being indifferent to his neighbors, and whose level of technology is quite simple, for they live in caves and possess no knowledge of agriculture or, for all their nearness to the sea, of sailing.

This assemblage of Cyclopes was visited by Odysseus and his companions on their way home from Troy, or rather the Greeks visited the cave of the Cyclops Polyphemos (Latinized form = Polyphemus). Despite his being a son of Poseidon, Polyphemos proved to be a cannibal with little respect for the Olympian gods and none at all for the laws of hospitality. After he ate several of Odysseus's men, the others survived by outwitting him. First they drove a stake into his single eye while he drunkenly slept, blinding him, and then they escaped from his cave by clinging individually to the bellies of his sheep as the animals exited from the cave to go to pasture for the day. Ancient vase-painters who illustrate this story select either the blinding of the seated Cyclops or the escape of the Greeks beneath the sheep. The story itself is the Greek form of an international folktale.

> *See also* Fabulous Peoples and Places; Giants; Monsters
>
> *Suggested reading:*
>
> Antti Aarne and Stith Thompson. *The Types of the Folktale: A Classification and Bibliography.* FF Communications, 184. 2nd revision. Helsinki: Academia Scientiarum Fennica, 1961, Type 1137: *The Ogre Blinded.*
>
> William Hansen. *Ariadne's Thread: A Guide to International Tales Found in Classical Literature.* Ithaca, NY: Cornell University Press, 2002, 289–301.
>
> Robert Mondi. "The Homeric Cyclopes: Folktale, Tradition, and Theme." *Transactions of the American Philological Association* 113 (1983): 17–38.
>
> Denys L. Page. *The Homeric Odyssey.* Oxford: Clarendon Press, 1955, 1–20.
>
> Odette Touchefeu-Meynier. "Kyklops, Kyklopes," in *LIMC* 6:154–159.

DEMETER (ROMAN CERES)

Goddess of grain and agriculture.

Demeter is a daughter of the Titans Kronos and Rhea. Kronos, having learned that he would be overthrown by a son, swallowed his children as they were born. When the grieving mother gave birth to Zeus, she hid her newborn son in a cave on Crete, giving her husband instead a stone wrapped in swaddling clothes, which he swallowed. Once Zeus was fully grown, Kronos was tricked into vomiting up the stone and his children, including Demeter, and presently Zeus led the younger gods in a war against the older gods, in which the younger gods emerged victorious. After Zeus vanquished another threat, the monster Typhon, the other Olympians invited him to be king of the gods. Thereupon Zeus entered into a series of seven marriages. His fourth wife was his sister Demeter, who bore him a daughter Persephonê (Hesiod *Theogony* 453–929).

According to the *Homeric Hymn to Demeter*, Zeus secretly gave his brother Hades permission to seize Persephonê to be his mate. One day as Persephonê gathered flowers in a meadow, the earth gaped open and Hades burst forth with his horses and chariot, seized her, and carried her down against her will to his kingdom. She cried out, and when her mother heard her voice, she rushed over land and sea in search of her daughter, but in vain. For nine days Demeter searched, torch in hand, tasting neither ambrosia nor nectar, until Helios (Sun) revealed to her that the girl's father, Zeus, had given her to his brother Hades, who had abducted

Demeter holding a sheaf of wheat.

her. In her anger at Zeus, Demeter avoided the company of the Olympians and, taking the form of an old woman, visited the cities of humans, coming in time to the house of Keleos, ruler of Eleusis, and his wife, Metaneira, where the latter engaged her as nurse for her own infant son. Demeter gave the boy neither grain nor milk; instead, she covertly anointed him with ambrosia and placed him nightly in the fire to burn away his mortal parts, and she would thus have made the boy ageless and immortal, but Metaneira saw her son lying in the fire and cried out, whereupon Demeter snatched him from the flames, and the boy remained mortal. The nurse revealed herself as the goddess Demeter, instructed the people to construct a temple for her, and promised to teach them her rites.

Persephonê in Erebos.

Resuming her true form, she departed from the house. The Eleusinians built a temple for the goddess, and she remained in it apart from the other gods, grieving for her daughter. She caused seeds not to sprout, keeping them hidden in the earth, and as a result agriculture came to a halt. The human race would have perished, and the gods would have been deprived of their sacrifices, had not Zeus intervened. He and the other gods tried to induce her to return to Olympos, but she angrily refused to return or to allow the seeds to sprout until she should see her daughter again.

So Zeus dispatched Hermes to the realm of the dead to persuade Hades to bring Persephonê back. Hades allowed it but secretly gave Persephonê a pomegranate seed so that she could not remain forever with her mother. Demeter and Persephonê were joyously reunited on earth, but when Demeter discovered that Persephonê had taken food in Erebos, she perceived that Persephonê would have to live a third of the year with her spouse and two-thirds of the year with her mother and the other immortals. Reconciled to this situation, however, Demeter was persuaded to allow seeds once again to grow for humans, so that the earth became laden with flowers and leaves. Then she revealed to the rulers of Eleusis how to perform her secret rites, the Eleusinian Mysteries. Whoever is initiated into these mysteries is blessed, and whoever is uninitiated does not share the same joys in Erebos. After that mother and daughter joined the other immortals on Olympos, where they dwell beside Zeus (*Homeric Hymn to Demeter*).

The hymnist's version of the myth is set at a time when human beings were already agriculturalists, for Demeter threatened the survival of the human population by bringing all agriculture to a stop; her great gift to humans, via the Eleusinians, who had received her in her grief, was the knowledge of her rites, the Eleusinian Mysteries. In other versions, however, her great gift to mankind at this point was grain and its cultivation. The historian Diodorus of Sicily reports that because the Athenians received Demeter more hospitably in her distress than any other people, Demeter gave the gift of wheat first to the Athenians and taught them how to prepare it for food, and the Athenians shared the seeds and knowledge of it with their neighbors, until agriculture spread throughout the inhabited world. In return for her gift, the Athenians honored the goddess by establishing the Eleusinian Mysteries (*Diodorus of Siculus* 5.4.4). So Demeter gave mortals the great gift of agriculture, just as subsequently Dionysos taught them viticulture.

An unwed goddess, Demeter has an occasional sexual encounter. In addition to her willing relationship with her brother Zeus, she paired unwillingly with her brother Poseidon. When she was wandering the earth in search of her daughter, Poseidon followed her, lusting after her. She turned herself into a mare and joined other mares in grazing, but Poseidon perceived the trick, turned himself into a stallion, and mated with her in that form. At first angry, Demeter in time accepted what had happened. She gave birth to a daughter, whose name may be mentioned only to the initiated, and to the famous horse Areion (Pausanias 8.25.4–10). Demeter also had an affair with a mortal, Iasion. According to Homer, she yielded to her passion and lay in love with Iasion in a thrice-plowed field, but Zeus soon learned of it and struck Iasion with a thunderbolt, killing him (*Odyssey* 5.125–128). The mythographer Apollodoros says rather that because Iasion tried to violate Demeter, Zeus killed him with a thunderbolt (Apollodoros *Library* 3.12.1). In any case she bore the god Ploutos (Wealth), who grants riches and prosperity (*Theogony* 969–974; *Diodorus of Sicily* 5.77.1).

Among her attributes in art are stalks of wheat, a torch, and a scepter.

See also Absent Deity; Culture Hero; Persephonê

Suggested reading:

Stefano de Angeli. "Ceres," in *LIMC* 4:893–908.

Luigi Beschi. "Demeter," in *LIMC* 4:844–892.

Jenny Straus Clay. *The Politics of Olympus: Form and Meaning in the Major Homeric Hymns.* Princeton, NJ: Princeton University Press, 1989, 202–266.

Helen Foley, ed. *The Homeric* Hymn to Demeter: *Translation, Commentary, and Interpretive Essays.* Princeton, NJ: Princeton University Press, 1994.

Timothy Gantz. *Early Greek Myth: A Guide to Literary and Artistic Sources.* Baltimore: The Johns Hopkins University Press, 1993, 63–70.

N. J. Richardson, ed. and comm. *The Homeric Hymn to Demeter.* Oxford: Clarendon Press, 1974.

DIONYSOS (ROMAN BACCHUS AND LIBER PATER)

God of wine.

Dionysos is the son of Zeus and Semelê, a mortal woman from Thebes with whom the god had an affair. According to the poet Ovid, Jove once consented to

Dionysos holding wine and thyrsus.

grant Semelê any wish, and she asked him to appear to her in the same form as he adopted when he appeared in love to his divine mate. Bound by his oath he reluctantly complied, but the intensity of his epiphany consumed the mortal Semelê in flames. Zeus removed from her womb the fetus that she was carrying and sewed it into his own thigh, from which in time the infant Bacchus was born (*Metamorphoses* 3.253–315).

Since Hera resented Dionysos as the offspring of her husband by another female, the newborn infant was in danger. Zeus turned him over to Hermes, who entrusted him in turn to Semelê's sister, Ino, and her husband, Athamas, persuading them to raise him as a girl; but Hera drove the couple mad, so that they became dangerously delusional. Zeus rescued the child, transforming him into a kid for his own safety, and Hermes delivered him to the Nysian nymphs to rear far away from Thebes (Apollodoros *Library* 3.4.3).

Both Dionysos and his mother attained godhood (Hesiod *Theogony* 940–942). In his case, despite his being the offspring of an immortal parent and a mortal parent, which normally is the recipe for a mortal demigod, he is somehow immortal from the first (*Homeric Hymn to Dionysos* 26.5–6). As for his mother, according to one tradition Semelê perished from Zeus's epiphany, Dionysos brought her out of Hades's realm, and they ascended together to Olympos (Apollodoros *Library* 3.5.3). According to another tradition, however, she was immortalized and translated to Olympos when she was struck by Zeus's lightning, which purified and sanctified her, raising her to a higher level of existence.

Dionysos discovered the grapevine and winemaking (Apollodoros *Library* 3.5.1), so that vines, wine, and intoxication became his special provinces. He traveled around the earth personally introducing the fruit and its use to humankind and also introducing himself as a divinity as well as his unusual rites, in which women and men left their homes, went to the mountains, and engaged in different ecstatic behaviors. Some myths emphasize the introduction of viticulture and others the introduction of the new cult, but not without problems: in the former case, misunderstanding of intoxication, and in the latter case resistance and hostility by some persons to the new god and his cult.

The first mortal to receive a plant from the god was Oineus, king of Calydon. Dionysos had visited him and, with Oineus's tacit consent, slept with his wife, Althaia. In return for his hospitality, the god gave Oineus a grapevine, naming "wine" (Greek *oinos*) after Oineus (Apollodoros *Library* 1.8.1; Hyginus *Fabulae* 129). Things did not always go so smoothly. When the god visited Ikarios in Attica, he gave him a vine cutting and taught him winemaking. Ikarios wished in turn to bestow this blessing upon other humans and so shared wine with some shepherds, who liked its taste so much that they drank a large quantity of it without water, became drunk, and killed Ikarios in the mistaken belief that they had been poisoned (Apollodoros *Library* 3.14.7; Hyginus *Fabulae* 130). Greeks customarily drank their wine diluted with water, but the shepherds, being inexperienced wine-bibbers, drank theirs neat.

Myths that emphasize the introduction of the new deity and his strange cult represent him traveling with a retinue of supernatural

Bacchante with wine and thyrsus.

celebrants in the form of satyrs and bacchantes. Dionysos's first mortal opponent was Lykourgos (Latinized form = Lycurgus), king of the Edonians in Thrace. Lykourgos chased Dionysos away, and the god sought refuge in the sea with the Nereid Thetis. The king also drove away the god's retinue of satyrs and bacchae, or took them prisoner. But presently the king, visited by madness, pruned off the limbs of his son Dryas in the belief that he was pruning vines, and the land became barren. When an oracle revealed to the Edonians that the soil would be fruitful again if Lykourgos should be put to death, they killed him (Homer *Iliad* 6.130–140; Apollodoros *Library* 3.5.1). Pentheus, king of Thebes, similarly opposed the god's orgiastic rites. When the monarch, encouraged by the god, went secretly to Mount Kithairon in order to spy on the bacchantes, they tore him to pieces in the belief that he was a wild animal (Euripides *Bacchae*).

Dionysos holding wine and ivy.

Often Dionysos toys with his persecutors, as if to mock them. Tuscan pirates once spotted a handsome, princely youth alone on a desolate shore and seized him. They tried tying him up, but he sat and smiled as the bonds fell from him. The helmsman perceived that the youth must be a god and urged his companions to set him free, but the captain disregarded him. As the ship sailed out to sea, strange things occurred. Wine started gushing over the ship. A grapevine spread out along the top of the sail, and grape clusters hung down, while ivy wrapped itself around the mast. As the men now begged the helmsman to bring the ship to land, the god suddenly transformed himself into a lion, and elsewhere on the ship a bear appeared. Presently the lion leaped upon the captain. The other sailors leaped into the sea in terror and were transformed into dolphins, but the god held the helmsman back and spoke to him, revealing himself to the man as Dionysos, son of Semelê and Zeus (*Homeric Hymn 7*).

On a different front, Dionysos had also to persuade the Olympians to accept him as one of their own. He won over his staunchest opponent, Hera, in the following way. Hera bore a son, Hephaistos, but she was ashamed of his lameness and cast him out of Olympos. So Hephaistos skillfully constructed a chair with invisible bonds, sending it as a gift to his mother, who happily sat down on it but could not get up from it again. Since only Hephaistos could free her, Dionysos made him drunk and brought him back to Olympos, where he released his mother. As a result of Dionysos's benefaction toward her, Hera changed her attitude toward him and persuaded the other Olympians that Dionysos was one of the celestial gods (Alcaeus frag. 349 MW), and he is usually regarded as one of the younger Olympians.

Dionysos's spouse is Ariadnê, daughter of King Minos of Crete and Pasiphaê. After Ariadnê had helped the hero Theseus overcome the monstrous Minotaur that lived in the Cretan labyrinth, she sailed away with him with the intention of accompanying him to Athens. But Dionysos fell in love with her, either taking her after Theseus had deserted her on the island of Naxos or telling Theseus to depart and leave the maiden; in any case Theseus sailed from Naxos without her. Dionysos made Ariadnê his wife, and Zeus granted her immortality (Hesiod *Theogony* 947–949).

Of Dionysos's epithets and alternative names, the best known is Bakchos (Latinized form = Bacchus), a word that is used both for the god and for his worshippers. He is Bakchos, and they are Bakchoi or Bakchai (respectively the masculine and feminine plural forms of the word, Latinized as Bacchi and Bacchae). Other names or epithets include Bromios (Noisy), Eiraphiotes (Insown?), and Twice-Born. In Rome he is Bacchus (a Latinization of Bakchos) and Liber (Free), or Liber Pater (Father Free).

In mythological art, Dionysos is often represented as a bearded youth in the company of satyrs and/or nymphs, customarily identified as maenads. His attributes include grape vines, ivy, kantharos (a kind of drinking cup), and thyrsus (a kind of wand). Among the frequently illustrated incidents in the life of the god is his birth from the thigh of Zeus.

See also Maenads; Satyrs and Silens; Translation

Suggested reading:

Marcel Detienne. *Dionysos at Large.* Trans. Arthur Goldhammer. Cambridge, MA: Harvard University Press, 1989.

P. M. C. Forbes Irving. *Metamorphosis in Greek Myths.* Oxford: Clarendon Press, 1990, 191–194, 316–317.

Timothy Gantz. *Early Greek Myth: A Guide to Literary and Artistic Sources.* Baltimore: The Johns Hopkins University Press, 1993, 112–119.

Carlo Gasparri. "Bacchus," in *LIMC* 3:540–566.

———. "Dionysos," in *LIMC* 3:414–514.

DIVINE GUILDS

Sets of divine or semidivine siblings of similar appearance and cosmic function.

Greek mythology features many small groups of homogeneous brothers or sisters such as the Hundred-Handers, the Graces, and the Hesperides, whose members are little distinguished from one another except by name and whose honor, or sphere of influence, if any, is shared. A divine guild typically has three members, although the numbers range from as few as two to as many as nine, and frequently the ancient sources disagree about their number as well as their individual names. Divine sisterhoods are far more common than divine brotherhoods.

I consider the sisterhoods first, assembling them for the sake of convenience into subgroups. In the discussions of both the sisterhoods and the brotherhoods, the subgroups are indicated by boldface type.

The three Hours.

Celestial Sisters

The three **Graces** (Latin *Gratiae*, a rendering of Greek *Charites*) are beautiful goddesses representing female charm and loveliness, as their name implies. The offspring of Zeus and the Oceanid Eurynomê, their individual names vary in different authorities. Hesiod calls them Aglaia, Euphrosynê, and Thalia (*Theogony* 907–911). The sisters dwell on Olympos next to the Muses (*Theogony* 64), which implies that they resemble each other, presumably in their shared focus upon the amenities of civilized life. Attendants of Aphroditê, they fashioned an ambrosial robe for her (Homer *Iliad* 5.338), and earlier, when the gods created the first woman, they joined Peitho (Persuasion) in adorning her with golden necklaces (Hesiod *Works and Days* 73–74). Ancient artists show the three Graces standing side by side, unclothed, in an interlocked pose.

In cult the three **Hours** (Greek *Horai*; Latin *Horae*) are divine personifications of the seasons. In the ordinary usage of ancient Greek, the term *hora* refers to a period of time, notably a subdivision of the year—that is, a "season," especially spring, and by extension the springtime of life—or a subdivision of the day, namely, an "hour." In mythology the Hours are personified seasons emblematizing the springtime of life with its youth and beauty, so that like the Graces they lend a pleasantly lovely and divine, if also somewhat indefinite, coloration to scenes. Daughters of Zeus and the goddess Themis (Order), their individual names vary, but Hesiod gives them as Eunomia, Dikê, and Eirenê (*Theogony* 901–903). The Hours attend various deities such as Aphroditê, much like the Graces, and they are the keepers of the cloud-gates that give access to Olympos (Homer *Iliad* 5.749–751), the clouds parting briefly to allow a deity to pass into the heavenly land of the gods, and then rejoining again.

Closely allied are the three **Fates** (Latin *Fata*, also called *Parcae*; Greek *Moirai*), who are sisters of the Hours, being offspring likewise of Zeus and Themis, inasmuch as the Fates, like the Seasons, have to do with cosmic regulation and order. They are goddesses of destiny, imagined concretely as weavers, wherefore they are called Klotho, Lachesis, and Atropos (*Theogony* 901–906), or Spinner, Allotter, and Unbending. The heavenly Fates are celestial versions of the ordinary Fates of folk belief who come to a household soon after the birth of a child in order to declare its fortune, as they do for example in the legend of Meleager, and much as the fairies do in Charles Perrault's *Sleeping Beauty* (indeed, English *fairy* derives, through French, from Latin *fata*). Details of the fates of several heroes other than Meleager were known, although without the dramatic portrayal of a scene in which the three sisters themselves announce it. Options or conditions were common features. Thus Achilleus was destined to live either a short and glorious life or a long and obscure one, suggesting that he could choose to remain at Troy, where he would win renown but die young, or he could choose to return home, where he would live a long but undistinguished life away from the battlefield. He wavered but eventually chose the former. Laios learned that if he begat a son, the boy would become his slayer. So he abstained from sexual intercourse with his wife, but he slept with her once when he was drunk, and she conceived a son, later named Oedipus. Subsequently, Oedipus himself was told by the Delphic oracle not to go to his homeland, else he would murder his father and have sexual intercourse with his mother. Like his father before him, he attempted without success to avoid the destructive option. Negotiation was a possibility. Apollon asked the Moirai that Admetos be released from death at the time at which he would otherwise die, if someone should volunteer to die in his place, and the Moirai granted it. When the time came, only Admetos's wife, Alkestis (Latinized form = Alcestis), was willing to die for him. She survived the ordeal because Persephonê sent her back, or when Thanatos (Death) came to fetch her, Herakles wrestled Alkestis away from him (Apollodoros *Library* 1.9.15). Just as the Fates spin the thread of an individual person's life at the time of his or her birth (Homer *Iliad*

Muse with lyre.

20.127–128), determining its length and quality, so also they determine the nature of complex events, even the course of the cosmos itself. The Moirai of ancient Greek tradition persist in modern Greek tradition (in folktales, for example) as the Moires.

The **Muses** (Greek *Mousai,* Latinized as *Musae;* also Latin *Camenae*) are nymphs of the arts. Usually represented as being nine in number, a sororal triad multiplied by three, the Muses are the offspring of Zeus and the goddess Mnemosynê (Memory), who lay together for nine nights in Pieria, north of Mount Olympos. The sisters have their homes on Olympos as neighbors of the Charites (Graces) and Himeros (Longing). They are Kleio, Euterpê, Thaleia, Melpomenê, Terpsichorê, Erato, Polymnia, Ourania, and, most eminent of them all, Kalliopê (Hesiod *Theogony* 1–103). Later authors assign individual Muses to individual arts, but without much consistency. Hesiod represents them as patrons of performative speech, both civic as when a king publicly judges a dispute among his subjects, but also and especially singing by musicians, a province that they share with Apollon, one of whose epithets is *Mousagetes,* or Leader of the Muses; after all, *mousikê,* the Muses' art, is "music." As goddesses, daughters of Memory, and patronesses of song, they are credited with knowing everything (Homer *Iliad* 2.485; Pindar *Paian* 6.54–55 in *The Odes*), that is, everything that a bard might wish to sing about. They teach singers their craft (Homer *Odyssey* 8.477–481), as they once did the shepherd Hesiod, appearing to him and breathing the knowledge and art of singing into him (Hesiod *Theogony* 22–35), or simply put a song into the breast of persons who sing a song (*Homeric Hymn to Apollon* 518–519). They themselves dance and sing the praises of the cosmos and the gods, sometimes accompanied by the lyre-playing of Apollon, to the delight of their father.

Some traditions attach to particular Muses, particularly genealogical traditions such as that the Muse Kalliopê was the mother by a mortal or by Apollon of the singer Linos and of the wondrous musician Orpheus. Both died violent deaths. Linos was Herakles's music teacher, but he once struck his pupil, who struck back at Linos with his lyre, killing him. Linos's brother Orpheus angered the maenads, who set upon him and tore him apart (Apollodoros *Library* 1.3.2, 2.4.9). In other traditions the Muses act collectively. On one occasion they encountered the Thracian singer Thamyris as he was coming from Oichalia. He boasted that he would win if they should have a contest in singing. In their anger the Muses paralyzed him, so that he lost his ability to sing songs and forgot how to play the lyre (Homer *Iliad* 2.594–600). Matters went further in the case of the Pierides, the nine hubristic daughters of Pieros, who similarly belittled the Muses' singing and challenged them to a contest in song. The Muses consented, nymphs were chosen as judges, and each chorus sang in turn. After the Muses were adjudged the victors, the Pierides became abusive, so that the goddesses changed them into magpies (Antoninus Liberalis 9; Ovid *Metamorphoses* 5.250–678). In a different realm of verbal art, the Muses taught the Sphinx the difficult riddle that she propounded to the Thebans.

Infernal Sisters: The Furies

The Furies (Latin *Furiae,* a rendering of Greek *Erinyes*) are implacable goddesses who take vengeance on behalf of a person who has been wronged. They are particularly fierce in the case of persons who have spilled the blood of their own kin, hunting them down and tormenting them during their lifetime, as they did Orestes after he had murdered his mother. Indeed, they themselves were born of blood, for drops of blood fallen from the severed genitals of

Fury pursuing Orestes.

Ouranos (Sky) had impregnated Gaia (Earth), who gave birth to the Erinyes (Hesiod *Theogony* 178–185). The sisters are three in number, namely Alekto, Tisiphonê, and Megaira (Apollodoros *Library* 1.1.4), and just as the celestial sisterhoods have their residences in Olympos, so the infernal sisterhood of Furies dwells in Erebos along with Hades and Persephonê (Homer *Iliad* 9.571–572, 19.259–260). They are attended by the orphaned daughters of Pandareos, whom the Harpies snatched away from the realm of the living and turned over to the Erinyes to be their servants (*Odyssey* 20.61–82). A mortal who wished not to call the Erinyes by name could refer to them by one of their conventional euphemisms such as Eumenides (Kindly Ones).

A distinction can be made perhaps between the particular three Furies of tradition, who are equipped with personal names and a mythic genealogy, and the personal Furies that each person has. After Oedipus's mother Epikastê

Furies pursuing Orestes.

learned that she had been married to her own son, she hanged herself in grief, going to Hades's realm and leaving behind for her son all the pains that the Erinyes of a mother could inflict (*Odyssey* 11.279–280). Even deities have personal Furies. After Kronos castrated his father, Ouranos, and swallowed his own children, his spouse, Rhea, meditated revenge in order that he pay the Erinyes of Ouranos and of his children (*Theogony* 472–473).

Snatchers: The Harpies

The Harpies (Greek *Harpyiai*), or Snatchers, are personified storm winds who carry persons away. Penelopê prays in her misery to Artemis to slay her with an arrow or, failing that, for a storm wind (*thyella*) to snatch her up and deposit her far away beside the River Ocean, just as storm winds (*thyellai*) once seized the daughters of Pandareos; for the Harpies once snatched up the daughters of Pandareos and gave them to the Furies to be their handmaidens (Homer *Odyssey* 20.61–82). Penelopê thus uses "storm winds" and "Snatchers" interchangeably, indicating their essential identity. In early Greek tradition, if a person's disappearance could not be accounted for, one could speculate that a storm wind or Harpy had carried him or her away.

According to Hesiod, the Harpies are two in number, Aello and Okypetê, daughters of Thaumas and the Oceanid Elektra (*Theogony* 265–269). They can snatch away not only mortal persons but also things, for the gods once sent them to Thrace to torment the blind seer Phineus. Whenever he sat down to eat, the Harpies flew down from the sky, snatched away most of his meal, and befouled the rest, leaving it inedible. When Jason and the Argonauts in the course of their quest for the Golden Fleece stopped in Thrace to consult Phineus, the diviner proposed to trade his information for their help in dealing with the Harpies. So Zetes and Kalais, the two winged sons of Boreas (North Wind), chased the Harpies permanently away, after which Phineus advised the Argonauts how to reach the land of the Golden Fleece (Apollodoros *Library* 1.9.21).

Although Harpies were usually represented as composite creatures, part bird and part woman, the Harpy Podargê seems to be a flying mare, for Zephyros (West Wind) lay with her as she grazed in a meadow beside the River Ocean, and she bore the horses Xanthos and Balios, who flew as swiftly as the winds (Homer *Iliad* 16.148–151).

Ambiguous or Monstrous Sisters

The **Sirens** (Greek *Seirenes*) are human-headed (or human-headed and human-breasted) birds and so are composite beings much like the Harpies. There are two of them in Homer, but in other representations they range from one to several, just as different authorities also offer different names and genealogies.

The best-known account of the Sirens is given by Homer (*Odyssey* 12:39–54, 158–200). When Odysseus and his companions, sailing home from Troy, reached the island of the Sirens, the weather became mysteriously calm. Having been warned by Kirkê what to do, Odysseus plugged the ears of his crew with wax in order that they might not hear and be charmed by the Sirens' song, and he had himself tied to the mast of his ship in order that he might hear it but not respond. The two Sirens addressed Odysseus by name and declared that they knew all that happened in the world. Although he wanted to get free, his men bound him all the tighter. After the ship had passed the isle, Odysseus was untied, and the plugs were removed from the ears of the crew.

It is not clear why the Sirens' song is dangerous to hear. Presumably a person under the spell of the Sirens will prefer to remain with them, enchanted by their song until he wastes away, somewhat in the way that a person who joins the Lotus-Eaters in consuming lotus loses all desire to continue his journey.

The **Hesperides** are nymphs who, along with a multiheaded dragon, guard the golden apples of the gods and the tree on which they grow. These precious apples were a wedding gift from Earth to Zeus on the occasion of his marriage to Hera (Apollodoros *Library* 2.5.11). The nymphs' collective name is related to the Greek word for "evening, west," as though they were daughters of Evening or West, and they do descend from darkness in that they are daughters of Nyx (Night), who bore them without a mate in the early era of the world (Hesiod *Theogony* 214–216). The Hesperides belong therefore to the great descent group headed by Chaos, which consists mostly of intangibles but also, as here, of things connected with darkness, in contrast to the descent group headed by Gaia (Earth). They dwell on the other side of the River Ocean at the limits of the earth toward Night, along with the Graiai, the Gorgons, and the Titan Atlas, who has been obliged by Zeus to hold up the sky (*Theogony* 270–276, 517–529). The sisters are three in number—Aiglê, Erytheia, and Hesperethousa (Hesiod frag. 360 MW).

The Hesperides' neighbors are two sets of hags, the **Graiai** and the **Gorgons**, all daughters of Phorkys and Keto. The Graiai are called Pemphredo and Enyo, and the Gorgons are Sthenno, Euryalê, and Medusa (Greek Medousa). Whereas the first two Gorgons are immortal and ageless, Medusa was born mortal and perished when the hero Perseus decapitated her. Before that, however, she lay with Poseidon and conceived the winged horse Pegasos and the hero Chrysaor, to whom she gave birth at the moment of her death (Hesiod *Theogony* 270–286). No explanation is offered why two Gorgon sisters are immortal and the third is mortal, but in any case the Perseus legend, in which Medusa's head functions as the hero's quest-object, requires that there be a Gorgon who can be decapitated. Since anyone who looks upon a Gorgon is transformed into stone, most persons who stumble into their land are converted into statues, but Perseus averted his glance as he slew Medusa, or looked at her only in the reflection of his shield, thereby escaping petrifaction. In art the Gorgons are portrayed as frighteningly monstrous, with snaky hair, tusklike teeth, protuberant tongue, round eyes (a characteristic of monsters in Greek painting) that stare at the viewer, and wings.

Their sisters the Graiai (Old Women), or Phorkides (daughters of Phorkys), are perhaps fair of face though gray-haired from birth, whence their collective name Old Women. Grotesquely and comically they have only a single eye between them, which they share by passing it back and forth as needed, at which point they are particularly vulnerable, and some authors say that they possess only a single tooth, which they likewise pass back and forth when they eat. The Graiai and the Gorgons differ from the divine sisterhoods discussed above in that they perform no manifest cosmic function. They are not in charge of anything and do not minister to anyone, except that the Graiai are perhaps the first line of defense for their sisters the Gorgons.

The fifty Nereids and the 3,000 Oceanids, marine daughters respectively of the sea-deity Nereus and of the river-deity Okeanos, as well as the 3,000 sons of Okeanos, the rivers of the world, might be added here as divine sisterhoods and brotherhoods. They neither have a focused job, however, nor, because of their very large numbers, work together as a group.

Divine Brothers

The cosmic parents Gaia (Earth) and Ouranos (Sky) had, in addition to the Titans, two sets of male offspring, the Cyclopes (Greek *Kyklopes*) and the Hundred-Handers (Greek *Hekatoncheires*). The three **Cyclopes**—Brontes, Steropes, and Arges—are identical in appearance and function. Each has one eye in the middle of his forehead, and together they supply Zeus with thunderbolts, the ultimate cosmic weapon, by means of which he maintains his position as ruler of mortals and immortals (Hesiod *Theogony* 139–146, 501–506).

The three **Hundred-Handers**—Kottos, Briareos, and Gyges—are similarly homogeneous in appearance and function. Each brother is a terrifying fighting machine, having fifty heads and a hundred arms, so that together they are able to throw 300 rocks simultaneously. By means of this firepower they overwhelmed the Titans in the battle between the Titans and the Olympians, driving them down into Tartaros, where subsequently the Hundred-Handers themselves took up residence, presumably in order to guard the Titans (*Theogony* 147–153, 617–735).

In classical mythology divine and semidivine brothers appear less commonly as triads than as dyads and less commonly in guilds than simply as similar or contrastive pairs. So, for example, the primordial mediators Prometheus and Epimetheus are respectively clever and foolish, and the city-founding twins Romulus and Remus are respectively rash and slow, whereas the winged Boreades Zetes and Kalais are all but indistinguishable from each other, as also are the giant Aloads Otos and Ephialtes.

See also Centaurs and Hippocentaurs; Ker; Monsters; Nymphs; Satyrs and Silens; Triads

Suggested reading:

Rolf W. Brednich. *Volkserzählungen und Volksglaube von den Schicksalsfrauen.* FFC 193. Helsinki: Academia Scientiarum Fennica, 1964.

A. Furtwängler. "Charis, Chariten," in Roscher 1:873–884.

Gerald Gresseth. "The Homeric Sirens." *Transactions of the American Philological Association* 101 (1970): 203–218.

William Hansen. *Ariadne's Thread: A Guide to International Tales Found in Classical Literature.* Ithaca, NY: Cornell University Press, 2002, 246–251 (Gorgons).

Georgios Megas. "Die Moiren als functioneller Faktor im neugriechischen Märchen," in *Märchen, Mythos, Dichtung: Festschrift zum 90. Geburtstag Friedrich von der Leyens am 19. august 1963,* edited by Hugo Kuhn and Kurt Schier. Munich: C. H. Beck, 1965, 47–62.

Walter F. Otto. *Die Musen und der göttliche Ursprung des Singens und Sagens.* 3rd ed. Darmstadt: Wissenschaftliche Buchgesellschaft, 1961.

Jean Rudhardt. *Themis et les Hôrai: Recherche sur les divinités grecques de la justice et de la paix.* Geneva: Librairie Droz, 1999.

EILEITHYIA

Goddess of childbirth, having the power to help or hinder delivery.

Eileithyia is one of the three children (Eileithyia, Hebê, Ares) of Zeus and his wife, Hera (Hesiod *Theogony* 921–923). Sometimes narrators speak in the plural of multiple Eileithyias (Greek *Eileithyiai*), who are likewise daughters of Hera (Homer *Iliad* 11.269–272). Roman names for the goddess are Ilithyia, a Latinized form of the Greek name, and Lucina (Ovid *Metamorphoses* 9.273–323).

Eileithyia plays a mostly negative role in mythological narrative, acting as an agent or dupe of Hera in her resentment against other females with whom Zeus has had a sexual relationship or against their offspring. Thus when Alkmenê was about to give birth to Zeus's son Herakles, Zeus declared to the other Olympian gods that on that day a descendant of Perseus would be born who would become ruler of Mycenae, but Hera jealously persuaded the Eileithyias to delay Alkmenê's delivery and arranged for the premature birth of a different descendant of Perseus, Eurystheus (Apollodoros *Library* 2.4.5). When the goddess Leto was about to deliver Apollon, her son by Zeus, she was obliged to endure nine days and nights of labor because Hera jealously distracted Eileithyia on Olympos, keeping her unaware of Leto's labor on the island of Delos. Finally the goddesses attending Leto dispatched Iris to bring Eileithyia. Iris ran through the air to Olympos, called Eileithyia aside from Hera, and bade her come, promising her a necklace as an inducement. Straightaway Eileithyia set out, and as soon as she set foot upon Delos, Leto felt an urge to bring forth her child, giving birth to Phoibos Apollon (*Homeric Hymn to Apollon* 91–119).

Suggested reading:

Timothy Gantz. *Early Greek Myth: A Guide to Literary and Artistic Sources.* Baltimore: The Johns Hopkins University Press, 1993, 81–83.

Ricardo Olmos. "Eileithyia," in *LIMC* 3:685–699.

ELYSION FIELD (LATINIZED FORM ELYSIUM) AND ISLES OF THE BLESSED

Legendary paradise to which certain persons of the heroic age were translated.

The first mention of the Elysion Field (Greek *Elysion pedion*), or Elysion Plain, occurs in Homer's *Odyssey* (4.561–569). In the course of his return home from Troy, Menelaos learned that he was not fated to die in his native Argos; rather, the gods would send him to the Elysion Field at the ends of the earth because he was married to Helen and so was a son-in-law of Zeus. There also Rhadamanthys dwells, and the living is very pleasant, for it neither snows nor rains, and the River Okeanos sends the refreshing breezes of Zephyros upon the people there.

The typical fate of a mortal person otherwise in the Homeric poems is eventually to die, whereupon the soul (*psychê*) of the deceased proceeds to the land of the dead, Erebos, and the body ceases its physical existence because of cremation, decay, or the like. The lot of Menelaos, Rhadamanthys, and their fellows is therefore exceptional in that they escape this cycle. Since they do not die, they do not experience the separation of soul and body; instead, they are transported alive and intact to a special preserve, an earthly paradise in the distant west characterized by perfect weather, there to live forever. As immortals who dwell in a paradise of eternal spring, the inhabitants of Elysion differ little from the immortal gods except for the fact that in their remoteness and lack of special powers they play no further role in human affairs.

The poet Hesiod has the same sort of place in mind when he mentions the Isles of the Blessed (*Works and Days* 156–173). In his Myth of the Ages he describes the fourth of five races of humans created in succession by Zeus: the race of heroes, a fine and just race, who were known also as demigods. Some of these men perished in war at Thebes or at Troy, but Zeus settled others apart from men and gods at the ends of the earth on the Isles of the Blessed (*makarôn nesoi*) beside the River Okeanos. There the soil produces three crops a year for them, and they live lives free of cares. Their king is Kronos, released by Zeus from his prison.

The Elysion Field and the Isles of the Blessed are different names for a paradise situated at the ends of the earth near the River Okeanos, far from the habitats of gods and ordinary humans. It is populated by a select group of persons who were active during the heroic age and have been translated there alive and intact by the gods or by Zeus in particular, to live carefree lives much like men of the Golden Age (who, like the inhabitants of the Isles of the Blessed, were ruled by Kronos) or like the gods. Indeed, the different names of the place are suggestive of something godlike, for the adjective "blessed" is applied typically to the gods and "Elysion" signifies a place that has been struck by Zeus's lightning, such places being regarded as sacred. The inhabitants are among the select not because of any moral or behavioral excellence on their part but because they are kinsmen of Zeus (in the case of Homer's Menelaos) or survivors of the great wars that characterized the age of heroes (in the case of Hesiod's fourth race of men) or because of other unstated reasons (in the case, for example, of Kadmos and Harmonia).

> **See also** Hero; Myth of the Ages; Promotion and Demotion; Translation
>
> **Suggested reading:**
>
> Walter Burkert. "Elysion." *Glotta* 39 (1960–1961): 208–213.
>
> Timothy Gantz. *Early Greek Myth: A Guide to Literary and Artistic Sources.* Baltimore: The Johns Hopkins University Press, 1993, 132–135.
>
> Arthur O. Lovejoy and George Boas. *Primitivism and Related Ideas in Antiquity.* Baltimore: The John Hopkins University Press, 1997 [1935], 290–303.
>
> Gregory Nagy. *The Best of the Achaeans: Concepts of the Hero in Archaic Greek Poetry.* Baltimore: The Johns Hopkins University Press, 1979, 167–168, 189–190, and passim.
>
> ———. *Greek Mythology and Poetics.* Ithaca: Cornell University Press, 1990, 140–141.
>
> Erwin Rohde. *Psyche: The Cult of Souls and Belief in Immortality among the Greeks,* trans. W. B. Hillis. London: Kegan Paul, French, Trubner; New York: Harcourt, Brace, 1925, 55–87.

EPITHET

Conventional adjective, especially one associated with a deity.

Greek tradition assigns a large number of epithets to the principal gods. An epithet can refer to one of the deity's provinces of influence, such as "Cloud Gatherer" for the sky-god Zeus and "Earthshaker" for the earthquake-god Poseidon; to a personal quality, such as "ox-eyed" for Hera and "golden" for Aphroditê; to a place associated with the deity, such as "Kyllenian" for Hermes (Mount Kyllenê in Arcadia is the site of the cave in which Hermes was born) and "Paphian" for Aphroditê (the town of Paphos on Cypress was an important cult-site of Aphroditê); to a particular epiphany of a deity, such as Apollon "Delphinios" (the epithet refers to the cult of Apollon of the Dolphin near Delphi, where the god once appeared in the form of a dolphin) and Aphroditê "Ourania" (the epithet distinguishes Heavenly Aphroditê from Aphroditê Pandemos, or Common Aphroditê); to an important event in the career of a deity, such as "Argeiphontes" (an obscure epithet of Hermes that was commonly interpreted in classical times as signifying "Argos-Slayer"); or to another aspect of the deity. A few epithets are euphemisms. Plouton (Wealthy One) is often employed for Hades, as Socrates comments: "Most persons, since they fear his [Hades's] name, call him Plouton" (Plato *Cratylus* 403a). Eumenides (Kindly Ones) is a common euphemism for the horrifying Furies.

Some epithets appear only in association with the deity's name (for example, "golden Aphroditê," "ox-eyed Hera"), whereas others ("Cloud Gatherer,"

"Earthshaker") can function independently as substantives in the manner of kennings, or metaphorical compound words. A few epithets are flexible in this respect. The goddess Athena can be called "Athena" (name alone) or "Pallas Athena" (epithet + name) or simply "Pallas" (epithet alone), with no essential difference in meaning, just as the god Apollon can be called "Apollon" or "Phoibos Apollon" (Latinized form = Phoebus Apollo) or "Phoibos." Some epithets are applied to more than one deity. Thus Phoibos is an epithet both of Apollon and of Helios, which leads readers sometimes to conclude that the two gods are one, but in classical mythology they are always separate characters.

Suggested reading:

C. F. H. Bruchmann. *Epitheta Deorum quae apud Poetas Graecos Leguntur.* Supplementband 1, to Roscher. Leipzig: B. G. Teubner, 1893.

Walter Burkert. *Greek Religion,* trans. John Raffan. Cambridge, MA: Harvard University Press, 1985, 184.

Iesse B. Carter. *Epitheta Deorum quae apud Poetas Romanos Leguntur.* Supplementband 2, to Roscher. Leipzig: B. G. Teubner, 1902.

Ingrid Waern. *Ges Ostea: The Kenning in Pre-Christian Greek Poetry.* Uppsala: Almqvist and Wiksells Bocktryckeri, 1951.

EPONYMY

Derivation of the proper name of a nation, town, river, and so on from a person of like name.

Greek tradition frequently derives the name of a nation or tribe from that of a founding ancestor of like name. The Hellenes, or Greeks, are said to descend from and be named for an ancestor Hellen; the branch of the Greek people called Dorians are descendants of a man named Doros, the Ionians from Ion, the Arcadians from Arkas, and so on, so that Hellen, Doros, Ion, and Arkas are eponyms of the Hellenes, Dorians, Ionians, and Arcadians respectively. Traditional Greek genealogies teem with eponymous ancestors.

Place-names may be traced to an eponym such as a nymph, if female, or a founder or conqueror, if male. Thus the land of Libya, or Africa, was named for the nymph Libya, daughter of King Epaphos of Egypt and his wife Memphis, a daughter of the Nile River (Apollodoros *Library* 2.1.4). The Greek peninsula known as the Peloponnesos, signifying "Pelops' Island," was named by the hero Pelops for himself after he gained control of the region. Similarly Rome was founded by a man named Romulus.

In contrast, the eponyms of rivers and bodies of water are regularly persons who, according to legend, drowned in them. The Hellespont acquired its name from the maiden Hellê, who fell from a flying ram and drowned in the waters below (Apollodoros *Library* 1.9.1), and the Icarian Sea similarly got its name from the youth Icarus (Greek Ikaros), who flew with artificial wings composed

Death of Icarus.

of feathers and glue but approached too closely to the sun, so that the glue of his wings melted and he plummeted to his death in the sea below, lending it his name (Apollodoros *Epitome* 1.13).

Stigler's Law of Eponymy states whimsically that "no scientific discovery is named after its original discoverer," if for no other reason than that great discoveries in science are ordinarily multiple rather than the work of a single person. Thus although the guillotine was named for the French physician Dr. Joseph Guillotin, who recommended its use as a painless and humane means of execution, contrary to common belief he did not invent the device, and he did not like the fact that his name became attached to it. Stigler's Law probably holds true also for mythological eponymy, which presents the past as a series of simple but memorable events.

See also Genealogy
Suggested reading:
   Morton S. Freeman. *A New Dictionary of Eponyms.* New York: Oxford University
      Press, 1997.
   Jim Holt. "Mistaken Identity Theory: Why Scientists Always Pick the Wrong
      Man." *Lingua Franca* (March 2000): 60.

EREBOS (LATINIZED FORM EREBUS)

Male binatural character who is both a living being and also the physical realm of the human dead.

The primordial being Chaos gave birth without sexual intercourse to Erebos (Darkness) and Nyx (Night), who then mated with each other, producing Aither (Brightness) and Hemera (Day), according to the poet Hesiod (*Theogony* 123–125). In this scheme Erebos is the principle of darkness, personified as a living creature, and Erebos and Nyx issued from Chaos because darkness is a quality of Chaos.

The anthropomorphic aspect of Erebos as male child and father appears only in this genealogical myth, for elsewhere in Greek mythology the physical aspect of Erebos is foregrounded as the cosmic repository for the human dead. The death realm is also known as the House of Hades, implying a kind of inn managed by Hades and his wife Persephonê as divine rulers of the kingdom of the dead. Although the two terms suggest different images, they were in practice interchangeable. A detailed picture of the place is given by Homer in the Eleventh Book of his *Odyssey*. The principal roles of

Danaides pouring water into a perforated jar.

Erebos as a realm in mythological narrative are to house the human dead and to serve as an extraordinary place for living heroes to visit, always with the intention of carrying away something: information (Odysseus), Hades's hound Cerberus (Herakles), Hades's wife Persephonê (Theseus and Peirithoos), his own wife (Orpheus).

Although the world of the dead is usually said to be located beneath the surface of the earth, like a cosmic basement, in which case it can properly be termed an underworld, in Homer's *Odyssey* it is found at the edge of the world in the distant west. But ancient narrators seem sometimes to treat a region at the edge of the earth and beneath the earth as the same thing.

See also Fabulous Peoples and Places; Tartaros

Suggested reading:

Lars Albinus. *The House of Hades: Studies in Ancient Greek Eschatology.* Aarhus: Aarhus University Press, 2000.

Timothy Gantz. *Early Greek Myth: A Guide to Literary and Artistic Sources.* Baltimore: The Johns Hopkins University Press, 1993, 123–128.

O. Gruppe. "Unterwelt," in Roscher 6:35–95.

L. von Sybel. "Erebos," in Roscher 1:1296.

FABULOUS PEOPLES AND PLACES

Wholly or partially imaginary communities and sites with unusual characteristics.

Fantastic peoples and places are generally located far away from Greece, such as at the ends of the earth alongside the River Ocean, where their existence is not readily subject to confirmation or disconfirmation. Some unusual peoples and places appear in one story only, whereas others recur. In this entry the names of the various peoples and places are indicated by boldface type.

In early Greek tradition, the **Ethiopians** are the most distant of men, dwelling in two widely separated communities, one where the Sun rises and the other where he sets (Homer *Odyssey* 1.22–25). Thus they live beside the River Ocean, half of them in the far east and the other half in the far west. Since Ethiopian (Greek *Aithiops*, "Burnt-Faced Person") was the ordinary Greek word for a dark-skinned person, the location of the Ethiopian communities at the sites of the Sun's rising and setting, where it comes closest to the earth, implies that the Ethiopians got (or get) their color from their nearness to the sun.

The Ethiopians are special favorites of the gods, who visit them frequently. Homer's *Iliad* recounts how Zeus and the other Olympians go to the River Ocean for twelve days to feast with the "blameless Ethiopians" (1.423–425), and his *Odyssey* reports that Poseidon goes off by himself to enjoy a sacrifice of bulls and sheep among them (1.22–26). The Ethiopians are therefore a privileged people whom the gods visit and to whom they appear openly, as they do also to the Phaeacians (*Odyssey* 7.199–206) and as they used to do to all humans. A divine visit to the Ethiopians is also a way for a narrator to motivate the absence of the gods or of a god, for when the gods feast with the distant Ethiopians, they are little aware of what is going on elsewhere in the world.

Ethiopians appear also in other mythological relations. The hero Perseus won the hand of the Ethiopian princess Andromeda by slaying the sea-monster to which she was being sacrificed (Apollodoros *Library* 2.4.3). The king of the Ethiopians at the time of the Trojan War was Memnon, son of Eos and Tithonos (Hesiod *Theogony* 984–985); he led a contingent of his countrymen to Troy to assist the Trojans and perished there. Geographically it makes sense for his mother Eos (Dawn), whose home lies in the extreme east, to have a connection of some sort with the eastern Ethiopians.

A different group of fabulous blacks are dwarfs known as **Pygmies** (Greek *Pygmaioi* "Persons-a-Cubit-in-Height," from *pygmê* "cubit"). Like the Ethiopians, they dwell beside the River Ocean. When the cranes fly south each winter, they attack the Pygmy folk, who bravely defend their homes against them (Homer *Iliad* 3.1–9).

While the blameless Ethiopians dwell in bilateral symmetry at the eastern and western boundaries of the world, the far north is held by the similarly pious and happy **Hyperboreans,** whose name (*Hyperboreioi*) the Greeks commonly understood to mean "Persons-beyond-Boreas," that is to say, inhabitants of a marvelously temperate region located beyond the cold North Wind. The poet Pindar describes the Hyperboreans as a "holy people" whom Apollon is fond of visiting; they pass their time in music and dance, enjoying lives that are happily free of toil, war, sickness, and old age (*Pythian* 10). For all their remoteness they interact at different times with the Greek world, as when they were persuaded

Pygmy (Pygmies) battling a crane (cranes).

by Herakles, founder of the Olympic Games, to let him have some of their olive trees to plant at Olympia, trees which thereafter provided shade for visitors and garlands for victors (Pindar *Olympian* in *The Odes* 3).

Odysseus visits different fabulous communities in the course of his journey home from Troy, among them the Lotus-Eaters, the Cyclopes, and the Phaeacians.

The **Lotus-Eaters** (Greek *Lotophagoi*) are a friendly community of persons whose principal characteristic is that they dine on a sweet fruit called lotus (edible plants called lotus are known, though they lack the special property of the mythological plant). They kindly shared their food with some of Odysseus's companions, who thereupon lost all desire to return home, wishing only to remain with the Lotus-Eaters and dine on lotus. These men had to be coerced to continue their journey (*Odyssey* 9.82–104).

The **Cyclopes** (Greek *Kyklopes*) are a community of one-eyed giants. Odysseus and a few of his companions visited the cave of one Cyclops, the lone shepherd Polyphemos. He proved to be a cruel but not terribly smart cannibal, who blocked the opening of his cave with a huge boulder that only he could move and proceeded to dine on his guests a couple at a time. Odysseus and the survivors managed to blind the ogre and to escape from his cave by means of a ruse (*Odyssey* 9).

The **Phaeacians** (Greek *Phaiakes*) were formerly neighbors of the Cyclopes but, having been oppressed by them, resettled in Scheria. They are descendants of the god Poseidon, who as it happens was also the father of Polyphemos by the nymph Thoosa (*Odyssey* 1.68–73,13.130). The Phaeacians devote their lives to carefree feasting, dancing, and athletics and sail the seas on magically intelligent ships that travel as swiftly as thought. They are on friendly and intimate terms with the gods, who visit them openly (*Odyssey* 9–13). Much like the Ethiopians and the Hyperboreans, then, the Phaeacians continue to enjoy conditions resembling those of the primordial Golden Age, which humanity has otherwise lost.

The **Amazons** (Greek *Amazones*) are a nation of female warriors who dwell somewhere to the east of the Greeks. According to different ancient authors, they had sexual intercourse with men from other nations but retained and reared only their female offspring. Folk etymology interpreted their name to signify "without breast," and there was accordingly a tradition that they removed their right breast in order to be unhampered in casting the javelin.

The Amazons make many appearances in heroic legend. On one occasion the hero Bellerophon fought them and vanquished them (Homer *Iliad* 6.186). One of the labors of Herakles was to acquire the Belt of Ares, which Hippolytê, queen of the Amazons, wore. The hero and his companions made their way to the country of the Amazons, where Hippolytê, upon learning of his mission, generously promised him the belt. But Hera, assuming the likeness of an Amazon, incited the other Amazons against the strangers, declaring that they were carrying away their queen. Thereupon the Amazons attacked the men, and the two sides fought, in the course of which Herakles slew the queen and took her belt (Apollodoros *Library* 2.5.9). Theseus, one of the companions of Herakles, carried off the Amazon Antiopê to be his wife and brought her to Athens, where she bore a son, Hippolytos. The abduction of Antiopê caused the Amazons to come to Athens, where they engaged the Athenians in battle. Alternatively, when Theseus deserted Antiopê and was celebrating his marriage to Phaidra (Latinized form = Phaedra), Antiopê and other Amazons marched against Athens (Apollodoros *Epitome* 1.16–17). The cyclic epic *Aithiopis* recounted how the Amazons fought at Troy as allies of the Trojans. The Amazons arrived there under the leadership of Penthesileia, a daughter of Ares. After impressive success on the battlefield, however, Penthesileia was slain by Achilleus. Depictions of the different Amazonomachies, or Battles with the Amazons, were popular in Greek art.

Sometimes a site is the center of interest. Thus the **Elysion Field** and the **Isles of the Blessed,** variant names for essentially the same concept, are special paradises for heroes, who are translated thither by the gods just before or just after death. Homer describes the Elysion Field (*Elysion pedion*), or Elysion Plain, as a delightful place located at the ends of the earth where the living is very pleasant, for it neither snows nor rains there, and the inhabitants enjoy the refreshing breezes of Zephyros (*Odyssey* 4.561–569). Hesiod has the same sort of place in mind when he mentions the Isles of the Blessed (*makarôn nesoi*) beside

Amazons and male warrior.

the River Okeanos, where the soil produces three crops a year and the fortunate inhabitants live lives free of care. They are ruled by Kronos, whom Zeus released from Tartaros for this purpose (Hesiod *Works and Days* 156–173). The inhabitants of these distant paradises, both male and female, are among the elect not because they excelled their fellow mortals in moral excellence but because they are kinsmen of Zeus or because they survived the great wars that marked the age of heroes or because they otherwise won the favor of the gods.

The divine counterpart to the Elysion Field and the Isles of the Blessed is the paradisal home of the Olympian gods, **Olympos,** represented sometimes as a dwelling place atop Mount Olympos in northern Greece and at other times as a site in the distant heavens. The contraries of these paradises are respectively **Erebos,** the gloomy abode of the human dead, and **Tartaros,** the dark and windy prison for defeated immortals.

A mythologically significant site need not be a habitation. The **Symplegades,** or Clashing Rocks, also called the **Planktai,** or Wandering Rocks, are huge cliffs in the sea that pull apart and clash together again in no predictable pattern, making it all but impossible for mariners to sail through. But one can pass through if one knows the trick. The crew of a ship confronting the Clashing Rocks must release a dove, and if it succeeds in flying through the rocks, the mariners should immediately attempt to row through, but if it fails, they must not venture it. Something rare and precious is found on the far side of the Clashing Rocks, either ambrosia (Homer *Odyssey* 12.59–72) or the fabled Golden Fleece (Apollonios of Rhodes *Argonautika* 2.317–612), so that they are not merely an isolated terror but a colorful obstacle.

In addition to sites with strange properties, some apparently unreal or perhaps forgotten places are noteworthy primarily for their mythic associations. Thus the mysterious islands of **Ortygia** (Quail Island) and **Syria,** located near each other, are places where "the turns of Helios (Sun) are." Syria is a miniparadise where famine and disease are unknown (Homer *Odyssey* 15.403–411). Eos (Dawn) once carried off the hero Orion to be her lover, arousing the jealousy of the gods, whereupon Artemis slew him on Ortygia (*Odyssey* 5.121–124), implying that she had brought him there. Aietes ("Landsman"), a son of Helios, is the ruler of a place called simply **Aia** ("Land"). He was the possessor of the Golden Fleece until the Argonauts took it from him and brought it to Greece. His sister, the witch Kirkê (Latinized form = Circe), dwells elsewhere on the similarly named island of **Aiaia.** Since Eos also has her house and dancing places on Aiaia, and Helios rises there (*Odyssey* 12.3–4), Aiaia lies in the far east. Another place with mythological resonance that belongs more to imagination than to geography is **Nysa.** Dionysos was born and reared by nymphs on Mount Nysa (*Homeric Hymns* 1 and 26), and it was at the Nysian Plain that the infernal deity Hades burst out of the earth in order to seize the maiden Persephonê (*Homeric Hymn to Demeter* 16–18).

See also Labyrinth

Suggested reading:

Josine H. Block. *The Early Amazons: Modern and Ancient Perspectives on a Persistent Myth.* Leiden: E. J. Brill, 1995.

Page duBois. *Centaurs and Amazons: Women and the Pre-History of the Great Chain of Being.* Ann Arbor: University of Michigan Press, 1982.

J. G. Frazer. "The Clashing Rocks," in *Apollodorus: The Library.* London: William Heinemann, 1921, 2: 355–358.

William Hansen. *Ariadne's Thread: A Guide to International Tales Found in Classical Literature.* Ithaca, NY: Cornell University Press, 2002, 45–49 (Pygmies).

Arthur O. Lovejoy and George Boas. *Primitivism and Related Ideas in Antiquity.* Baltimore: The John Hopkins University Press, 1997 [1935], 303–314, 348–351.

James S. Romm. *The Edges of the Earth in Ancient Thought.* Princeton, NJ: Princeton University Press, 1992, 49–77.

Frank M. Snowden Jr. *Blacks in Antiquity: Ethiopians in the Greco-Roman Experience.* Cambridge, MA: Harvard University Press, 1970.

Wm. Blake Tyrrell. *Amazons: A Study in Athenian Mythmaking.* Baltimore: The Johns Hopkins University Press, 1984.

FLOOD MYTH AND LEGEND

Story featuring a great deluge sent by the gods as a punishment for evil or inhospitable mortals.

The flood narrative is one of a number of catastrophe stories that portray an excess or dearth of something useful such as water, fire, or food. The flood narrative is found in two branches in Greek and Roman tradition, a naval subtype set in Greece in which the flood heroes are Deukalion and Pyrrha, and a pedestrian subtype set in Phrygia in which the heroes are Philemon and Baucis.

In the *naval form* of the story, when Zeus decided to destroy the Bronze Generation of persons, Prometheus advised his son Deukalion to build a chest, fill it with provisions, and embark on it with his wife, Pyrrha. Zeus flooded most of Greece, destroying all human life with the exception of a few persons who escaped to the mountains. Deukalion floated in his chest for nine days and nights, coming to Mount Parnassos. When the rains ceased, he disembarked and sacrificed to Zeus Phyxios (Zeus of Escape). Zeus sent Hermes to Deukalion and allowed him to make a wish, and Deukalion wished to have people. So Zeus told Deukalion and Pyrrha to throw stones over their head; those that Deukalion threw became men, and those that Pyrrha threw became women. For this reason they were called people (*laoi*) metaphorically from stones (*laas*) (Apollodoros *Library* 1.7.2).

Ovid's telling of the Greek myth differs in a few details. Human beings became so evil that Jupiter decided in anger to destroy them. So he sent down rain from above, and his brother Neptune sent up waters from the rivers and seas, so that the world became a single sea in which nearly all life was destroyed. Sailing in a little boat, Deucalion and his wife, Pyrrha, landed on Mount Parnassus, whose highest peaks rose above the waters. There the couple worshipped the Corycian nymphs, Themis, and other deities. When Jove saw that only two human beings had survived the deluge and that both were reverent and upright persons, his anger faded and he let the flood subside. Since Deucalion and Pyrrha felt lonely, being the last two humans on earth, they went to Themis's oracle and asked how the human race might be restored. Moved, the goddess instructed them to throw behind them the bones of their Great Mother. Perceiving that their Great Mother was the earth and that the stones in her body were her bones, they cast stones behind them, and those that he cast turned into men and those that she cast became women. That is why human beings are hard and enduring. Earth herself presently produced other forms of life (*Metamorphoses* 1.125–437).

According to the *pedestrian form* of the story, as recounted by Ovid, there was a particular place in Phrygia in which an oak tree and a linden tree stood beside each other, surrounded by a low wall, a short distance from a marsh. At an earlier time Jupiter and Mercury had come to this region in the guise of humans and sought shelter at a thousand homes before finally one household admitted them. The inhabitants of that small cottage were a pious, elderly couple, Philemon and Baucis, who hospitably shared with the disguised gods their own meager fare. When their wine bowl kept refilling itself regardless of how many times it was drained, the amazed Philemon and Baucis perceived that their guests must be divine, uttered a prayer, and asked forgiveness for their modest food. Jupiter and Mercury now disclosed that they were gods, that the impious neighborhood would be punished, but that Philemon and Baucis would be spared. The gods bade the old couple follow them on foot up a nearby mountain. As they neared the top, the old couple turned around and saw that every house in the region except theirs was covered with water, and while they wept for the destruction of their neighbors, their cottage turned into a fine marble temple. Then Jupiter asked them what they might wish for, and they chose to serve as priests in the temple and, when their time came to die, not to outlive each other. Their requests were granted. Philemon and Baucis tended the temple until one day they metamorphosed into two neighboring trees, which the local peasants thereafter venerated with offerings (*Metamorphoses* 8.620–724).

In the naval branch of the flood story, the deluge is a cosmic catastrophe. The world, or at least the known world, is covered with water and virtually all living creatures perish. The pious couple survives and reaches safety by means of a boat. The deluge is a virtual return to chaos, and human beings are created anew, as though the gods did not get things right the first time. It is also a virtual purification of the earth on a vast scale, a warning that the gods have it in their power to destroy the earth by means of natural catastrophes if they are sufficiently offended by human misbehavior. In contrast, the pedestrian branch of the story recounts a regional catastrophe, in which a community is covered with water, killing the local inhabitants. A pious couple survives and reaches safety by walking up a nearby mountain. One story has cosmic significance, whereas the other has regional significance; that is, the Greek, or naval, form of the story is a myth, and the Phrygian, or pedestrian, form of the story is a legend.

That the myth and legend are ultimately forms of the same story-type is shown clearly by the agreement of their plots in all essentials. (1) Human beings behave impiously, so that (2) the gods decide to destroy them. (3) They warn a particular pious couple, however, telling them what to do in order to survive. (4) Then the gods send a cosmic (local) deluge, (5) in which all the living beings on the earth (in a town) drown, (6) except for the pious couple, (7) who survive by embarking on a boat, which lands on a mountain (by climbing a local mountain). (8) The gods offer the pious couple a boon of their choice, (9) the couple makes a wish, and (10) their wish is fulfilled. The story concludes with a transformative and aetiological element (stones are transformed into people, whence "people" from "pebbles" or whence our hardness; or the pious humans are transformed into trees, for which reason the trees are regarded as sacred).

The Flood Myth/Legend is an international migratory story attested also in Hebrew, Mesopotamian, and Indian tradition.

Suggested reading:

Gian Andrea Caduff. *Antike Sintflutsagen.* Göttingen: Vandenhoek and Ruprecht, 1986.

Alan Dundes, ed. *The Flood Myth.* Berkeley: University of California Press, 1988.

Joseph Fontenrose. "Philemon, Lot, and Lycaon." *University of California Publications in Classical Philology* 13 (1945): 93–119.

James George Frazer. *Folk-Lore in the Old Testament: Studies in Comparative Religion, Legend, and Law.* London: Macmillan, 1919, 1:104–361.

William Hansen. *Ariadne's Thread: A Guide to International Tales Found in Classical Literature.* Ithaca, NY: Cornell University Press, 2002, 219–222.

FOLK ETYMOLOGY

Popular, unscientific derivation of a word.

Popular etymologies, based upon the observation of superficial resemblances between words, underlie or play a role in many myths and legends in ways that are not apparent when the narratives are translated or retold in another language.

Thus a chance similarity between the Greek noun *aphros* ("foam") and the first part of the divine name Aphroditê, which has no obvious meaning in Greek, can suggest that the goddess's name may signify "Foam + (something)," an etymology that contributed to the strange myth according to which Aphroditê was born from foam. In the same way, a superficial resemblance between the Greek noun *myrmekes* ("ants") and the ethnic substantive *Myrmidones* (Myrmidons, a term for inhabitants of Phthia) underlies the story according to which Zeus transformed certain ants into humans, the first Myrmidons.

When the sense of divine epithets became obscure over time, their original import having been forgotten, Greeks often reinterpreted them on the basis of their resemblance to familiar words. Hermes's epithet Argeiphontes was taken to mean "Slayer of Argos" and connected with a myth in which Hermes slew a many-eyed monster named Argos, whom he had lulled to sleep. Athena's obscure epithet Tritogeneia was understood variously, such as "Born by [the River] Triton."

The attention of folk etymologists was not restricted to proper nouns. When the lonely survivors of the Great Deluge, Deukalion and Pyrrha, were instructed to cast stones behind them, those thrown by him became men and those thrown by her turned into women, wherefore (the narrative claims) humans are termed *laos* ("folk"), having originated from *laas* ("stones"). That is, humans are called "people" because they came from "pebbles."

Suggested reading:

William Hansen. "Foam-Born Aphrodite and the Mythology of Transformation." *American Journal of Philology* 121 (2000): 1–19.

Martin L. West, ed. and comm. *Hesiod: Works and Days.* Oxford: Clarendon Press, 1978, 366–375.

GENEALOGY

Grouping of beings into descent groups based upon mating and offspring.

Mythological genealogies differ from ordinary genealogies in that they may include both humans and divine beings. Among the latter are purely anthropomorphic deities such as Zeus, elements of the physical cosmos such as Gaia (Earth), and personified abstractions such as Phobos (Fear), all three classes being treated as living creatures capable of mating.

In practice, like tends to mate with like: mortals mate mostly with mortals and immortals with immortals, and among the latter, cosmic parts are inclined to mate with other cosmic parts (thus Gaia "Earth" mates with Ouranos "Sky"), and purely anthropomorphic beings with other such beings (Zeus mates with Demeter). When a mortal mates with an immortal, the latter is regularly a purely anthropomorphic deity, as in the affair of the human woman Semelê and the god Zeus. Many matches are found between human males and nymphs and between male gods and nymphs, the nymphs holding a place in the cosmic hierarchy between immortal gods and ordinary mortals. Although monstrous beings sometimes aspire to mate with Olympian goddesses, they do not succeed. So the huge serpentine monster Typhon once had designs upon Hera that were not realized, and the prodigiously huge mortals Otos and Ephialtes, known as the Aloads, wooed Hera and Artemis without success.

As in real life, mythological parents tend to produce offspring like themselves, anthropomorphic deities producing anthropomorphic deities, humans producing humans, Cyclopes producing Cyclopes, and so on, in self-reproducing communities. But many exceptions are found. Some groups such as satyrs are made up entirely of males, whereas others such as nymphs are all females, so that it is not possible to have a self-reproducing community of satyrs or nymphs. The fathers of different nymphs range from the anthropomorphic god Zeus to a particular river-deity to the sun-god Helios, and their mothers similarly vary. Since unique and limited-edition creatures cannot by definition be members of self-reproducing communities, they are worked into genealogical relationships as fittingly as possible so that they will not be entirely anomalous with respect to the species of their parents and siblings. Some of these genealogies are more convincing than others. Gaia (Earth) and Ouranos (Sky) produced three sets of dissimilar siblings, the Titans, the Cyclopes, and the Hundred-

Handers, who have little in common with their parents beyond divinity and great size. The monstrous Minotaur, morphologically part-android and part-bull, was appropriately the offspring of a human woman and a bull, but the god Pan, a similarly composite being who is part-android and part-goat, is the son of the rustic god Hermes and a nymph, so that the Minotaur's bestial component is more clearly accounted for than Pan's.

The primary function of mythological genealogies is to suggest relationships between the constituents of the universe, organizing real and imagined things into kinship relationships on the model of human families. People or things that are perceived to be similar in nature are usually grouped together, and conversely dissimilar peoples and things are separated. This is the basic principle of mythological genealogies. Similarity can be expressed linearly by descent or laterally in segmented genealogies or both, as in the pedigree reported by Hesiod (*Theogony* 295–325).

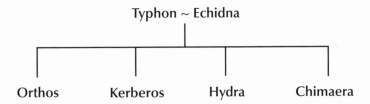

The parents are monsters, and they bear monstrous children. Typhon and Echidna are morphologically similar in being partly serpentine and partly humanoid, and their four offspring share the peculiarity of being, like their father, multiheaded: Orthos is a two-headed dog, Kerberos is a fifty-headed dog, Hydra is a multiheaded water snake, and the Chimaera is a tricephalic creature having the heads of a lion, goat, and snake. Here different relationships of similarity are expressed both linearly and laterally.

Genealogies can also express quality, status, and privilege, or relationships of high and low. For example, descent from a deity is more estimable than descent from a human, descent from royalty is more desirable than descent from commoners, and descent from free parents is better than descent from slaves.

Since the god Zeus mated with the nymph or maiden Kallisto, who bore a son Arkas, eponymous ancestor of the Arcadians, the inhabitants of Arcadia can boast descent from an Olympian deity.

Eponymy is a common device in traditional genealogies. A nation or tribe is often traced to an ancestor of like name. Thus Hellenes, or Greeks, descend from an ancestor named Hellen, just as subdivisions and neighbors of the Hellenes have their own eponymous founders: Aeolians come from Aiolos (Latinized form = Aeolus), Dorians from Doros, Ionians from Ion, Macedonians from Makedon, and so on.

A different kind of claim appeals to autochthony.

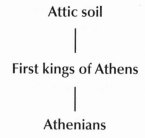

Attic soil

First kings of Athens

Athenians

According to Athenian tradition, the earliest kings of Athens are autochthonous, sprung from the very soil of Attica like plants; accordingly, their descendants the Athenians are natives, indigenous in the most literal sense, and not immigrants, and their relationship to the land is that of offspring to mother. As a homeland, then, Attica is inalienable from Athenians. Although other persons may occupy it, it can never really be theirs.

Filiation, especially in conceptual genealogies, can express a variety of logical relationships.

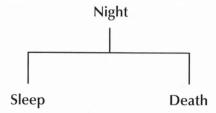

Night

Sleep   **Death**

In the traditional Greek genealogem, Nyx (Night) begets two sons: Hypnos (Sleep) and Thanatos (Death). The similarity of sleep and death is expressed by their representation as siblings: sleep is a weak form of death, just as death a strong form of sleep. Since night is ordinarily a precondition of sleep, Night is represented genealogically as preceding and begetting Sleep.

Fashioners of mythological genealogies assume that everything should and can make sense genealogically. The genealogist reasons matters out and organizes beings into families the way they should be in order appropriately to reflect the present, as he or she perceives, imagines, or desires it to be.

See also Eponymy

Suggested reading:

Jaakko Aronen. "Genealogy as a Form of Mythic Discourse: The Case of the Phaeacians," in *Myth and Symbol I: Symbolic Phenomena in Ancient Greek Culture,* edited by Synnøve des Bouvrie. Bergen: Norwegian Institute at Athens, 2002, 89–111.

Claude Calame. "Spartan Genealogies: The Mythological Representation of a Spatial Organisation," trans. by A. Habib, in *Interpretations of Greek Mythology,* edited by Jan Bremmer. London: Routledge, 1988, 153–186.

Robert Fowler. "Genealogical Thinking, Hesiod's *Catalogue,* and the Creation of the Hellenes." *Proceedings of the Cambridge Philological Society* 44 (1998): 1–19.

Paula Philippson. *Genealogie als mythische Form: Studien zur Theogonie des Hesiod.* Oslo: Brøgger, 1936.

Martin L. West, ed. and comm. *Hesiod: Theogony.* Oxford: Clarendon Press, 1966, 31–39.

———. *The Hesiodic Catalogue of Women: Its Nature, Structure, and Origins.* Oxford: Clarendon Press, 1985.

GIANTS (GREEK GIGANTES)

Hubristic warriors born of Gaia (Earth).

According to Hesiod, when the Titan Kronos cut off the genitals of his father, Ouranos (Sky), with a sickle and threw them behind him, drops of blood landed upon Gaia (Earth), who in time gave birth to the Erinyes (Furies), the "great Giants, shining in their armor and holding long spears in their hands," and the Meliai (*Theogony* 176–187), or nymphs of ash trees, a way of saying that ash trees came into being, since the nymphs and the trees are one. The three sets of siblings share a connection with blood and violence. The Erinyes specialize in persecuting mortals who have spilled the blood of their own kin, the Giants are warriors, and ash trees furnished the wood from which spears were made. Just as the warrior goddess Athena was born fully grown and armed from the head of Zeus, and just as a crop of armed warriors called Spartoi (Sown Men) emerged fully grown from the earth after it was sown with dragon's teeth (Apollodoros *Library* 1.3.6, 3.4.1), so here the Giants are born fully grown and ready for battle. Hesiod describes them as "great," referring perhaps to their stature, but the Giants are not always represented as being huge. Although our word *giants* derives ultimately from the Greek *Gigantes,* the most persistent traits of the Gigantes are strength and hubristic aggression.

The Giants' principal myth is that of the Gigantomachy (Greek *Gigantomachia*), or battle of the Giants against the Olympian gods and their allies. The mythographer Apollodoros recounts that Gaia (Earth), upset at the Olympians' conquest of the Titans, gave birth to the Giants, who were fathered by Ouranos, in Phlegrai or Pallenê. They had bodies of great bulk and strength and were frightening to look upon, with long hair hanging down from their heads and with the scaly feet of dragons. The Giants cast boulders and burning trees at the sky. One of them, Alkyoneus, was immortal so long as he did battle in the land in which he was born. The Olympians knew from an oracle that the Giants could not be killed by the gods alone but only with the help of a mortal. Gaia, knowing this as well, began searching for a drug by means of which her sons might be protected also from a mortal, but Zeus outwitted her by forbidding Eos (Dawn), Selenê (Moon), and Helios (Sun) to shine, allowing him to harvest the plant himself in the dark before she might do so; then he summoned Herakles to help the gods. The hero shot Alkyoneus with an arrow, but when he fell upon the earth, he revived a bit, so that, upon the advice of Athena, Herakles dragged him outside of the land of his birth, where he expired. The Giant Porphyrion tore Hera's clothing, intending to rape her, but Zeus struck him with a thunderbolt and Herakles finished him off with an arrow. Other gods overcame other Giants, often with a characteristic weapon or tool, in a series of individual combats. Thus Apollon and Herakles killed Ephialtes with arrows, Dionysos slew Eurytos with his thyrsus (a kind of wand), Hekatê killed Klytios by means of torches, and so on. With the help of Herakles, all the Giants were finally killed (*Library* 1.6.1–2).

According to Apollodoros, the Gigantomachy took place after the Titanomachy and before the combat of Zeus and Typhon. Therefore it was one in a series of violent challenges that the Olympians had to face before they could establish their sovereignty in the cosmos.

Being similar to one another, the Titanomachy and the Gigantomachy were not always clearly distinguished. Another mythic assault on the gods, that made by the huge brothers Otos and Ephialtes, or Aloads, added to the confusion. Ovid seems to mix the Giants with the Aloads (*Metamorphoses* 1.151–162).

Homer makes several obscure references to the Giants. A certain Eurymedon, king of the arrogant Giants, led his people and himself to destruction. Poseidon mated with Eurymedon's daughter Periboia, begetting Nausithoos, king of the Phaiakians (*Odyssey* 7.58–60). Alkinoos, son of Nausithoos, remarks that the gods come to them, not concealed, but openly, for the Phaiakians are close to the gods, "just as are the Kyklopes [Latinized form = Cyclopes] and the wild tribes of Giants" (*Odyssey* 7.201–206). On the one hand the Giants are arrogant and wild, and on the other hand they are among the ancestors of the very civilized Phaiakians and enjoy the favor of the gods. Homer relates elsewhere that Odysseus and his companions, having arrived at the land of the Laistrygonians, entered the palace of the chief and found his wife to be as big as a mountain. Presently they were surrounded by hostile, boulder-hurling Laistrygonians, who are described as being more like Giants than men (*Odyssey* 10.105–120).

> **See also** Aloads; Titans
>
> **Suggested reading:**
>
> Claude Calame. "Le figures grecques du gigantesque," *Communications* 42 (1985): 147–172.
>
> Timothy Gantz. *Early Greek Myth: A Guide to Literary and Artistic Sources.* Baltimore: The Johns Hopkins University Press, 1993, 445–454.
>
> Francis Vian. "Gigantes," in *LIMC* 4:191–270.
>
> ———. *La Guerre des Géants: Le mythe avant l'époque Hellénistique.* Paris: Librairie C. Klincksieck, 1952.

Hades with cornucopia.

HADES (ALSO AIDONEUS)
(ROMAN DIS AND ORCUS)

God of the death realm.

Hades, along with his wife, Persephonê, is the ruler of the dead. The couple have no offspring. Hades was one of six children of the Titans Kronos and Rhea. He and his siblings were swallowed alive by their father as they were born, except for Zeus, who was smuggled away and raised secretly in a cave on Crete. A year after Zeus's birth, Kronos was induced to take an emetic, causing him to spew up the children he had swallowed. A great battle, the Titanomachy, between the older gods and the younger gods followed in which the younger gods, led by Zeus, emerged as victors.

According to one tradition, the three brothers Hades, Zeus, and Poseidon drew lots for the sovereignty of different parts of the world. Since Hades drew the lot for Erebos, he became lord of the death realm (Homer *Iliad* 15.187–193). But according to a different tradition, Zeus allotted honors, or offices, to the individual deities after he became king of the gods (Hesiod *Theogony* 881–885).

Hades's kingdom is Erebos or the House of Hades, one term referring to the gloomy land of the dead and the other to the death lord's residence, although in practice the names are used interchangeably. The House of Hades is imagined as a house, or group of houses, with a yard and gate. In the yard is found Hades's multiheaded hound, Cerberus (Greek Kerberos), a kind of reverse watchdog, for he attacks persons who attempt to leave rather than those who wish to enter. Early authors occasionally transfer the name Hades from the ruler to his domain, a usage that becomes more common in later authors.

Apart from the myth of how Hades acquired his particular honor in the cosmic organization, the major myth in which he plays a role is that in which he acquires his spouse, Persephonê (Latinized form = Proserpina). In the mythological past Zeus acquired a mate, Hera, and Poseidon got a wife, Amphitritê, so that of the three brothers only Hades lacked a spouse. At this juncture, according to the *Homeric Hymn to Demeter*, Zeus secretly consented to give the maiden Persephonê to Hades as his bride. She was the daughter of Zeus and Demeter, and Zeus as the girl's father had the right to determine her mate, but he said nothing to his daughter herself or to her mother, doubtless because he knew neither would welcome the match. One day as Persephonê frolicked in a meadow with her companions, Hades suddenly burst out of the earth upon his chariot, seized her, and took her down to his dark kingdom to be his bride. In distress, Demeter searched for her daughter, becoming furious when she learned that Hades had abducted her with the connivance of her own father. Zeus had Hermes conduct Persephonê out of Erebos to see her mother again, but because Hades had induced her to eat a pomegranate seed before she departed, she had to return eventually to Erebos. In the end Zeus arranged a compromise between the realms of life and death such that Persephonê would spend part of the year with her mother and part with her husband.

Hades otherwise plays secondary roles in mythology, acting mostly as the possessor of quest-objects that one or another living mortal wishes to carry away. In one legend, the adventurous heroes Theseus and Peirithoos decided to marry only daughters of Zeus. First Peirithoos helped Theseus abduct the young maiden Helen from Sparta. Then Theseus accompanied his companion to Erebos in order to woo Persephonê for him. Their caper came to an end when the crafty Hades, as though offering them hospitality, invited the pair to sit down on a particular chair, the Chair of Forgetfulness, and when they did so, they became bound to it by coils of snakes. And there they remained until the day that

Persephonê and Hades, with cock and sheaf of wheat.

Herakles showed up, released Theseus, and brought him back up with him; Herakles was forbidden to liberate Peirithoos (Apollodoros *Epitome* 1.23).

Herakles had business of his own in Plouton's realm, for he went there in order to accomplish one of the labors assigned to him by Eurystheus, to bring back Hades's dog Cerberus. After releasing Theseus, Herakles asked Hades for Cerberus, and the god agreed that he might take the dog if he could overpower it without any weapons. Protected by his lion's skin, which was invulnerable, the powerful Herakles crushed Cerberus in his arms until the dog yielded. He carried the beast up, showed it to Eurystheus, and then returned it to its owner (Apollodoros *Library* 2.5.12).

Similarly, when Orpheus descended to the realm of the dead in the hope of carrying back his recently deceased wife Eurydikê (Latinized form = Eurydicê), the god promised that she might return, provided that during his own return home Orpheus not look behind him. Orpheus failed to keep Hades's condition, so that Eurydikê remained in Erebos (Apollodoros *Library* 1.3.2).

Hades's role in myth and legend would be greater if he were the sole divinity representing the interests of the death realm, but although he alone is the ruler of the dead, the role of the death spirit is distributed among several characters, including Ker and Thanatos. Ker appears in Homer's *Iliad* as eagerly carting off warriors alive or dead. In the legend of the wily Sisyphos and in the legend of the kindly Alkestis, the spirit of death who shows up when it is time for a particular mortal to die, eager to carry him or her away to the world of the dead, is Thanatos (Death). Homer also alludes to a story in which the hero Herakles shot Hades among the dead at Pylos, forcing the god to go to Olympos to seek treatment for his painful wound (Homer *Iliad* 5.395–404). Perhaps Hades was busy collecting the souls of the dead for his kingdom. Regardless of their name, representatives of the death realm are regularly represented as being eager to add to the inhabitants of Erebos and as being disinclined to release any who are there.

The Cap of Invisibility is not properly a tool of this god, although folk etymology reinterpreted its Greek name (*aidos kyneê*) as Cap of Hades, and one mythographer attributes the helmet to him, saying that the Cyclopes forged it for him when they made the thunderbolt for Zeus and the trident for Poseidon, in order that they might overcome the Titans (Apollodoros *Library* 1.2.1). Apart from this passage, Hades is never said to possess or use it, nor are the gods and heroes who do use it said to have borrowed it from him.

As the implacable and unconquerable lord of death, Hades is the god most hateful to mortals (Homer *Iliad* 9.158–159). Since his very name is ill-omened, euphemisms were in common use. "Most persons, since they fear his [Hades's] name, call him Plouton," writes Plato (*Cratylus* 403a). The euphemism Plouton (Latinized form = Pluto), that is, Wealthy One, refers to the agricultural and mineral wealth of the earth, which is located beneath the surface or issues from below, and so belongs to the god within the earth.

The Romans had several names for the death lord. One was Pluto, simply the Roman adaptation of the Greek euphemism Plouton, and another was Dis, or Wealthy One, presumably a translation of Greek Plouton. A third name was

Orcus (from which via French we perhaps get our word *ogre*), which like the Greek Hades could be employed also to refer to the death realm.

Among Hades's attributes in art are a scepter, cornucopia, and rooster.

See also Personified Abstractions

Suggested reading:

Timothy Gantz. *Early Greek Myth: A Guide to Literary and Artistic Sources.* Baltimore: The Johns Hopkins University Press, 1993, 70–73.

Ruth Lindner. "Hades," in *LIMC* 4:367–394.

———. "Pluto," in *LIMC* 4:399–406.

HEPHAISTOS (ROMAN VULCAN)

Divine smith and craftsman.

In the Homeric poems, Hephaistos is a son of Zeus and Hera (*Iliad* 1.577–578, 14.338–339, *Odyssey* 8.312). According to a different tradition, however, Zeus first married Metis, but when she was about to give birth to their daughter Athena, he swallowed her and kept her in his belly in order that he might retain his position as king of the gods, for he had learned that Metis was fated to give birth to a daughter who would be Zeus's equal in strength and counsel, and after that to an arrogant son who would be king of gods and men. After successive marriages to Themis, Eurynomê, Demeter, Mnemosynê, and Leto, Zeus wed his seventh and present spouse, Hera, who bore him three children. But Zeus himself bore from his head Athena, after which, without sexual intercourse, Hera in anger bore Hephaistos (Hesiod *Theogony* 886–929). Since Zeus swallowed his pregnant wife and gave birth to Athena, he played both the male role (insemination) and the female roles (gestation and parturition) in the production of Athena, and Hera regarded him as sole parent, for her own jealous response to Athena's birth was to produce a son entirely by herself, countering Zeus's parthenogenesis with her own. Athena and Hephaistos are similar in their interest in craftsmanship, being the ultimate sources of human knowledge about the making of beautiful or intricate objects (Homer *Odyssey* 6.232–234; *Homeric Hymn to Hephaistos*).

After Zeus and Hera bore Athena and Hephaistos respectively, Athena stood out among the gods, whereas Hephaistos proved to be a weakling with withered legs, so that Hera picked him up and threw him into the sea. To her disappointment, Thetis and other Nereids took him in and looked after him. Hera contrived to produce another son without sexual intercourse, one she hoped would be superior to Zeus, giving birth to Typhon, a creature unlike either gods or mortals, whom she entrusted to a female dragon to rear (*Homeric Hymn to Apollon* 305–355). Homer agrees that Hera cast her son out of Olympos because she wanted to conceal him on account of his lameness and that he fell into the sea. There the Nereid Thetis and the Oceanid Eurynomê took care of him. The poet adds that for nine years Hephaistos remained with them hidden in a cave beside the River Ocean fashioning all manner of intricate objects—pins, clasps, cups, and necklaces—and no god or mortal knew where he was, except for his two rescuers (Homer *Iliad* 18.394–405).

Among the marvelous objects that Hephaistos fashioned was a chair with invisible bonds, which he sent as a present to his mother. Delighted with the gift, she sat down but became stuck, and no one was able to release her. The gods began to talk about bringing Hephaistos back up to Olympos, inasmuch as he alone could set her free. When they were at a loss what to do, Ares promised to bring him back but returned in disgrace after Hephaistos frightened him away with torches. Since Hera was in distress, Dionysos now went equipped with wine, got Hephaistos drunk, and brought him back in that state, and Hephaistos freed his mother. This act won Dionysos the goodwill of Hera, who dropped her hostile attitude toward him and persuaded the other celestial deities that Dionysos was one of them (Alcaeus frag. 349c MW; Pausanias 1.20.3).

Surprisingly, Hephaistos was cast out of Olympos a second time. Hera once sent a powerful storm after the hero Herakles as he was sailing away from Troy, and in his anger Zeus hung Hera by her wrists from the edge of Olympos, her hands tied with a golden chain and an anvil dangling from each foot, and Zeus threw from Olympos to earth any god who tried to come to her aid. Thus when Hephaistos wished to help her, Zeus took him by the foot and threw him out of the sky, and he fell all day, landing on the island of Lemnos (Homer *Iliad* 1.584–594, 15:18–33; Apollodoros *Library* 1.3.5, 2.7.1). Hephaistos (says Homer) had little life left in him after his fall, and the islanders took care of him. More drastically (according to Apollodoros), the fall caused him to be lame in the legs, and Thetis rescued him. The two occasions of Hephaistos's being cast out of Olympos and Hera's being bound are presumably doublets, that is, different developments of the same narrative ideas, which were worked into the mythology as successive incidents.

Hephaistos is lame, either congenitally or as a result of his day-long fall to earth, but his physical defect is balanced by his cleverness in general and by his wondrous skill in the fashioning of intricate objects in particular. All these traits play a role in the mythic novella of the love affair of Ares and Aphroditê, in which Hephaistos and Aphroditê are represented as being husband and wife, a dissonant coupling that all but guarantees instability. And indeed Ares carried on a secret affair with Aphroditê in Hephaistos's own house. After all-seeing Helios advised Hephaistos of the affair, the god went to his smithy and angrily forged invisible, unbreakable chains, which he draped over his bed. Having laid this trap, he pretended to make an excursion to Lemnos, and Ares immediately went to Hephaistos's house, Ares and Aphroditê went to bed, and the invisible net fell upon them so that they could not move. Then the lame god returned and invited all the gods to view the adultery of his wife, saying that she has always despised him for being lame and loved Ares for being handsome and sound of limb. Although the goddesses modestly stayed away, the male gods viewed and commented upon the spectacle, and eventually Hephaistos released the lovers, whereupon Ares dashed up to Thrace and Aphroditê went to Cyprus (Homer *Odyssey* 8.266–366). Just as Hephaistos fashioned a chair with invisible chains for his mother so that she could not rise until he released her, so also he surrounded his bed with invisible chains that kept his adulterous wife and her lover immobile until he chose to free them. Actually, the mythical tradition disagrees about the identity of Hephaistos's spouse. She is Aphroditê in the *Odyssey*, Charis in the *Iliad* (18.382), and Aglaia, one of the Charites (Graces), in Hesiod's *Theogony* (945–946).

Hephaistos too can be lustful. When Athena once came to him to have some weapons made, Hephaistos was erotically attracted to her and pursued her, lame though he was. She fled, and although the god managed to catch up with her, she effectively fought him off, with the result that he ejaculated on her leg. She wiped the semen off and threw it on the earth, but from the seed there grew a child, Erichthonios, whom Athena reared. He became a king of Athens (Apollodoros *Library* 3.14.6). Overall, Hephaistos is unfortunate with the women in his life.

Apart from his dealings with women, Hephaistos's principal role in mythology is to play the master craftsman, fashioning marvelous objects, especially from metal. For his own house he manufactured different kinds of automatons, including servants in the form of golden female manikins that possess intelligence as well as the power of speech (Homer *Iliad* 18.372–77, 417–21). For his fellow celestial gods he built individual palaces on Olympos (*Iliad* 1.605–608); helped to deliver Athena by splitting open Zeus's head with an axe (Apollodoros *Library* 1.3.6), though not of course in the version of the myth in which he himself was born after Athena; nailed Prometheus to Mount Caucasus (*Library* 1.7.1); and fashioned the first human female out of earth and water, working closely with Athena (Hesiod *Theogony* 570–612, *Works and Days* 53–105). Furthermore, he made fire-breathing bulls with brazen feet for King Aietes (Apollodoros *Library* 1.9.23); the bronze man Talos for King Minos (*Library* 1.9.26); a golden breastplate for the young hero Herakles (*Library* 2.4.11); bronze castanets for Athena, who gave them to Herakles for one of his labors (*Library* 2.5.6); a necklace for Kadmos, who gave it to Harmonia (*Library* 3.4.2); and an underground house for Poseidon for the use of the mortal Oinopion (*Library*

1.4.4). Any wondrous artifact is likely to be attributed to him, including living or quasi-living creations such as the female manikins employed in his own house, the partly metallic bulls for King Aietes, and the bronze man for King Minos.

The Romans called the god Vulcan (Latin *Vulcanus* or *Volcanus*), one of whose epithets was Mulciber.

In art Hephaistos can be portrayed as a deformed smith in his smithy. An axe, mule, and *pilos*, or workman's cap, are among his attributes.

> *See also* Athena
> ***Suggested reading:***
> Timothy Gantz. *Early Greek Myth: A Guide to Literary and Artistic Sources.* Baltimore: The Johns Hopkins University Press, 1993, 74–78.
> Antoine Hermary and Anne Jacquemin. "Hephaistos," in *LIMC* 4:627–654.
> Erika Simon and Gerhard Bauchhenss. "Vulcanus," in *LIMC* 8:283–298.

HERA (ROMAN JUNO)

Queen of the gods.

Hera's parents are the Titans Kronos and Rhea. Having learned from Gaia and Ouranos that he would be overthrown by a son, Kronos swallowed his children, including Hera, as they were born. When the grieving mother was about to bear Zeus, she hid her newborn son in a cave on Crete, giving her husband instead a stone wrapped in swaddling clothes, which he swallowed. A year later when Zeus was fully grown, Kronos was tricked into vomiting up the stone and his children, including Hera, and presently Zeus led a war in which the younger gods overcame the older gods. After Zeus vanquished the monster Typhon in a cosmic battle, the other Olympians invited Zeus to be king of the gods (Hesiod *Theogony*).

One of the elder Olympians, Hera is the wife of Zeus in the mythological present. According to Hesiod, she is his seventh wife, for Zeus swallowed his first wife, Metis, when she was about to give birth to a daughter, Athena, after which he mated in turn with Themis, Eurynomê, Demeter, Mnemosynê, Leto, and finally his sister Hera. She bore him three children: Hebê (Youth), Ares, and Eileithyia. But Zeus himself bore Athena from his head, after which Hera in anger and without sexual intercourse bore Hephaistos (*Theogony* 886–929).

According to a different text, Zeus gave birth to Athena from his head, after which Hera produced Hephaistos on her own, but since Athena was distinguished among the gods, whereas Hephaistos was crippled and weak, Hera cast him out of Olympos, and he fell into the sea, where Thetis and other Nereids took care of him. Hera next uttered a prayer that she also produce a child who would be distinguished among the gods, a child neither by Zeus nor by another but entirely of her own, a child who would be stronger than Zeus. She abstained from Zeus's bed, and a year later she bore the monster Typhon (*Homeric Hymn to Apollon* 305–354; cf. Homer *Iliad* 18.394–405). In this version Hera produced two children parthenogenically, first Hephaistos, who proved to be defective, and then the monstrous Typhon. She seemed to wish not only to match Zeus's accomplishment but also to produce a child who would be stronger than Zeus and overthrow him, as Zeus had overthrown his father, Kronos, and Kronos his father, Ouranos.

Hera and Zeus compete again in another unusual myth, although they vie in losing, as it were. For they once argued with each other whether males or females derived the greater pleasure from sexual intercourse, Zeus declaring that females did, and Hera saying that males did. Finally they asked Teiresias to judge the dispute, since he had lived for some years as a woman and so had had personal experience both as male and as female. Teiresias declared that if the pleasure of lovemaking should be divided into ten parts, men enjoyed one tenth and women enjoyed nine. In her anger Hera blinded him, but Zeus in compensation gave him second sight, making him a soothsayer (Hesiod frag. 275 MW).

Hera.

For the most part Hera plays an unattractively reactive role in mythological narrative, the unaccepting wife of a philandering husband who jealously persecutes her husband's amours and their offspring. When, for example, Zeus was having an affair with the mortal woman Semelê, Hera deceptively persuaded Semelê to ask Zeus to come to her in the form in which he had wooed Hera. Zeus reluctantly agreed to do so, and Semelê perished, overwhelmed by the power of his epiphany (Apollodoros *Library* 3.4.3). The love child of this affair was Dionysos, whose acceptance among the Olympians was for a long time obstructed by Hera. Another lover of Zeus, but an unwitting one, was Alkmenê. Zeus once came to her bed in the likeness of her husband, Amphitryon, and she bore Herakles. When the child was eight months old, Hera tried to kill him by sending two huge snakes to his bed, but he strangled them. After he grew up, Hera made life difficult for him in different ways throughout his life, driving him temporarily mad, inspiring false rumors against him, sending a violent storm against his ship, and so on (Apollodoros *Library* 2.4.8–2.7.7). Hera's sending a storm against Herakles so exasperated Zeus that he suspended Hera from the edge of Olympos, tying an anvil to each foot and a golden cord around her hands. She hung there in the air among the clouds, and Zeus cast down from Olympos any god who tried to set her free (Homer *Iliad* 15.18–30; Apollodoros *Library* 1.3.5, 2.7.1).

Still, as king and queen of heaven, Zeus and Hera are the type of the beatific couple. Hera bathes annually in a particular spring called Kanathos, which restores her virginity (Pausanias 2.38.2), so that she is at once matron and maiden. The human couple Keyx and Alkyonê expressed their own marital happiness by likening themselves to the Olympian couple, Keux calling his wife Hera and Alkyonê calling her husband Zeus. But because of their hubris in comparing themselves to gods, Zeus changed them into birds (Apollodoros *Library* 1.7.4).

Nonetheless, as queen of the gods or at least as spouse of the king of the gods, Hera is the supreme imaginable mate for a cosmically ambitious male or the supremely unattainable female for a lustful male. Thus the monster Typhon once stole Zeus's thunderbolts, and since the ruler of the universe was now unarmed and helpless, Typhon planned to journey to Olympos, replace him as sovereign, and make Hera his own bed partner. To his assistant he offered a choice of Athena, Leto, Charis, Aphroditê, Artemis, or Hebê as reward (Nonnos *Dionysiaka* 1.145–480). The huge brothers Otos and Ephialtes decided to do battle with the gods, and piling several mountains on top of one another they threatened to ascend to the sky. Naturally they wished also to obtain goddesses as wives, so that Ephialtes wooed Hera and Otos wooed Artemis (Apollodoros *Library* 1.7.4). In the battle of the gods and the Giants, Hera was lustfully attacked by Porphyrion, who tore her clothes in his desire to rape her (Apollodoros *Library* 1.6.2). The mortal Ixion also attempted to assault Hera sexually, and when she reported the matter to Zeus, he made an image of his wife out of cloud and lay it down beside Ixion. After having sexual intercourse with it, Ixion boasted he had slept with Hera (Apollodoros *Epitome* 1.20). The aspirants to Hera's bed, all of them unsuccessful, are monsters or mortals.

Hera does play a positive role in some narratives. For example, there was a time when the gods competed to be patrons of the different cities on earth, for if a god possessed a particular city, he or she would be honored there with a special cult. So it was that Athena and Poseidon competed for the city that subsequently would be called Athens, and she was awarded it (Apollodoros *Library* 3.14.1). A less well-known myth recounts how Hera and Poseidon competed for the possession of Argos, and the Rivers Inachos, Kephisos, and Asterion, serving as judges, declared that the land belonged to Hera. Poseidon angrily dried up the waters in the region so that these rivers now flow only after a rain (*Library* 2.1.4; Pausanias 2.15.5). Hera also helped Jason and the Argonauts in their difficult quest for the Golden Fleece, somewhat as Athena championed the interests of Odysseus.

Hera plays a role in the Judgment of Paris. After Eris (Strife) cast an apple of beauty among the goddesses Athena, Hera, and Aphroditê, Zeus instructed Hermes to conduct the goddesses to the Trojan youth Alexander, or Paris, on Mount Ida in order that he might judge them. The goddesses each offered him a bribe, Hera promising him kingship, Athena offering victory in war, and Aphroditê holding out marriage with Helen. Paris chose Aphroditê (Apollodoros *Epitome* 3.2). Aphroditê's reward led to the seduction of Helen and thus to the massive military campaign against Troy to retrieve her. Paris's choice endeared him to Aphroditê, who thereafter favored the Trojans, but it earned him the hostility of Athena and Hera, who accordingly supported the Achaeans, or Greeks.

Hera's epithets include "white-armed" and "ox-eyed," the latter corresponding perhaps to Athena's epithet *glaukopis,* which is rendered variously as "owl-eyed" and "gray-eyed." She is also called "Argive Hera" because of her important cult at Argos.

Among Hera's attributes are symbols of sovereignty such as a scepter and crown. Her chariot is drawn by peacocks, her special bird (Ovid *Metamorphoses* 1.722–723, 2.531–533), and in later art a peacock often serves to identify her.

See also Hephaistos; Zeus

Suggested reading:

Timothy Gantz. *Early Greek Myth: A Guide to Literary and Artistic Sources.* Baltimore: The Johns Hopkins University Press, 1993, 61–62.

Anneliese Kossatz-Diessmann. "Hera," in *LIMC* 4:659–719.

Eugenio La Rocca. "Iuno," in *LIMC* 5:814–856.

HERAKLES (LATINIZED FORM HERCULES)

Hero of great strength and endurance.

According to the mythographer Apollodoros, Amphityron wooed Alkmenê (Latinized form = Alcmena), who agreed to marry him after he had avenged the death of her brother. He did so, but before he returned to Alkmenê in Thebes,

Infant Herakles strangling the snakes.

Zeus assumed Amphitryon's likeness and lay with Alkmenê, lengthening the night threefold. After the god departed, the real Amphitryon reached home and found he was not received as warmly as he had expected. Subsequently, he learned from the seer Teiresias of Zeus's imposture. Alkmenê bore a son Herakles by Zeus and, a day later, a son Iphikles by Amphitryon. When the babes were eight months old, Hera sent two immense serpents to their bed, wishing to destroy Zeus's son. But Herakles, holding one serpent in each hand, strangled them.

Young Herakles had many tutors. His father taught him to drive a chariot, Autolykos to wrestle, Eurytos to shoot with the bow, Kastor to wield sword and javelin, and Linos, a brother of Orpheus, to play the lyre. When Linos once struck him, Herakles hit him back with the lyre, killing him, whereupon Amphitryon, fearing that he might do the same again, sent him out to tend the cattle. Herakles presently exceeded all others in size and strength, and it became obvious that he was a son of Zeus. His body was huge, his eyes flashed fire, and he never missed with either the bow or the javelin.

When he was eighteen years old, the Cithaeronian Lion, a lion using Mount Kithairon (Latinized form = Cithaeron) as its base, was killing cattle belonging to Amphitryon and Thespios, a nearby ruler. Wishing to catch the lion, Herakles went to Thespios, in whose house he stayed for fifty days while hunting the creature. Thespios had fifty daughters, and each night he bedded one of his daughters with Herakles, wishing them all to have children by him. Herakles, thinking he was with the same girl each night, lay with them all. Eventually he overcame the lion and dressed himself in its skin, using its gaping scalp as a helmet.

After Herakles distinguished himself in a conflict between Thebans and Minyans, King Kreon (Latinized form = Creon) of Thebes gave him his daughter Megara in marriage. Hermes moreover gave him a sword, Apollon a bow and arrows, Hephaistos a breastplate of gold, and Athena a peplos, or robe. He equipped himself with a club, which he had cut at Nemea. But Hera in her jealousy drove Herakles mad, and in this state he killed his own children as well as those of his brother Iphikles by flinging them into the fire. Condemning himself to exile, he went to Thespios, who purified him of the killings. Then he went to Delphi to ask the god where he should live. The Pythia, or priestess, instructed him to dwell in Tiryns, where he should serve Eurystheus for twelve years, performing ten tasks that Eurystheus would assign him, and when the tasks were completed, he would become immortal. She also addressed him for the first time as Herakles, for his given name was Alkides.

Herakles went to Eurystheus at Tiryns. His first task was to bring the skin of the Nemean Lion, which was invulnerable. Herakles caught up with the animal in Nemea, put his arm around its neck, choked it to death, and carried the beast back to his taskmaster. Astonished at Herakles's manliness, Eurystheus forbade him henceforth to enter the city, instructing him rather to display the results of his tasks before the city gates. Furthermore, Eurystheus concealed himself in a subterranean bronze jar and from then on conveyed his commands via a herald.

As his second task Herakles was commanded to kill the Lernaean Hydra, or water-serpent, which lived by a swamp at Lerna and used to sally out to kill cattle. It had an immense body and nine

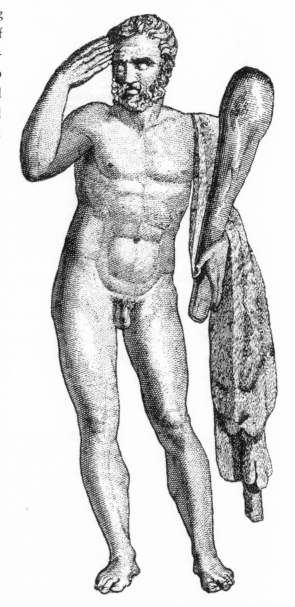

Herakles with club.

heads, one of which was immortal. Herakles grappled with the monster, smashing its heads with his club, but for every smashed head two new ones sprouted. So he told his companion Iolaos to cauterize each smashed head with fire in order to prevent new heads from growing, which he did. Then Herakles cut off the immortal head and buried it under a heavy rock. Before departing he dipped his arrows in the gall of the hydra's body. Eurystheus said, however, that this task should not count, since Herakles overcame the hydra with the aid of a helper.

His third labor was to capture the Cerynitian Hind and bring it back alive. The animal had golden horns and was sacred to Artemis. Not wishing to kill or wound it, Herakles chased it for a year, but finally he shot it with an arrow and captured it alive. As he was carrying it on his shoulders, he encountered Artemis, who rebuked him for trying to kill an animal that was sacred to her, but he soothed the goddess's anger by pointing out that Eurystheus was to blame. Then he carried the animal alive to Eurystheus.

Next he was ordered to fetch the Erymanthian Boar alive. Using Mount Erymanthos as its base, this beast caused much harm. On his way there Herakles was entertained by the centaur Pholos, whom he persuaded to open the jar of wine that belonged to the centaurs in common. Smelling the wine, the other centaurs presently arrived at Pholos's cave armed with rocks and sticks. Herakles repelled them, and when they retreated to Cheiron's cave at Malea, he shot an arrow at them that happened to strike Cheiron, who received thereby an incurable wound but, being immortal, could not die. Zeus transferred Cheiron's immortality to another, and Cheiron died. The other centaurs fled in all directions, but Pholos drew one of Herakles's arrows from the body of a slain centaur, wondering how so small a thing could kill such large beings, and the arrow slipped from his hand and landed on his foot, killing him also. After that Herakles resumed his hunt for the boar, exhausted it, trapped it, and conveyed it alive to Eurystheus.

His fifth task was to remove the cattle dung from the cattle yard of King Augeias of Elis in a single day. Herakles offered to clear out the dung in return for a tenth of the cattle, a proposal to which the incredulous king agreed. Herakles did not mention that he was obliged to clear away the dung anyway. Then he diverted the course of two rivers through the cattle yard, which got rid of the dung. But when Augeias learned that Herakles had acted at the command of Eurystheus, he refused payment, and when Eurystheus learned that Herakles had performed the task for hire, he did not accept it as one of the ten.

Herakles's sixth labor was to chase away the Stymphalian Birds from Lake Stymphalis, where they had taken refuge. When he was at a loss how to do so, Athena provided him with brazen castanets, which she had gotten from Hephaistos. Clashing these together, Herakles frightened the birds away.

Eurystheus then ordered him to bring the Cretan Bull. He captured it, showed it to Eurystheus, and set it free.

His eighth task was to bring the cannibalistic mares that belonged to Diomedes the Thracian, ruler of the fierce Bistones. Herakles overpowered the men in charge of the mares, drove them away, and turned them over to Eurystheus, who let them go.

Herakles's ninth labor was to fetch the Belt of Ares, which belonged to Hippolytê, queen of the warlike Amazons. Coming to the land of the Amazons,

Herakles was visited by Hippolytê, who learned of his quest and promised him the belt. In the meantime Hera, in the likeness of an Amazon, spread a false rumor among the Amazons that Herakles and his companions were carrying away their queen. When the Amazons attacked, Herakles believed that Hippolytê was acting treacherously, so that he killed her, took her belt, and sailed away. He went to Troy, where he found that Hesionê, daughter of King Laomedon, was being sacrificed to a sea-monster. Apollon and Poseidon had wished secretly to test Laomedon's hubris, so that disguised as humans they had hired themselves out to the king to fortify Pergamon, but when they had finished the job and the monarch refused to pay them their wages, Apollon sent a pestilence and Poseidon sent a monster from the sea. Oracles foretold that the people could escape these misfortunes if Laomedon should set out his daughter as food for the monster. Herakles now offered to rescue her in return for certain mares, and when Laomedon agreed to this condition, the hero killed the monster. But Laomedon once again reneged on his agreement, and as Herakles sailed away he said he would come back and make war on Troy. Returning to Eurystheus for the time being, he gave him the belt.

Next he was ordered to bring the Cattle of Geryon from Erythia, an island near the River Ocean. Geryon had the bodies of three men fused together. His cattle were herded by Eurytion, who was aided by his two-headed watchdog, Orthos. As Herakles was crossing from Europe to Libya (Africa), he set up two pillars as signs of his journey. When he was heated by Helios (Sun), he aimed his bow at the god, and Helios in admiration of his courage gave him a golden goblet, by means of which Herakles crossed the River Ocean. Reaching Erythia, Herakles smote both Orthos and his master, Eurytion, with his club, killing them, and when Geryon attacked him, Herakles killed him, too. Taking the cattle, he crossed back over the River Ocean on the golden goblet, returning the goblet to the sun-god and giving the cattle to Eurystheus.

Since Eurystheus did not acknowledge the task concerning Augeias's cattle or that concerning the hydra, he now ordered Herakles to perform an eleventh labor, to fetch golden apples from the Hesperides. These apples, a gift from Gaia (Earth) to Zeus upon his marriage to Hera, were guarded by an immortal hundred-headed dragon and by the Hesperides. Learning the location of the sea-god Nereus from certain nymphs, Herakles seized Nereus as he was sleeping. Nereus changed himself into all sorts of forms, but the hero did not let him go until he had learned where to find the apples. On his way through Libya he encountered Antaios (Latinized form = Antaeus), a son of Poseidon who ruled Libya at that time. Antaios killed strangers by making them wrestle with him. Since Antaios's strength increased every time he touched the earth, Herakles lifted him off the ground with a hug and crushed him to death.

Reaching the Caucasus, Herakles shot the eagle that devoured the liver of Prometheus and unbound the Titan. On Prometheus's advice, Herakles relieved Atlas of the sky and sent him after the golden apples, but Atlas, returning with three apples from the Hesperides and not wishing to resume his support of the sky, said he himself would deliver them to Eurystheus. Advised by Prometheus once again, Herakles asked Atlas to take back the sky until he should place a pad on his head. After Atlas set the apples on the ground and took the sky, Herakles picked up the apples and departed. He gave them to Eurystheus, who gave them back as a gift to Herakles, but he passed them on to Athena, who returned them to their rightful place, for it was improper for them to be laid down anywhere.

Herakles's twelfth labor was to bring from Hades's realm Cerberus (Greek Kerberos), a three-headed dog with the tail of a dragon. Herakles descended down to the realm of the dead through Tainaron (Latinized form = Taenarum), a cave in Laconia. Plouton told him he could take Cerberus away, provided that he overcame the hound without the use of weapons. So Herakles put his arms around the animal's head and squeezed, despite his being bitten by the dragon at the dog's tail, until Cerberus gave in. He carried the dog up to the earth's surface, showed it to Eurystheus, and returned it to Hades's realm.

After he had completed his labors, he returned to Thebes and bestowed his wife, Megara, on Iolaos and sought the hand of Iolê, daughter of Eurytos, ruler of Oichalia. But his madness recurred, and he killed a son of Eurytos. As a result of the killing he contracted a disease, and an oracle revealed that in order to be cured he must be sold and serve someone for three years. So Hermes sold him to Omphalê, queen of Lydia, and Herakles served her as a slave for three years, after which he was rid of his sickness.

Gathering volunteers, Herakles went to Troy and took the city, killing King Laomedon. He had many other adventures and accomplishments, including helping the gods in their war against the Giants and founding the Olympic Games. In time he went to Calydon in order to woo Deianeira, for whom the river god Acheloos (Latinizied form = Achelous) was also a suitor. Herakles and Acheloos wrestled for her hand. Although Acheloos transformed himself into a bull, Herakles overcame him and wed Deianeira. Traveling together, Herakles and Deianeira came to the Euenos River, across which the centaur Nessos ferried travelers for a fee. Herakles crossed it on his own, but he entrusted his wife to the centaur, who attempted to rape her as he carried her across. When she screamed, Herakles fatally shot Nessos. But before he died, the centaur privately told Deianeira that if she wanted a love potion to give her husband, she could make one by mixing the semen that the centaur had ejaculated and the blood that was flowing from his wound. Deianeira did so.

Herakles now gathered together an army to attack Oichalia in order to punish Eurytos, and he and his companions killed Eurytos and his sons, captured the city, and took Iolê captive. Deianeira, learning about Iolê and fearing that Herakles might love her more than herself, resorted to the love potion made from Nessos's blood and semen, which she smeared on one of her husband's garments. When Herakles donned it, however, the hydra's poison began to mortify his flesh. The poisoned clothing clung to his skin so that when he ripped it off, he tore his flesh. When Deianeira saw what had happened, she hanged herself. After arranging for one of his sons to marry Iolê, Herakles climbed Mount Oitê, built a pyre, mounted it, and had someone set it afire. As it burned, a cloud came down and, with a peal of thunder, carried him up to the sky, where he obtained immortality and was reconciled with Hera, who gave him her daughter Hebê in marriage (*Library* 2.4.6–2.8.5).

The numerous deeds of Herakles, only a selection of which are included in the foregoing summary, were classified by late Greek mythographers into three groups, namely, tasks, byworks, and deeds. The "tasks" (*athloi*) are the canonical twelve labors that Eurystheus assigns the hero. In English they are conventionally known as "labors" because English borrows from the Latin, and the Romans rendered *athloi* as *labores*. The content and sequence of the labors vary according to the ancient source. The "byworks" (*parerga*) are deeds that Herakles does on the side, as it were, while engaged in one or another labor, such as his rescuing the Trojan princess Hesionê from a sea-monster, which he executes in the course of his expedition to acquire Hippolytê's belt, his ninth labor according to Apollodoros. And the "deeds" (*praxeis*) are his accomplishments before or after his labors, such as his slaying of the Cithaeronian Lion.

Herakles is the strong man par excellence, with an enormous appetite for action, food, drink, and sex. His strength is such that he can crush a monstrous animal with his bare arms or kill a person unintentionally. He typically acts rather than deliberates. If the sun is too hot, his impulse is to aim an arrow at it. By ridding the earth of many monstrous beings, Herakles serves as a culture hero who facilitates civilized life, but at the same time he is destructively violent, a killer of men and a rapist of women. This brutish nature is emblematized by his lion skin and club, although it is not the only weapon he employs. His quasi-Paleolithic style is not the result of his being an early hero, for he lives three generations later than the hero Perseus, whose great-grandson he is, and Perseus displays none of Herakles's primitivism.

Occasionally Herakles is also the clever man, as when he devises a strategy for cleaning the cattle yard of King Augeias, rerouting two rivers through the yard in order to carry away the accumulated dung. But more often strategic ideas are assigned to a second, conventionally clever character, and Herakles's

role is to execute the plan, as when Athena provides him with castanets in order to drive away the Stymphalian Birds and Prometheus advises him how to
acquire the golden apples of the Hesperides.

The Herakles legend is parallel in many respects to an international folktale known as "Strong John." Like Herakles, the protagonist of the tale is a
prodigiously strong man with an enormous appetite. The central action of the
tale is a labor contract between the hero and a man who assigns him dangerous
or seemingly impossible tasks to perform.

Herakles was very popular in ancient art, in which he is usually represented as a male wearing a lion skin, the lion's head serving him as a helmet.
Ancient artists are careful not to show him wearing a lion skin if the adventure
they illustrate takes place prior to his slaying of the Cithaeronian (or Nemean)
Lion. As a weapon he may carry a bow or spear or club.

> ***See also*** Hero; Promotion and Demotion
>
> ***Suggested reading:***
>
> Antti Aarne and Stith Thompson. *The Types of the Folktale: A Classification and
>   Bibliography,* FF Communications, 184. Helsinki: Academia Scientiarum
>   Fennica, 1961, Type 650A: *Strong John.*
>
> John Boardman et al. "Herakles," in *LIMC* 4:728–838, 5:1–192.
>
> Frank Brommer. *Heracles: The Twelve Labours of the Hero in Ancient Art and
>   Literature,* trans. by S. Schwartz. New Rochelle, NY: Caratzas, 1986.
>
> G. Karl Galinsky. *The Herakles Theme: The Adaptations of the Hero in Literature
>   from Homer to the Twentieth Century.* Totowa, NJ: Rowman and Littlefield,
>   1972.
>
> Timothy Gantz. *Early Greek Myth: A Guide to Literary and Artistic Sources.*
>   Baltimore: The Johns Hopkins University Press, 1993, 374–463.
>
> Nicole Loraux. "Herakles: The Super-Male and the Feminine," in *Before Sexuality:
>   The Construction of the Erotic Experience in the Ancient Greek World,* edited
>   by David M. Halperin, John J. Winkler, and Froma Zeitlin. Princeton, NJ:
>   Princeton University Press, 1990, 21–52.

HERMES (ROMAN MERCURY)

God of thieves, heralds, and herds.

Hermes is the most prodigious of Greek tricksters, practicing deceit almost
from the moment of his birth. An anonymous hymn relates how the god was
born and acquired his honors, or divine spheres of interest. Zeus used to mingle
in love with the nymph Maia in her cave in Mount Kyllenê in Arcadia, while
Hera slept, and in time the nymph bore a son who was crafty of mind, thievish,
and a bringer of sleep. On the morning he was born, the infant god secretly left
his cradle, came upon a tortoise, killed it, and using its shell and other materi-
als made the first lyre, upon which he improvised a song.

Longing for meat, baby Hermes ran to Pieria, where cattle belonging to the immortal gods had their pasture, and stole fifty cattle belonging to his older brother Apollon, driving them backward to a fold in a distant cave, so that their footprints would not betray their place of concealment, while he himself walked forward, having invented wicker sandals that made his own tracks confusing to interpret. After rubbing two pieces of wood together, thereby inventing fire-sticks, Hermes slaughtered two cows and roasted their meat. Though he was a god he was tempted to feast upon the meat, but he did not do so, storing the meat in the cave instead as a sign of his theft. Then he burned up the heads and feet of the slaughtered cattle, threw his sandals into a river, put out the fire, and smoothed over the soil. By dawn of the following day he was back at the cave on Mount Kyllenê, where he lay down in his cradle with apparent innocence.

Hermes with caduceus.

In the meantime Apollon noticed that he had lost some cattle and presently learned who the thief was. He confronted Hermes, threatening to hurl him into Tartaros, but Hermes denied stealing the cattle, pleading that he was a day-old baby who cared only for sleep and mother's milk. Apollon smiled at the infant's lies, declaring that Hermes would have thievery and thieves as his divine province. They took the dispute to their father, Zeus. Although Zeus also found Hermes's denials amusing, he ordered him to lead the way to the cattle, which he did. Once there, the two young gods made peace. Hermes gave Apollon the lyre he had invented, adding this instrument to Apollon's repertory as god of music, and Apollon gave Hermes a whip as token of his becoming patron of cattle-herding. Hermes immediately invented a different musical instrument for himself, shepherd's pipes. Apollon declared that since Zeus gave Hermes thievery as one of his honors, Hermes should swear an oath not to steal from Apollon, and Hermes so swore. Then Apollon presented him with a golden caduceus, or herald's staff, in acknowledgment of his new honor as messenger of the gods. He announced also that Hermes would be in charge of cattle, horses, mules, sheep, dogs, and certain wild animals and that Hermes alone would be messenger to Hades (*Homeric Hymn to Hermes*).

As a latecomer among the gods, Hermes was eager to acquire domains for himself in order to secure a niche in the Olympian bureaucracy. Happily he was a gifted thief and liar from the start and also a brilliant inventor, combining the roles of trickster and culture hero. He made peace with Apollon by giving him the lyre he had invented and by swearing not to steal from him and acquired from Zeus and Apollon the patronage of herds and flocks, thieves, and heralds, becoming himself a herald of the gods, by virtue of which he acquired a caduceus, or herald's staff, and in particular becoming the sole messenger of the upper gods to Hades. So when Zeus needs to send a message to Hades, he dispatches Hermes (*Homeric Hymn to Demeter* 334–339), and when a god is needed to conduct the souls of the newly deceased to Erebos, Hermes leads them there with his golden wand (Homer *Odyssey* 24.1–14).

Many myths of the mature Hermes employ him as a trickster. After the monster Typhon stole Zeus's sinews, hid them in a cave, and stationed the dragon Delphynê to guard them, Hermes and Pan stole the sinews and refitted them to Zeus (Apollodoros *Library* 1.7.3). When the Aloads imprisoned the god Ares, Hermes surreptitiously freed him (Homer *Iliad* 5.385–391). On another occasion Jove (Zeus) transformed his unfortunate lover Io into a heifer, and Juno (Hera) appointed Argus (Argos) to guard her. Argus had 100 eyes, some of which were always alert. When Jove bade Mercury (Hermes) slay Io's guard, Mercury put Argus soundly asleep with his magic wand and slew him. Juno placed his many eyes on the feathers of her bird, the peacock (Ovid *Metamorphoses* 1.588–723).

Hermes often conveys a message or an object, especially for Zeus. For example, after the flood-heroes Deukalion and Pyrrha survived the great deluge, landed upon Mount Parnassos, and performed a pious sacrifice, Zeus sent Hermes to grant them whatever they should wish (Apollodoros *Library* 1.7.2). When Zeus wanted Kalypso (Latinized form = Calypso) to release the hero Odysseus, whom she was holding in erotic captivity, he dispatched Hermes (Homer *Odyssey* 5). After the birth of Dionysos from Zeus's thigh, Zeus handed the infant over to Hermes to take to Ino and Athamas in order that they might rear him. When that plan did not work out, Zeus had Hermes take Dionysos away to distant Nysa and entrust him to the local nymphs (Apollodoros *Library* 3.4.3). It was Hermes who conducted Hera, Athena, and Aphroditê to the Trojan shepherd Alexander, or Paris, in order that the shepherd might decide which of the three merited the apple of beauty (Apollodoros *Epitome* 3.1). And Hermes gave to Nephelê the golden ram (*Library* 1.9.1), whose fleece the Argonauts would later seek.

Hermes frequently lends aid to heroes. For example, he joined Athena in helping Perseus (Apollodoros *Library* 2.4.2), gave a sword to the young Herakles (*Library* 2.4.11), and provided Odysseus with the plant known as moly that he needed in order to neutralize the spell of the witch Kirkê (Homer *Odyssey* 10.275–309).

He had several children, notably the rustic god Pan (*Homeric Hymn to Pan*), the master-thief Autolykos (Apollodoros *Library* 1.9.16), the hunter Kephalos (*Library* 3.14.3), and the deceitful charioteer Myrtilos (*Epitome* 2.6). In a particularly unpleasant story, Hermes conceived a passion for the maiden Apemosynê but was unable to catch her because she was a swift runner. So he placed across her path the hides of freshly skinned animals, and when she slipped, he raped her. The girl told her brother of her experience, but not believing her, he kicked her to death (*Library* 3.2.1).

Hermes's epithets include Argeiphontes (commonly interpreted as "Slayer of Argos"), Diaktoros (Guide?), and Kyllenian (Latinized form = Cyllenian), referring to his place of birth. The Romans identified him with their deity Mercury (Latin *Mercurius*).

In art Hermes is sometimes a bearded man, sometimes a youth. Among his attributes are the caduceus (herald's wand), petasos (broad-rimmed traveler's hat), winged footwear, and winged hat.

See also Culture Hero; Trickster

Suggested reading:

Jenny Strauss Clay. *The Politics of Olympus: Form and Meaning in the Major Homeric Hymns.* Princeton: Princeton University Press, 1989, 95–151.

Timothy Gantz. *Early Greek Myth: A Guide to Literary and Artistic Sources.* Baltimore: The Johns Hopkins University Press, 1993, 105–112.

Gérard Siebert. "Hermes," in *LIMC* 5:285–387.

Erika Simon and Gerhard Bauchhenss. "Mercurius," in *LIMC* 6:500–554.

HERO (GREEK HEROS)

Greek term with mythological and cultic significances in antiquity.

In mythological narrative, the term *hero* (Greek *heros*) is employed by the poets Homer, Hesiod, and others to refer to men of free status who lived in the heroic age, that is to say, the generations of humans who lived during the time that culminated in the great wars at Thebes and Troy. This period follows the age of the gods, when the basic features of the cosmos were formed and organized, and is succeeded in turn by the human age, our own time. The sense of the word when we first encounter it was probably no more precise than this, but the usage may have developed from an earlier, more focused sense such as "warrior" or "preserver" (that is, warriors as preservers of the community).

More or less synonymous with this usage, though etymologically different, is the term *demigod* (Greek *hemitheos*), which the early poets apply to the same population (for example, Hesiod *Works and Days* 156–173). Some of the heroes were strictly demigods in the sense of having one divine parent and one human parent; for example, Achilleus was the son of the Nereid Thetis and the mortal

Peleus, Sarpedon was the son of the god Zeus and the mortal Deidameia, and Aineias was the son of the goddess Aphroditê and the mortal Anchises. But most heroes were not strictly demigods in terms of their immediate parents, so that the application of the word must have been extended from the demigods in the literal sense to include their peers. Many heroes had an additional divine connection in that they were raised or trained by nature spirits in their early lives. Aineias was nurtured by nymphs for his first five years, and the centaur Cheiron reared many Greek heroes in his cave, teaching them the art of hunting or healing.

In Greek cult, however, the term *hero* signifies rather a mortal who died, became a powerful dead person, and received worship, ordinarily at the site of his or her supposed grave, because he or she was able to affect human affairs for good or bad. Heroes in this second sense can overlap with heroes in the first sense, since a personage of the heroic age can be the recipient of a hero cult in historic times, but the two groups are not identical, since on the one hand not every member of the heroic age received cultic worship after death as a hero, and on the other hand heroes could be men, women, or children and need not have lived their lives during the period of the demigods.

The following narratives exemplify a variety of cultic heroes.

As Odysseus and his companions wandered homeward after the capture of Troy, they came to the Greek city of Temesa in Italy. One of the men raped a local girl while he was drunk, for which crime the inhabitants stoned him to death. Odysseus and his men sailed on, but the spirit (*daimon*) of the executed man remained active at Temesa, attacking and killing local persons young and old. The Temesans were on the point of abandoning their city and resettling elsewhere, but they consulted Apollon's oracle at Delphi, where the Pythian priestess instructed them rather to placate the Heros, as he came to be called, building him a shrine and giving him every year the most beautiful Temesan maiden for his wife. The citizens did so, and the spirit ceased bothering them. The Olympic boxer Euthymos happened to come to Temesa at the time of the annual ritual, inquired about what was taking place, and went inside the shrine to see the maiden. He fell in love with her, and she swore to marry him if he rescued her. So Euthymos awaited the arrival of the Heros, fought him, and drove him out of the land. The athlete and the maiden married, and the Temesans had no further trouble from the Heros (Pausanias 6.6.7–11). In this legend an ordinary man of the heroic age was executed for committing a crime, but returned after death as a revenant, or embodied ghost, to plague his executors. His depredations ceased only when a hero cult was established in his honor, including the annual offering of a maiden to satisfy his lust.

Agamedes of Stymphalos and his son Trophonios were outstanding craftsmen who constructed a number of notable buildings, including a treasury for

King Augeias of Elis. In making the treasury, however, they secretly left a particular stone loose in order that, unknown to Augeias, they might enter the treasury and steal from it, which they did. The puzzled Augeias set a snare for the thieves. It caught Agamedes, who perished. In order that the identity of the thieves not be discovered, Trophonios cut off Agamedes's head and departed with it. Nevertheless, Augeias set out in pursuit. Trophonios fled to Lebadia in Boiotia, where he constructed for himself an underground dwelling. When he died, Trophonios's underground dwelling became an oracle (Charax of Pergamon *FGH* 103 F 5). That is, after Trophonios died he carried on an existence as a hero, giving oracular responses to persons who consulted him in his subterranean home.

The Corinthians stoned to death Jason and Medeia's children Mermeros and Pheres because of the role they had played in the death of the daughter of the Corinthian king, bringing her gifts that unbeknownst to them were lethal. The murdered boys thereafter caused Corinthian infants to die until the folk learned from an oracle the cause of their misfortune and instituted annual sacrifices to Mermeros and Pheres in order to appease them (Pausanias 2.3.6).

In many legends of heroization, the person dies an untimely death such that he or she might be supposed to resent his or her lot and is placated with ritual honors. As the legends of the Heros and Trophonios illustrate, the heroized person need not have lived a virtuous or meritorious life.

See also Elysion Field and Isles of the Blessed; Promotion and Demotion; Translation

Suggested reading:

Walter Burkert. *Greek Religion,* trans. John Raffan. Cambridge, MA: Harvard University Press, 1985, 203–208.

Joseph Fontenrose. "The Hero as Athlete." *California Studies in Classical Antiquity* 1 (1968): 73–104.

Jennifer Larson. *Greek Heroine Cults.* Madison: University of Wisconsin Press, 1995.

Deborah Lyons. *Gender and Immortality: Heroines in Ancient Greek Myth and Cult.* Princeton, NJ: Princeton University Press, 1997.

Gregory Nagy. *The Best of the Achaeans: Concepts of the Hero in Archaic Greek Poetry.* Baltimore: The Johns Hopkins University Press, 1979.

Vinciane Pirenne-Delforge and Emilio Suárez de la Torre, eds. *Héros et Héroïnes dans les Myths et les Cultes Grecs.* Liège: Centre International d'Étude de la Religion Grecque Antique, 2000.

Erwin Rohde. *Psyche: The Cult of Souls and Belief in Immortality among the Greeks,* trans. by W. B. Hillis. London: Kegan Paul, French, Trubner; New York: Harcourt, Brace, 1925, 115–155.

Martin L. West, ed. and comm. *Hesiod: Works and Days.* Oxford: Clarendon Press, 1978, 370–373.

HESTIA (ALSO HISTIA) (ROMAN VESTA)

Goddess of the hearth.

Hestia (Hearth) is a member of the older generation of Olympians, offspring of the Titans Kronos and Rhea (Hesiod *Theogony* 453–500). Indeed, she is said to be both the eldest and the youngest of her siblings (*Homeric Hymn to Aphrodite* 22–23), eldest because she was the first-born, but also youngest, for Kronos swallowed his children as they were born, and when subsequently he was given an emetic and disgorged them, they reappeared in reverse order, so that Hestia emerged last. Hestia's residence in her father's belly is therefore treated as a second period of gestation, and his spewing her up, as a second parturition.

Although the elder Olympian Poseidon and the younger Olympian Apollon each wooed Hestia, she turned them down, swearing an oath that she would remain a virgin forever. In place of marriage, Zeus granted her the privilege of enjoying the fat of sacrificial meats in the center of each house, and she is honored in all temples and enjoys honor among all mortals as the eldest of the gods (*Homeric Hymn to Aphrodite* 22–32). So, like the younger Olympians Artemis and Athena, Hestia chooses to remain a maiden, and Zeus allots to her the cosmic honor of being the hearth, the locus of sacrificial rites. Accordingly she is binatural, being at once the physical hearth with its fire and also an anthropomorphic goddess who can enjoy the rich juices that issue from a sacrificial victim. Since her name signifies simply "hearth," a *hestia* (hearth) derives its name from the given name of the goddess or, like Atlas (Bearer), the goddess was named proleptically.

Important in cult but not in mythology, Hestia appears in few myths. Her Roman equivalent is Vesta.

> *Suggested reading:*
> Marcel Detienne. *The Writing of Orpheus: Greek Myth in Cultural Contact*, trans. by Janet Lloyd. Baltimore: The Johns Hopkins University Press, 2003, 59–69.
> Tobias Fischer-Hansen. "Vesta," in *LIMC* 5:412–420.
> Timothy Gantz. *Early Greek Myth: A Guide to Literary and Artistic Sources.* Baltimore: The Johns Hopkins University Press, 1993, 73–74.
> Haiganuch Sarian. "Hestia," in *LIMC* 5:407–412.

HONOR (GREEK TIMÊ)

A deity's sphere of influence in the cosmos.

The gods are officials in a cosmic bureaucracy that covers all imaginable territory, each deity having an honor, or focused sphere of influence, in the cosmic order. Zeus is in charge of the sky, Poseidon in charge of the waters, Hades in charge of the death realm, Demeter in charge of grains, Aphroditê in charge of erotic love, and so on.

The usual Greek word for a deity's area of responsibility in the cosmic order is *honor* (*timê*), a word that in the corresponding human context refers to an office held by a civic official. Other terms for a Greek deity's sphere of influence are *portion, lot, allotment* (*moira*), and *honor-gift* (*geras*).

The distribution of offices in the mythological present is owed to Zeus, who assigned the gods new honors or confirmed their old ones as in the case of Styx (Hesiod *Theogony* 389–403, 775–806), after the other Olympians acclaimed him king of the gods, following his victory over the monster Typhon (Hesiod *Theogony* 389–396, 881–885). The kingship of the gods is itself such an office, which previously belonged to Zeus's father, Kronos. According to a different tradition, however, the three brothers Zeus, Poseidon, and Hades drew lots to determine their respective honors. As his province and residence, Poseidon got the sea, Hades obtained Erebos, Zeus acquired the sky, and they were to share the earth and Olympos (Homer *Iliad* 15.187–193). Gods can have several provinces. Poseidon is responsible not only for the waters but also for horses and earthquakes, although the latter two honors are of little importance in mythology.

A popular theme of Greek myths is how individual deities acquired their provinces of concern. Since the significance and number of provinces and cult-sites are an index of a deity's importance, the gods place great value upon the personal validation that the possession by them of one or more provinces signifies. They may even compete for them, as when Athena and Poseidon each vied for the possession of the city that, after Athena won, acquired the name Athens. Younger gods such as Apollon and Hermes, who were born after Zeus's distribution and confirmation of honors, were concerned to establish what role, if any, they would play in the cosmic bureaucracy (*Homeric Hymn to Apollon; Homeric Hymn to Hermes*).

One way for a human to please a god is to give due acknowledgment to the deity's cosmic honor (*timê*) or to augment the deity's cult or worship (also called *timê*). A mortal cannot allot to a deity an additional sphere of influence, which is a matter for the gods to determine, but a mortal can increase a deity's cultic honor by extending the worship that the deity receives. So when the hero Odysseus set out to placate the sea-god Poseidon, whom he had offended, he did so by introducing the god's cult to a community of persons who lived so far inland that they knew nothing of the sea or of the god of the sea, thereby augmenting his honor (scholiast on Homer *Odyssey* 11.121, 130). The other side of the coin is that because the gods are very sensitive to the respect that is their due, they resent any slight by human beings, in the form either of cultic neglect or of competition from a mortal in the deity's special area of competence. When King Oineus of Calydon made an offering of first-fruits to all the gods but forgot Artemis alone, she in her anger sent against the Calydonians a great wild boar that caused much devastation. And when Agamemnon felled a stag with a single shot of his bow and exclaimed that not even Artemis could have shot so well, the archer goddess avenged this hubristic slight by causing the winds to strand Agamemnon's fleet at Aulis, preventing the Greeks from setting out to Troy.

Suggested reading:

Gregory Nagy. *The Best of the Achaeans: Concepts of the Hero in Archaic Greek Poetry.* Baltimore: The Johns Hopkins University, 1979, 118–119.

Jean Rudhardt. "À propos de l'hymne homérique à Déméter." *Museum Helveticum* 35 (1978): 1–17.

HUBRIS

Insolent or presumptuous behavior such as arises from an excessive sense of self-importance.

The cosmic status of characters is ordinarily persistent, immortals remaining immortals, mortals remaining mortals, and so on, although a few mortals are elevated to a higher status in the cosmic hierarchy. For the most part, however, a being remains in the cosmic category of birth and is expected to behave accordingly. Any mortal who acts as though he or she were equal or superior to a deity in some respect is likely to incur the wrath of the deity, and the same is true of a minor deity who ventures to compete with a major deity. "Know thyself," as the Delphic maxim expresses it. That is, understand your place in the scheme of things.

Many mythological narratives portray the hubristic behavior of a mortal (or minor divinity) who offends a deity by acting above his station, often in an insolent manner, prompting the deity to punish the offender in some way (or a third character takes up the cause).

Boasting

Mortal women often boasted that they were more beautiful than this or that goddess. Among them was Kassiepeia, queen of Ethiopia, who once boasted that her beauty exceeded that of all the Nereids, thereby angering the Nereids and along with them Poseidon, who sent a sea-monster against the Ethiopian kingdom (Apollodoros *Library* 2.4.3).

The proud matron Niobê audaciously compared her prowess in child-bearing with that of a goddess. Niobê drove away the Theban women who were sacrificing to Latona (Greek Leto) and to her children Apollo and Diana (Greek Artemis), declaring that she herself had more claim to worship than did Latona, for she herself was mother to fourteen children, whereas Latona had borne a mere two. The goddess angrily dispatched her son and daughter to avenge the insult, and Apollo presently felled all seven of Niobê's sons with his arrows. Niobê's husband, Amphion, took his own life in his grief, but Niobê herself only cried out to the goddess that, for all her losses, she still had more children than Latona. So Diana now slew Niobê's daughters, until only Niobê remained, utterly alone. In the end Niobê was transformed into a weeping rock (Ovid *Metamorphoses* 6.165–312).

Just as hubristic women may boast of their beauty or fertility, insolent men may boast of something of traditional interest to men, such as hunting. While the Achaean fleet lay at anchor at Aulis, ready to sail against Troy, Agamemnon killed a deer with an arrow and vaunted: "Not even Artemis could have shot so well." As a result the angry goddess prevented the fleet from sailing (Apollodoros *Epitome* 3.21). Even more outrageous was Orion, who while hunting on Crete with the goddesses Artemis and Leto boasted that he would kill every single animal on the surface of the earth. Gaia (Earth) was infuriated and sent against him a giant scorpion, which stung Orion, killing him (Hesiod frag. 148a MW).

Contesting

If it is unwise to compare oneself to a god or goddess, it is more brazen to engage in an actual contest. Arachnê (Spider) was a gifted weaver who denied that she had been taught by Minerva (Greek Athena), and indeed she challenged Minerva to a contest. The mortal and the goddess then competed in weaving on the loom, and Arachnê's web was faultless. In frustration, Minerva beat Arachnê until the wretched girl started to hang herself. Pitying her, the goddess transformed her into a spider, and as such she has continued to hang and to weave (Ovid *Metamorphoses* 6.1–145). The male hero Orion was killed, according to one version of his legend, as a result of his challenging Artemis to a contest in throwing the discus (Apollodoros *Library* 1.4.5).

Musical challenges are issued both by females and by males. The Pierides, or nine daughters of Pierus, arrogantly challenged the nine Muses to a contest in song, with nymphs to serve as judges. After one member of each chorus sang in turn, the nymphs awarded the prize to the Muses, but since the challengers continued to behave abusively, the Muses transformed them into magpies, in which form they continue their raucous babble (Ovid *Metamorphoses* 5.294–678). On another occasion, the Muses were accosted by the Thracian singer Thamyris, who challenged them to a singing contest on the condition that, if he should win, he could have sex with each of them, and if they should win, they might take from him what they wished. The Muses won and deprived him not only of his sight but also of his minstrelsy, causing him to forget how to sing and to play the lyre (Homer *Iliad* 2.594–600; Apollodoros *Library* 1.3.3). The satyr Marsyas once entered into a music contest with the god Apollon, agreeing that the winner might do what he wished with the loser. When Apollon played his lyre upside-down but Marsyas could not do the same with his pipe, the satyr lost the contest, and Apollon chose to flay him alive (*Library* 1.4.2).

Presumption

Some gifted beings take their skills too far, threatening the prerogatives of the gods. The seeress Ocyrhoê, daughter of the centaur Cheiron, revealed too much of the future, thereby offending the Fates. By Jove's will she was metamorphosed into a mare, silencing her prophetic voice (Ovid *Metamorphoses* 2.633–679). The healer Asklepios was a son of Apollon and a mortal woman, Koronis. He was raised by the centaur Cheiron, who taught him the art of healing. Asklepios became so great a surgeon that he was able to recall the dead to life, whereupon Zeus killed him with a thunderbolt, fearing that other persons might learn this treatment from him (Apollodoros *Library* 3.10.3).

Some mortals identified themselves with the gods. Thus a number of happily married couples called themselves Zeus and Hera, implying that they were as happy as the blessed king and queen of the gods. Keyx called his wife Hera, and his wife Alkyonê called him Zeus. Because of their excessive pride, Zeus turned them both into birds, Keyx (gannet) into a gannet and Alkyonê (kingfisher) into a kingfisher (Hesiod frag. 15 MW; Apollodoros *Library* 1.7.4). More arrogantly, a certain Salmoneus, declaring he was Zeus, ordered the citizens of his city to sacrifice to him rather than to Zeus. As he drove around in his chariot he dragged bronze kettles, saying that he was thundering, and threw torches at the sky, saying that he was making lightning. For his impiety, Zeus struck him with a real thunderbolt and destroyed his fellow citizens as well (Apollodoros *Library* 1.9.7).

Narratives that link a particular behavior with a negative outcome, as though to illustrate the harmful consequences of a form of action, lend themselves to being used as cautionary, or apotreptic, narratives, told by a narrator with the purpose in mind of dissuading a hearer from a particular kind of behavior. But occasionally a character behaves outrageously and gets away with it. In the course of his journeys, the hero Herakles was once suffering so much from the heat that he aimed his bow at Helios (Sun), preparing to shoot the god, but Helios in fear bade him stop. A short time later Herakles similarly prepared to shoot Okeanos (River Ocean), who was causing Herakles's boat to toss uncomfortably (Pherekydes frag. 18a Fowler; Apollodoros *Library* 2.5.10). Herakles's threatening behavior toward these deities is presented as forgivable audacity rather than as insolence.

The contrary of legends of mortals acting above their station are myths of deities acting beneath theirs, such as when goddesses take mortal men as lovers. The Olympians were outraged when Eos (Dawn) fell in love with the hero Orion, so that Artemis slew him with her arrows. And as soon as Zeus learned that Demeter lay in a field making love with Iasion, he killed Iasion with a thunderbolt (Homer *Odyssey* 5.116–129). Such stories are relatively few in number.

See also Transformation

HUNTERS

Hunters and huntresses play a major role in Greek mythology.

Hunting brings characters of different sorts into the untamed countryside with its potential for adventure and danger, such as wild animals, centaurs, supernatural beings, and unregulated sexuality.

Since hunting as a sport required leisure, not to mention equipment, among real-life mortals it was a pastime associated particularly with aristocrats, and being understood as symbolic warfare it was an activity deemed appropriate to males. But classical mythology features also huntresses, notably Artemis on the divine level and Atalantê (Latinized form = Atalanta) on the human level, females who by adopting male pursuits and sometimes a male style are anomalies among immortals and mortals.

Hunting was invented by the archers Apollon and Artemis, who gave the art as a gift to the centaur Cheiron, and he in turn taught it to individual heroes, including Nestor, Hippolytos, Achilleus, Meleager, Odysseus, and Palamedes, whence it passed to the rest of mankind (Xenophon *On Hunting* 1). Alternatively, different kinds of hunting had different inventors, centaurs inventing it for their own use as an after-dinner pastime, whereas among humans the first hunter was Perseus, the inventor of hunting with bow and arrows was Atalantê, hunting with nets was first devised by Hippolytos, hunting at night was invented by Orion, and so on (Oppian *Cynegetica* 2.1–30). Deities of the mountains and countryside—Artemis, Apollon, Pan, Hermes, and the nymphs—are the principal hunters among the gods (Arrian *Cynegetica* 35.4). Pan spends his day roaming the mountains and hunting in the company of nymphs (*Homeric Hymn to Pan*), and Artemis wanders in the wilds armed with her bow and arrows, alone or in the company of nymphs.

Although hunters are found in both the immortal and the mortal spheres, mythological narratives focus primarily upon mortal hunters, either as individuals or in parties. Among heroes they range from Orion and Herakles, grotesque figures of extreme strength, size, and appetite who do much hunting, to the more conventional Perseus (slayer of the Gorgon Medusa), Bellerophon (slayer of the Chimaera), and Theseus (slayer of the Minotaur), each noted for overcoming a particular monster. In some hunting narratives, the romantic intertwines with the tragic, as when the hunter Kephalos (Latinized form = Cephalus) unwittingly slew his own wife Prokris, and the hunter Adonis, Aphroditê's lover, was killed by a wild boar.

As a sample I give the legend of Orion, although none of the stories is typical of the lot. Orion was a son of a mortal maiden, Euryalê, and the god Poseidon. His father gave him the ability to walk on the sea as easily as upon the land. The hero once visited Oinopion on Chios and, while drunk, raped his daughter Meropê, for which act Oinopion put out Orion's eyes and ejected him from the island. Orion made his way to the island of Lemnos, where Hephaistos, pitying him, lent the hero his servant Kedalion as a guide. Carrying Kedalion upon his shoulders and following his directions, Orion went east, where he met Helios (Sun), who healed his blindness, whereupon Orion returned to Chios with the intention of punishing Oinopion, but the locals had hidden the man under the earth. So Orion went to Crete, where he passed his time hunting with Artemis and Leto. When, however, he threatened to slay every animal on the surface of the earth, Gaia (Earth) angrily sent forth a huge scorpion that stung him, causing his death. At the bidding of Artemis and Leto, Zeus placed both Orion and the scorpion among the stars in commemoration of his bravery (Hesod frag. 148a MW).

Orion is a hunter with an immoderate appetite for drink, sex, and slaying, whose excesses finally cause his divine execution, although the gods also admire and memorialize his courage. Intemperate behavior characterizes other hunters as well. The *Kypria*, a poem belonging to the Epic Cycle, relates that when the Achaean forces gathered together at Aulis, about to sail for Troy, Agamemnon felled a deer during a hunt and boasted that he had surpassed even Artemis. The wrathful goddess responded by sending a storm that prevented the Achaeans from sailing, and the seer Kalchas explained that in order to placate the goddess's anger, Agamemnon must sacrifice to her his daughter Iphigeneia (Proklos *Chrestomathia* p. 104 Allen).

Among individual hunters, the followers of Artemis constitute a special category, being passionate hunters who with equal passion reject sexuality, a combination that tends to attract rather than to discourage the sexual interest of others. This group includes the huntresses Atalantê and Kallisto (Latinized form = Callisto) and the hunters Melanion and Hippolytos (Latinized form = Hippolytus).

The legend of Atalantê can serve as an illustration. She was the daughter of Iasos and Klymenê. Since Iasos wanted sons, he exposed her, but a she-bear nursed the infant girl until some hunters chanced upon her and adopted her. When Atalantê grew up, she chose to remain virginal and to pass her time hunting in the wilderness. Once the centaurs Rhoikos and Hylaios tried to rape her, but she shot and killed them with her bow and arrows. She participated in the hunt for the Calydonian boar, and in the funeral games held in honor of Pelias she overcome the hero Peleus in a wrestling match. In time she discovered her biological parents, and her father urged her to wed, but she agreed to marry only the man who could beat her in a footrace. She gave her suitor a head start, and she herself pursued him in arms, killing him if she caught up with him. Many hopefuls perished in this way. Eventually a certain Melanion won the race by means of a trick, for having gotten golden apples from Aphroditê, he cast them down during the race, and since Atalantê paused to gather them up, Melanion won. Atalantê and Melanion wed. But once while they were out hunting, they had sexual intercourse with each other in a sanctuary of Zeus, and for this behavior they were transformed into lions (Apollodoros *Library* 3.9.2).

Nursed by a she-bear and raised by hunters, the semiferal Atalantê grows up to be fiercely independent and self-reliant, pursuing a characteristically male life of hunting and athletic competition, and distinguishing herself in both. Her downfall is her inability to govern her sexuality appropriately, for she knows only total abstinence or total yielding. In the end she gives in to an impulse to have sexual intercourse in a holy sanctuary, incurring divine anger. Immoderation is her fatal flaw, as it is for Orion.

In addition to individual hunters, there are hunting parties, the most famous of which is the hunt for the Calydonian boar, an enterprise involving many hunters, indeed all the heroes of Greece at the time. According to the mythographer Apollodoros, King Oineus of Calydon once neglected to include Artemis when he was performing the annual sacrifice of first-fruits to all the gods. In her wrath, the goddess sent against Calydon a boar of extraordinary size and strength, which not only prevented the inhabitants from sowing their crops but also caused destruction among cattle and humans. Oineus summoned to Calydon all the finest men in Greece, promising to give the boar's skin as a prize to the person who should slay the animal. Many prominent men gathered for the hunt, among them Meleager, Idas and Lynkeus, Kastor and Polydeukes, Theseus, Admetos, Kepheus, Jason, Peirithoos, Peleus, Telamon, Amphiaraos, the sons of Thestios (Meleager's maternal uncles), and also a woman, Atalantê. Oineus feasted the hunters for nine days, but on the tenth day some of the men refused to set out hunting with a woman. Meleager, who was sexually attracted to Atalantê, forced them all to set out together. Several men perished in the hunt. Atalantê was the first to hit the boar with an arrow, Amphiaraos was the second, and finally Meleager dispatched it, winning the boar's skin. He gave the prize to Atalantê, but his uncles took it from her, deeming it disgraceful for a woman to take the prize when men were present and claiming the skin belonged to them as kinsmen of Meleager if he declined it. But Meleager angrily killed his uncles and once again gave the skin to Atalantê (*Library* 1.8.2). As often the hunter becomes the hunted.

A less conventional form of hunting party consists of bacchantes, or maenads, who collectively become hunters in the course of their Dionysiac rites when they ecstatically tear apart a wild animal with their bare hands. Sometimes their victim is a human being, as in the case of King Pentheus of Thebes, who while stalking the bacchantes on Mount Kithairon in order to spy upon them suddenly found his role changed from predator to prey (Euripides *Bacchae*). Another intruder who suffered a like fate on the same mountain was the unfortunate hunter Actaeon (Greek Aktaion), who happened upon Diana and her nymphs bathing in a grotto, was transformed by the indignant goddess into a stag, and was torn apart by his own hounds (Ovid *Metamorphoses* 3.138–252).

See also Meleager

Suggested reading:

Judith M. Barringer. *The Hunt in Ancient Greece.* Baltimore: The Johns Hopkins University Press, 2002, 125–173.

Marcel Detienne. *Dionysos Slain,* trans. by M. Muellner and L. Muellner. Baltimore: The Johns Hopkins University Press, 1979, 20–52.

Joseph Fontenrose. *Orion: The Myth of the Hunter and the Huntress.* University of California Publications: Classical Studies, 23. Berkeley: University of California Press, 1981.

P. M. C. Forbes Irving. *Metamorphosis in Greek Myths.* Oxford: Clarendon Press, 1990, 80–90.

Pierre Vidal-Naquet. *The Black Hunter: Forms of Thought and Forms of Society in the Greek World,* trans. by Andrew Szegedy-Maszak. Baltimore: The Johns Hopkins University Press, 1986, 106–128.

ICHOR

Fluid in the bodies of immortals corresponding to blood in mortals.

According to Homer, the gods do not eat bread or drink wine, for which reason they do not have blood and do not die; instead, they have ichor. Thus when the goddess Aphroditê is wounded, ichor runs from her body (*Iliad* 5.337–342). Evidently a diet of bread and wine leads to the production of blood, which in turn is characteristic of beings who are subject to death.

This mythological significance of ichor is a special application of an ordinary Greek word that is otherwise found mostly in technical contexts. In the medical writers, *ichor* means approximately "blood serum," and in the realm of cuisine it refers to the juice of roasted meat. In short, it denotes a watery liquid that exudes from pierced flesh.

A mortal being whose body has ichor instead of blood is Talos, a unique brazen man with a single vein running from his neck to his ankles that is plugged with a bronze nail. The witch Medeia tricked him into allowing her to unplug the vein, after which the ichor drained out so that he died (Apollodoros *Library* 1.9.26).

Suggested reading:

J. Jouanna and P. Demont. "Le sens d'ichor chez Homère et Eschyle en relation avec les employs du mot dans la *Collection Hippocratique.*" *Revue des Études Anciennes* 83 (1981): 335–354.

Nicole Loraux. "Le corps vulnérable d'Arès." *Le Temps et la Réflexion* 7 (1986): 335–354.

Bruno Z. Quirini. "ICHOR, 'il Sangue' degli Dèi." *Orpheus* 4 (1983): 355–363.

IRIS

Personified rainbow and divine messenger of the Olympian gods.

Iris is a divine personification of the rainbow, the Greek noun *iris* signifying "rainbow." But her principal roles in narrative are those of divine messenger and occasionally escort. She is especially a messenger for Zeus (Hesiod *Theogony* 780–787), but she can also convey a message for a mortal, for when Achilleus utters a prayer to the winds, Iris takes it upon herself to convey his message to the wind-gods personally (Homer *Iliad* 23.198–212). When Aphroditê is wounded in the fighting at Troy, Iris escorts her away from the battle (*Iliad* 5.353–354).

She is therefore a female counterpart to the divine male messenger and escort, Hermes, although her cosmic range is mostly restricted to sky and earth, like that of the rainbow, for unlike Hermes she does not escort the souls of the dead or travel to the realm of the dead. On rare occasions, however, Zeus dis-

Iris with child and caduceus.

patches her to fetch a golden pitcher of water from Styx, which the gods employ to swear their oaths (Hesiod *Theogony* 780–787).

Genealogically Iris is a daughter of the Titan Thaumas and the Okeanid Elektra and a sister of the Harpies (*Theogony* 265–269). The sisters share a relationship with the winds, for Iris runs as fast as the wind, as her epithet "wind-footed" declares, and the Harpies are personified storm winds.

In art she can be shown as a winged female bearing a caduceus, or herald's staff, in her hand, as Hermes regularly does. Among her attributes in art is winged footwear.

See also Hermes

Suggested reading:
Timothy Gantz. *Early Greek Myth: A Guide to Literary and Artistic Sources.* Baltimore: The Johns Hopkins University Press, 1993, 17–18.
Anneliese Kossatz-Diessmann. "Iris," in *LIMC* 5:741–760.

JASON (GREEK IASON)

Youth who went in search of the Golden Fleece.

According to the mythographer Apollodoros, Jason was the son of Aison and Polymedê and lived in Iolkos, which was ruled by his paternal uncle, Pelias. The king received an oracle warning him to beware of the man wearing one sandal. Once Pelias was sacrificing to Poseidon and summoned many persons to attend, including Jason, who lived in the country. The youth lost one of his sandals as he crossed the Anauros River, and when Pelias saw him, he recalled the oracle. The king asked Jason what he would do if he had gotten an oracle saying that he would be murdered by a fellow-citizen, and Jason replied: "I would order him to bring me the Golden Fleece." So Pelias ordered Jason to bring him the fleece, which hung from a tree in a grove of Ares in Kolchis, guarded by a dragon that never slept.

Jason sought the aid of Argos, who constructed a fifty-oared ship, named the *Argo* after its builder, and Athena fitted to its prow a piece of wood from the oracular oak at Dodona that had the power of speech. When Jason consulted an oracle about the enterprise, the god told him he could sail after he had gathered together the best men in Greece. After many adventures, Jason and the Argonauts reached Kolchis.

Jason approached the local king, Aietes, asking for the fleece, and Aietes promised to give it to him if he could yoke two bronze-footed bulls and then sow a field with dragon's teeth. Jason was at a loss how to do so, but Aietes's daughter Medeia, who was a witch, fell in love with him and secretly offered her help if Jason would swear to marry her and take her with him at his departure, which Jason agreed to do. So she gave him a potion that would make his body and weapons safe from fire or iron for one day, and she told him what to do after sowing the dragon's teeth. Then Jason yoked the bulls and sowed the teeth, after which armed men sprang up from the ground. Jason cast stones at them, causing them to fight among themselves, so that Jason easily dispatched them. Although he had accomplished the tasks, the king refused to hand over the fleece and plotted against Jason and his companions. So during the night Medeia led Jason to the grove of Ares, drugged the dragon, took the fleece, and accompanied by her brother Apsyrtos proceeded to the *Argo*. The ship set out in the darkness.

When Aietes discovered what had happened, he pursued the *Argo*. But Medeia killed her brother Apsyrtos, cut him into pieces, and scattered them in the sea. Aietes paused to gather the limbs of his son, so that the Argonauts escaped. After further adventures, they reached Iolkos, where Jason learned that Pelias, not expecting Jason to return, had planned to kill his father, Aison, in his absence. So Aison had killed himself by drinking bull's blood, and Jason's mother had hanged herself after cursing Pelias. Jason now turned over the fleece to his uncle and awaited an opportunity for revenge. He asked Medeia for her help. She went to the palace and told Pelias's daughters that she could restore their aged father's youth by means of her drugs. She demonstrated by cutting up a ram and placing the pieces in a cauldron, after which a lamb leaped out. So Pelias's daughters chopped him up and boiled the pieces in Medeia's cauldron. After Pelias was buried, Jason and Medeia were banished from Iolkos.

They settled in Corinth and for ten years lived happily. But then King Kreon of Corinth offered his daughter Glaukê to Jason, who divorced Medeia and wed Glaukê. After reproaching Jason for ingratitude, Medeia exacted her revenge. First she sent as a gift to Glaukê a poisonous robe. When the princess put it on, she was consumed by fire, as also was Kreon when he tried to help her. Then Medeia killed her two sons by Jason and fled to Athens on a chariot drawn by winged dragons, which her grandfather Helios had provided. There she married Aigeus, father of Theseus. But after she plotted against Theseus, Aigeus expelled her from Athens, and she returned to Kolchis (*Library* 1.9.16–28).

The legend of Jason and Medeia is a Greek development of an international tale, "The Girl as Helper in the Hero's Flight," in which an ogre assigns the protagonist one or more seemingly impossible tasks, but he is helped by the ogre's daughter, who has fallen in love with him.

The principal literary treatment of the legend in antiquity is Apollonios of Rhodes's *Argonautika,* or *Voyage of the Argonauts,* an epic poem written in the third century B.C.

> ***See also*** Argonauts; Biographical Pattern; Tasks; Wondrous Objects
>
> ***Suggested reading:***
>
> Antti Aarne and Stith Thompson. *The Types of the Folktale: A Classification and Bibliography.* FF Communications, 184. 2nd revision. Helsinki: Academia Scientiarum Fennica, 1961, Type 313C: *The Girl as Helper in the Hero's Flight + The Forgotten Fiancée.*
>
> Timothy Gantz. *Early Greek Myth: A Guide to Literary and Artistic Sources.* Baltimore: The Johns Hopkins University Press, 1993, 340–373.
>
> William Hansen. *Ariadne's Thread: A Guide to International Tales Found in Classical Literature.* Ithaca, NY: Cornell University Press, 2002, 151–166, 263.
>
> Jenifer Niels. "Iason," in *LIMC* 5:629–638.

KADMOS (LATINIZED FORM CADMUS)

Phoenician youth who slew a dragon and founded Thebes.

According to the mythographer Apollodoros, Agenor went to Phoenicia, where he wed Telephassa and begat a daughter Europê and three sons: Kadmos, Phoinix, and Kilix (Latinized forms = Europa, Cadmus, Phoenix, and Cilix). Zeus, erotically attracted to Europê, turned himself into a tame bull and induced Europê to climb onto his back, whereupon he conveyed her to Crete. They lay together, and she bore him several sons, including Minos.

Upon the disappearance of Europê, Agenor dispatched his sons to look for her, telling them not to return until they found her. Unable to locate her, the three brothers settled in different places, Phoinix in Phoenicia and Kilix in Cilicia, giving their names to these lands, and Kadmos in Thrace.

Subsequently, Kadmos asked the Delphic oracle about his sister, but the oracle instructed him rather to follow a cow as guide, and where the cow should lie down from weariness, there he should found a city. So he followed a particular cow through Boiotia (Cow-Land), and the cow rested at the site of present-day Thebes. Wishing to sacrifice the cow to Athena, Kadmos sent several of his companions to fetch water from the Spring of Ares, but the spring was guarded by a dragon, an offspring of Ares, and it destroyed most of his men. In anger Kadmos slew the dragon. Upon Athena's advice he sowed the teeth in the ground, and there arose from the earth armed men, whom they called Spartoi (Sown-Men). When Kadmos saw them arising from the ground, he threw stones at them, and the men—thinking that the stones were thrown by one another—engaged in battle with one another. Five survived: Echion, Oudaios, Chthonios, Hyperenor, and Peloros. In atonement for his action, Kadmos was obliged to serve Ares for a period of eight years. Afterward Athena procured the kingdom of Thebes for Kadmos, and Zeus gave him as wife Harmonia, daughter of Ares and Aphroditê, and the celestial gods left the heavens and joined in celebrating their marriage in the Kadmeia, or citadel of Thebes. In their old age Kadmos and Harmonia were turned into serpents by Zeus and sent to the Elysion Field (*Library* 3.1.1–3.5.4).

> *See also* Combat Myth and Legend; Eponymy; Transformation; Translation
> *Suggested reading:*
> Ruth B. Edwards. *Kadmos the Phoenician: A Study of Greek Legends and the Mycenaean Age.* Amsterdam: Adolf M. Hakkert, 1979.
> Timothy Gantz. *Early Greek Myth: A Guide to Literary and Artistic Sources.* Baltimore: The Johns Hopkins University Press, 1993, 467–473.
> Michalis A. Tiverios. "Kadmos I," in *LIMC* 5:863–882.
> Francis Vian. *Les origines de Thèbes: Cadmus et les Spartes.* Paris: Librairie C. Klincksieck, 1963.

KER (OR KERES)

Death goddess, found singly as a Ker and multiply as Keres.

Ker, or a Ker, is a personified spirit of death, especially the violent death of battle. She is black in appearance (Homer *Odyssey* 17.500) and cannot be outrun (Homer *Iliad* 18.117). On the battlefield Ker is described as mingling horribly with other goddesses such as Eris (Strife) and dragging away a dead man by his feet, her clothing stained with men's blood (*Iliad* 18.535–540; Hesiod *Shield of Herakles* 156–160). On one occasion "Keres of death" bring a man who has died an apparently natural death to the House of Hades (*Odyssey* 14.207–208), much as Hermes escorts the souls of Penelopê's slain suitors to Erebos (*Odyssey* 24.1–14). According to Hesiod, "black Ker" is a daughter of Nyx, or Night (*Theogony* 211).

Functionally, Ker is an ineluctable spirit of death who, like Thanatos (Death), eagerly pursues her victims and collects the newly dead and is also, like the psychopomp Hermes, an escorter of the newly dead to the death realm. As a character, Ker remains austere, at home mostly in early Greek poetry, and like other divine guilds such as the Graces or the Hours or the Muses, the Keres are not much personified beyond their basic underlying idea, in this case death or doom.

> *See also* Divine Guilds; Hades; Personified Abstractions
> *Suggested reading:*
> O. Crusius. "Keres," in Roscher 2:1136–1166.
> Rainer Vollkommer. "Ker," in *LIMC* 6:14–23.

Kouretes dancing, with infant Zeus in the background.

Kouretes dancing around infant Zeus.

KOURETES
(LATINIZED FORM CURETES)

Male nature deities.

The Kouretes are obscure minor divinities, nature spirits of some sort, for according to Hesiod (frag. 123 MW) the oreads, or mountain nymphs, are their sisters and the satyrs are their brothers. He describes the Kouretes as "playful dancers."

Kouretes and nymphs worked together to nurture and protect baby Zeus. When Rhea gave birth to her youngest child, Zeus, she hid him in a cave on Crete in order to conceal him from her husband Kronos, who otherwise swallowed each of their children as they were born. She placed her infant in the charge of the Kouretes and certain nymphs. While the nymphs nourished the child with the milk of the goat Amaltheia, the Kouretes guarded him and beat their spears against their shields in order to drown out his voice so that Kronos would not hear him (Apollodoros *Library* 1.1.6–7; cf. Hyginus *Fabulae* 139).

Suggested reading:

Timothy Gantz. *Early Greek Myth: A Guide to Literary and Artistic Sources.* Baltimore: The Johns Hopkins University Press, 1993, 147–148.
Ruth Lindner. "Kouretes, Korybantes," in *LIMC* 8:736–741.

KRONOS (ROMAN SATURN)

Titan god who preceded Zeus as ruler of the gods.

Kronos was the youngest of the twelve Titans, offspring of Ouranos and Gaia. He overthrew his father Ouranos (Sky) as ruler of the gods and was overthrown in turn by his own son Zeus.

In his *Theogony*, Hesiod recounts how Ouranos, hating his children, prevented each new child from being born, apparently by engaging in continual sexual intercourse with Gaia. Groaning from the pain of unending labor, Gaia created a great adamantine sickle with teeth and conspired with her children to punish their father. Only the youngest Titan was willing to undertake the task. From within his mother, the crafty Kronos lopped off his father's genitals with the sickle. Presumably this act effected the permanent separation of Gaia and Ouranos, or Earth and Sky, allowing Gaia space to give birth, thereby liberating the Titans.

Now king of the gods, Kronos mated with his sister Rhea, who bore him six children. Having, however, learned from his parents, Gaia and Ouranos, that his own son was fated to overthrow him, Kronos swallowed each of his children as they were born. Rhea in grief appealed to her parents to help her bear her next son in secret and to punish Kronos for his behavior toward his father, Ouranos, and toward his children. Gaia and Ouranos revealed to her what was fated, sending her to Crete to deliver her child, and Gaia hid the babe in a cave. Rhea gave Kronos a stone wrapped in swaddling clothes, which he swallowed in the belief that it was his son.

A year later, when Zeus was fully grown, Kronos was tricked into taking an emetic, which caused him to vomit up what he had swallowed, first the stone and then his children. A battle for supremacy took place between the older gods or Titans, led by Kronos, and the younger gods or Olympians, led by Zeus, which the Olympians and their allies eventually won, imprisoning the Titans in Tartaros.

Although Kronos was a tyrant among the immortals, he was a benevolent monarch among mortals, for it was during his reign that the Golden Generation lived (Hesiod *Works and Days* 111), a happy period of peace, leisure, and abundance. Consequently, Kronos now rules as king of the Isles of the Blessed (*Works and Days* 173a), since life in the Isles of the Blessed is much like life as it was in the Golden Age. Zeus had released his father from Tartaros and granted him this honor.

Some ancient scholars derived the name Kronos from the Greek word *chronos* ("time"), so that Kronos, personified as Father Time, was sometimes represented as an old man carrying a scythe. The two words are not etymologically related, however.

The Romans identified their god Saturn (Latin *Saturnus*) with Greek Kronos.

See also Elysion Field and Isles of the Blessed; Luminaries; Myth of the Ages;
    Succession Myth; Titans

Suggested reading:

François Baratte. "Saturnus," in *LIMC* 8:1078–1089.
Maximilian Mayer. "Kronos," in Roscher 2:1452–1573.
Eleutheria D. Serbet. "Kronos," in *LIMC* 6:142–147.

LABYRINTH (GREEK LABYRINTHOS)

Fabulous building structured as a maze.

The Labyrinth was constructed by the ingenious inventor Daidalos (Latinized form = Daedalus) for King Minos of Crete, who employed it as a kind of prison. It is the site of several notable mythological adventures.

According to the mythographer Apollodoros, the Labyrinth was a building constructed on Crete by the clever craftsman and inventor Daidalos. The complexity of its passageways prevented anyone who entered it from discovering the way out again. Minos kept the monstrous Minotaur imprisoned in it. With the help of Minos's daughter Ariadnê, however, the Athenian youth Theseus managed to kill the Minotaur and find his way out of the maze, for at the advice of Daidalos she gave Theseus a clew of thread, one end of which he tied to the door of the Labyrinth when he entered it. After locating the Minotaur deep within the maze and killing him, Theseus traced the thread back to the door again and was able to exit.

Holding Daidalos responsible for Theseus's success, Minos imprisoned him and his son Ikaros (Latinized form = Icarus) in the Labyrinth. But the clever Daidalos constructed wings from feathers and glue for himself and his son, warning him to fly neither too high where the sun might melt the glue, nor too low where the moisture might loosen the feathers. But Ikaros ignored his father's instructions, flew higher and higher until the glue melted, and plunged to his death in the sea below, which thereafter was called after him the Icarian Sea (Apollodoros *Library* 3.1.4, 3.15.8, *Epitome* 1.7–9, 12–13).

Theseus and the Minotaur are often shown in ancient art, and the Cretan Labyrinth is represented as a formal maze or its nature is suggested by a mazelike pattern. As a common noun in the classical period, *labyrinthos* referred either to a building of intricate and potentially confusing design or to an actual maze.

See also Fabulous Peoples and Places; Theseus

Suggested reading:

Arthur B. Cook. *Zeus: A Study in Ancient Religion.* Cambridge: Cambridge University Press, 1914–1940, 1:472–490, 3:1086–1087.

Penelope Doob. *The Idea of the Labyrinth from Classical Antiquity through the Middle Ages.* Ithaca, NY: Cornell University Press, 1990.

William Hansen. *Ariadne's Thread: A Guide to International Tales Found in Classical Literature.* Ithaca, NY: Cornell University Press, 2002, 158–159.

O. Höfer. "Labyrinthos," in Roscher 2:1778–1783.

Wm. Henry Matthews. *Mazes and Labyrinths: A General Account of Their History and Developments.* London: Longmans, Green, 1922.

LUMINARIES

Bright celestial phenomena visible from earth.

In Greek mythology the planets and stars are mostly living beings, either gods who have been in the sky ever since they first came into existence or human beings whom the gods have placed in the sky.

The principal divine luminaries of mythological interest are Helios (Sun), Selenê (Moon), and Eos (Dawn), who are siblings, offspring of the Titans Hyperion and Theia.

Eos pursuing Kephalos.

Sometimes also Hemera (Day) and its complement Nyx (Night) are treated as independent divine beings rather than as states connected with the presence or absence of sunlight. In both Greek and Latin, the noun *sun* is grammatically masculine, whereas *moon, dawn, day,* and *night* are feminine, so that Sun is a male deity, whereas Moon, Dawn, Day, and Night are female deities.

Helios is the personified sun, and similarly his Roman name, Sol, is simply the Latin word for *sun.* He traverses the sky daily in his chariot. The ancients were no more troubled about how Helios's chariot travels in the sky than Americans today are troubled about how Santa Claus's sleigh flies through the air. Since the Greeks did not picture the earth as a sphere, they did not envision Helios as traveling in an orbit around a globe, but rather as crossing the sky daily from east to west and then returning nightly to his eastern starting place by sailing halfway around the flat earth on the River Okeanos. Helios has a view of

Helios riding in his chariot.

all that transpires upon the earth, rather like a modern spy-satellite, so that he "sees and hears everything," as Homer says (*Odyssey* 12.323). Consequently it is natural for him to play the role of informant in narratives. In the myth of Ares and Aphroditê, Helios is aware of the covert affair of the two lovers and informs the cuckolded husband Hephaistos (*Odyssey* 8.270–271, 302), and in the myth of Demeter and Persephonê he knows of the abduction of Persephonê by Hades (*Homeric Hymn to Demeter* 62–89).

Helios possesses herds of cattle and flocks of sheep on the island of Thrinakia, and he takes pleasure in seeing them each day as he rises and sets in the sky. They are tended by two nymphs, Phaethousa and Lampetiê, daughters of Helios by Neaira (Homer *Odyssey* 12.131–136). When Odysseus's starving companions slaughter some of the animals, Helios demands revenge, threatening to leave the sky, descend to Hades' realm, and shine instead for the dead. Zeus quickly agrees to avenge Helios's loss (*Odyssey* 12.374–388). As the daily bearer of light to the world, Helios is a manifest part of the order of the cosmos, so that a threat to cease bringing light to the world is a threat to overturn cosmic order itself.

The sun-god has sons and daughters by different mates. The Okeanid Perseis bore him the sorceress Kirkê (Latinized form = Circê) and a son Aietes, father in turn of the sorceress Medeia (Latinized form = Medea) by the Okeanid Idyia (*Theogony* 956–962). Aietes became king of Kolchis, where in a sacred grove the famed Golden Fleece was kept. Another daughter of Helios and Neaira was Pasiphaê, who wed King Minos of Crete (Apollodoros *Library* 3.1.2–4). Another notable offspring of the deity was Phaethon, born to him by the nymph Clymenê (Greek *Klymenê*). Doubting that the sun was indeed his father, Phaethon sought out the god in his palace, and as proof of his paternity Phoebus swore to grant him any wish. The youth unwisely chose to drive the chariot of the sun across the sky. The attempt ended in near disaster for the cosmos and in death for the daring youth (Ovid *Metamorphoses* 1.750–2.400).

Among the god's epithets is Phoibos (Latinized form = Phoebus), which is also an epithet of Apollon. It signifies "radiant." The shared epithet has fostered the notion that Apollon is a sun-god, but in classical mythology Helios and Apollon are always distinct characters. Hyperion is sometimes the name of Helios's father but at other times an epithet of Helios himself.

Selenê is the personified moon, called Luna (moon) by the Romans. She crosses the sky during the night on her chariot or wagon, or sitting astride a horse. Selenê fell in love with Endymion, an exceptionally handsome youth, and bore him fifty daughters. When Zeus permitted Endymion to choose whatever he wished, he chose to sleep forever, unaging and deathless (Apollodoros *Library* 1.7.5; Pausanias 5.1.4).

Selenê riding a mule.

Selenê riding a ram.

Endymion sleeping.

Eos is the personified dawn, with the memorable Homeric epithets "rosey-fin-gered" and "saffron-robed." To the Romans she is Aurora (dawn). Rising from her bed each morning, she brings light to mortals and immortals. According to Homer, Eos has her house and dancing places on Aiaia (*Odyssey* 12.3–4) and dwells beside

Eos carrying away a child.

the River Ocean (*Iliad* 11.1–2, 19.1–2). The principal winds—Zephyros (west wind), Boreas (north wind), and Notos (south wind)—are the offspring of Eos and Astraios (Hesiod *Theogony* 378–380). Eos is an unusually erotic goddess who carries different mortal men away, usually to be her lovers. Once she bore off the handsome hunter Orion and enjoyed his love. But Artemis slew him because of the jealousy the gods felt at Eos's having a mortal lover (Homer *Odyssey* 5.118–124). On another occasion she took the mortal male Tithonos, a member of the Trojan royal house, to her bedside to be her spouse in her distant dwelling place, and according to Homer she arises each morning from her bed beside him (*Iliad* 11.1–2, *Odyssey* 5.1–2). She asked Zeus that Tithonos be granted immortality, and Zeus fulfilled her wish. But she forgot to ask that Tithonos also have eternal youth. So long as he was young, she delighted in his bed, but when he became an old man, she avoided his embrace, and when finally he lacked the strength even to lift a limb, she put him away in a chamber (*Homeric Hymn to Aphrodite* 216–238). Tithonos and Eos had a son, Memnon, who perished in the Trojan War. She still weeps for him, her tears appearing on the earth as dew.

Although individual stars such as the Morning Star (the planet Venus) are the offspring of Eos and Astraios (*Theogony* 381–382), constellations are humans, animals, and objects that the gods have translated from the earth to the sky and made immortal. Among those mentioned by the early poets are the Pleiades, the Hyades, Orion, and the Great Bear, the easily recognized constellation Ursa Major, part of which is known familiarly today as the Big Dipper or as the Wain or Wagon. Each constellation is the result of a catasterism in the mythological past, a translation by the gods of someone or something earthly to a station among the stars. The celestial wonders move across the vault of the sky, some chasing another or concluding their descent along the vault of the sky with a dip into the waters of the River Ocean. So Zeus once transformed the nymph Kallisto into a bear and subsequently placed her in the sky as the Bear, where now the hunter Orion, who also was placed there by a god, pursues her but never catches her.

Eos and Tithonos.

See also Catasterism; Translation

Suggested reading:

Fr. Boll and Hans Georg Gundel. "Sternbilder, Sternglaube und Sternsymbolik bei Griechen und Römern," in Roscher 6:867–1071.

Theony Condos. *Star Myths of the Greeks and Romans: A Sourcebook.* Grand Rapids, MI: Phanes Press, 1997.

Joseph Fontenrose. "Apollo and Sol in the Latin Poets of the First Century B.C.," *Transactions of the American Philological Association* 70 (1939): 439–455.

———. "Apollo and the Sun-God in Ovid." *American Journal of Philology* 61 (1940): 429–444.

Alfred Jeremias. "Sterne," in Roscher 4:1427–1500.

A. Rapp. "Eos," in Roscher 1:1252–1278.

———. "Helios," in Roscher 1:1993–2026.

W. H. Roscher. "Selene," in Roscher 4:642–650.

MAENADS (GREEK MAINADES)

Bacchantes, or ecstatic female worshippers of Dionysos.

Etymologically the term *maenads* signifies "mad women" or "raving women," and in the same spirit they are also known as *thyiades* (frenzied women). In contrast, the term *bacchae* (Greek *bakchai*), connected with Bacchus (Greek *Bakchos*), a name of Dionysos, refers to their connection with their god rather than to their behavior or state of mind, and *bacchantes*, derived from Latin, has the same meaning. Regardless of the term employed, legends and an-

Maenads reveling with satyrs.

cient commentators ascribe various extreme behaviors to the female votaries of Dionysos.

In mythological Bacchanalia, the bacchantes go in groups to the mountains (Greek *oreibasia* "mountain-going"). Dressed in fawn-skins (*nebrizein*), carrying a special wand called a thyrsus (*thyrsos*), and surrounded by the music of castanets, drums, and the *aulos*, a clarinet-like instrument traditionally translated as "flute," they loosen their hair, shake their heads, utter cries such as "euhoi," and dance, entering a trancelike state of ecstasy and enthusiasm (*enthousiasmos*, "possession"). Honey flows from their thyrsi, which can also serve as magical conduits. If a maenad strikes the ground with her thyrsus, milk or wine or honey springs forth; if she strikes a man, he is wounded as though by a weapon (Euripides *Bacchae* 704–713, 762–764). In the climax of the rite, at least in mythological narrative, the maenads take hold of an animal, tearing it apart with their bare hands (*sparagmos*, "tearing apart") and consuming it raw (*omophagia*, "raw-eating"). Their homeward descent may be frenzied, for Demeter is once described as rushing down a mountain like a maenad (*Homeric Hymn to Demeter* 386).

In some mythological narratives, Dionysos tours the world spreading his cult, and in these stories the inhabitants of a community respond positively or negatively to the sudden appearance in their community of the god and his unusual rites, either celebrating or opposing Dionysos. Persons who deny his divinity or disparage the nature of his worship may be divinely punished. Thus when King Pentheus opposed Dionysos on the occasion of his arrival at Thebes, the very home of Dionysos's mother Semelê, the god induced

Pentheus to spy upon the rites of the Bacchae and then caused the Bacchae to perceive Pentheus as a animal, with the result that the frenzied celebrants discovered Pentheus and tore him apart in the belief that he was a lion (Euripides *Bacchae*). Thus the role of the victim in the shocking rite of *sparagmos* is played, not by a wild animal, but by the god's opponent. The fate of Pentheus is much like that of another intruder, the hunter Aktaion, whom the goddess Artemis actually transformed into an animal, after which his own hounds tore him apart in the belief that he was a stag.

Orpheus was similarly torn apart by maenads, whether in the context of a Bacchanalia or not is unclear. After Orpheus lost his beloved wife Eurydikê a second time, he avoided all dealings with women, giving his love instead to young men. When once a group of maenads spot-

Orpheus attacked by maenads.

ted him, they rushed at him and tore him apart in their anger at his rejection of women (Apollodoros *Library* 1.3.2; Ovid *Metamorphoses* 10.78–85, 11.1–84).

In addition to human worshippers of Dionysos, satyrs and Bacchae or maenads also accompany the deity regularly as a part of his comitatus (Apollodoros *Library* 3.5.1; Ovid *Metamorphoses* 11.89). These females, understood as supernaturals, possibly include nymphs from Mount Nysa, who nursed Dionysos as an infant. Maenads, or at least female figures classified by modern scholars as maenads, are commonly represented in vase paintings as frolicking with satyrs.

See also Dionysos; Orpheus

Suggested reading:

Synnøve des Bouvrie. "Euripides' *Bakkhai* and Maenadism." *Classica et Mediaevalia* 48 (1977): 75–114.

Jan Bremmer. "Greek Maenadism Reconsidered." *Zeitschrift für Papyrologie und Epigraphik* 55 (1984): 267–286.

E. R. Dodds, comm. *Euripides: Bacchae.* 2nd ed. Oxford: Clarendon Press, 1960.

———. *The Greeks and the Irrational.* Berkeley: University of California Press, 1951, 270–282.

Timothy Gantz. *Early Greek Myth: A Guide to Literary and Artistic Sources.* Baltimore: The Johns Hopkins University Press, 1993, 142–143.

Albert Henrichs. "Greek Maenadism from Olympias to Messalina." *Harvard Studies in Classical Philology* 82 (1978): 121–160.

Ingrid Kranskopf et al. "Mainades," in *LIMC* 8:780–803.

MELEAGER (GREEK MELEAGROS)

Youth fated to live only so long as a particular piece of wood was not consumed by fire.

According to the mythographer Apollodoros, a son, Meleager, was born to King Oineus of Calydon and his wife, Althaia. When Meleager was seven days old, the Moirai (Fates) came to the house and declared that Meleager would die when a particular piece of wood in the hearth was burned up. Hearing this, Althaia picked up the firebrand and stored it away in a chest. Meleager grew up invulnerable. One day when Oineus was sacrificing to the gods, however, he neglected Artemis, who in her anger sent a huge boar into the land of the Calydonians. In the course of the boar-hunt that had been organized to slay the animal, Meleager got into an angry dispute with his maternal uncles and killed them. In her grief at the destruction of her brothers, Althaia deliberately burned the firebrand, whereupon Meleager immediately died (*Library* 1.8.2–3).

The Calydonian legend of Meleager is a form of the international story of a person whose life span is mystically bound up in something consumable such as a candle.

> **See also** Divine Guilds; Hunters
> **Suggested reading:**
> Antti Aarne and Stith Thompson. *The Types of the Folktale: A Classification and Bibliography.* FF Communications 184. Helsinki: Academia Scientiarum Fennica, 1961, Type 1187: *Meleager.*
> Rolf W. Brednich. *Volkserzählungen und Volksglaube von den Schicksalsfrauen.* FF Communications 193. Helsinki: Academia Scientiarum Fennica, 1964, 17–31.
> William Hansen. "Homer and the Folktale," in *A New Companion to Homer,* edited by Ian Morris and Barry Powell. Leiden: Brill, 1997, 452–453.
> Jennifer R. March. *The Creative Poet: Studies on the Treatment of Myths in Greek Poetry.* London: University of London, Institute of Classical Studies, 1987, 27–46.
> Susan Woodford et al. "Meleagros," in *LIMC* 6:414–435.

MIDAS

King who was granted the power to turn whatever he touched into gold.

According to Ovid, King Midas of Lydia did Bacchus a favor, in return for which the god offered to grant him anything he wished. Midas asked that anything he touched should turn to gold, and Bacchus reluctantly gave him the gift he sought. At first Midas delighted in seeing everything he touched change to gold, but when he found to his dismay that also food and drink turned to gold at his touch, so that he was unable to eat or drink, he prayed to Bacchus to restore him to his former condition, which the kind god did, instructing him to wash in the stream that flowed past Sardis. Midas did so and was cured, his golden touch passing into the waters, so that to this day the neighboring fields are hard and yellow.

But Midas's folly brought him to harm a second time. Pan and Apollo once engaged in a contest of music, Pan playing his rustic pipes and Apollo his refined lyre. Although the judge declared Apollo to be the winner, Midas disagreed. Apollo, concluding that such insensitive ears did not deserve to be human, changed them into ass's ears. Ashamed of his bestial ears, Midas kept them concealed under a turban. Only the slave who cut his hair knew his secret, and since he did not dare to reveal it but also was unable to keep to himself, he dug a hole in the ground and whispered the truth about his master's ears in it. Reeds grew up from the ground, and stirred by gentle breezes they repeated the buried words, giving Midas's secret away (*Metamorphoses* 11.100–193).

The story of the golden touch and the story of the ass's ears are both morality tales about foolish behavior and its consequences. The former is built upon the theme of the foolish wish, which appears frequently in classical mythology: Semelê's unwisely asking her lover, Zeus, to appear to her as he appears to Hera; Phaethon's unwisely asking his father, Helios, to let him drive the solar chariot; Eos's asking Zeus to grant her lover, Tithonos, immortality without also asking that he not age. In the latter, Midas's poor judgment in music induced Apollo to give him ass's ears because the donkey was a conventional symbol of stupidity.

The two stories are international tales that became attached to Midas as a king of Phrygia. Since they are set in the historical period, the Midas legends belong to a later period than that in which most mythological narratives are set. Their frequent inclusion in compilations of classical mythology is probably due to their inherent appeal as stories and to their appearance in Ovid's much-read *Metamorphoses*.

Suggested reading:

Antti Aarne and Stith Thompson. *The Types of the Folktale: A Classification and Bibliography.* FF Communications 184. Helsinki: Academia Scientiarum Fennica, 1961, Types 775: *Midas' Short-Sighted Wish* and 782: *Midas and the Ass's Ears.*

Maja Bošković-Stulli. "Midas," in *Enzyklopädie des Märchens.* Berlin: Walter de Gruyter, 1999, 9:633–641.

W. Crooke. "King Midas and His Ass's Ears." *Folk-Lore* 22 (1911):183–202.

Margaret C. Miller. "Midas," in *LIMC* 8:846–851.

Lynn Roller. "The Legend of Midas." *Classical Antiquity* 2 (1983): 299–313.

MONSTERS

Fabulous and usually frightening beings that typically are unnaturally large in size and/or composed of elements proper to more than one natural being.

Morphologically speaking, nearly all monsters appearing in classical myth and legend can be generated by three or fewer rules, namely, increase the size of a naturally occurring creature, multiply a body part, and/or combine body parts from two or more creatures. In short: magnification, multiplication, and mixing.

By and large the messages of monster morphology are straightforward (cf. Burkert 1979, 20). Largeness in a hostile being is frightening because it is overwhelming. Since qualities are often represented quantitatively in traditional story, multiple body parts convey intensity in a particular respect (many eyes = wondrous eyesight, many arms = wondrous strength, and so on). Composite beings combine the properties of different beings, such as the strength of a lion, the terrifying aspect of a serpent, and a bird's ability to fly. In addition, monsters can possess unusual properties that are not morphological. The hide of the Nemean Lion is invulnerable, so that the animal cannot be pierced; Typhon's eyes and mouth emit fire. The most elemental narrative function of evil monsters is to threaten order and safety by means of their frightening, formidable, and aggressive power, providing an opportunity for heroes to overcome them and so to manifest thereby their strength or cleverness in the service of good.

Characters in a traditional story tend to have little interiority, especially secondary characters, and monsters are particularly likely to be opaque. What was the Sphinx thinking when she proposed her riddle to the Thebans? What motivates dragons to guard springs?

Animals that are monstrous in the sense only of great magnitude appear in many legends. An example is the Calydonian Boar, a huge wild beast that Artemis in her anger sent against the Calydonians, prompting their king to form a hunting party of youths from all over Greece. Simple monsters often take their name from their locality. So the Calydonian Boar, the Krommyon Sow, the Marathonian Bull, the Teumessian Fox, and so on.

Stranger than unnaturally huge creatures are beings with multiple body parts, such as the three-headed hound of the death realm, Kerberos (Latinized form = Cerberus), and the Hundred-Handers (Greek *Hekatoncheires*), equipped with fifty arms on each side of their body.

Most striking of all are composite beings that mix parts of several natural creatures, such as the Minotaur, which has the body of a man and the head of a bull. Composite beings can be classified according to the complexity of the mix, ranging from those that draw upon two different creatures to those that draw upon three or even four. Monsters and other fabulous creatures that are mixes of two beings include centaurs (horse + man), Harpies (bird + woman), Minotaur (bull + man), Pan (man + goat), Pegasos (horse + bird), satyrs (man + horse), Sirens (bird + woman), and Scylla (dog + woman). Monsters drawing upon three different beings include the Chimaera (lion + goat + serpent), the Sphinx (lion + woman + bird), and Typhon (man + serpent + bird). Few monsters draw upon four, but a Gorgon (woman + serpent + bird + boar) is an example. Some monsters vary in recipe. Thus a Sphinx may be represented in one place as having a leonine body and bird's wings but no human face, and in another place as possessing a leonine body and woman's face but no wings.

A glance at the recipes reveals a cultural preference for certain animals and an avoidance of others. Lions, serpents, and birds, which offer respectively strength, terror, and flight, are favorite ingredients, whereas insects, so popular in modern science fiction, are entirely ignored in Greco-Roman tradition. Overall, monstrosity often implies greater quantity—bigger size, more limbs, borrowed parts—rather than the contrary, but the Cyclopes with their single eye are the exception. Several composite monsters attested in ancient lore play no role in mythology. Examples are the griffin (Greek *gryps*), a mix of eagle and lion, and the hippalectryon, a mix of horse and rooster.

Here follows a brief survey in alphabetical order of the better known monsters of classical mythology, indicated by boldface type.

In form, **Argos** (Latinized form = Argus) is an android with 200 eyes. He functions as a guard in the story of Io, difficult to deceive because he has no blind spot and never fully sleeps, many eyes always being open. Mercury, however, lulled Argos to sleep with music and beheaded him (Ovid *Metamorphoses* 1.624–723). In mythological art, Argos is depicted as a humanoid male with eyes distributed over his body.

Cerberus (Greek Kerberos), the multiheaded dog of the death realm, allows persons to pass into Erebos but not to exit (Hesiod *Theogony* 305–312, 767–774), acting as a kind of watchdog in reverse. In narrative he figures only in the legend in which Herakles, as one of his labors, fetched the monstrous hound from the land of the dead and later returned it. **Orthos** is a two-headed watchdog belonging to the herdsman Eurytion, both of whom figure in a labor of Herakles, the fetching of the Cattle of Geryon (Apollodoros *Library* 2.5.10).

The **Chimaera** (Greek Chimaira) is a composite being having the body and head of a lion, the tail of a serpent, and, arising from its back, a goat's head (the Greek noun *chimaira* signifies "she-goat"). The semiotics of the goat is unobvious and has been variously explained. Like several other monsters, the Chimaera breathes fire. The creature appears in the legend of Bellerophon, who slew it (Homer *Iliad* 6.178–183).

According to Homer, the huge, one-eyed, cannibalistic **Cyclopes** (Greek Kyklopes) dwell in a community somewhere on the shores of the Mediterranean Sea, where Odysseus visited them in the course of his return home from Troy. They are haughty in nature, display minimal political or social organization, and have little technology, emblematized by the fact that they live in caves. The particular Cyclops whose cave Odysseus came upon was Polyphemos, a son of Poseidon (Homer *Odyssey* 6.1–6, 9.105–564), which shows that a Cyclops can be produced by a non-Cyclopean parent. But Hesiod represents the Cyclopes as three huge, one-eyed sons of Ouranos and Gaia named Brontes, Steropes, and Arges, brothers of the similarly huge Hundred-Handers. They supply Zeus with the thunderbolts upon which his cosmic supremacy depends (Hesiod *Theogony* 139–146, 501–506).

Dragons (Greek *drakon*, "serpent") are found in a number of myths and legends. Ancient authors use the term of any large serpent or any composite creature with a large proportion of serpent. The huge serpent Python appears in the myth of the foundation of Delphi by Apollon, who slew him, and similarly the Dragon of Ares, likewise a huge serpent, appears in the legend of Kadmos (Latinized form = Cadmus) and was killed by him. The dragon Delphynê, part woman and part serpent, plays a role in the myth of Typhon and Zeus. Frequently dragons are the solitary, terrifying guardians of something desirable, such as a place that is suitable for a city or sanctuary. The Dragon of Ares guarded a spring at the site of the future city of Thebes; the dragon Python guarded the site of the future sanctuary of Apollon at Delphi; Delphynê guarded Zeus's sinews, which her consort Typhon had removed from the god; and the multiheaded serpent Ladon still guards the Golden Apple Tree of the gods. Although dragons appear in several myths and legends, they are individually unique creatures, not being related to one another and not forming a community.

Part lovely nymph and part monstrous serpent, **Echidna** dwells by herself in a cave. With her consort, Typhon, she is the mother of many monsters (Hesiod *Theogony* 295–332).

Geryoneus, or **Geryon**, is a three-headed android whom Herakles kills (Hesiod *Theogony* 287–294).

The **Gorgons**, daughters of Phorkys and Keto, possess bodies like those of human women, snakes as hair, boar's tusks, and wings. Whereas the Gorgons Sthenno and Euryalê are immortal and ageless, Medusa (Greek *Medousa*) was born mortal and perished when she was decapitated by the hero Perseus (Hesiod *Theogony* 270–286). Anyone who looks upon a Gorgon is transformed into stone, becoming in effect a statue. A Gorgon's head, or at least that of Medusa, has other unusual properties also. Displaying a lock of hair from a Gorgon can cause an army to scatter in fright, and Gorgon's blood was used by the physician Asklepios sometimes to heal and sometimes to injure his patients (Apollodoros *Library* 2.7.3, 3.10.3)

The **Harpies** (Greek *Harpyiai*, "Snatchers") are two sisters, Aello and Okypetê, who are part bird and part woman (Hesiod *Theogony* 265–269). In art they are represented as having the face and breasts of a woman and the body of a bird, like Sirens. They snatch humans and carry them away so that they are never seen again; thus they carried off the daughters of Pandareos (Homer *Odyssey* 20.77). The Harpies play a different role in the legend of the Argonauts. Angry at the seer Phineus for a particular offense, the gods blinded him and also dispatched the Harpies, "hounds of great Zeus," to torment him, which they did by snatching up much of his food and befouling the rest (presumably they defecated upon it). When the Argonauts wished to consult Phineus about their route, he offered to help them in return for their ridding him of the Harpies, whereupon two of the Argonauts, Zetes and Kalais, chased the Harpies off (Apollonios of Rhodes *Argonautika* 2.178–300).

The **Hundred-Handers** (Greek *Hekatoncheires*) are three powerful sons of Ouranos (Sky) and Gaia (Earth) named Kottos, Briareos, and Gyges. They each possess a hundred arms and fifty heads, making them formidable warriors in the Titanomachy, or battle of the Olympians against the Titans (Hesiod *Theogony* 147–153, 617–735). Monstrous in form but not in character, the Hundred-Handers are allies of the Olympian gods.

The **Hydra of Lerna** is a huge, nine-headed water snake slain by Herakles as one of his labors (Hesiod *Theogony* 313–318; Apollodoros *Library* 2.5.2).

The **Minotaur** (Greek *Minotauros*, "Minos-Bull") is the monstrous offspring of a bull and a human woman. King Minos of Crete once sacrificed to Poseidon, asking the god to send him a bull from the sea and promising to sacrifice it. Poseidon sent up a fine bull, but Minos kept it and sacrificed a different bull. So Poseidon angrily made the original bull savage and caused Minos's wife, Pasiphaê, to conceive a sexual passion for it. She satisfied her passion with the aid of the clever craftsman Daidalos, who constructed a hollow cow out of wood, covered it with cowhide, and placed it in a meadow, instructing Pasiphaê to enter it. The bull had sexual intercourse with her, and she gave birth to a creature that had the face of a bull and the body of a human male. He was called the Minotaur, though his given name was Asterios. Minos shut him up and kept him under guard in the Labyrinth (Apollodoros *Library* 3.1.3–4). His only narrative role is in the legend of Theseus, in which the hero slew him. The form of the Minotaur is exceptional among Greek mixes of human and beast, which favor a human upper body and a bestial lower body.

Scylla (Greek *Skylla*) and **Charybdis** are two neighboring monsters, the former a mix of woman and dogs, the latter a personified whirlpool. A ship passing their way had to choose to sail close either to Scylla or to Charybdis, a predica-

Sphinxes.

ment that became proverbial for a dilemma in which neither option is attractive. High upon a sheer cliff there was a cave that ran down to Erebos, and in it dwelled Scylla. Her upper body protruded from her cave, her twelve feet and her six long necks dangling in the air, each neck ending in a head with three rows of teeth. Making a sound like that of a newborn puppy (the name Scylla resembles the Greek word for "puppy"), she fished from her lair for passing dolphins, seals, and men, and indeed she captured and ate several of Odysseus's companions as they sailed by. A short distance away there was another rock, below which was an even worse danger, Charybdis, who three times a days sucked the water down and three times a day spewed it back up again (Homer *Odyssey* 12.73–126, 201–259, 426–446).

Like the Harpies, the **Sirens** (Greek *Seirenes*) have the body of a bird and the visage of a human woman. Their best-known appearance in mythology is their encounter with Odysseus and his companions as the men sailed past them on their homeward journey from Troy. They sing an alluring song, which for some reason is dangerous for men to hear, or at least to respond to, for Odysseus was instructed to plug his men's ears with wax as they sailed by; he himself, if he wished to hear the Sirens' song, had to be tied securely to the mast of his ship (Homer *Odyssey* 12:39–54, 158–200).

The **Sphinx** is a composite female monster, having the body of a lion, the face of a woman, and the wings of a bird. Hera sent her against the Thebans. Perched on a nearby mountain, she propounded a riddle that she had learned from the Muses, and each time the citizens failed to solve her riddle, she devoured a male Theban. But Oedipus solved it, whereupon the monster killed herself (Apollodoros *Library* 3.5.8).

Sphinxes.

Talos is an oddity among Greek monsters, being a man of bronze and so not a composite of natural creatures. Either a lone survivor of the Bronze Generation or a creature presented to King Minos by Hephaistos, Talos guarded Crete by running around it three times a day, pelting with stones any person who would land there. Talos perished when, by deceit or magic or accident, his single vein was opened up so that his ichor gushed out (Apollonios of Rhodes *Argonautika* 4.1636–1686; Apollodoros *Library* 1.9.26). Other legendary monsters with metallic parts are the two huge **bulls** in Kolchis that Jason had to

Sphinx with victim.

yoke as a prerequisite for receiving the Golden Fleece from King Aietes. The bulls, a gift to Aietes from Hephaistos, had bronze hooves and breathed fire (*Library* 1.9.23). The fact that the brazen-hoofed bulls were a gift from the god Hephaistos, as in one tradition the brazen Talos also was, indicates that they were created by the craftsman god himself.

Typhon (also Typhaon, Typhoeus) is a monster par excellence. He is so tall that his head brushes the stars, and his reach is so great that with his outstretched arms he touches the east and the west. Typhon's upper body is that of a man, while his arms and lower body are bestial. His arms end in a hundred dragons' heads, and beneath his waist his body consists of immense, coiled, hissing vipers. Fire flashes from his eyes and mouth. Powerful, aggressive, and violent,

Zeus, thunderbolt in hand, battling Typhon.

Leto, holding her infants, flees from Python.

Typhon challenged the gods and temporarily overcame Zeus, but in the end Zeus vanquished him, casting Mount Etna upon him, which still smolders from the thunderbolts thrown by the god (Apollodoros *Library* 1.6.3). Hesiod connects Typhon with destructive winds (*Theogony* 869–880), tempting one to see an etymological connection between the word *typhoon* and Typhon, but *typhoon* derives ultimately from Chinese.

Most monstrous beings in classical mythology are unique creatures rather than members of self-reproducing communities and play a role in a single myth or legend. Thus Python belongs to the myth of Apollon, the Chimaera to the legend of Bellerophon, the Gorgons to the story of Perseus, and so on. A very few make up self-reproducing communities such as the Cyclopes, whose land Odysseus visited on his way home from Troy.

See also Centaurs and Hippocentaurs; Divine Guilds; Satyrs and Silens

Suggested reading:

Catherine Atherton, ed. *Monsters and Monstrosity in Greek and Roman Culture.* Nottingham Classical Literature Studies, Midland Classical Literature Studies, 6. Bari: Levante, 2002.

John Boardman. "'Very Like a Whale'—Classical Sea Monsters," in *Monsters and Demons in the Ancient and Medieval Worlds: Papers Presented in Honor of Edith Porada*, edited by Ann E. Farkas, Prudence O. Harper, and Evelyn B. Harrison. Mainz on Rhein: Philipp von Zabern, 1987, 73–84.

W. Deonna. "Essai sur la genèse des monstres dans l'art." *Revue des Études Grecques* 28 (1915): 288–349.

Lowell Edmunds. *The Sphinx in the Oedipus Legend.* Beiträge zur klassischen Philologie, 127. Königstein: Verlag Anton Hain, 1981.

Ann E. Farkas, Prudence O. Harper, and Evelyn B. Harrison, eds. *Monsters and Demons in the Ancient and Medieval Worlds: Papers Presented in Honour of Edith Porada.* Mainz on Rhein: Philipp von Zabern, 1987.

Joseph Fontenrose. *Python: A Study of Delphic Myth and Its Origins.* Berkeley: University of California Press, 1959.

Gerald Gresseth. "The Homeric Sirens." *TAPA* 101 (1970): 203–218.

Bengt Holbek and Iørn Piø. *Fabeldyr og Sagnfolk.* Copenhagen: Politikens Forlag, 1967.

Adrienne Mayor. *The First Fossil Hunters: Paleontology in Greek and Roman Times.* Princeton: Princeton University Press, 2000.

Simone Mühlemann. "Monstrum," in *Enzyklopädie des Märchens.* Berlin: Walter de Gruyter, 1999, 9:823–829.

Paul Perdrizet. "Hippalectryon." *Revue des Études Anciennes* 6 (1904): 7–30.

MOUNTAINS

Mountains figure prominently as sites of mythological activity.

In contrast to towns, where people live, and plains, where they tend their crops, mountains are mostly wild places. As such, they are the haunts of supernatural beings as well as places where, at a distance from human habitation and cultivation, unusual things happen.

Foremost among mountains as divine residences is Mount Olympos (Latinized form = Olympus), on whose summit the Olympian gods dwell. Although many mountains bore this name anciently, the Olympos of mythological significance is a mountain range in northern Greece around 10,000 feet high, often reaching into the clouds. The Titanomachy, the great battle between the Olympians and the Titans for cosmic dominion, took place on Mount Olympos and on nearby Mount Othrys, where the Titans had their headquarters.

Other mountains are also frequented by supernatural and fabulous beings. The huntress Artemis and the rustic gods Hermes and Pan roam the mountains, and nymphs, satyrs, and centaurs have their homes there. "Give me all the mountains," Artemis asked of her father, Zeus, when she sought her honors and attributes (Kallimachos *Hymn to Artemis* 18). Mount Helikon (Latinized form = Helicon) in particular is a haunt of the Muses, according to Hesiod, who once encountered them there as he pastured his sheep (*Theogony* 1–35). Hermes was born on Mount Kyllenê (Latinized form = Cyllenê), the highest mountain in Arcadia, and Zeus was reared by nymphs on Mount Diktê or Mount Idê (Latinized forms = Dictê, Ida) on Crete. On the Phrygian Mount Idê, the Trojan cowherd Anchises was seduced by Aphroditê, and their child Aineias was reared by the oreads there. Similarly, the centaur Cheiron reared many young heroes in his cave on Mount Pelion, instructing them in the art of hunting and in other matters. Since most hunting took place on mountains, it was while hunting that the youth Aktaion (Latinized form = Actaeon) chanced to come upon Artemis bathing on Mount Kithairon (Latinized form = Cithaeron), just as on a different occasion the youth Teiresias and his hounds similarly came upon Athena as she was refreshing herself in a spring on Mount Helikon.

Wild places can be violent places. Hunters who stumble upon bathing goddesses come to a bad end. The angry Artemis transformed Aktaion into a deer, whereupon his own hounds, not recognizing him, tore him apart (Apollodoros *Library* 3.4.4), and Athena blinded Teiresias for having viewed her unclothed, but yielding to the pleas of his mother, she compensated for his loss of sight by making him a seer and granting him a long life (Kallimachos *Hymn* 5). It was on Mount Kithairon that the maenads, celebrating the mountain-rites of Dionysos, tore apart another quasi-voyeur, King Pentheus, in the mistaken belief that he was a wild animal (Euripides *Bacchae*).

All in all, the usual rules do not apply on mountains. Supernatural beings abound, females hunt and roam freely, and sex is unregulated. Mountains offer more adventure and more danger than do towns and plains.

Although mountains function in classical mythology primarily as sites, they can also be actors. In his *Theogony* (126–132), Hesiod relates how Gaia (Earth) gave birth by parthenogenesis to Ouranos (Sky), Ourea (Mountains), and Pontos (Sea). Some mountains came into existence later. The god Atlas was transformed into Mount Atlas by Perseus, who petrified him by means of the Gorgon's head after Atlas rudely refused Perseus hospitality (Ovid *Metamorphoses* 4.625–662). Sometimes poets personify a mountain, representing it as responding with grief or fear or joy to a striking event.

See also Hunters
Suggested reading:
Richard Buxton. "Imaginary Greek Mountains." *Journal of Hellenic Studies* 112 (1992): 1–15.
Anneliese Kossatz-Diessmann. "Montes," in *LIMC* 8:854–860.

MYTH OF THE AGES

Myth according to which the cosmos passes through a number of discrete periods of different quality, beginning with a paradisal Golden Age and generally declining thereafter.

According to Hesiod, the gods first made a Golden Race of mortals, who lived when Kronos ruled the world. Their lives were carefree like those of the gods, without pain or old age or toil, for the earth produced abundant food on its own. Eventually the earth hid them away, and they are now benevolent spirits who watch over human deeds upon the earth. After that the Olympians made a Silver Race, much inferior to the preceding. Their childhood lasted a hundred years, after which they lived only a short time as adults, for they were fools and violent to one another, and they ignored the gods. So Zeus angrily hid them away too, and they are blessed mortals beneath the earth. Now Zeus made a third race of mortals from ash trees, a Bronze Race, who were immensely strong and terribly violent. Their armor and houses were of bronze. Conquered by their own hands, they went nameless to the House of Hades. After the earth hid them also, Zeus made a fourth race, which was better and more just, a Race of Heroes, also called demigods. They perished in battle, some at Thebes and other at Troy. Although death was the end for some of them, Zeus settled others on the Isles of the Blessed at the ends of the earth beside the River Ocean. There the earth bears three crops a year, and the heroes live prosperous, carefree lives with Kronos as their king, for Zeus released him.

Next Zeus made a fifth race of mortals, an Iron Race, the present race, and Hesiod says he wishes he had died before or was born after it. This race is marked by toil, pain, and oppression, though some good is mixed with the evil. Zeus will eventually destroy this race also when infants are born with gray hair, when there is strife within families and between friends, when violence and evil dominate and the hubristic man is honored. Then Aidos (Reverence) and Nemesis (Indignation) will abandon human beings in order to join the immortal gods, and only pains will be left for mortal men, and there will be no cure for evil (*Works and Days* 109–201).

Seven centuries later the Roman poet Ovid recounts a different version of the myth. The first humans lived in peaceful leisure in the Golden Age, an age without laws, compulsion, punishments, or weapons. Spring was everlasting, and the earth spontaneously produced abundant food. But after Saturn (Greek Kronos) had been banished and Jove (Greek Zeus) came into power, the Silver Race succeeded its predecessor, less precious than gold but better than bronze. Jove replaced spring with four different seasons, and because of the heat of summer and the cold of winter, humans moved from caves to houses for the sake of shelter, and first worked the soil to produce crops. Third came the Bronze Race, men who more readily resorted to arms but were not evil. Last was the Iron Race, who lived in an age of evil. Truth and Faith fled the earth, replaced by Dishonesty and Violence. Humans sailed the seas, turned commons into private lands, and dug into the earth's interior, revealing hidden wealth, which then provoked men to crime. Wars raged, and respect within families and among friends ceased to exist, until finally Astraea (Justice), the last of the gods, abandoned the earth (*Metamorphoses* 1.89–150).

In the Myth of the Ages, world history is presented as a succession of discrete populations or periods of time, each (except for Hesiod's Race of Heroes) named for a metal. To some extent these ages coincide with historical reality in that there really were a Bronze Age and an Iron Age in the sense of periods during which the principal metal in use was bronze or iron, but of course there never was a golden or silver age in the same sense. The principal significance of the metals is therefore not literal but metaphoric, and the metaphor is one of relative value and desirability: just as gold is better than silver, and silver than bronze, so also the Golden Race/Age was better than the Silver, and so on. Ovid's scheme features four units (Gold, Silver, Bronze, Iron), called indifferently ages or races, whereas Hesiod has five races (Gold, Silver, Bronze, Heroes, Iron), since a Race of Heroes has been interpolated into the metallic series, dividing the militant mortals who lived between the Silver Race and Iron Race into two subgroups, one hubristically violent and the other nobly violent. The

Golden Race/Age was entirely good and the Iron Race/Age was, or will become, entirely bad. The overall movement is therefore one of deterioration and decline, consistently so in Ovid though not in Hesiod.

Kronos (Latin Saturn) was the ruler of the world during the Golden period, and Zeus (Jove) thereafter. Thus the Myth of the Ages has been synchronized with the Succession Myth, an essentially unrelated story according to which the world has had a series of three divine rulers: Ouranos, Kronos, and Zeus. The synchronization has its costs, since Kronos's reign during the Golden era and his later rulership of the Isles of the Blessed do not make a good fit with his tyrannical behavior in the Succession Myth.

The series of ages suggests a development much like the life cycle of a living organism, its youth characterized by abundant energy (everlasting spring) and fertility (spontaneous crops) and its old age by their absence. In the Myth of the Ages, all aspects of the cosmos behave in sympathy, for the decline of the physical world is accompanied by a concomitant deterioration in human biology (eventually humans are born old) and human society (all human bonds disintegrate into violence), until the entire system breaks down and comes to an end. The notion of cosmic senescence accounts not only for the mix of bad and good in the world but also for the apparently ongoing deterioration of things. The pessimistic Hesiod sees himself as having the misfortune of being a member of the Iron Race, but for Ovid the Iron Age has long ago been destroyed, and humanity now lives in a post-ages era.

The devolutionary model that underlies the Myth of the Ages is essentially the opposite of the evolutionary, or progressive, model that underlies the tradition of culture heroes, whose activities led to improvements in the conditions of human life.

See also Culture Hero

Suggested reading:

Sue Blundell. *The Origins of Civilization in Greek and Roman Thought.* London: Croom Helm, 1986, 135–164.

W. K. C. Guthrie. *In the Beginning: Some Greek Views on the Origins of Life and the Early State of Man.* Ithaca, NY: Cornell University Press, 1957.

Arthur O. Lovejoy and George Boas. *Primitivism and Related Ideas in Antiquity.* Baltimore: The John Hopkins University Press, 1997 [1935].

Gregory Nagy. *The Best of the Achaeans: Concepts of the Hero in Archaic Greek Poetry.* Baltimore: The Johns Hopkins University Press, 1979, 151–173.

Martin L. West, ed. and comm. *Hesiod: Works and Days.* Oxford: Clarendon Press, 1978.

Eviatar Zerubavel. *Time Maps: Collective Memory and the Social Shape of the Past.* Chicago: University of Chicago Press, 2003, 11–36.

NECTAR (GREEK NEKTAR)

Wondrous beverage, or sometimes food, of the gods.

Nectar and ambrosia are the drink and food of the Olympian gods, maintaining them in an ageless state.

When Hermes visited the nymph Kalypso, she placed ambrosia on a table and mixed red nectar for him, after which he ate and drank (Homer *Odyssey* 5.92–94), as a mortal might serve another mortal food and wine. On Olympos, nectar is dispensed for the gods by the goddess Hebê, or Youth (Homer *Iliad* 4.2–3), or by the handsome Ganymedes (*Iliad* 20.231–235; *Homeric Hymn to Aphrodite* 202–206).

Although the etymology of the word *nectar* is disputed, it is likely to be similar to that of *ambrosia* ("undeath").

See also Ambrosia

Suggested reading:

Jenny Strauss Clay. *The Wrath of Athena: Gods and Men in the* Odyssey. Princeton, NJ: Princeton University Press, 1983, 145–148.

Paul Kretchmer. "Nektar." *Anzeiger der Österreichischen Akademie der Wissenschaften, philosophisch-historische Klasse* 4 (1947): 13–26.

Saul Levin. "The Etymology of Nektar: Exotic Scents in Early Greece." *Studi micenei ed egeo-anatolici* 13 (1971): 31–50.

Gregory Nagy. *Greek Mythology and Poetics.* Ithaca, NY: Cornell University Press, 1990, 139.

R. B. Onians. *The Origins of European Thought about the Body, the Mind, the Soul, the World, Time, and Fate.* Cambridge: Cambridge University Press, 1951, 292–299.

Rüdiger Schmitt. "*Nektar—*und kein Ende," in *Antiquitates Indogermanicae,* edited by Manfred Mayrhofer et al. Innsbrucker Beiträge zur Sprachwissenschaft, 12. Innsbruck: Institut für Sprachwissenschaft der Universität Innsbruck 1974, 155–163.

Paul Thieme. "Nektar," in *Indogermanische Dichtersprache,* edited by Rüdiger Schmitt. Darmstadt: Wissenschaftliche Buchgesellschaft, 1968, 102–112.

NYMPHS (GREEK NYMPHAI)

Female deities of the wild.

In the sphere of ordinary Greek life, the word *nymphê* meant "an unwed girl of marriageable age" or "a young bride," that is, a nubile female just before or just after marriage. In the sphere of the supernatural the term denoted a goddess of lower rank, youthful and lovely in aspect, who lived a life of freedom in one of the uncultivated places of the earth, away from human habitation.

Nymphs are classified mostly in accordance with their habitat. The best-known terrestrial nymphs (indicated by boldface type) are dryads or hamadryads

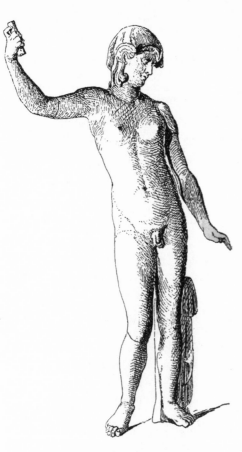

Hermaphroditos.

(nymphs of trees), naiads (nymphs of springs), and oreads (nymphs of mountains), but we also hear of alseids (nymphs of groves), meliai (nymphs of ash trees), potamiads (nymphs of rivers), and several others who do not figure much in mythology. The classification is loose in that some terms may include others. For example, a dryad may be a type of oread, and ancient authors frequently refer to a female character simply as a nymph without further specification. But some nymphs are labeled in accordance with their parentage. Thus, nymphs of the sea (indicated by boldface type) are known as Nereids (daughters of Nereus) and Okeanids (daughters of Okeanos, or Ocean). The different terrestrial nymphs are said to be daughters of Zeus (for example, Homer *Odyssey* 9.154) or of other gods such as particular rivers, whereas sea nymphs are daughters of particular marine and river gods. Some nymphs are sisters or nieces of the satyrs (Hesiod frag. 123 MW), and the meliai were conceived by Gaia (Earth) after she was impregnated by the blood of Ouranos (Sky). By and large nymphs are associated with different natural phenomena that for the most part lie outside of towns and cities.

Although nymphs are often called goddesses, the usual view seems to have been that they rank between the immortal gods and mortal humans, enjoying long lives but not immortality. Thus a dryad lives only so long as does the tree whose spirit she is, and a naiad similarly coexists with her spring. The poet Hesiod represents a nymph as saying that a crow lives for nine human generations, a stag lives four times as long as a crow, a raven three times as long as a stag, a phoenix nine times as long as a raven, and a nymph ten times as long as a phoenix (Hesiod frag. 304 MW).

Terrestrial nymphs are often represented as living carefree lives, enjoying their youth, beauty, and freedom unconstrained by husbands and children. Their sexuality tends to the extremes of overindulgence or underindulgence. Some nymphs shun the company of males entirely, living independently or belonging to the retinue of the chaste huntress Artemis, but others dance and indulge in sex promiscuously with satyrs and the rural gods Hermes and Pan, and mythic genealogies record many matings between terrestrial or marine nymphs on the one hand and gods or human males on the other, resulting in offspring. In addition, nymphs are sometimes represented as kindly nurturers of the young. When the goddess Aphroditê, impregnated by the mortal Anchises, bore a son Aineias, she entrusted the infant to the dryads on Mount Ida to rear (*Homeric Hymn to Aphrodite* 273–275), just as Zeus turned over baby Dionysos to the nymphs of Mount Nysa to rear. A group of nymphs who are not closely specified are keepers of wondrous objects including winged sandals and the Cap of Invisibility, which they lent to the hero Perseus to equip him for his quest for the Gorgon's head (Apollodoros *Library* 2.4.2–3).

There are many other minor divinities in Greek tradition who are called nymphs or can be so regarded, including the relatively isolated Kirkê and Kalypso, who were hosts and lovers of Odysseus in the course of his journey home from Troy. Others are celestial, such as the three Graces (attendants of Aphroditê), the three Hours (keepers of the gates of heaven), the Hyades (a constellation), the three Fates, and the nine Muses (divine patrons of speech, music, and dance). Like terrestrial and marine nymphs, they are lovely females who are indefinitely young, but unlike them they are defined by their particular cosmic function. If these goddesses are celestial nymphs, then the three Furies (avengers of certain blood crimes) can be deemed infernal nymphs. The three nymphs known as the Hesperides, daughters of Nyx (Night) and guardians of the golden apples of the gods, dwell in the distant west at the edge of the world, near Night.

Dryads (Greek *dryades*) and **hamadryads** (Greek *hamadryades*) are nymphs of trees. Individual dryads are associated or identified with individual trees (the name dryad is connected with the Greek root signifying "tree," especially oak tree). A dryad is born at the same time as a particular tree and her life is bound to that of the tree; when it dies, she too perishes (*Homeric Hymn to Aphrodite* 256–273). She can exit from the tree, and like other nymphs she has the appearance of a lovely female of human form. The relationship of a dryad to her tree is the same as that of a naiad, or freshwater nymph, to her spring or stream.

Different legends recount humans treating particular trees and their associated dryads with kindness or unkindness. Rhoikos came to the aid of a threatened oak tree and was rewarded for his gesture by the hamadryad whose life was bound to the tree (scholiast on Apollonios of Rhodes 2.477), whereas the impious woodcutter Erysichthon cut down a sacred oak tree, for which disrespect he was severely punished (Ovid *Metamorphoses* 8.738–878).

The meliai (ash tree nymphs) are a particular kind of tree nymph who, according to Hesiod, came into being when Gaia (Earth) became impregnated by blood fallen from the genitals of Ouranos (Sky), which Kronos had cut off. The

Naiads abducting Hylas.

centaur Pholos was the son of the satyr Silenos and a melian nymph (Apollodoros *Library* 2.5.4).

Naiads (Greek *naiades* or *naides*) are nymphs of springs, streams, and ponds (the name is formed from a Greek root meaning "flow"). As nymphs of freshwater, naiads can be distinguished from nymphs of the sea, the Oceanids and the Nereids. Moreover, individual naiads are associated or identified with individual bodies of water. A naiad is at once the water itself and also the spirit of the water. Her life is bound to a particular stream or spring; if it dries up, the naiad perishes with it. As the spirit of the water, she inhabits it and can exit from it. Like other nymphs, naiads have the appearance of lovely females of human form. Genealogically, naiads are said to be daughters of Zeus or of particular rivers.

Naiads are represented in some mythological narratives as an undifferentiated swarm and in others as named individuals. They often mate with mortal men; for example, Homer mentions two warriors at Troy "whom a naiad nymph once bore to blameless Boukolion" (*Iliad* 6.21–22). Indeed, naiads may be sexually aggressive toward youths they find attractive. So a naiad of a spring was erotically attracted to the youth Hylas, who had come to the spring to draw water, and she drew him into the water, where he drowned or became her consort (Apollonios of Rhodes 1.1207–1357). The naiad Salmacis fell in love with the youth Hermaphroditus, and once when he came to bathe in the spring she clung to him, refusing to release him and praying to the gods that they might never be separated, whereupon their bodies fused (Ovid *Metamorphoses* 4.285–388).

Oreads (Greek *oreiades*, connected with the word for "mountain") are nymphs of the mountains who roam the wilds, enjoying a life of dancing, hunting, and the like, free of husbands and children and the other constraints that characterized the domestic life of ordinary Greek women. The designation oread is employed loosely, there being no sharp classificatory distinction between oreads on the one hand and dryads and naiads and the other. All are youthful, attractive females in human form who frolic in rural and mountainous regions.

Oreads fall into two extreme groups with regard to their attitude toward sexuality, which they either indulge in with abandon or seek to avoid entirely. Lusty oreads are found in the company of males such as the rural deities Hermes and Pan and the satyrs, with whom they enjoy dancing and sexual play. But other oreads show an aversion to sexual intercourse in general and to males in particular. This attitude characterizes especially the companions or attendants of the chaste huntress Artemis. Perhaps for this reason male deities find them all the more attractive; in any case, most myths about individual oreads feature nymphs such as Arethousa (Ovid *Metamorphoses* 5.572–641), Daphnê (1.452–567), Kallisto (2.409–531), and Syrinx (1.689–712) who try, successfully or unsuccessfully, to avoid having dealings with males. The nymph Kallisto, for example, was a huntress, a member of Artemis's band in Arcadia. Zeus saw her once day and was erotically attracted to her. Taking the form of Artemis, he embraced the unsuspecting nymph affectionately and then, resuming his true form, forced himself upon her sexually. When the band later discovered her pregnancy, she was driven away.

Nereids (Greek *Nereïdes*) and **Okeanids** (Greek *Okeanides*) are nymphs or goddesses of the sea, or mermaids. The former are the fifty daughters of the sea-god Nereus and the Okeanid Doris, and the latter are the 3,000 daughters of Okeanos and Tethys. Dwelling in the depths of the sea with their father, Nereus, the Nereids are lovely in appearance and generally kindly to humans. Like their fellow sea-nymphs the Okeanids, they are entirely human in form, not a mix of woman and fish as in the case of some mermaid traditions.

Sometimes the Nereids are represented as a swarm. Thus when Kassiepeia, queen of Ethiopia, boasted that she was more beautiful than the Nereids, she enraged them, and as a result the god Poseidon angrily sent a sea-monster against the inhabitants of Ethiopia. Although most Nereids are little more than names, several individual Nereids such as Amphitritê, Galatea, and Thetis have myths of their own. Thetis is a kindly Nereid who came to the aid of Dionysos, Hephaistos, and her own son Achilleus when they were in distress. She was wed to the mortal hero, Peleus, who won her by lying in ambush for her and, finding her asleep in a cave at the edge of the sea, bound her and held her close as she transformed herself first into a bird, then a tree, and next a tigress, finally resuming her original form, whereupon she was his. They were parents of the mortal warrior Achilleus (Ovid *Metamorphoses* 11.217–265). Thetis's reluctance to mate and remain with a mortal man is a characteristic trait of mermaids in the sea lore of many lands.

> *See also* Centaurs and Hippocentaurs; Divine Guilds; Satyrs and Silens
> *Suggested reading:*
> P. M. C. Forbes Irving. *Metamorphosis in Greek Myths.* Oxford: Clarendon Press, 1990.
> J. G. Frazer. *Apollodorus: The Library.* London: William Heinemann; New York: G. P. Putnam's Sons, 1921, 2:383–388.

Timothy Gantz. *Early Greek Myth: A Guide to Literary and Artistic Sources.* Baltimore: The Johns Hopkins University Press, 1993, 139–142.

Monique Halm-Tisserant and Gérard Siebert. "Nymphai," in *LIMC* 8:891–902.

Noëlle Icard-Gianolio and Anne-Violaine Szabados. "Nereides," in *LIMC* 6:785–824.

Jennifer Larson. *Greek Nymphs.* Oxford: Oxford University Press, 2001.

Walter F. Otto. *Die Musen und der göttliche Ursprung des Singens und Sagens.* 3rd ed. Darmstadt: Wissenschaftliche Buchgesellschaft, 1961, 7–20.

Laura M. Slatkin. *The Power of Thetis: Allusion and Interpretation in the* Iliad. Berkeley: University of California Press, 1991.

ODYSSEUS

Hero renowned for his cleverness.

Homer's *Odyssey* represents Odysseus as the son of Laertes, once ruler of the island of Ithaca in western Greece, and his wife, Antikleia. A less respectable tradition, however, makes Odysseus the son of Sisyphos, who seduced Antikleia before her marriage to Laertes (Hyginus *Fabulae* 201), accounting for Odysseus's resourcefulness as a trait inherited from the wily Sisyphos, son of the thief Autolykos, who got his cunning from his father, the divine trickster Hermes.

As a youth Odysseus was one of many suitors for the hand of Helen. Her father, Tyndareus, was afraid to select a husband for his daughter for fear that the unsuccessful suitors would become unruly, but Odysseus promised to solve this problem if Tyndareus in turn would help Odysseus win the hand of Ikarios's daughter Penelopê. When Tyndareus agreed, Odysseus told him to make all of Helen's suitors swear beforehand to come to the aid of the eventual bridegroom if he should come to harm as a result of the marriage. Tyndareus made the suitors so swear, selected Menelaos as Helen's bridegroom, and then asked Ikarios to give Penelopê in marriage to Odysseus (Apollodoros *Library* 310.8–9).

After Helen had been abducted by, or had run off with, the Trojan prince Paris, her husband, Menelaos, asked his brother Agamemnon to gather a military force to attack Troy. Agamemnon accordingly sent heralds to the former suitors of Helen, reminding them of their oath. Although most of them were eager to join the expedition against Troy, not all were. When envoys came to Ithaca, Odysseus played the fool in order to avoid conscription, yoking different kinds of animal to his plow, but one of the envoys, Palamedes, snatched up Odysseus's infant son Telemachos from the lap of his mother and placed him in front of the plow, obliging Odysseus to stop his plowing and thereby reveal his sanity. But Odysseus later brought about the death of Palamedes at Troy, and so avenged himself (Apollodoros *Epitome* 3.6–8; Hyginus *Fabulae* 95).

Another draft dodger was Achilleus, whose mother, Thetis, dressed him in girl's clothes and entrusted him to King Lykomedes to be raised at court as a maiden. His whereabouts were eventually discovered, although Lykomedes denied that Achilleus was there and allowed the envoys to search his palace. Since they were unable to discover which maiden was Achilleus, Odysseus deposited in the forecourt a few gifts such as girls might like along with a shield and spear, and then had a trumpeter sound a signal and other men clash their weapons and shout. Thinking that the enemy had come, Achilleus tore off his female clothing and picked up the weapons Odysseus had planted, thereby giving himself away (Apollodoros *Library* 3.13.8; Hyginus *Fabulae* 96).

After these preliminaries, Odysseus and a contingent of Ithacan men joined the Achaean, or Greek, expedition against Troy. The war went on for ten years without a decisive result, after which Odysseus made crucial contributions toward its resolution. First, when the seer Kalchas prophesied that the Achaeans could not take Troy unless they possessed the bow of Herakles, Odysseus sailed to the island of Lemnos, gained possession of the bow from Philoktetes by means of trickery, and induced Philoktetes to join the fighting; presently Philoktetes killed Paris. Next, when Kalchas revealed that the Trojan soothsayer Helenos knew the secret oracles that protected Troy, Odysseus captured Helenos, from whom the Achaeans learned that they might capture the city if the bones of the hero Pelops were brought there, if Achilleus's son Neoptolemos joined the campaign, and if the Achaeans stole the Palladion, an image that had fallen from the sky, from the Trojans. So the Achaeans had the bones of Pelops brought to their camp, Odysseus and Phoinix persuaded Neoptolemos to join the war, and Odysseus, disguised as a beggar, entered Troy and stole the Palladion. Finally, it was Odysseus who devised the strategy of the wooden horse. He suggested that a hollow horse be constructed, with an opening at one side and an inscription explaining that the animal was an offering to Athena for the safe return home of the Greeks. The bravest Achaean warriors concealed themselves inside the horse while the others burned their tents and sailed away, pretending to give up the campaign. The Trojans fell for the ruse, taking the horse inside their city and celebrating the end of the long war. But that night the men in the horse, led by Odysseus, exited from the structure and opened the gates of the city for their comrades, who had returned. The Achaeans overcame the Trojans, sacked the city, and distributed the spoils among the victors (Apollodoros *Epitome* 5.8–25).

The Achaean survivors of the campaign now set out individually for home. For Odysseus the journey took ten years. In the course of his return he encountered many unusual beings, including the Lotus-Eaters, the one-eyed

Odysseus sailing past the Sirens.

Odysseus offering wine to the Cyclops.

Cyclopes, Aiolos the keeper of the winds, the savage Laistrygonians, the witch Kirkê, the ghosts of the dead in Erebos, the enticing Sirens, the monsters Scylla and Charybdis, the Cattle of the Sun, the erotic nymph Kalypso, and the luxury-loving Phaiakians (Homer *Odyssey* 9–12).

When Odysseus finally reached Ithaca, however, his palace was beset with arrogant suitors who for several years had been pressing Penelopê to remarry, since it seemed unlikely that Odysseus would ever return. Odysseus made himself known to his son Telemachos, and disguised as a beggar he went to the palace, observing the situation and testing the loyalty of the household. When Penelopê instituted an archery contest for her hand, the disguised Odysseus took advantage of the occasion to win the contest and with the help of his allies disposed of the suitors, after which Odysseus and Penelopê were at last reunited (*Odyssey* 12–24).

Odysseus turned his attention to his last task, walking inland with an oar over his shoulder in quest of a community whose inhabitants were ignorant of the sea and seafaring. He found such a place when a local man mistook his oar for a winnowing shovel. There he performed a sacrifice to Poseidon in order to propitiate him for the blinding of Poseidon's son Polyphemos. Then Odysseus returned to Ithaca and enjoyed a prosperous reign, eventually dying peacefully (*Odyssey* 23.247–284).

Throughout many of his trials Odysseus enjoyed the support of the goddess Athena, who energetically acted as a divine champion on behalf of Odysseus and his son.

Ulixes is the Roman name for Odysseus, deriving apparently from a Greek dialectal form of the name, whence also the Latin and modern form Ulysses.

See also Cyclopes; Trickster; Trojan War

Suggested reading:

Antti Aarne and Stith Thompson. *The Types of the Folktale: A Classification and Bibliography*, FF Communications 184. Helsinki: Academia Scientiarum Fennica, 1961, Type 974: *The Homecoming Husband*.

Timothy Gantz. *Early Greek Myth: A Guide to Literary and Artistic Sources.* Baltimore: The Johns Hopkins University Press, 1993, 703–713.

William Hansen. *Ariadne's Thread: A Guide to International Tales Found in Classical Literature.* Ithaca, NY: Cornell University Press, 2002, 201–211 (Odysseus and Penelope), 371–378 (Odysseus and the oar).

———. "Homer and the Folktale," in *A New Companion to Homer*, edited by Ian Morris and B. B. Powell. Leiden: E. J. Brill, 1997, 442–462.

W. B. Stanford. *The Ulysses Theme: A Study in the Adaptability of a Traditional Hero.* 2nd ed. Ann Arbor: University of Michigan Press, 1963.

W. B. Stanford and J. V. Luce. *The Quest for Ulysses.* New York: Praeger, 1974.

Odette Touchefeu-Meynier. "Odysseus," in *LIMC* 6:943–970.

OEDIPUS (GREEK OIDIPOUS)

Youth who killed his father and wed his mother.

According to the mythographer Apollodoros, King Laios of Thebes married a woman who some say was named Iokastê (Latinized form = Jocasta), and others Epikastê. An oracle instructed him not to beget a child, for if the child was a son, he would become his father's killer. But on a particular occasion Laios, drunk with wine, had sexual intercourse with his wife, and she bore him a son. Laios pierced the infant's ankles with pins and entrusted him to a shepherd to expose in the wilderness, and the shepherd exposed the child on Mount Kithairon. Cowherds of King Polybos of Corinth, however, found the infant and brought him to the king's wife, Periboia, who adopted him, passing him off as her own child. After healing his ankles, she gave him the name Oedipus (Swollen-Foot) because of the condition of his feet.

When Oedipus grew up and excelled his peers in strength, they jealously declared that he was not the genuine son of his supposed parents. He asked his mother but was unable to learn anything from her. So he traveled to Delphi to ask the oracle of Apollon about his parents. The god told him not to travel to his own country, else he would slay his father and have sexual intercourse with his mother. Believing that his nominal parents were his true parents, he left Corinth. Traveling by chariot through Phokis, he encountered Laios traveling by chariot on a narrow road. Laios's herald told him to move out of the way, and when Oedipus did not immediately do so, the herald killed one of Oedipus's horses, whereupon Oedipus angrily slew the herald and Laios, and proceeded to Thebes.

Laios was buried, and Kreon became king. During his reign Hera sent the Sphinx, offspring of Echidna and Typhon. She had the face of a woman, the breast and feet and tail of a lion, and the wings of a bird. Having learned a riddle from the Muses, she sat on Mount Phikion and propounded it to the Thebans: what is it that becomes four-footed, three-footed, and two-footed but has only one voice? The Thebans had an oracle that declared they would be rid of the Sphinx when they should solve her riddle. Accordingly, they often gathered in an effort to solve it, but whenever they failed to do so, she seized one of them and devoured him. After many persons perished, including finally the king's son Haimon, Kreon announced that if someone should solve the riddle, he would give him the kingdom and Laios's widow. Oedipus solved it, giving the answer "human being" (Greek *anthropos*), for an infant travels on four limbs, a grown person on two, and an old person using a staff on three. The Sphinx cast herself down from the acropolis, and Oedipus succeeded to the kingdom and unwittingly wed his own mother, begetting children by her, the brothers Polyneikes and Eteokles and the sisters Ismenê and Antigonê. When the hidden facts later came to light, Iokastê hanged herself and Oedipus blinded himself. Expelled from Thebes, he cursed his sons for not coming to his aid as he was driven out. With Antigonê's help, he made his way as a suppliant to the precinct of the Eumenides at Kolonos (Latinized form = Colonus) in Attica and died shortly thereafter (*Library* 3.5.7–9).

Laios's motive in piercing the ankles of the infant is presumably to disable the child's eventual ghost, but in the narrative economy of the story the scarring serves to mark the infant, setting up the later recognition of the son by his mother, who—perceiving the scar—realizes to her horror that the infant whom she and her husband exposed long ago must have survived, that this must be he, and that she has therefore married her own son. Apollodoros's version omits the recognition scene.

Oedipus and the Sphinx.

The Oedipus story is most familiar today in its performative treatment by the tragedian Sophokles in his drama, *Oedipus the King*, often called by its Latin title of *Oedipus Rex*. The underlying legend is the Greek form of an international story in which a man is fated to kill his father and wed his mother. The Riddle of Man is similarly an international riddle that is known independently of the Oedipus legend.

See also Biographical Pattern

Suggested reading:

Antti Aarne and Stith Thompson. *The Types of the Folktale: A Classification and Bibliography*, FF Communications 184. Helsinki: Academia Scientiarum Fennica, 1961, Type 931: *Oedipus.*

Rolf W. Brednich. *Volkserzählungen und Volksglaube von den Schicksalsfrauen.* FFC 193. Helsinki: Academia Scientiarum Fennica, 1964, 42–56.

Lowell Edmunds. *Oedipus: The Ancient Legend and Its Later Analogues.* Baltimore: The Johns Hopkins University Press, 1985.

Lowell Edmunds and Alan Dundes, eds. *Oedipus: A Folklore Casebook.* New York: Garland Publishing, 1983.

Timothy Gantz. *Early Greek Myth: A Guide to Literary and Artistic Sources.* Baltimore: The Johns Hopkins University Press, 1993, 490–506.

Ingrid Kranskopf. "Oidipous," in *LIMC* 7:1–15.

Jennifer R. March. *The Creative Poet: Studies on the Treatment of Myths in Greek Poetry.* London: University of London, Institute of Classical Studies, 1987, 119–154.

Walter Puchner. "Ödipus," in *Enzyklopädie des Märchens.* Berlin: Walter de Gruyter, 2002, 10:209–219.

Stith Thompson. *A Motif-Index of Folk-Literature*, Vol. 3. Bloomington: Indiana University Press, 1955–1958, H 761: *Riddle of the Sphinx: What is it that goes on four legs in the morning, on two at midday, and on three in the evening.*

OLYMPIANS (GREEK OLYMPIOI)

Family of gods, the principal deities of Greek mythology.

The Olympian gods consist of an older generation and a younger generation. The elder Olympians are the siblings Zeus, Poseidon, Hera, Demeter, and Hestia, and the younger Olympians are Zeus's sons Hermes, Hephaistos, Ares, Apollon, and Dionysos and Zeus's daughters Athena, Aphroditê, and Artemis. (Aphroditê is a daughter of Zeus and Dionê, although according to a different tradition she emerged from the semen of the god Ouranos.) Hades, a sibling of the elder Olympians, resides in Erebos and so is not accounted one of the Olympians. In addition, other immortals dwell on Olympos who are not ordinarily classified as Olympians, notably the Hours, Herakles (after his apotheosis) and his wife Hebê, and Ganymedes. There was a tradition that when Zeus was about to enroll Herakles among the twelve Olympians, Herakles declined the honor, since one of the present Olympians would have to be ejected (Diodorus of Sicily 4.39.4).

Although the Greeks generally agreed that the Olympian gods were twelve in number, they did not always agree which were the twelve. In lists or works of art representing all the Olympians, Dionysos or Hestia is likely to be omitted, since the number of Olympians otherwise amounts to thirteen. Since the number twelve was a pattern number, or culturally favored number, as in the twelve labors of Herakles, the persistent idea of a group of twelve gods was to some extent independent of the idea of the Olympian family. In any case, the notion of twelve gods was more important in cult than in mythological narrative, where it is mentioned only occasionally (*Homeric Hymn to Hermes* 126–137; Apollodoros *Library* 3.14.1–2).

As a family the Olympians are the younger gods, in contrast to the Titans, the older family of gods. When the Titan Kronos became king of the gods, he mated with his sister Rhea, who bore him five children: Hestia, Demeter, Hera, Hades, and Poseidon. But he swallowed each as it was born, since he had learned that he was fated to be overthrown by his own son. In her grief, Rhea appealed to her parents to help her bear her next son in secret and to punish Kronos for his behavior. Upon the advice of Gaia and Ouranos, she went to Crete to deliver her sixth child, Zeus, whom Gaia hid in a cave. Rhea deceived her husband by giving him a stone wrapped in swaddling clothes, which he swallowed in the belief that it was his infant son. When Zeus was fully grown, Kronos was tricked into taking an emetic, causing him to disgorge what he had swallowed. Presently a ten-year battle for supremacy took place between the older gods, led by Kronos, and the younger gods, led by Zeus, in which the Olympians and their allies overcame the Titans, whom they imprisoned in Tartaros. The Olympians had their name from Mount Olympos, where they had taken their stand during the Titanomachy, and eventually they settled there. After Zeus vanquished in single combat the dragon Typhon, the other gods urged him to be king of the gods, so that he became ruler of the cosmos and distributed to the other gods their honors, or spheres of influence.

Now Zeus presides over the other deities on Olympos, either the summit of Mount Olympos in northern Greece or the celestial Olympos in the sky. The Olympians pass their mostly carefree lives with one another in their heavenly homes, attend to their different cosmic chores, pay friendly visits to earthly favorites such as the Ethiopians, observe terrestrial events like spectators at the theater, and sometimes insert themselves into the lives of mortals in order to help or harm them or to take sexual liberties.

See also Triads

Suggested reading:

Gratia Berger-Doer. "Dodekatheoi," in *LIMC* 3.1:646–658.

Walter Burkert. *Greek Religion,* translated by John Raffan. Cambridge: Harvard University Press, 1985.

Timothy Gantz. *Early Greek Myth: A Guide to Literary and Artistic Sources.* Baltimore: The Johns Hopkins University Press, 1993, 120–123.

Stith Thompson. *A Motif-Index of Folk-Literature,* Vol. 3. Bloomington: Indiana University Press, 1955–1958, Z71.8: *Formulistic number: twelve.*

O. Weinreich. "Zwölfgötter," in Roscher 6:764–848.

ORACLES

Revelations of what is fated to happen or not to happen or of how events are fated to happen.

In Greek tradition the course of cosmic, divine, and human events relies ultimately upon fate, details of which may be known to the gods, or to particular gods such as Zeus (as ruler of the cosmos) and Apollon (as the chief god of prophecy), and may therefore guide their behavior. The gods generally avoid trying to effect something that is contrary to fate. Oracles play an important role in legend, in which a human may learn some details of fate by one means or another and act accordingly; however, since human understanding is limited, humans often act inappropriately.

In myths of the gods, a deity who is privy to fate transmits this information to another deity, who acts accordingly. For example, Gaia and Ouranos informed Kronos that he was fated to be overthrown by his own son, so that he swallowed each of his children as it was born (Hesiod *Theogony* 453–465). Despite this drastic action, Kronos was overthrown by his son in the end. As usual, efforts made by a character to thwart a fated outcome are in vain. But occasionally an exception occurs. When Zeus took Metis as his first wife, Gaia and Ouranos advised him to swallow her, since she was fated to bear a son who would be king of gods and men. Zeus did so, and Metis never bore the son who was fated to replace him (*Theogony* 886–900).

A similar destiny was attached to the Nereid Thetis. Jove wished to have sexual intercourse with Thetis, but Prometheus alone knew that she was fated to bear a son who was greater than his father. Prometheus, who was in chains on Jove's order, offered to exchange useful information for his freedom. When Jove agreed, Prometheus advised him not to lie with Thetis, else he might beget a son who would drive him from his throne. So Thetis was given in marriage to the hero Peleus, and Jove arranged for Prometheus's release (Hyginus *Fabulae* 54).

For the narrator, a great advantage of oracles is that their content requires no justification. An oracle is beyond question since what is fated is fated, no matter how bizarre or unfair it may be. Fate is a special rule applied to the future, and special rules are by their nature arbitrary. A narrator rarely feels obliged to explain why one deity knows what it fated, and another does not, just as here we are asked simply to accept that, for no obvious reason, Prometheus possesses this information whereas Jove does not.

Human beings become privy to fate ordinarily by consulting a god at an oracular shrine, such as Apollon's renowned oracle at Delphi, or by consulting a seer. Such information may serve to get a story started or to lend it structure. Thus in the legend of Oedipus (Greek Oidipous), King Laios of Thebes received an oracle in which the god warned him not to beget a son, for if he did so, his son would kill him. So Laios abstained from sexual intercourse with his wife, but once when he was drunk he slept with her, and she bore a son. The legend goes on to relate how the parents, in an effort to avert fate, tried to do away with the child, but failed, for the child survived, was reared in nearby Corinth, and eventually slew his father, as the oracle had foretold.

Frequently the oracular message is deceptive in that it is true but only in an unobvious way. The consultant interprets it in the obvious way and so gets it wrong. Thus when Oedipus was a youth, his peers suggested that he was not a legitimate child. When he consulted the Delphic oracle about his true parents, the god told him not to go to his native land, for if he did he would murder his father and lie with his mother. Since Oedipus believed himself to be the son of Corinthian parents, he decided not to return to Corinth and went instead to Thebes where, in the course of time, he unwittingly killed his father and wed his mother. Although the oracle was true, Oedipus did not possess sufficient information to understand it properly, so that it did not benefit him.

In a unique case a human learns what is fated by overhearing the conversation of supernatural beings. Althaia bore a son Meleager (Greek *Meleagros*), and when he was seven days old the Fates came to the house to declare his fate.

They said that he would die when the piece of wood burning in the hearth should burn up. Chancing to hear this, Althaia snatched the brand from the hearth, and as a result Meleager grew up to be invulnerable. He met his end when he angered his mother, who then retrieved the firebrand and kindled it.

An oracle can serve to prolong a story by motivating additional episodes. Thus oracles foretold that Troy could not be captured unless three things should happen: the bones of Pelops had to be brought to Troy, Achilleus's son Neoptolemos had to join the fight, and the Palladion, which was in the possession of the Trojans, had to be stolen away. Having learned these oracles from a captured Trojan seer, the Greeks proceeded to satisfy the preconditions one by one (Apollodoros *Epitome* 5.9–13). The reason for these oracles is to motivate a sequence of episodes in which the Greeks first capture the Trojan seer Helenos and then meet the conditions.

> ***See also*** Seers; Special Rules and Properties
> ***Suggested reading:***
> Joseph Fontenrose. "The Oracular Response as a Traditional Narrative Theme." *Journal of Folklore Research* 20 (1983): 113–120.

ORPHEUS

Marvelous musician whose music moved gods, humans, animals, plants, and even stones.

The mythographer Apollodoros relates that Orpheus, a son of Oiagros and the Muse Kalliopê, was a musician who affected even stones and trees when he sang. He wed Eurydikê (Latinized form = Eurydicê), who perished soon after-

Orpheus charming the wild animals.

ward from a snake bite. Wishing to retrieve her, Orpheus descended to Hades's realm to persuade its ruler to release her. Hades promised to do so on the condition that Orpheus not turn around during his return journey until he should reach his own house. But Orpheus disobeyed the injunction. When he looked back he saw his wife, but she thereupon returned to the death realm (Apollodoros *Library* 1.3.2).

Orpheus was inconsolable in his grief for having twice lost Eurydikê. He himself eventually died a violent death, being torn apart by maenads celebrating the nocturnal rites of Bacchus (Virgil *Georgics* 4.507–527). Ancient authors generally agree on the manner of Orpheus's death but attribute different motives to the maenads. Some say that the women were offended at Orpheus's faithfulness to the memory of Eurydikê, for after losing her a second time he avoided all women; a few authorities add that he came to prefer the love of males. According to a different tradition, Orpheus was devoted to the sun as the greatest of the gods and arose early each day to see the sunrise from the top of Mount Pangaion. His reverence for Helios angered Dionysos, who caused his maenads to tear the bard apart limb from limb (*Pseudo-Eratosthenes Catasterisms* 24).

Among his attributes in art is a lyre.

See also Maenads; Romantic Narratives

Suggested reading:

Timothy Gantz. *Early Greek Myth: A Guide to Literary and Artistic Sources.* Baltimore: The Johns Hopkins University Press, 1993, 721–725.

Maria-Xeni Garezou. "Orpheus," in *LIMC* 7:81–105.

PAN

God of shepherds and flocks, at home in Arcadia in the central Peloponnese.

In form Pan is a composite being, partly human and partly goat. According to the *Homeric Hymn to Pan,* he has two horns, goat's feet, and a beard, together with long unkempt hair. As a god of shepherds, he wanders the mountains and hills. The hymnist says that the deity spends his days roaming the wilderness and hunting animals, and in the evenings he joins the nymphs, playing his reed pipes while they sing and dance. Pan was born in Arcadia to the god Hermes and the daughter of Dryops. When the infant's nurse saw the infant's beard, horns, and hooves, she fled in fear, but Hermes delighted in him and so did the other immortals, especially Dionysos.

As a god of flocks, Pan has power over the fertility of goats and sheep, and he is the hidden cause of panic (Greek *panikon*), the apparently groundless terror that can suddenly come over animals or humans (Pausanias 10.23.7). A lusty god himself, he can inspire sexual desire; indeed, he is in a frequent if not constant state of sexual arousal, and ancient art depicts him engaged in making a pass at Aphroditê, chasing after a shepherd lad, or having sexual intercourse with a goat.

His approach to love is coarse and rustic, and he is not fortunate in it. Thus he once propositioned the nymph Syrinx as she was tending her goats, playing with other nymphs, and singing, as nymphs do. Though he promised to make all her goats give birth to twins every year, she only mocked his love, saying that she would not take as her lover one who was neither fully goat nor fully human. Pan then set out after her with the intention of taking her by force, but Syrinx fled, eventually disappearing in a grove of reeds. Pan angrily cut up the reeds in an attempt to

Pan.

locate her, but since he did not find the nymph, he bound together reeds of unequal length, since their love was unequal, and so invented a new musical instrument, the reed pipe (Greek *syrinx*). So the beautiful maiden is now a musical pipe (Longos *Daphnis and Chloe* 2.34). Pan's presence and good disposition can enhance the fertility of Syrinx's goats, as happened when Apollon worked as a herdsman for the mortal Admetos, whose cows all gave birth to twins (Apollodoros *Library* 3.10.4).

In a humorous tale of cross-dressing and sexual frustration, Faunus (that is, Pan) once spied from a distance Hercules escorting Omphalê and immediately lusted after the woman. That evening, as Hercules and Omphalê prepared to dine together in a cave, she disrobed and gave him her clothes to wear, and she took his club, lion pelt, and arrows. Thus attired they dined and went to bed. Faunus crept into the cave, felt his way to Omphalê's delicate clothing, climbed into the bed, lifted up her clothing, but to his surprise found rough calves and coarse hair. Hercules woke up and threw Faunus from his cot, and presently everyone awoke and laughed at the embarrassed god (Ovid *Fasti* 2.303–358). Roman narrators sometimes retain the Greek name and sometimes identify Pan with the Roman deity Faunus.

Pan and a youth.

As in sexual activity, Pan's taste in music is unrefined, for he prefers the rustic pipe to the aristocratic lyre. He once remarked how much superior his music was to that of Apollo, and the comment led to a contest with Apollo, with Tmolus serving as judge. Pan played a crude song on his reed pipes, after which Phoebus Apollo skillfully played his sweet lyre. Tmolus readily acclaimed Apollo the winner (Ovid *Metamorphoses* 11.153–171).

A strange legend tells how a certain Epitherses was on a ship with many other passengers, sailing from Greece to Italy. In the evening as they were passing the island of Paxos, they heard a voice calling for Thamous, who, it turned out, was pilot of the ship. The caller asked him to report, as the ship sailed past the harbor Palodes, that the great Pan was dead. The passengers discussed the mysterious message, and Epitherses decided that if the wind was calm as they sailed past, he would deliver the message. Since the wind was calm, he faced land and said: "The great Pan is dead." Before he even finished speaking, a great lamentation arose, the voices of many beings. News of the event quickly reached Rome, where the emperor Tiberius made inquiries. The emperor's scholars conjectured that the Pan in question was the god Hermes's son (Plutarch *On the Obsolescence of Oracles* 17). The underlying story is an international legend, still told today of elves, trolls, and fairies, who employ an unwitting human being to deliver a message that a particular supernatural being has died. Pan, being a god, is not elsewhere treated as mortal.

Ancient iconography agrees for the most part with the portrayal of Pan in the *Homeric Hymn*. Typically he is shown with goat's horns and a goatee, standing upright on two legs that end in hooves, but illustrations vary in their relative emphasis on the bestial and the human, ranging from early representations in which he is little more than an upright goat to later depictions in which he is almost fully human in aspect. He is often ithyphallic and in any case possesses large genitals. Pan is frequently shown in the company of Hermes or nymphs, dancing or playing reed pipes (that is, panpipes, his special instrument) or a double flute. Multiple Pans also appear in art and literature, like satyrs (Ovid *Metamorphoses* 14.637–641). In time, Pans and satyrs become difficult to distinguish from each other, since satyrs come to be represented with goat features. But swarms of Pans play little role in mythology.

See also Centaurs and Hippocentaurs; Satyrs and Silens; Sexual Myths and Legends

Suggested reading:

Philippe Borgeaud. *The Cult of Pan in Ancient Greece.* Trans. by Kathleen Atlass
and James Redfield. Chicago: University of Chicago Press, 1988.

Frank Brommer. *Satyroi.* Wurzburg: Konrad Triltsch Verlag, 1937.

Timothy Gantz. *Early Greek Myth: A Guide to Literary and Artistic Sources.*
Baltimore: The Johns Hopkins University Press, 1993, 110–111.

William Hansen. *Ariadne's Thread: A Guide to International Tales Found in
Classical Literature.* Ithaca, NY: Cornell University Press, 2002, 131–136 (death
of Pan).

Peter Weiss. "Pan," in *LIMC* 8:923–941.

PANDORA

First mortal woman.

Pandora was created by the gods in order to punish mortal men.

According to Hesiod, the primordial human community consisted only of
men, who lived lives of ease and health, enjoying a neighborly relationship with
the gods; however, the relationship soured after Prometheus twice deceived the
Olympian gods on behalf of mankind. For when gods and men met to decide
once and for all time what parts of a slaughtered animal would belong to immortals and what parts would belong to mortals, Prometheus tricked Zeus into
selecting the less desirable portion for the gods. After Zeus angrily withheld fire
from mankind, thereby preventing humans from cooking their meat,
Prometheus stole it and made it easily available. In retaliation, Zeus arranged
for Prometheus to be bound and tortured, and Zeus schemed to punish men by
inserting woman into their community, along with the miseries that she en-
tailed. So Hephaistos made a maiden from earth, Athena dressed her, the Graces
and Peitho (Persuasion) ornamented her with necklaces, the Hours placed a garland of flowers on her head, and Hermes put lies and deceit in her breast, gave
her a voice, and named her Pandora (All-Gift), since all the gods had gifted her.
Zeus told Hermes to take this irresistible gift to Epimetheus, who accepted her,
perceiving the evil only after he had done so. For he neglected the advice of his
brother Prometheus not to accept any gift from Zeus. Pandora took the lid off a
great jar, scattering countless evils among mankind, such as toil and diseases.
The only spirit to remain in the jar was Hope, for Zeus had Pandora replace the
lid before Hope escaped (*Works and Days* 53–105).

Since according to this myth mortal women are an inherent source of misery for their husbands, the first woman is made to be physically attractive in order to induce a foolish man to accept her. This fool is Epimetheus (Afterthought), the unwise brother of Prometheus (Forethought). In addition to the
misery that she herself incarnates (Hesiod *Theogony* 570–612), the maiden re-
moves the lid from a jar, the origin of which is not explained, with the result

that countless miseries in the form of silent spirits enter the world, introducing mortal men for the first time to hard work and to sickness. Since Hesiod calls the jar a *pithos,* or large storage jar that was typically five or six feet tall, Pandora cannot have carried it with her. The modern expression "Pandora's box" rests ultimately upon a mistranslation by Erasmus of Rotterdam, who recounting the myth in Latin in 1508 rendered Pandora's *pithos* "jar" as *pyxis* "box" (Panofsky 1965, 14–26).

A similar tale is recounted elsewhere in Greek literature, not as a myth but as an Aesopic fable. In this form of the story, the character who lifts the lid off the jar is described simply as a person (that is, not specifically female or male), and the jar contains good things rather than evils. According to the fable, Zeus once gathered together everything good, placed it in a *pithos,* put a lid on it, and set it down beside a human being. But the person, eager to know what was inside, opened the jar, so that the good things flew up to the habitation of the gods, and only Hope remained below, for it was still in the jar when he or she replaced the lid. And so only Hope remains among humans, promising us each of those good things that escaped (Babrios *Fabulae* 58).

The message of the myth as well as of the fable is the same, or intended to be the same, more or less that at some time in the past humans enjoyed conditions of ease like that of the gods, but thanks to human agency all that changed such that mortals now have lives of misery, although we carry on because we have the hope of something better. The difference between them is that one image presents the idea in terms of evils (there used to be no evils, and now there are), whereas the other presents it in terms of good things (there used to be all good things, and now there are not), and depending upon which image is employed, the jar either protects humans from its contents (the evils imprisoned in the jar do not affect us) or does not (the good things residing in the jar affect us). It is clear, however, that the motif of Hope makes good sense only in the second kind of jar, the jar of blessings, for only in this form of the story do things within the vessel affect persons outside of it (Panofsky 1965, 6–8). Although Hesiod's meaning is clear enough, his narrative mixes the two images, employing the idea of a jar of evils from the first image and the idea of Hope from the second.

See also Anthropogony

Suggested reading:

Ernst Heitsch, ed. *Hesiod.* Darmstadt: Wissenschaftliche Buchgesellschaft, 1966, 327– 435.

Manfred Oppermann. "Pandora," in *LIMC* 7:163–166.

Dora and Erwin Panofsky. *Pandora's Box: The Changing Aspects of a Mythical Symbol.* 2nd ed., revised New York: Harper and Row, 1965.

PERSEPHONÊ (LATINIZED FORM PROSERPINA; ALSO KORÊ)

Goddess of the dead.

Persephonê is the daughter of Zeus and Demeter, who was the fourth in Zeus's succession of seven wives (Hesiod *Theogony* 912–914). According to the *Homeric Hymn to Demeter*, Zeus gave his unmarried brother Hades permission to seize Persephonê, saying nothing of this arrangement to the girl or her mother. One day as Persephonê gathered flowers in a meadow with a number of Oceanids, the earth in the Nysian Plain gaped open and Hades burst forth on his golden chariot, seized her, and carried her away against her will to his gloomy kingdom. She cried out, but by the time her mother heard her voice, the girl had disappeared. While Persephonê dwelled with Hades in Erebos, Demeter in grief searched the earth for her, and when she learned what had happened, she was furious. She kept herself apart from the other gods in her grief and anger, keeping the seeds concealed in the ground, so that agriculture came entirely to a halt. Had not Zeus intervened, the human race would have perished and the gods would have been deprived of their sacrifices.

Since Demeter angrily refused to return to Olympos or to allow the seeds to emerge until she should see her daughter, Zeus dispatched Hermes to the House of Hades to persuade the god to bring Persephonê back. Hermes went beneath the earth to Hades's mansions, where he found the lord and his consort sitting on a couch. Persephonê was longing for her mother. Hades said Persephonê was free to visit her mother, but he also pointed out that he was no unsuitable husband for her, since he was a brother of her own father, Zeus, and since as Hades's spouse she would become mistress of everything that lived and would acquire great honors among the gods. But secretly he gave Persephonê a pomegranate seed to eat before her departure so that she would not remain forever with her mother. Demeter and Persephonê were joyously reunited, but when Demeter discovered that Persephonê had eaten in Erebos, she perceived that Persephonê would have to live a third of the year with her spouse and two-thirds of the year with her mother and the other immortals. Zeus gave his approval to this plan. After Demeter caused the fields once again to luxuriate in produce, she and her daughter went to Olympos to join the other gods, where they dwell beside Zeus (*Homeric Hymn to Demeter*).

The myth recounts how Hades got a wife and how the maiden Persephonê acquired her cosmic honor, the queenship of the dead. Since the death realm might have little appeal to a prospective bride as a future home, her father and suitor did not broach the marriage arrangement openly; instead, Hades was permitted to abduct her, and in the end Persephonê had no choice whether to remain or depart, for she had eaten a small amount of food in the death realm, becoming thereby bound to it forever. Zeus, Hades, and Demeter play active roles in the events, but Persephonê is primarily a character to whom things happen. The myth is similar to that of the Athenian maiden Oreithyia, who was abducted by Boreas (North Wind) as she played beside a stream and carried off by him to his cold and distant kingdom, where he made her his wife, and she bore him children (Apollodoros *Library* 3.15.2; Ovid *Metamorphoses* 6.675–713). But Hades and Persephonê, rulers of the sterile realm of the dead, produce no offspring.

Persephonê reappears in other stories, always in her role as queen of the dead, for once she assumes this position, mythological narrative assumes her constant presence in the death realm, despite the fractional living arrangement announced in the *Homeric Hymn to Demeter* and in other narrations. Persephonê once disputed with Aphroditê for the possession of Adonis, a myth that is reminiscent of her own story. When Adonis was born, he was so beautiful that Aphroditê concealed the infant in a chest without the knowledge of the other gods and entrusted it to Persephonê. But when she saw the child, she would not give him back. The dispute was referred to Zeus, who decreed that Adonis should live one-third of the year with himself, one-third with Persephonê, and one-third with Aphroditê. But Adonis gave his share to Aphroditê, so that he lived with her for two-thirds of the year. Later he perished while hunting (Apollodoros *Library* 3.14.4). As in the myth of Persephonê, the world of the living and the world of the dead dispute the possession of a beautiful young being. Zeus resolves the matter such that the being resides among the living for two-thirds of the year and among the dead for the remainder.

Persephonê could show compassion. The Moirai (Fates) agreed that when Admetos was about to die, he would be released from death if another person should be willing to die in his place. Only his wife, Alkestis, volunteered, but after she died, Persephonê sent her back up again (Apollodoros *Library* 1.9.15). The goddess could also be frightful. When Odysseus visited Erebos on his way home from Troy, the fear suddenly seized him that Persephonê might dispatch against him the terrible head of a Gorgon, so that he quickly took his leave of the place (Homer *Odyssey* 11.633–640).

Persephonê could be a prized mate for a mortal because of her status as a goddess. When the bold heroes Theseus and Peirithoos made a pact with each other to marry daughters of Zeus, Peirithoos helped Theseus carry off Helen from Sparta, and Theseus accompanied Peirithoos down to the House of Hades in order that Peirithoos might woo Persephonê, in the hope of making her his bride. But Hades tricked the two youths, inviting them to sit on the Chair of Forgetfulness. Expecting hospitality, they did so but were unable to rise again. Although Peirithoos remained there forever, Theseus was eventually rescued by

Herakles (Apollodoros *Epitome* 1.23–24). It is unclear how Peirithoos expected to win over Persephonê, who was already married, or why the two youths expected Persephonê's husband to treat them hospitably.

Persephonê is known also as Korê (Daughter, Maiden), but the title is less common in mythic narrative than in cultic contexts. Among her epithets are "venerable" and "awesome."

In art she is often shown with her mother or with her husband. Among her attributes are a torch and a scepter.

> **See also** Demeter; Erebos; Hades
>
> **Suggested reading:**
>
> Helene Foley, ed. *The Homeric* Hymn to Demeter: *Translation, Commentary, and Interpretive Essays.* Princeton, NJ: Princeton University Press, 1994.
>
> Timothy Gantz. *Early Greek Myth: A Guide to Literary and Artistic Sources.* Baltimore: The Johns Hopkins University Press, 1993, 64–68.
>
> Susan Gubar. "Mother, Maiden, and the Marriage of Death: Women Writers and an Ancient Myth." *Women's Studies* 6 (1979): 301–315.
>
> Gudrun Güntner. "Persephone," in *LIMC* 8:956–978.
>
> N. J. Richardson, ed. and comm. *The Homeric Hymn to Demeter.* Oxford: Clarendon Press, 1974.

PERSEUS

Youth who slew the Gorgon.

When King Akrisios of Argos learned from an oracle that his daughter Danaê would give birth to a son who would kill him, he secluded Danaê in an underground chamber. But Zeus, pouring through the roof in the form of a stream of gold, had sexual intercourse with her, and she bore a son, Perseus. After Akrisios learned of the child, he placed mother and son in a chest and cast it into the sea. The chest came ashore at the island of Seriphos, where Diktys gave a home to mother and child.

Diktys's brother, King Polydektes, fell in love with Danaê, and in order to get rid of Perseus he ordered him to fetch the Gorgon's head. With Hermes and Athena as helpers, Perseus went first to the Graiai, three women who were old from birth and had among them but one eye and one tooth, which they passed from one to another. Perseus got hold of their eye and tooth, agreeing to return them only when the old women had told him the way to the nymphs who possessed winged sandals, a certain kind of pouch, and the Cap of Invisibility. Having gotten these items, Perseus flew to the River Ocean, where he found the three Gorgon sisters sleeping: Sthenno, Euryalê, and Medusa, of whom only the last was mortal. Anyone who saw them was turned to stone. Guided by Athena and looking only at the reflection of the Gorgons in his shield, Perseus beheaded Medusa. From her sprang the winged horse Pegasos and the hero Chrysaor, with whom she had been preg-

Perseus slaying the Gorgon Medusa, with Hermes looking on.

nant. Perseus placed Medusa's head in his pouch and flew away. The two remaining Gorgons attempted pursuit but in vain because of Perseus's Cap of Invisibility.

As he was returning, Perseus came to Ethopia, ruled by King Kepheus. There he saw the king's daughter, Andromeda, exposed to a sea-monster. Kepheus's wife, Kassiepeia, had boasted that she was more beautiful than the Nereids, a vaunt that had angered the Nereids and the sea-god Poseidon, who then sent a flood and a sea-monster against the land. When an oracle revealed that the Ethiopians would be freed of the monster if Andromeda should be set out as food for the monster, the Ethiopians forced the king to bind his daughter to a rock as a sacrifice to the creature. But Perseus fell in love with her and promised to slay the monster if the king should give him Andromeda as wife. After the god agreed, Perseus killed the monster and released Andromeda. The princess had originally been betrothed to Phineus, who now conspired against her rescuer. Perseus showed the Gorgon's head to Phineus and his allies, turning them all into stone.

Returning to Seriphos, Perseus displayed the Gorgon's head to King Polydektes and his supporters, who all turned to stone. After appointing Diktys ruler of the island, Perseus returned the borrowed sandals, pouch, and cap, and gave the Gorgon's head to Athena, who placed it in the middle of her shield. Then he proceeded to the mainland to see King Akrisios. There Perseus competed in a pentathlon, but when he threw the discus it struck Akrisios, killing him. The oracle was thereby fulfilled. Ashamed to assume the rule of Argos, Perseus traded kingdoms with King Megapenthes of Tiryns, so that Megapenthes ruled Argos and Perseus reigned over Tiryns. Perseus had five sons by Andromeda, including Perses, from whom the kings of Persia were descended (Apollodorus *Library* 2.4.1–5).

The legend of the monster-slayer Perseus, the princess Andromeda, and the false hero Phineus is a Greek version of the international tale of the Dragon-Slayer, which is found in many lands.

Perseus and Andromeda.

In mythological art, Perseus is often depicted as a youth, eyes averted, slaying the Gorgon Medusa or as a youth with winged sandals fleeing the pursuing Gorgons.

See also Biographical Pattern; Divine Guilds; Hero; Monsters

Suggested reading:

Antti Aarne and Stith Thompson. *The Types of the Folktale: A Classification and Bibliography,* FF Communications 184. Helsinki: Academia Scientiarum Fennica, 1961, Type 300: *The Dragon-Slayer.*

Timothy Gantz. *Early Greek Myth: A Guide to Literary and Artistic Sources.* Baltimore: The Johns Hopkins University Press, 1993, 300–311.

William Hansen. *Ariadne's Thread: A Guide to International Tales Found in Classical Literature.* Ithaca, NY: Cornell University Press, 2002, 119–123, 246–251.

Linda Jones Roccos. "Perseus," in *LIMC* 7:332–348.

Jocelyn M. Woodward. *Perseus: A Study in Greek Art and Legend.* Cambridge, UK: The University Press, 1937.

Eros.

PERSONIFIED ABSTRACTIONS

Concepts treated as living, supernatural beings.

Greek culture is replete with abstract notions that are personified and treated as divine beings. Some are emotions or forces such as Atê (Mental Blindness), Eros (Erotic Love), Himeros (Longing), Metis (Cleverness), Nemesis (Indignation), Peitho (Persuasion), Phobos (Fear), and Tychê (Fortune). Others are conditions such as Eirenê (Peace), Eris (Strife), Nikê (Victory), Nyx (Night), and Thanatos (Death). And still others are institutions such as Horkos (Oath) and Themis (Divine Law/Custom). The gender of the being is determined by the grammatical gender of the noun; for example, *eros* is a masculine noun so that Eros is a male deity, and *eris* is a feminine noun so that Eris is a female deity. Since most abstract nouns in Greek are feminine, most personified abstractions are feminine.

Personified abstractions are especially frequent in mythic cosmogonies, in which a number of concepts may be placed in genealogical relationships with one another. Thus a large number of the characters in Hesiod's *Theogony* are personified abstractions grouped into families. Hesiod assigns most of the constituents of the universe to one of two descent-groups, the Chaos group and the Gaia (Earth) group, the descendants of Chaos being for the most part impalpable things that we regard as forces or conditions; that is, they are abstractions. Thus Chaos gave birth to Erebos and Nyx (Darkness and Night), who in turn begot Aither and Hemera (Brightness and Day). Night herself then produced many offspring including Moros (Doom), Thanatos (Death), Hypnos (Sleep), Oneiroi (Dreams), Momos (Blame), Moirai (Fates), Nemesis (Indignation), Geras (Old Age), and Eris (Strife), and Eris likewise had many children, among them Lethê (Forgetfulness), Limos (Famine), Phonoi (Killings), and Horkos (Oath).

Some personified abstractions do no more than fill a slot in a mythic genealogy or receive a passing mention by an author, whereas others play a role in a story and so are more personalized. For example, the goddess Eris (Strife) stirred up strife among the immortals by casting among them an apple that was to be given to the most beautiful goddess, an exquisitely destabilizing gesture that led ultimately to the Trojan War. The Moirai (Fates) came to Meleager's house several days after his birth and declared that he would live until a particular stick should be consumed by fire, a motif of central importance in the Meleager legend. In several stories, Thanatos (Death) stalks living beings in his eagerness to acquire additional souls for the realm of the dead, as when he came to carry Sisyphos away. In this respect Thanatos and Hades are interchangeable. Indeed, when Alkestis was about to die, the particular deity who came to fetch her was Thanatos in one source (Euripides's *Alkestis*) and Hades in another (Apollodoros's *Library*). The same redundancy is found among the divine inciters of love; functionally, Thanatos is to Hades as Eros is to Aphroditê.

The role of certain personified abstractions is to accompany a major deity. Thus the entourage of the goddess Aphroditê may include Eros (Erotic Love) and Himeros (Longing), and the god Ares has his assistants Phobos (Fear) and Deimos (Terror). The satellites serve not only to signal the importance of the deity but also to externalize attributes of the deity and his or her sphere of influence. Aphroditê is the cause of love and longing in living creatures, just as fear and terror are inevitably present in warfare.

Not all the personified abstractions found in classical mythology received worship, nor do all deified abstractions honored in cult appear as characters in story. Thus the personified abstraction Freedom was a deity, had temples, and was represented on coins. She was conceived as being female, since the word for the concept "freedom" is grammatically feminine in both Greek (*eleutheria*) and Latin (*libertas*). The ultimate inspiration for the Statue of Liberty created by the French sculptor Frédéric-Auguste Bartholdi in 1886, she is familiar to every American today. But she appears in no ancient myth or legend.

Eros.

See also Divine Guilds

Suggested reading:

Walter Burkert. *Greek Religion,* trans. John Raffan. Cambridge, MA: Harvard University Press, 1985, 184–186.

K. J. Dover. *Greek Popular Morality in the Time of Plato and Aristotle.* Indianapolis, IN: Hackett, 1994, 141–144.

Stewart Guthrie. *Faces in the Clouds: A New Theory of Religion.* Oxford: Oxford University Press, 1993.

Kurt Heinemann. *Thanatos in Poesie und Kunst der Griechen.* Munich: Kastner and Callwey, 1913.

Victoria T. Larson. "The Statue of Liberty: An American Symbol in Its Classical Context." *Omnibus* 33 (January 1997): 29–32.

Emma Stafford. *Worshipping Virtues: Personification and the Divine in Ancient Greece*. London: Duckworth and the Classical Press of Wales, 2000.

Martin L. West, ed. and comm. *Hesiod: Theogony*. Oxford: Clarendon Press, 1966, 33–34.

POSEIDON (ROMAN NEPTUNE)

God of waters, especially the sea.

Poseidon is ruler of the sea, where he dwells in an underwater palace with his wife, the Nereid Amphitritê. Triton is their son, a merman having an android upper body and a piscine lower body. The Romans identified their deity Neptune (Latin *Neptunus*) with Poseidon.

One of six children of the Titans Kronos and Rhea, Poseidon along with his siblings was swallowed alive by his father upon his birth. The exception was the youngest sibling, Zeus, who was smuggled away and raised secretly in a cave on Crete. Later Kronos was induced to take an emetic, causing him to spew up the children he had swallowed. There followed a great battle, the Titanomachy, between the older gods and the younger gods, in which the younger gods, led by Zeus, emerged victorious.

According to one tradition, the three brothers Hades, Zeus, and Poseidon drew lots for the sovereignty of different parts of the world, and Poseidon drew the lot for the gray sea (Homer *Iliad* 15.187–193), but according to a different tradition Zeus allotted honors, or offices, to all the deities after he became king of the gods (Hesiod *Theogony* 881–885). As an emblem of his lordship of the sea, Poseidon carries a trident, or three-pronged fishing spear, which he wields not as a fishing tool but as a magic wand, focusing his power. Actions attributed to the god in different stories reflecting his role as ruler of waters include sending floods, creating storms at sea, sending sea-monsters (or other animals) forth from the sea, drowning men at sea, turning a ship to stone, creating an inland pool of seawater, and creating (or revealing the location of) freshwater springs.

Although Poseidon is also lord of horses and of earthquakes in Greek tradition, these honors are not foregrounded in mythological narrative. True, he does take the form of a horse for a particular purpose in a story and he does beget a horse, but so do other deities. Among his epithets is Dark-Haired One, or more precisely Dark-Blue-Haired One (*kyanochaites*), an epithet applied also to horses with reference to the mane. His association with earthquakes finds little mythic expression other than in the frequent use by narrators of his epithets Earthshaker and Earth-Holder.

Among honors that Poseidon sought but failed to acquire were the lordship over certain cities, for there was a time when the gods individually took possession of particular cities, places where they would be specially honored. In some cases, two gods competed for the honor of possessing a particular city. Thus Poseidon and Athena each came to Attica, claiming the right to it. Poseidon struck a place on the Acropolis with his trident, causing salt water to appear. Then Athena planted an olive tree. Acting as judges, the gods awarded the region to Athena, who named the city Athens after herself and became its patron. Poseidon angrily responded by sending a flood (Apollodoros *Library* 3.14.1). Poseidon similarly contested with Hera for possession of Argos, losing to her as well.

Poseidon had numerous erotic encounters, including some with an equine theme. When Demeter was searching for her abducted daughter, Poseidon pursued her, desiring to have sexual intercourse with her, and in order to escape him Demeter changed herself into a mare and grazed among the mares belonging to a certain Arcadian king named Onkios. But Poseidon perceived the deceit, changed himself into a stallion, and coupled with her in that form. The offspring of their union was the divine horse, Areion, whose first owner was Onkios (Pausanias 8.25.4–10). On another occasion Poseidon mated with the Gorgon Medusa, who at the moment of her beheading by Perseus bore the hero Chrysaor and the winged horse Pegasos (Hesiod *Theogony* 279–286). But myths are also recounted of other deities who assume the form of a horse for the purpose of engaging in sexual intercourse (Kronos, Zephyros, Boreas), and of course Demeter takes equine form in the present myth in order to avoid a sexual encounter. As a god, Poseidon enjoys the general power of metamorphosis into any form, but unlike lesser sea deities such as Thetis and Proteus, he does not manifest rapid, serial transformation, perhaps because serial transformation is usually a defensive maneuver.

Among his many other erotic encounters, two may be mentioned. Caenis (Greek Kainis) was a lovely Lapith maiden who received many offers of marriage and turned them all down. One day as she walked by herself along the seashore, she was ravaged by Neptune. He offered then to grant her any wish, and she wished to become a man, so that the sea god transformed her from female to male, and Caenis became Caeneus (Greek *Kaineus*), the masculine form of the name. Neptune also made him invulnerable, so that Caeneus enjoyed a long career as a warrior in his homeland of Thessaly (Ovid *Metamorphoses* 12.169–209, 459–535). After Poseidon lost the contest for Argos to Hera, he angrily caused all the springs there to dry up. Amymonê, a daughter of Danaos, was sent by her father in search of water, and in the course of her search she spotted a deer, cast her javelin at it, but hit instead a sleeping satyr.

Pelops racing Oinomaos for the hand of Hippodameia.

The satyr leapt up and lustily pursued her but fled when Poseidon suddenly appeared. Then Amymonê and Poseidon slept together, after which the god revealed to her the springs at Lerna. She bore a son, Nauplios (Apollodoros *Library* 2.1.4–5).

In a different sort of story, Poseidon and Apollon once went disguised as mortals to King Laomedon of Troy and offered to build a wall around the city for certain wages. The gods' object was to test Laomedon's reputed hubris. And indeed after the gods fortified Troy, Laomedon refused them their promised wages. In punishment, Apollon sent a pestilence against the city and Poseidon sent a sea-monster (Apollodoros *Library* 2.5.9).

Poseidon's connections with mortal heroes are many and varied. Tantalos's son Pelops was a handsome youth, to whom Poseidon felt erotically attracted, so that he carried him off to Olympos, where the two were lovers for a time. Later, in return for Pelops's favors, Poseidon helped the youth win his wife, Hippodameia (Pindar *Olympian* 1). Poseidon was the father of the Athenian hero Theseus. For on the night when King Aigeus of Athens lay with Aithra, Poseidon also had sexual intercourse with her. She bore Theseus, whose putative father was Aigeus but whose biological father was Poseidon (Apollodoros *Library* 3.15.7). Poseidon fathered many other heroes, including the great hunter Orion and the giant Aloads. He was the principal divine opponent of the hero Odysseus during his journey home following the Trojan War. For when Odysseus and his companions visited the land of the Cyclopes, they blinded the Cyclops Polyphemos, a son of Poseidon. The blinded giant cursed Odysseus, asking his father to punish him, and the angry Poseidon complied by obstructing Odysseus's homeward journey at sea (for example, Homer *Odyssey* 5.287–381). Upon his return Odysseus was obliged to propitiate the god by performing a sacrifice to him at an inland community whose inhabitants were entirely unfamiliar with the sea (*Odyssey* 11.121–137), that is, to increase Poseidon's honor by introducing his cult among persons who had not before heard of him.

In mythological iconography, Poseidon is typically represented with long hair and a beard, holding his trident, often in the company of his wife, Amphitritê, and sometimes surrounded by sea creatures such as fish or dolphins or mermen. These last are Tritons, who are sometimes treated as a genus of sea-deity, like male Nereids, rather than as a single male being. Poseidon's sea-chariot is drawn by hippocampi (Greek *hippokampoi*), sea-horses having the forepart of a horse and the tail of a fish. But in literature his chariot is drawn by horses, sometimes described as winged, who fly above the waters (Homer *Iliad* 13.17–31).

> **See also** Waters
> **Suggested reading:**
> Joseph Fontenrose. "The Building of the City Walls: Troy and Asgard." *Journal of American Folklore* 96 (1983): 53–63.
> Timothy Gantz. *Early Greek Myth: A Guide to Literary and Artistic Sources.* Baltimore: The Johns Hopkins University Press, 1993, 62–63.
> Erika Simon. "Poseidon," in *LIMC* 7:446–479.
> ——— and Gerhard Bauchhenss. "Neptunus," in *LIMC* 7:483–500.

PROMOTION AND DEMOTION

Raising or lowering of a character's cosmic status.

The cosmic status of characters is ordinarily persistent, immortals remaining immortals, mortals remaining mortals, and so on. A few characters, however, are elevated to a higher status in the cosmic hierarchy by becoming a higher life-form (a human becomes a god, and so on), acquiring immortality, undergoing heroization, or the like, whereas others are downgraded to a lower status by losing immortality, by becoming a lower life-form (a human becomes an animal, and so on), or by losing their lives. Promotion may be a divine reward for merit, and demotion a divine punishment for hubris, although this is far from always the case.

The most important kinds of mythological promotion and demotion are exemplified below, beginning with apotheosis, or deification.

Promotion

The gods occasionally admit a human to their number, transforming him or her into a fellow divine being. Thus the hero Herakles, a son of Zeus and a human female, Alkmenê, was born a mortal, enjoyed a heroic career as a mortal, and became a god at the end of his life. After Herakles was unwittingly poisoned by his wife, Deianeira, he made his way to Mount Oitê, built a funeral pyre, climbed onto it, and had someone light it. As the flames burned away his mortal parts, Zeus's son was wafted up to the heavens by a cloud and became a god. He married the goddess Hebê (Youth) and dwelled thereafter among the Olympians (Homer *Odyssey* 11.601–604; Hesiod *Theogony* 950–955; Apollodoros *Library* 2.7.7; Lucian *Hermotimos* 7; Ovid *Metamorphoses* 9.239–272), though he was not accounted an Olympian. Except to wed a goddess and live among the gods, the deified Herakles plays no real role as a deity in mythological narrative.

The greatest success story of this sort may be that of Dionysos, a son of Zeus and a mortal woman Semelê, for although the offspring of a god and a human is regularly a mortal, however outstanding he or she may otherwise prove to be, both Dionysos and his mother, Semelê, become gods (Hesiod *Theogony* 940–942; Pindar *Olympian* 2.25–27; Nonnos *Dionysiaka* 8.413–418), and Dionysos even joins the ranks of the Olympians as their youngest and last member. But it is unclear whether Dionysos was made immortal (Hyginus *Fabulae* 224), since he had only one divine parent, or was immortal from the first (*Homeric Hymn to Dionysos* 2.5–6), since from another perspective he had two divine parents. Zeus in a sense was Dionysos's mother as well as his father, for upon the death of his pregnant lover, Zeus removed the fetus from Semelê's womb and sewed it into his own thigh as a quasi-womb until the infant was ready to be born. The principal concern of Dionysiac mythology moreover is his struggle not to acquire divinity but to win acknowledgment of it.

There is no ambiguity in the apotheosis of the human woman who was transformed into Leukothea, or White Goddess, a marine deity who along with her son Palaimon helps sailors in distress. Homer relates that Kadmos's daughter Ino, or Leukothea, spotted Odysseus when he was trying to stay afloat on a battered raft while Poseidon was making a serious effort to drown him. Previously Leukothea had been a mortal woman but now dwelled in the sea as a goddess, an honor granted her by the gods. Having noticed Odysseus, then, she emerged from the sea like a bird, perched upon Odysseus's raft, instructed him what to do in order to save himself, lent him a magic veil to guarantee his safety, and dove back into the stormy sea (Homer *Odyssey* 5.333–364). Before Leukothea was a goddess she had been a human being, Ino, one of Semelê's sisters. Ino and her husband, Athamas, offended Hera, who in her anger caused Athamas (or both Athamas and Ino) to be dangerously delusional. Ino leaped into the sea with her son Melikertes, after which she was known as Leukothea and he as Palaimon (Apollodoros *Library* 3.4.3; Ovid *Metamorphoses* 4.447–542). It is also possible for a human woman to become a nymph. Dryopê was beloved by the hamadryads, or tree nymphs, who took her away from the world of humans and made her one of their own (Antoninus Liberalis 32).

Several nondivine male beings aspire not to godhead as such but to this or that divine privilege such as having a goddess as wife or sexual partner. Thus the huge Aloads, Otos and Ephialtes, piled several mountains on top of one another, threatening to reach the sky. Wishing to obtain goddesses as wives, Ephialtes wooed Hera and Otos wooed Artemis (Apollodoros *Library* 1.7.4). Ixion attempted to assault Hera sexually, and when she reported Ixion's intentions to Zeus, he made an image of Hera out of cloud and placed it beside Ixion, who had sexual intercourse with it, boasting that he had slept with Hera (Apollodoros *Epitome* 1.20). For a male monster or human a goddess is the supreme female, and of goddesses Hera is the most desirable because, as the wife of Zeus, she enjoys the highest possible cosmic status and so is the unattainable female par excellence. Human females can also aspire to sexual relationships with male deities, but they tend to invite rather than to assault. Thus Iphimedeia fell in love with Poseidon and would often visit the sea, pouring seawater onto her lap with her hands, and in time Poseidon lay with her (Apollodoros *Library* 1.7.4).

Promotion to divine status of some sort and promotion only to immortal status were distinguished conceptually, if not always in narration. It was possible for a character to acquire passive features of divinity (immortality, agelessness, life of ease, residence among the gods, and so on) but not active ones (general supernatural powers, a particular sphere of influence, and so on). Really there were three principal possibilities: a human could be elevated to being an active god, a passive god, or simply a being who was immortal and ageless. When Ino became Leukothea, she became a full divinity with divine powers and a defined role in the cosmic organization. When Herakles and Semelê were deified, they became passive divinities, at least so far as mythological narrative is concerned, acquiring the status and lifestyle of deities but no roles in the cosmic system, and so figuring in no myths in their new status. When Zeus carried off the handsome Trojan youth Ganymedes to Olympos to be cupbearer for the gods, he made the youth "immortal and ageless like the gods" (*Homeric Hymn to Aphrodite* 202–217), but only like the gods, not a god as such.

Particular instances can be fuzzy because once a character becomes immortal and ageless, the distinction between divine and nondivine status may be narratively unimportant. When a deity weds a mortal, the mortal must be made immortal and ageless at the least, or else the relationship is doomed to be brief, for one partner will age and eventually die while the other will remain physically unchanged forever, as in the case of the mortal Peleus and the Nereid Thetis (Homer *Iliad* 18.428–435). So when Dionysos took the human maiden Ariadnê to wife, she was made immortal and ageless (Hesiod *Theogony* 947–949), though she perhaps was not made a divinity and in any case not an active one so far as myth is concerned. Similarly, in the mythologized folktale of Cupid and Psychê, when Jove confirmed the marriage of the two lovers on Olympus, he told Cupid's mother, Venus, not to concern herself with the fact that her son's mate was a mortal, for he himself would make the match equal. Jove handed Psychê a cup of ambrosia and declared her immortal, so that the marriage might last forever (Apuleius *Metamorphoses* 6.22–23). Events turn out differently in the story of Marpessa, who was courted both by the human Idas and the god Apollon. When Zeus permitted the maiden to choose which of the two she preferred, she picked her mortal suitor, fearing that Apollon would leave her when she grew old (Apollodoros *Library* 1.7.8).

Many human beings acquire immortality coupled with agelessness. This is probably the experience of all persons whom the gods translate from one cosmic realm to another, such as Ganymedes. Thus toward the end of his life Menelaos will not die in Argos, but the gods will transport him to a special paradise, the Elysion Field, because as Helen's husband he is a son-in-law of Zeus (Homer *Odyssey* 4.562–569). There he will presumably dwell forever like a god but not as a god. Similarly, persons who are catasterized, whether they are regarded as divine or not, necessarily become immortal and unchanging. The hunter Arkas once pursued a bear into a sanctuary, not knowing that the animal was actually his mother Kallisto, whom a god had transformed into a bear. Before he could slay the animal, or before the angry Arcadians could kill them both for their intrusion, Zeus placed them in the sky as constellations, the one as the Bear and the other as the Bear-Keeper (Ovid *Metamorphoses* 2.496–530; Hyginus *Poetic Astronomy* 2.1). In the list of persons who acquired immortality compiled by the mythographer Hyginus (*Fabulae* 224), most instances are catasterisms.

Sometimes a deity tries to render a human infant immortal and ageless but fails. So Demeter attempted to give these qualities to the human baby Demophoön, but the infant's mother interrupted the supernatural process, the goddess did not complete it, and the child remained mortal (*Homeric Hymn to Demeter* 213–264). Also other things can go wrong. The goddess Eos (Dawn) wed the mortal man Tithonos, whom at her request Zeus made immortal, but inasmuch as she neglected to ask also for eternal youth for him, Tithonos continued to age and eventually wasted away until he was no more than a voice (*Homeric Hymn to Aphrodite* 218–238). Immortality and aging thus run on separate tracks, so that it is possible for a human to escape death without enjoying concomitant youthfulness. It can also happen that a mortal rejects the opportunity, as when the nymph Kalypso offered immortality to the hero Odysseus if he would remain with her as her mate, but he declined, wishing instead to return to his mortal wife, Penelopê, which in the end he managed to do (Homer *Odyssey* 23.333–337).

Immortality can be granted after death. The cyclic epic *Aithiopis* recounts that after Eos's son Memnon was slain by Achilleus, Eos secured Zeus's permission to make him immortal. Later, after Achilleus himself was killed, his mother, Thetis, translated him from his funeral pyre to Leukê, or the White Isle, to dwell. Similarly, persons may already be dead when the gods decide to place them in the sky as a star group. Apollodoros relates that the huntress Artemis shot and killed Kallisto, her companion in hunting, because the latter had not preserved her virginity. Zeus then turned Kallisto into a constellation, the Bear (*Library* 3.8.1).

A different kind of postmortem promotion is heroization, that is, elevation upon death to the status of hero or heroine in the cultic sense of a powerful dead person, or ghost. Although a hero or heroine must always be a mortal who has died, only a few deceased persons become heroes. Some heroes are persons who suffered an untimely death, as in the case of Jason's and Medeia's children Mermeros and Pheres, whom the Corinthians stoned to death because of the role the children had played in the death of Glaukê, daughter of the Corinthian king, bringing her gifts that, unknown to the children, were lethal. The two murdered boys then caused Corinthian infants to die until the Corinthians learned the cause of their misfortune from an oracle and instituted annual sacrifices to Mermeros and Pheres in order to appease them (Pausanias 2.3.6). In this tradition the murdered children become heroes, powerful dead persons who can affect for good or bad the lives of those who dwell in the vicinity of their remains. The heroized children angrily plague the Corinthians with the loss of their own young until the community honors the slain children.

Finally, changes of sex can be mentioned in this connection, for a transformation from female to male was deemed an elevation, if perhaps not a cosmic one. For example, Caenis (Greek Kainis) was the loveliest maiden in Thessaly. Many suitors sought her, but she refused them all. She used to take walks along the solitary shore, where one day Neptune raped her. Afterward he offered to grant any wish, and thinking of the injury she had suffered, she chose to remain a woman no longer. So the god transformed her into a man, and not only a man but an invulnerable man. Caenis changed his name to Caeneus (Greek Kaineus) and, being invulnerable, became a formidable warrior. Since he could not be pierced, his enemies eventually put an end to him by crushing him (Ovid *Metamorphoses* 12.189–535).

Demotion

Although many mortal characters acquire immortality, perhaps only one immortal loses this quality. The good centaur Cheiron chanced to be struck by one of Herakles's poisoned arrows, and although the distressed Herakles withdrew the shaft and treated the wound with medicine given him by Cheiron, the painful wound proved to be incurable. Since Cheiron wished only to die but being immortal could not, with the centaur's permission Zeus transferred his immortality to another, allowing Cheiron to die (Apollodoros *Library* 2.5.4).

More common is the radical metamorphosis of a human to a lower lifeform, either an animal or a plant. That the change is a downgrade is clear when the transformation is a divine punishment. Thus the Maeonian maiden Arachnê (Spider) was a skillful spinner and weaver of wool who refused to acknowledge Minerva's superiority in this art. Eventually Arachnê and Minerva engaged in a contest of weaving, in which Arachnê performed flawlessly. Frustrated and angry, the goddess beat Arachnê over the head with her shuttle until Arachnê, unable to bear it any longer, placed a noose around her neck. Pitying her, the goddess changed the girl into a spider as a punishment for her and her descendants, so that as a hanging spider Arachnê continued her weaving (Ovid *Metamorphoses* 6.1–145). In another story the nine daughters of Pierus and Euippê were masterful singers who challenged even the nine Muses in a contest of singing skill. After nymphs were chosen to be judges, each group performed. The nymphs unanimously declared the goddesses to be the winners, but when the Pierides continued their insults, the Muses punished them for their continued offensiveness, turning them into hoarse and noisy magpies (*Metamorphoses* 5.294–678). Arachnê and the Pierides not only descend in the cosmic hierarchy but also are condemned to repeat endlessly the offensive behavior that brought about their demise in the first place. Not all transformations, however, are demotions.

The transformation of a living person into a dead one, and so the relegation of a human from the realm of the living to the realm of the dead, is a different form of downgrade, for which there are many instances. Thus Asklepios was the son of Apollon and a human maiden but was raised by the centaur Cheiron, who taught him the art of medicine. Asklepios grew up to be a renowned surgeon who could not only prevent persons from dying but even raise them from the dead. Zeus, fearing that other humans would acquire this art, slew Asklepios with a thunderbolt. In retaliation Apollon angrily killed the Cyclopes, forgers of Zeus's thunderbolts (Apollodoros *Library* 3.103–4). On another occasion, Demeter, yielding to her desire, lay with a mortal man Iasion in a field, but Zeus learned of it and killed him with a thunderbolt, since the gods are jealous of goddesses consorting with mortal men (Homer *Odyssey* 5.125–128f).

Immortals are often attracted romantically or sexually to mortals. For an unmarried god, there are rarely repercussions, but erotic dealings between an unmarried goddess and a mortal man may provoke the jealousy and anger of other deities (Homer *Odyssey* 5.118–140). In the case of a married god, there are few repercussions, except in the case of Zeus, whose erotic encounters with other females result in his wife's displeasure, which she may take out on the woman and her offspring, if any. Married goddesses tend to avoid sexual encounters with mortal men.

Cosmic promotions and demotions are mostly understandable after the fact but usually not predictable in advance.

See also Catasterism; Sex-Changers; Transformation; Translation

ROMANTIC NARRATIVES

Myths and legends focusing upon love, especially idealized love.

Romantic narratives, emphasizing love over sexuality, frequently achieve closure with the union (or reunion) of two lovers, either happily in life or tragically in death.

A common initial situation is that of a beautiful maiden (or handsome youth) who attracts many suitors. Atalantê (Latinized form = Atalanta) was both an extraordinary athlete and an independent-minded maiden. When her father persuaded her to wed, she made her suitors compete with her individually in a footrace. The youth was given a head start, and she followed dressed in full armor. If she caught up with him, he was killed then and there, but if he reached the goal first, he could marry her. Many suitors had perished when a certain Melanion, who had fallen in love with her, came to race her. He had the foresight of obtaining from Aphroditê some golden apples, which he tossed aside as she pursued him, and since Atalantê paused to pick them up, she lost the race. So Melanion married her (Apollodoros *Library* 3.9.2; cf. Ovid *Metamorphoses* 10.560–680). The strategy of distracting one's pursuer by throwing down something valuable, known as a *diversion flight,* is found in legends and folktales worldwide.

A sculptor named Pygmalion became disgusted with women and so lived his life without a consort. But when he carved a statue of a beautiful maiden from ivory, he fell in love with her. During the festival of Venus he prayed to the goddess to obtain a wife like his ivory maid, but the goddess understood his true intent, so that when he returned home and kissed his ivory maid, she became flesh. They married, and she bore a daughter, Paphos (Ovid *Metamorphoses* 10.243–297). In a form of the legend that foregrounds lust rather than romance, Pygmalion fell in love with a statue of Aphroditê, treating it though it were his wife, which included his employing it as his sexual partner (Arnobios *Adversus Gentes* 6.22), one of several ancient stories of men who fall in love with statues, usually of Aphroditê, and make love to them.

Perhaps the most lovely tale in ancient literature is that of Cupid and Psychê, which is probably a mythologized folktale. Like the story of Odysseus and Penelopê, as related in Homer's *Odyssey*, it portrays the painful separation of a loving husband and wife and concludes with their reunion. A king and queen had three daughters, of which the youngest, Psychê (Soul), was so beautiful that people honored her as they would a goddess, neglecting Venus. Angry at this, Venus bade her son Cupid make Psychê fall in love with some impoverished man. When Psychê's father consulted an oracle of Apollo about a prospective husband for her, the god responded that he must leave her on a certain cliff attired for marriage, and that her husband would be a fierce, winged being whom even the gods fear. The wedding procession sorrowfully conducted the girl to the cliff and left her there weeping, but gentle Zephyur wafted her up and placed her in a valley below, where she came upon a palace full of treasure and invisible servants. During the night her unknown husband joined her in bed, making her his wife, but left again before it was light. Meanwhile Psychê's family grieved for her, and Psychê asked her husband to allow her to see her sisters in order to comfort them. He agreed but told her that they would try to persuade her to discover what he looked like and warned her that such curiosity would be disastrous. The sisters, envious of Psychê's good fortune, deceitfully told her that her husband might be something monstrous, as the oracle implied, and persuaded her to kill him as he slept. That evening, as she approached her sleeping husband with a knife in hand, she saw by the light of her lamp that he was Cupid, and she accidentally spilled a drop of hot oil on him, awakening him. He explained that although his mother Venus had told him to wed Psychê to some poor wretch, he had married her himself, but since Psychê had obeyed her sisters rather than him, her punishment would be his flight. So saying, he flew away. After Psychê punished her evil sisters for ruining her happiness, she wandered from country to country in quest of her husband in the hope of soothing his anger. Eventually she surrendered to her hostile mother-in-law, Venus, who assigned her a number of seemingly impossible tasks to accomplish. As she was attempting the last of them, Cupid intervened, having recovered from his oil burn, and asked Jupiter to set things aright. The god decreed that Psychê should be Cupid's wife and made her immortal in order that Venus not be offended by her son's marrying beneath his station. In time Psychê gave birth to a daughter Voluptas, or Pleasure (Apuleius *Metamorphoses* 4.28–6.24). Like some other romantic stories set in the historical period or in a vaguely timeless past in the manner of folktales, the tale of Cupid and Psychê came at some point to be included in compilations of classical mythology (first in Fulgentius's *Mythologies*) and so became an honorary mythological narrative.

Narcissus gazing at his own reflection, with Eros looking on.

The legend of Narcissus (Greek *Narkissos*) is a romantic story without a romantic conclusion, since the protagonist falls in love with himself, making a final union impossible. The youth Narcissus, offspring of a nymph and a river-god, was sought in love by many youths and maidens, but he coldly rejected them all. Finally one scorned youth prayed to the gods that Narcissus too might fall in love but not attain his beloved. Presently when Narcissus sought to refresh himself at a spring, he fell in love with the sight of his own reflection, which he tried in vain to embrace and kiss, thinking it to be another being. Although in time he perceived that he had fallen in love with himself, nothing could induce him to stop gazing at his reflection, and he gradually wasted away. In place of his body a new kind of flower sprang up (Ovid *Metamorphoses* 3.339–510).

In tragic love stories the loving couple may be united in death. In Assyria there lived a handsome youth Pyramus and a lovely maiden Thisbê, who loved each other but were forbidden by their parents to marry. Living next door to each other, they managed to communicate secretly through a chink in the party wall. One night they decided to run away together and agreed to meet at the Tomb of Ninus, near a mulberry tree with its white fruit. Thisbê reached the tomb first, but a lioness also made her way there fresh from a kill, and when Thisbê spotted her she ran away, dropping her veil, which the lioness chewed upon. In the meantime Pyramus showed up, saw the animal tracks and the bloody veil, and concluding that his beloved had perished, plunged his sword into his body. When Thisbê returned, she perceived what had happened and chose to join Pyramus in death. Their blood caused the berries of the mulberry tree to turn red, and so they remain to this day. The two lovers were buried by their parents in a single tomb (Ovid *Metamorphoses* 4.55–166).

A youth Leander (Greek *Leandros*) lived in Abydos, near Troy, and a maiden Hero, a priestess of Aphroditê, lived across the sound in a tower beside the sea in the city of Sestos. Once at a festival of Adonis and Aphroditê, Leander and Hero met and fell in love. Since they dwelled in different cities, he offered to swim across the sound nightly, instructing her to hold aloft a lamp to guide him. For many a summer night, Leander swam to Hero's tower, guided by the light of her lamp, after which they enjoyed each other's love. One night in winter during a storm Hero lit her lamp and Leander set out, but the rough sea overcame him and the bitter wind blew out her lamp. In the morning, seeing his drowned body at the base of her tower, Hero cast herself down in order to join him in death (Musaios *Hero and Leander*).

Several stories muse upon the implications of a committed relationship between a mortal and an immortal. Marpessa was wooed by both the mortal Idas and the god Apollon. When Zeus allowed the maiden to choose which of the two she wished to marry, Marpessa, fearing that Apollon would leave her when she grew old, chose Idas as her husband (Apollodoros *Library* 1.7.8). The same choice is made by Aphroditê when she is faced with the prospect of a mortal spouse. She declined to take the mortal Anchises as her husband, reasoning that he would inevitably grow old and she would then feel sorrow (*Homeric Hymn to Aphrodite* 239–248). The consequences anticipated by the mortal Marpessa and the immortal Aphroditê are realized in the relationship of Eos (Dawn) and the mortal Tithonos. Eos snatched up Tithonos and carried him off to be her lover, and upon her request Zeus made him immortal, but she neglected to ask that he also make Tithonos ageless. When Tithonos grew old and became too weak to move, being now little more than a voice, she placed him in a room and closed the door (*Homeric Hymn to Aphrodite* 218–238).

> **See also** Sexual Myths and Legends
>
> **Suggested reading:**
>
> Antti Aarne and Stith Thompson. *The Types of the Folktale: A Classification and Bibliography.* FF Communications, 184. Helsinki: Academia Scientiarum Fennica, 1961, Type 425B: *The Disenchanted Husband: The Witch's Tasks* and Type 666: *Hero and Leander.*
>
> Hans Färber. *Hero und Leander: Musaios und die weiteren antiken Zeugnisse.* Munich: Ernst Heimeran, 1961.
>
> Michael Grant. *Myths of the Greeks and Romans.* New York: Mentor, 1964, 373–378 (Hero and Leander).
>
> William Hansen. *Ariadne's Thread: A Guide to International Tales Found in Classical Literature.* Ithaca, NY: Cornell University Press, 2002, 100–114 (Cupid and Psychê), 258–259 (Narcissus).

Noëlle Icard-Gianolio. "Psyche," in *LIMC* 7:569–585.

Jaromir Jech. "Hero und Leander," in *Enzyklopädie des Märchens.* Berlin: Walter de Gruyter, 1990, 6:845–851.

Jane M. Miller. "Some Versions of Pygmalion," in *Ovid Renewed,* edited by Charles Martindale. Cambridge: Cambridge University Press, 1988, 205–214.

Louise Vinge. *The Narcissus Theme in Western European Literature Up to the Early Nineteenth Century.* Lund, Sweden: Gleerup, 1967.

Satyr.

SATYRS (GREEK SATYROI) AND SILENS (GREEK SILENOI)

Composite male beings of the countryside, partly human and partly equine in form.

The basic structure of satyrs, including the fact that they walk upright on two legs, is that of a human male, whereas their bestial face, ears, manelike hair, ithyphallic (or at least large) genitalia, tail, and feet are usually those of a horse. Morphologically a satyr is therefore much like Pan, except that the latter is a mix of man and goat. The term *silen* came into use among Greeks for a while and was employed more or less interchangeably with *satyr.* Sometimes Silenos or Papposilenos (Grandfather Silen) was treated as the proper name of a particular silen.

In mythological illustration, satyrs are represented sometimes as more bestial (for example, with horse legs) and sometimes as more human (for example, without mane or tail), and the artistic trend over time was to portray them as more and more human, as also in the case of Pans, with whom they were frequently associated. Indeed the iconography of satyrs (that is, horse-men) and that of Pans (that is, goat-men) gradually influenced each other so that by the Hellenistic period satyrs may display goat features. Typical scenes show them playing the double flute, dancing, pursuing nymphs, or accompanying Dionysos. Like other male nature-spirits, satyrs are usually represented as being unclothed. The depiction of satyrs in art came to be influenced by contemporary performances of satyr plays, a genre of Athenian drama in which the chorus consisted of actors costumed as satyrs and silens.

According to Hesiod (frag. 123 MW), Phoroneus had five granddaughters, who bore oreads (mountain nymphs), satyrs, and Kouretes. The poet calls the nymphs "goddesses" and the Kouretes "playful gods, dancers," whereas the satyrs are "worthless" creatures who are "unsuited to work." According to the poet Nonnos, satyrs were the offspring of Iphthimê, a daughter of Doros, and the rustic god Hermes (*Dionysiaka* 14.105–117). The god's role here as a begetter of partly anthropomorphic and partly theriomorphic beings agrees in spirit with the tradition in which Hermes and a nymph are the parents of Pan, a mix of man and goat according to the same recipe according to which satyrs are a mix of man and horse. But there may be more than one way to produce a satyr, as there is to produce a Cyclops or a centaur, since the father of the satyr Marsyas is given by mythographers as being Olympos or Oiagros. By and large the pedigree of satyrs is partly divine and rustic. Since there were no female satyrs, they could not be a self-reproducing group. The question of whether they were mortals or immortals evidently was unclear to the ancients, as we can judge from the Greek traveler Pausanias, who, seeing several graves of silens, concluded that silens must be born mortal (6.24.8). This conclusion is supported by the fate of the satyr Marsyas, who perished at the hands of Apollon.

For all their colorfulness and popularity in mythological art, few stories were told of satyrs, and those mostly of individuals. The best known of these concerns the Phrygian satyr or silen Marsyas, who engaged in a musical contest with Apollon. Athena devised a double flute but discarded it when she found that it distorted her face while she played it. Marsyas found it, taught himself to play it, and challenged Apollon to a musical contest. They agreed in advance that the winner could do whatever he wished with the loser. In the course of the contest, Apollon played his lyre upside down and bade Marsyas to do the same, and since the satyr was unable to do so, he was judged the loser. Apollon hung him from a pine tree and flayed him alive. The nymphs and satyrs of the countryside mourned for him, and either their tears or Marsyas's blood became the River Marsyas (Apollodoros *Library* 1.4.2; Pausanias 10.30.9; Hyginus *Fabulae* 165). This myth is one of several narratives of a contest between a god and a lesser being, usually a human, in the god's own sphere of expertise.

A satyr or silen appears in the legend of Midas. The Phrygian king captured the wild creature by mixing wine in the spring from which it was wont to drink (Herodotos 8.138; Xenophon *Anabasis* 1.2.13), or Silen, old and drunken, wandered away from other satyrs and bacchae in Dionysos's retinue and was captured by peasants, who turned him over to their king. Midas, however, treated him hospitably and returned him to Dionysos (Ovid *Metamorphoses* 11.89–99).

> **See also** Centaurs and Hippocentaurs; Nymphs; Pan
>
> **Suggested reading:**

Frank Brommer. *Satyroi.* Würzburg: Konrad Triltsch Verlag, 1937.

J. G. Frazer. *Pausanias's Description of Greece.* London: Macmillan, 1898, 2:289–294.

Timothy Gantz. *Early Greek Myth: A Guide to Literary and Artistic Sources.* Baltimore: The Johns Hopkins University Press, 1993, 135–139.

William Hansen. *Phlegon of Tralles' Book of Marvels.* Exeter: University of Exeter Press, 1996, 171–174.

François Lissarrague. "The Sexual Life of Satyrs," in *Before Sexuality: The Construction of the Erotic Experience in the Ancient Greek World*, edited by

David M. Halperin, John J. Winkler, and Froma Zeitlin. Princeton, NJ: Princeton University Press, 1990, 53–82.

———. "Why Satyrs Are Good to Represent," in *Nothing to Do with Dionysos? Athenian Drama in Its Social Context,* edited by John J. Winker and Froma Zeitlin. Princeton, NJ: Princeton University Press, 1990, 228–236.

Erika Simon. "Silenoi," in *LIMC* 8:1108–1133.

SEERS

Human specialists in the hidden knowledge of the past, present, and future.

Like gods, seers have some insight into what is fated to happen in the future as well as into unobvious details of the present and the past, such as the influence of divine forces upon human events. Individual seers are able to interpret omens sent by the gods, or have a kind of second sight, or understand the language of animals, or possess a variety of skills. Often their gift is god-given. Homer (*Iliad* 1.68–72) describes a particular Achaean seer as

> Kalchas, son of Thestor, by far the best of augurs,
>
> who knew the present, the future, and the past,
>
> and led the ships of the Achaeans to Troy
>
> by means of his divination, which Phoibos Apollon had given him.

Seers figure prominently in mythological narratives set in the heroic era, in which they are classified as professionals in the same category as doctors, carpenters, bards, and heralds (Homer *Odyssey* 17.382–385, 19.135) and are treated respectfully as persons who genuinely have privileged access to important information. Thus when the Achaeans at Troy were suffering from a sudden and mysterious plague, they assumed that it was sent by Apollo, whose divine spheres of influence include sickness and healing, and that the god was expressing his anger at them. What they did not know was why he was angry and what they could do to set things right again. For this information they sought the help of a seer. Kalchas explained that certain actions of Agamemnon had angered Apollon and that Agamemnon must propitiate the god in certain ways. Agamemnon responded angrily to this, accusing the seer of always making unwelcome revelations (*Iliad* 1). Agamemnon does not accuse Kalchas of incompetency or deceit, merely of being a regular bearer of bad news. Only in nonmythological genres such as jokes and comedy are seers, like doctors, treated as incompetents and frauds.

Just as Hesiod became a bard when the Muses suddenly appeared to him one day while he was shepherding his flocks and breathed into him the power of mythological song (*Theogony* 22–34), so a man or a woman becomes a seer as a result of unforeseeable circumstances. Several seers were given, or taught, their art by Apollon, divine prophet par excellence. An unusual case was the Trojan princess Kassandra (Latinized form = Cassandra), whom Apollon courted, offering to teach her the art of prophecy in exchange for her sleeping with him. But after he had taught her, she still refused to lie with him, so that he caused her prophetic utterances to lack persuasion (Apollodoros *Library* 3.12.5); that is, she could foretell the future, but no one would believe her. Similarly, a person could be made a seer by Zeus. The mortal Teiresias was once asked by Zeus and Hera to settle a dispute, but in so doing he angered Hera, who blinded him. In compensation Zeus gave him the gift of divination as well as a life span of seven generations (Hesiod frag. 275 MW). Teiresias became the great and long-lived seer of Theban legend, retaining his extraordinary mental powers even after death. The association of soothsayers and long life spans was a traditional idea. The Erythraean Sibyl lived even longer—ten life spans, over a thousand years (Phlegon of Tralles *Makrobioi* [*FGH* 257 F 37] 5). Like any other craft, the art of divination could be taught by a mortal practitioner, as when the seer Polyidos was forced by King Minos of Crete to instruct his son Glaukos in the art. Polyidos complied, but as he was leaving Crete he told Glaukos to spit in his mouth, and when Glaukos did so he forgot all that he had learned (Apollodoros *Library* 3.3.2). A number of persons acquired the gift of prophecy when snakes licked their ears, which unblocked latent powers. Thus after servants of Melampous killed a nest of snakes near his dwelling, Melampous respectfully cremated the dead creatures and reared their young. Later, while Melampous slept, the snakes cleansed his ears by licking them, after which Melampous was able to understand the speech of different animals, whereby he learned the future (Apollodoros *Library* 1.9.11). Since several seers were descendants of other seers, the power of divination, once established, was sometimes transmitted in families. Teiresias's daughter Manto could foresee the future, and her offspring included the seer Mopsos. Among the descendants of the seer Melampous were the seers Polyidos, Amphiaraos, and Theoklymenos.

The potential for irony in the careers of soothsayers is perhaps greater than that in any other profession. Thus the blind seers Teiresias and Phineus were unable to see what other mortals saw but were able to discern things that were obscure to others. A favorite irony is the seer who foresees his or her own ill fortune. Melampous helped his brother Bias rustle cattle, although he knew that he would be caught in the act and imprisoned. The diviner Amphiaraos joined the expedition of the Seven against Thebes reluctantly, perceiving that it would fail and that all but one of the Seven would perish. Euchenor, son of the Corinthian seer Polyidos, learned from his father that he would either die from a painful illness at Corinth or be killed by a Trojan at Troy. Knowing this, he chose to go to Troy, where he was felled by Paris (Homer *Iliad* 13.660–672). Euchenor's choice was therefore much like that of Achilleus. And the Trojan seeress Kassandra, brought by Agamemnon to Greece as a captive after the war, foresaw that she and Agamemnon would presently be murdered but was incapable of communicating her foreknowledge to anyone else.

See also Oracles

Suggested reading:

Luc Brisson. *Le mythe de Tirésias: Essai d'analyse structurale.* Leiden: E. J. Brill, 1976.

Timothy Gantz. *Early Greek Myth: A Guide to Literary and Artistic Sources.* Baltimore: The Johns Hopkins University Press, 1993, 528–530 (Teiresias).

SEX-CHANGERS

Characters who experience an actual or apparent change of sex.

Change of sex, a particular form of the common theme of transformation, is a frequent and sometimes striking feature of Greek myths and legends.

When a deity changes sex, as divine beings have the inherent ability to do, the change is merely a temporary expedient for good or bad, as with any other divine metamorphosis or disguise. At the beginning of Homer's *Odyssey*, the goddess Athena wished to suggest a certain course of action to Odysseus's son Telemachos, so that she took the form of Mentes, a Taphian chieftain who was an old friend of Odysseus's family. A little later she assumed the appearance of a different mortal man, Mentor, a local resident and trusted friend of Odysseus, in order to facilitate the voyage of Telemachos. And presently she adopted a third male disguise, assuming the form of Telemachos himself, so that she might go around town gathering a crew for the trip (*Odyssey* 1–2). In each instance Athena takes mortal form, speaking with mortals as an apparent mortal and not confronting them as a deity, in order to work within the realm of natural causation; and although she is herself female, she chooses to appear in the guise of a man because the roles she plays are male roles in Ithacan society.

Zeus, on the other hand, employs the same sort of tactic for personal gain. Conceiving a passion for the nymph or human maiden Kallisto, a hunting companion of Artemis who had sworn to remain a virgin, he took the form of Artemis in order that he might easily approach Kallisto and raped her (Apollodoros *Library* 3.8.2). Like Athena, Zeus temporarily adopts a guise that is expedient for the matter at hand, which in this instance involves his taking the form of a deity of the opposite sex.

Since humans cannot change their sex at will, a human who wishes temporarily to pass as a member of the opposite sex is obliged to assume a disguise, which consists usually of cross-dressing. The mortal Leukippos conceived a passion for Daphnê, a virgin huntress dear to Artemis and therefore a maiden much like Kallisto. Having no other means of getting close to her, he assumed the guise of a girl by donning female clothing, and eventually won Daphnê's innocent affection. This happy situation was sabotaged by the jealous god Apollon, who, being similarly attracted to Daphnê, caused her and her fellow maidens to conceive a desire to bathe in a certain spring. When they disrobed, they discovered Leukippos's ruse and killed him (Parthenios 15).

The young Achilleus was once disguised as a girl by his mother Thetis. When conscription for the campaign against Troy was under way, Thetis was fearful, knowing that Achilleus was fated to die at Troy if he should join the campaign. So she disguised him as a maiden and entrusted him to the care of King Lykomedes of Skyros, at whose court the boy passed as a girl until the Achaeans learned that he was hidden there, though they did not know which of the apparent maidens was actually Achilleus. So the clever Odysseus had a trumpeter sound the alarm, whereupon Achilleus, believing the enemy was at hand, stripped off his female clothing and seized a spear and shield, thereby giving himself away (Hyginus *Fabulae* 96).

One mortal did actually undergo a temporary change of sex; indeed, he did so twice. The youth Teiresias once saw two snakes copulating, and struck the female with his staff, whereupon he was transformed into a woman. After living some years as a female, he spotted the same snakes copulating, struck the male, and regained his original form. Consequently, when Zeus and Hera were disputing with each other about whether males or females derived the greater pleasure from sexual intercourse, Zeus declaring that females did, and Hera saying the opposite, they asked Teiresias to judge the matter, inasmuch as he had had experience as a female and as a male. He declared that if the pleasure of lovemaking should be divided into ten shares, men enjoyed one share and women enjoyed nine. Hera angrily blinded him, but Zeus in compensation gave him second sight, making him a soothsayer (Hesiod frag. 275 MW).

More characteristic, however, are stories of mortals who undergo a permanent change of sex, which is always from female to male. Legends were told of different girls who were covertly raised as boys and then, when they reached the age of marriage, were miraculously transformed by a deity into a male. Thus on Crete a poor shepherd named Lampros took a wife, Galateia. When she became pregnant, he instructed her to expose the child if it was a girl. Unknown to her husband, she gave birth to a girl. She pitied her child, and since dreams and seers instructed her to raise her as a boy, she gave her the name Leukippos and treated her as a son. As she grew up, Leukippos became so beautiful that Galateia feared she could no longer conceal her true sex, and in desperation the mother went to the temple of Leto and prayed that her daughter might become a boy. The goddess granted her prayer. In commemoration of this miracle, the citizens of Phaistos on Crete performed sacrifices to Leto the Grafter because she had grafted male organs onto a maiden (Antoninus Liberalis 17). Ovid tells basically the same story in his *Metamorphoses* (9.666–797) of a girl named Iphis. Greek and Roman authors also report many cases of historical persons who spontaneously experienced a change of sex from female to male, often at the age of marriage.

More violent is the legend of the Thessalian maiden Caenis, who was transformed into a man, taking the male name Caeneus. According to the Roman poet Ovid, Caenis was a beautiful maiden with many suitors. Once as she walked alone by the sea, Neptune ravished her, after which he offered to grant her any wish she should care to make. She asked to become a man in order that she might never again have to endure rape. The god not only changed her into a man but also made her invulnerable, so that she could not be pierced by weapons. The invulnerable Caeneus became a renowned warrior, who finally perished in the battle of the Lapiths and centaurs. Since he could not be pierced, the centaurs crushed him to death (Ovid *Metamorphoses* 12.189–535).

Hermaphroditos (Latinized form = Hermaphroditus) should also be mentioned. Although according to one tradition this child of Hermes and Aphroditê was androgynous from birth, combining male and female sexual characteristics (Diodorus of Sicily 4.6.5), another tradition recounts that he was originally a male child who was reared by naiads. When he was an adolescent, he set out traveling, coming eventually to Caria, where he bathed in a certain spring. The naiad of the spring, Salmacis, conceived a passion for the youth, and once he entered her waters, she held him fast and prayed to the gods that they might never be separated. The gods granted her wish, merging them into one body (Ovid *Metamorphoses* 4.285–388).

> ***See also*** Sexual Myths and Legends; Transformation
> ***Suggested reading:***
> Luc Brisson. *Sexual Ambivalence: Androgyny and Hermaphroditism in Graeco-Roman Antiquity*. Trans. by Janet Lloyd. Berkeley: University of California Press, 2002.
> P. M. C. Forbes Irving. *Metamorphosis in Greek Myths*. Oxford: Clarendon Press, 1990, 149–170.
> William Hansen. *Phlegon of Tralles' Book of Marvels*. Exeter: University of Exeter Press, 1996, 112–126.

SEXUAL MYTHS AND LEGENDS

Mythological narratives focusing upon the fulfillment or frustration of sexual desire.

Stories of divine sexuality, other than purely genealogical narratives, are numerous and extremely varied. Many myths feature an aggressive god who acts upon his erotic desire for a goddess, nymph, or mortal or, less commonly, an aggressive goddess or nymph who acts upon her desire for a mortal male. The best known of these are the many encounters in which Zeus transforms himself into the form of someone or something else in order to gain erotic access to a female or male. Thus he took the form of a tame bull in order to attract the attention of the Phoenician princess Europê. After she climbed upon its back, the bull leaped into the sea and swam to Crete, where Zeus lay with Europê. She bore Minos, Sarpedon, and Rhadamanthys (Apollodoros *Library* 3.1.1). In order to gain sexual access to Callisto (Greek Kallisto), a virginal huntress and follower of Diana, Jupiter (Greek Zeus) assumed the form of Diana herself. First caressing Callisto in the guise of Diana, he then ravished her in the form of Jupiter. She gave birth to a son, Arcas, eponym of the Arcadians (Ovid *Metamorphoses* 2.401–530). Similarly he mated with Leda in the form of a swan, Antiopê in the form of a satyr, Alkmenê in the form of her husband, Amphitryon, and Danaê in the form of a shower of gold, producing in each case one or more offspring. Nor were his erotic interests exclusively heterosexual. Taking the form of an eagle, or dispatching an eagle as his agent, he seized the handsome Trojan youth Ganymedes and carried him up to Olympos. No other deity was so sexually active and predatory as Zeus.

But straightforward rape or abduction is more typical of deities than shape-changing for sexual advantage. Thus Poseidon ravished the maiden Kainis as she strolled along the seashore. When he thereafter offered to grant her any wish, she chose to become a man so that she would never again be raped. Although aggressive male gods characteristically seek single encounters rather than relationships, some exceptions are found. Hades erupted through the earth on his chariot and seized the maiden Korê, taking her down to Erebos to be his bride and co-ruler of the death realm. Similarly the north wind, Boreas, abducted the Athenian princess Oreithyia and brought her up to his northerly kingdom to be his spouse.

Likely to fail in their lustful aims are monstrous beings who aspire to a sexual encounter or marital relationship with a nonmonstrous being, especially with a lovely goddess. The huge Tityos, a son of Gaia (Earth), attempted to assault Leto as she was traveling to Pytho. As a result he now lies tormented in Erebos, where vultures continually peck at his liver (Homer *Odyssey* 11.577–581). The horrible monster Typhon temporarily disabled Zeus by removing his sinews. Typhon planned to take Zeus's place on Olympos and to make Hera his spouse, but Zeus recovered his sinews and overcame the pretender (Nonnos *Dionysiaka* 1.145–2.712). The gigantic brothers Otos and Ephialtes, who had a human mother and a divine father, piled Mount Ossa upon Mount Olympos and Mount Pelion atop Mount Ossa in an attempt to reach the sky. Among other things they wished to have Olympian goddesses as wives, for Otos wooed Artemis and his brother wooed Hera. But Artemis slew them both (Apollodoros *Library* 1.7.4).

Aggressive goddesses typically seek relationships rather than encounters. The busiest goddess sexually is Eos, or Dawn, who carries men away to be her lovers. Thus she bore off the handsome hunter Orion and enjoyed his love, but Artemis slew him because the gods disliked Eos's having a mortal lover (Homer *Odyssey* 5.118–124). Eos carried off the mortal Tithonos to the eastern edge of the world to be her mate, though she lost interest in him when he grew old (*Homeric Hymn to Aphrodite* 216–238). On another occasion she seized Kephalos and bore him up to Olympos to be her lover (Euripides *Hippolytos* 454–456), and yet again she carried Kleitos up to Olympos to dwell among the gods on account of his beauty (Homer *Odyssey* 15.249–251).

Among male nature spirits, centaurs take the prize for sexual aggression, responding to situations with primitive immediacy. When the centaur Nessos was ferrying Herakles's wife Deianeira across the river Euenos, he tried to rape her in mid-river, but the enraged Herakles killed him with an arrow (Apollodoros *Library* 2.7.6). Similarly, when a pair of centaurs named Rhoikos and Hylaios saw the athletic maiden Atalantê, they intended to rape her, but she slew them both (*Library* 3.9.2). The wildness of the centaurs was exhibited most memorably at the wedding of the Lapith Pirithous (Greek *Peirithoos*) and his bride, Hippodamê (Greek *Hippodameia*). Overcome with wine and lust, the centaurs tried to make off with the bride as well as the other females in attendance, an act that led to warring between the Lapiths and the centaurs (Ovid *Metamorphoses* 12.210–525). The most erotically aggressive nymphs are probably the naiads. When the youth Hylas, one of the Argonauts, went to a particular spring to fetch water, he attracted the attention of the resident naiad, who emerged from the water, placed an arm around him, and drew him into the water, where she made him her husband (Apollonios of Rhodes *Argonautika* 1.1207–1325). The naiad Salmacis, erotically attracted to the youth Hermaphroditus, seized him when he was refreshing himself in her spring. She prayed that her body might be fused with his, and the gods granted her prayer. Having become a hermaphrodite, Hermaphroditus in turn prayed that hereafter the spring should effeminize any man who bathed in it, and the gods granted this prayer as well (Ovid *Metamorphoses* 4.285–388).

A different sort of aggressive initiative appears in a story-type that can be labeled the Pursuit Myth, for its plot of erotic pursuit, flight, and transformation is told of different sets of characters. Thus Apollo fell in love with the nymph Daphnê and pursued her, but she fled from him, having no interest in any suitors. In order to avoid losing her virginity she prayed to her father, the river-god Peneus, to change her shape into something else, and he assented, turning her into a laurel tree (Greek *daphnê* = laurel), whereupon Apollo declared that if Daphnê would not be his wife, then at least the laurel would be his special tree (Ovid *Metamorphoses* 1.452–567). So Daphnê remained a maiden, and Apollo sublimated his frustrated erotic relationship into a relationship of a different sort. In the same way Pan once pursued the Arcadian hamadryad Syrinx with erotic intent, and she fled, escaping him by a transformation into reeds, which Pan bound together, creating a pipe (Greek *syrinx* = pipe), his special musical instrument (*Metamorphoses* 1.689–712). Similar stories were told of the pursuit of the nymph Arethousa by the river-god Alpheios, of the pursuit of the nymph Lotis by the phallic god Priapos, and of the pursuit of Pleionê and the Pleiades by the lustful hunter Orion.

A group of businesslike myths recounts how the divine initiator attempts and fails to win over his beloved by means of negotiation. Wishing to sleep with the Trojan princess Kassandra, Apollon offered to teach her to foretell the future. After she learned the art but still refused to sleep with him, he brought it about that, though she might prophesy, no one would ever believe her (Apollodoros *Library* 3.12.5). The same god propositioned the Cumaean Sibyl, offering to grant her any wish. She asked to live as many years as there were grains in a particular heap of sand, neglecting to ask also to be ageless. When the deity now offered to grant her this also, she still rejected his love, so that she lived many centuries, aging all the while and unable to die (Ovid *Metamorphoses* 14.130–153).

In addition to the many myths in which desire and aversion are confronted, there are of course also instances of consensual sex. A ribald myth tells how Aphroditê was married to the lame god Hephaistos but secretly carried on an affair with Ares. When, however, Helios (Sun) informed the cuckolded husband of his wife's infidelity, Hephaistos laid a cunning trap for the lovers in his bedroom, netting them flagrante delicto and displaying them thus in public (Homer *Odyssey* 8.266–366). Poseidon enjoyed a love affair with the hero Pelops when Pelops was a handsome boy and later in life helped him win a wife (Pindar *Olympian* 1). Zeus and a Theban woman, Semelê, had an affair, resulting in the birth of Dionysos. The relationship ended tragically when the jealous Hera tricked Semelê into asking Zeus to appear to her in the same form as he appeared to Hera; reluctantly Zeus did so, but the power of his divine manifestation destroyed Semelê.

Occasionally a human aspires to an erotic encounter with a deity, in which case the mortal initiates matters. Wishing to have sexual intercourse with Hera, the mortal Ixion tried to take her by force. Hera reported the assault to Zeus, who wanted to learn if Ixion really was trying to have sex with his wife. So he fashioned the likeness of Hera out of cloud-matter and set the phantom down beside Ixion, who not only engaged in sexual intercourse with the image but also boasted that he had slept with Hera. Zeus punished him by affixing him to a wheel that spun through the air (Apollodoros *Epitome* 1.20). Aloeus's wife, Iphimedeia, in love with Poseidon, went frequently to the sea where she would pour seawater onto her lap with her hands. Eventually Poseidon lay with her, and she gave birth to two sons, Otos and Ephialtes (Apollodoros *Library* 1.7.4).

Not surprisingly, narratives of human sexuality are less fantastic than those involving supernatural beings. Many stories explore forbidden sexual relations such as adultery, incest, or rape. Antiquity's most frequently recounted legend of human passion is the triangle tale of the lustful matron, the calumniated youth, and the gullible husband, told of many different sets of characters and known generically as the Potiphar's Wife motif from the biblical legend featuring Joseph, Potiphar, and his wife (*Genesis* 39:1–20). Theseus's wife, Phaidra (Latinized form = Phaedra), fell in love with and propositioned her stepson Hippolytos, who felt an aversion to all women, however, and in any case rejected her advances. Fearing that Hippolytos might reveal the matter to his father, Phaidra accused the youth of having assaulted her. Believing her fabrication, Theseus prayed to Poseidon that Hippolytos might perish for this horrible deed. So while Hippolytos was driving his chariot along the seashore, Poseidon sent forth a bull from the sea that terrified the young man's horses, causing him to become entangled in the reins, after which he was dragged to death. Later the truth came out (Apollodoros *Epitome* 1.18–19).

The theme of witting and unwitting incest was treated in different ways. Byblis fell in love with her own brother Kaunos, begging him to alleviate her misery, but feeling only repulsion for her he went away to another land, after which she hanged herself (Parthenios 11; cf. Ovid *Metamorphoses* 9.453–664). The maiden Smyrna had no interest in her many suitors because of the secret lust she felt for her father, which was driving her mad. She finally confessed her passion to her nurse, who contrived to solve the problem by telling the girl's father, Theias, that a girl of good parents desired to sleep with him, but secretly. At night the man awaited the girl in his bed, and after a time the nurse escorted Smyrna into the room, her identity hidden by the darkness and by a covering of clothes. Their meetings continued until Smyrna became pregnant and Theias longed to discover who the mother of his child was. When he held up a light he learned that his lover was his own daughter. Smyrna prayed to be seen neither among the living nor among the dead, whereupon Zeus transformed her into a tree, called *smyrna* ("myrrh," another form of the same word) after her, which annually weeps tears. Theias killed himself. But the child, Adonis, grew into a handsome youth, becoming eventually a lover of Aphroditê (Antoninus Liberalis 34; cf. Ovid *Metamorphoses* 10.298–532). Women are more often than men portrayed as slaves to inappropriate sexual passion because according to ancient gender stereotypes women were more subject to lust than were men, since, like children and slaves, they were less able to control their emotions and wants. Appropriate self-governance was deemed to be a characteristic of free, adult males.

The most horrifying Greek legend of forced sexual intercourse is that of Tereus, Proknê, and Philomela. King Pandion of Athens had two daughters, Proknê and Philomela. Proknê wed Tereus, a Thracian ally of her father, and they had a son, Itys. But Tereus conceived a passion also for his wife's sister and arranged for her to visit Thrace, where he raped her, cut out her tongue, and hid her away in the country. Unable to speak, Philomela wove her story onto cloth. After Proknê understood what had happened, she conspired with Philomela to get revenge by cooking Itys and serving him to his father to eat. When Tereus perceived the nature of his cannibalistic meal, he pursued the two sisters. The gods resolved the situation after a fashion by transforming the three into birds, Proknê into a nightingale, Philomela into a swallow, and Tereus into a hoopoe (Apollodoros *Library* 3.14.8; Ovid *Metamorphoses* 6.424–674).

> **See also** Romantic Narratives; Sex-Changers
> **Suggested reading:**
> Richard Buxton. "Blindness and Limits: Sophokles and the Logic of Myth. *Journal of Hellenic Studies* 100 (1980): 22–37.
> William Hansen. *Ariadne's Thread: A Guide to International Tales Found in Classical Literature*. Ithaca, NY: Cornell University Press, 2002, 332–352.
> W. R. Johnson. "The Rapes of Callisto." *Classical Journal* 92 (1996): 9–24.
> Amy Richlin. "Reading Ovid's Rapes," in *Pornography and Representation in Greece and Rome*, edited by Amy Richlin. Oxford: Oxford University Press, 1992, 158–179.
> Froma Zeitlin. "Configurations of Rape in Greek Myth," in *Rape*, edited by Sylvana Tomaselli and Roy Porter. Oxford: Basil Blackwell, 1986, 122–151.

SPECIAL RULES AND PROPERTIES

Arbitrary or logically capricious assignment of properties to an entity or rules to an event. The association of the quality with the thing or of the rule with the event does not rest upon inherent probability or necessity but exists for the convenience of the narrative.

Probably the most straightforward instance of the arbitrary rule is the theme of the precondition. Success in a particular matter may be said to depend upon the satisfaction of a condition that has no rhyme or reason within the world of the story; however, on the level of narrative composition, the theme of the precondition may offer one or another payoff such as to justify an additional event and so prolong the story enjoyably. In classical mythology the authority for conditional events generally rests ultimately upon fate or other mysterious operations of the unseen world, and the usual conduit for such information is prophecy in the form of an oracle or seer. Thus the Trojans knew from secret oracles that their city could not be captured unless three things should happen: the bones of Pelops had to be brought to Troy, Achilleus's son Neoptolemos had to join the fight against them, and the Palladion, an object that had fallen from the sky and was in the possession of the Trojans, had to be stolen away (Apollodoros *Epitome* 5.9–13). The raison d'être of this odd assortment is to motivate a sequence of episodes in which the Greeks first capture the Trojan seer Helenos in order to learn the secrets of Troy's vulnerability and then meet the three conditions one by one. The rule is really comprehensible only on the backstage level of story composition; on the front-stage level, it adds an enjoyable atmosphere of mystery to the events. Similarly, in the Gigantomachy, or battle of the gods and the giants, the gods learn from an oracle that they can triumph only with the help of a mortal, so that they call upon the help of Herakles.

Since mythological oracles reveal matters that are beyond human ken anyway, they need not make much sense in and for themselves. An oracle revealed to Oedipus that he would murder his father and have sexual intercourse with his mother if he should return to his homeland, and Oedipus, learning this, attempted in vain to avoid his fate. But why should these arbitrary rules attach to his life? The legend offers no explanation within itself. Although one may infer that at Oedipus's birth the Moirai (Fates) so ordained the conditions of his life, their allotment is no less arbitrary. On the level of story composition, however, the theme controls the overall story, setting the initial action in motion, motivating the protagonist's behavior, and lending closure at the end. Somewhat similar is the theme of the curse. When one mythological character curses another character (or his descendants), bad things inevitably happen to the accursed, as though a special property now attached to him (or them) requiring that he (or they) suffer. When King Oinomaos, about to die, perceived that his charioteer Myrtilos had betrayed him, he cursed Myrtilos, who presently was murdered by Pelops. Before Myrtilos perished, however, he cursed the family of Pelops (that is, the descent line headed by Pelops). The lives of Pelops's sons Atreus and Thyestes were characterized by internecine struggles, with scheming and betrayals continuing into the next generation. When Oedipus felt slighted by his sons Eteokles and Polyneikes, he cursed them to die by each other's hands, and so it happened.

An arbitrary property commonly attached to monstrosities equipped with a single trick is that if anyone beats them at their trick, they cease to function or even self-destruct. When therefore the Argonauts successfully sailed through the Symplegades, or Clashing Rocks, the rocks stood motionless thereafter, for it was fated that if a ship should pass through them, they would remain still (Apollodoros *Library* 1.9.23). And after Oedipus correctly answered the Sphinx's riddle, the monster cast herself down from an acropolis (*Library* 3.5.8).

Things, like actions, can have their own special properties. The legend of Kephalos and Prokris features a dog that could not be outrun as well as a spear that never missed its prey, a hunter's fantasy, but also a fox that was fated to elude any pursuer. There is no reason why the two animals should have these qualities other than to pose the intriguing problem: what would happen if this dog should pursue this fox? The problem was resolved (or avoided) by Zeus's transforming the two beasts into stone (Antoninus Liberalis 41), freezing their pose of pursued and pursuer forever.

The special property most frequently assigned to privileged persons or objects is invulnerability, signifying that the person or object cannot be penetrated. In an age in which the principal kinds of weapon—swords, javelins, arrows—did their work by piercing the flesh, impenetrability was a virtual guarantee against harm from warriors or hunters. Consequently, in the game of war or hunting, invulnerability posed an interesting problem: how can such a person, animal, or object be harmed? There were two possible solutions. One was to squeeze the creature to death. A labor of Herakles was to acquire the skin of the Nemean Lion, but the lion, offspring of a supernatural parent, was invulnerable. How was the hero to slay a beast whose skin could not be pierced by the weapons of hunting? His solution was to strangle it (Apollodoros *Library* 2.5.1). Similarly, to kill the hero Kaineus, who had been granted invulnerability by the god Poseidon, his enemies had to crush him into the earth.

The other solution was to take advantage of a loophole. The Nereid Thetis, holding her infant son Achilleus by his heel, dipped him into the waters of the Styx in order to make his flesh invulnerable, since she feared for his death, but he remained vulnerable in one small spot, the place where she had held him. The hero Aias was also invulnerable, which posed a difficulty when he wished to fall upon his sword in order to take his own life, until he found the one spot on his body that was vulnerable.

Many other instances of fantastic properties are found. The maiden Mestra could transform herself into anything she wished. During sexual intercourse Minos ejaculated snakes and scorpions. Any property, it seems, can potentially be attached to any being or object. In addition to the color that such unusual motifs add to stories, some of them serve as a structuring device (for example, the preconditions for the capture of Troy, the fate of Oedipus), some are like a thought experiment (what would happen if someone could transform herself at will?), and others pose an apparently insoluble problem that begs for an answer (how does one overcome a warrior who is invulnerable? how does one have sexual intercourse with a man who ejaculates scorpions?).

See also Wondrous Objects

Suggested reading:

Joseph Fontenrose. "The Oracular Response as a Traditional Narrative Theme." *Journal of Folklore Research* 20 (1983): 113–120.

William Hansen. *Ariadne's Thread: A Guide to International Tales Found in Classical Literature.* Ithaca, NY: Cornell University Press, 2002, 481–489.

SUCCESSION MYTH

Myth recounting the successive reigns of the first rulers of the gods.

The first ruler of the gods was Ouranos (Sky), who mated with his mother Gaia (Earth), begetting the twelve Titans, the three Cyclopes, and the three Hundred-Handers. To Gaia's great distress, Ouranos did not allow his children to be born, either because he engaged in continual sexual intercourse with Gaia or because he shoved them back into their mother, imprisoning them within her (our principal source for the myth, Hesiod, somewhat confusingly conflates these two images). So she secretly invited her children to overthrow their tyrannical father, giving Kronos, the youngest of the Titans, a sickle and placing him in ambush. When later Ouranos covered Gaia in a sexual embrace, Kronos lopped off his genitals with the sickle, thereby deposing his father and ending the imprisonment of the Titans in their mother.

Succeeding his father as ruler, Kronos took his sister Rhea as mate. But since he had learned from his parents, Ouranos and Gaia, that he would beget a son who would overthrow him, he swallowed each of his children as soon as Rhea bore them. Distressed, Rhea consulted her parents, who advised her to bear her forthcoming child in Crete and to conceal him there in a cave (that is, in the earth, Gaia), which she did. Instead of her baby son, Rhea gave Kronos a stone wrapped in swaddling clothes to swallow. Baby Zeus grew up and gave his father an emetic, forcing him to vomit up his brothers and sisters as well as the stone, which Zeus placed at Pytho (Delphi). Zeus and his siblings, collectively known as the Olympians, fought a ten-year-long war with the Titans, the younger gods ranged on Mount Olympos and the older gods on Mount Othrys. The conflict dragged on with no resolution until Zeus released from within the earth first the Cyclopes, who furnished him with thunderbolts as weapons, and then the Hundred-Handers, who joined the battle as formidable combatants, whereupon the Olympians succeeded in driving the Titans down into the earth, imprisoning them permanently in Tartaros, where they are guarded by the Hundred-Handers.

Following his victory in the Titanomachy (Battle with the Titans), Zeus was acclaimed king by the other gods, becoming the third ruler of the gods. But there were still threats to face. The first was the huge dragon Typhon, the monstrous offspring of Gaia and Tartaros, whom Zeus overcame in a battle of cosmic proportions. Then Zeus took Metis (Cleverness) to wife, but he learned from Gaia and Ouranos that Metis was fated to bear two children, the goddess Athena and then a son who would become king of gods and men, so that when she was about to bear Athena, Zeus swallowed Metis, who remained within him as a counselor. Sometime later he himself gave birth to Athena, who emerged from his head. But since he had swallowed Metis before a son had been conceived, the succession came to an end. Stronger and wiser than his predecessors, thanks to his possession respectively of thunderbolts and Metis, Zeus consolidated his rule, which was characterized by relative moderation, and he remained king of gods and men.

The myth of the successive reigns of Ouranos, Kronos, and Zeus is the Greek form of the Succession Myth, an international migratory story of which ancient Mesopotamian, Hittite, and Phoenician variants are also known. The principal source for our knowledge of the Greek variant is Hesiod's *Theogony*.

See also Combat Myth and Legend

Suggested reading:

Richard S. Caldwell. "The Psychology of the Succession Myth," in Richard S. Caldwell, *Hesiod's Theogony*. Cambridge, MA: Focus, 1987, 85–100.

C. Scott Littleton. "The 'Kingship in Heaven' Theme," in *Myth and Law among the Indo-Europeans: Studies in Indo-European Comparative Mythology*, edited by Jaan Puhvel. Berkeley, Los Angeles, London: University of California Press, 1970, 83–121.

Martin L. West. *The East Face of Helicon: West Asiatic Elements in Greek Poetry and Myth*, Oxford: Clarendon Press, 1997, 276–305.

Martin L. West, ed. and comm. *Hesiod: Theogony*. Oxford: Clarendon Press, 1966, 18–30.

TARTAROS (LATINIZED FORM TARTARUS)

Male binatural character who is both a living being and also a prison for defeated supernaturals.

According to Hesiod (*Theogony* 116–119), Tartaros is one of four primordial entities, the others being Chaos, Gaia, and Eros. He subsequently mates with Gaia, begetting the huge, serpentine monster Typhon (*Theogony* 820–822).

At the same time Tartaros is a cosmic realm, the lowest of the three or four cosmic worlds, located beneath Gaia (when Erebos is regarded as part of Tartaros) or beneath Erebos (when Erebos is distinguished from Tartaros). The principal function of Tartaros in mythic narrative is to serve as a holding tank for defeated immortals, who must be stored somewhere since they cannot be killed. So the Battle of the Olympians and Titans, or Titanomachy, concludes with the Olympian forces driving the Titans down into Tartaros, and the combat between Zeus and Typhon similarly ends with Zeus throwing the monster down into Tartaros (Hesiod *Theogony* 717–731, 868). A common threat among supernaturals is for a stronger deity to cast a weaker deity into Tartaros (*Homeric Hymn to Hermes* 256; Apollodoros *Library* 3.10.4).

Physically Tartaros is a vast pit, a world of darkness and winds, surrounded by bronze walls (Homer *Iliad* 8.13–16; Hesiod *Theogony* 720–819).

> **See also** Erebos; Fabulous Peoples and Places
>
> **Suggested reading:**
>
> Timothy Gantz. *Early Greek Myth: A Guide to Literary and Artistic Sources.* Baltimore: The Johns Hopkins University Press, 1993, 128–132.
>
> Martin L. West, ed. and comm. *Hesiod: Theogony.* Oxford: Clarendon Press, 1966, 356–359.

TASKS

Important jobs undertaken by a character, usually of a difficult or seemingly impossible nature.

A task and its accomplishment (in effect, a problem and its solution) are among the basic building blocks of traditional narrative.

A task may have the form of disposing of a dangerous creature (Herakles had to kill the Hydra of Lerna), of acquiring or retrieving a particular object (Jason had to bring back the Golden Fleece; Zeus had to retrieve his stolen thunderbolts), of solving a difficult problem (Oedipus had to solve the riddle of the Sphinx), or of accomplishing some other deed (Kadmos had to found a city where a particular cow lay down to rest; Odysseus had to consult the ghost of the seer Teiresias in the death realm). The journey of a living person to the realm of the dead, known in Greek as a *katabasis* (descent), was a task peculiar to heroes and always involved a quest for something. Herakles went to Erebos to bring back the monstrous hound Cerberus; Peirithoos and Theseus journeyed there to bring back Persephonê as a wife for Peirithoos; Orpheus traveled there to retrieve his own wife Eurydikê; and Odysseus sailed there for the sake of information he needed for his return home. In the instance of Odysseus, the term *katabasis* is not quite fitting, since he reached the death realm not by going down to an underworld but by sailing to the western edge of the world.

The quest for a particular thing necessarily implies the existence of a desirable quest-object of one kind or another, and many Greek legends are structured around the idea of the quest for a rare or precious object or creature, the acquisition of which appears to be too dangerous or otherwise difficult to be feasible. Examples are the quest of Jason and the Argonauts for the Golden Fleece, which was located in the distant land of Colchis, ruled by the hostile wizard Aietes; the quest of Perseus for the head of Medusa, one of three Gorgon sisters who dwelled at the edges of the earth and had a dangerous quality, namely that anyone who looked upon them turned immediately to stone; and the different quests of Herakles for the belt of the Amazon queen Hippolytê, for the death-realm dog Cerberus, for the golden apples belonging to the gods, and so on.

Frequently a character assigns a task to another in the belief that it is impossible of fulfillment so that he or she will inevitably fail, but the character triumphs, relying upon his or her own talents or upon the crucial help of another character. King Polydektes ordered Perseus to bring him the head of the Gorgon Medusa, expecting that he would perish in attempting so difficult and dangerous a task. King Aietes ordered Jason to yoke a pair of bronze-footed, fire-breathing bulls and with them to sow a field with dragon's teeth, in the belief that he could not possibly do so. But Perseus succeeded in slaying the Gorgon without being petrified because he cleverly looked, not at her, but at her reflection as he cut off her head, and he escaped the Gorgons who pursued him because of the special, wondrous equipment that he had borrowed, including the Cap of Invisibility and winged sandals, which allowed him to fly. And Jason succeeded in his seeming impossible task because his taskmaster's daughter Medeia, offering to help him, gave him a salve that protected him against fire and also instructed him precisely what to do. Although tasks are usually assigned to a particular character by another, hostile character, a character can assign a task to himself or herself, as when Theseus volunteered to be among the youths and maidens sent to the Minotaur.

The accomplishment of a task can be retarded by the presence of one or more obstacles, which delay the protagonist's progress. The quest of Jason and the Argonauts for the Golden Fleece features a rich series of obstacles that the heroes must overcome before they can address the main task. Thus even to reach the land where the Golden Fleece is kept, the Argonauts must somehow sail successfully through the treacherous Symplegades, or Clashing Rocks. An obstacle can take the form of preliminary tasks that constitute preconditions to the accomplishment of the principal task, such as that the Achaeans cannot retrieve Helen (principal task) until they should conquer Troy (preliminary task), and they cannot take Troy before they should fulfill certain other requirements, including acquiring the Palladion (preliminary task). Similarly, Perseus cannot obtain the Gorgon's head (principal task) until he should borrow winged sandals and the Cap of Invisibility from certain nymphs (preliminary task), but before he can do this he must learn the location of these nymphs, which is known to the Graiai (preliminary task). In the same way Herakles cannot acquire the golden apples from the Hesperides (main task) before he should learn from Nereus where they are located (preliminary task), but first he must discover the location of Nereus from certain nymphs (preliminary task).

Sisyphos rolling the stone uphill.

Altogether different are the strange tasks carried out by several characters in Erebos, the death realm, for the characters never succeed but rather repeat the same actions endlessly with the same results. Sisyphos (Latinized form = Sisyphus) rolls a stone up a hill, but as soon as it nears the top, it rolls down again, after which he starts over. The Danaides (daughters of Danaos) or other persons carry water in sieves, from which it leaks out, or they pour water into a perforated jar, which they never succeed in filling, since the water flows out the bottom as quickly as they pour it into the top.

See also Herakles; Jason; Perseus

Suggested reading:

José Luis Calvo Martínez. "The *Katábasis* of the Hero," in *Héros et Héroïnes dans les Myths et les Cultes Grecs,* edited by Vinciane Pirenne-Delforge and Emilio Suárez de la Torre. Liège: Centre International d'Étude de la Religion Grecque Antique, 2000, 67–78.

Stith Thompson. *A Motif-Index of Folk-Literature,* Vol. 3. Bloomington: Indiana University Press, 1955–1958, H900-H1199: *Tests of prowess: tasks,* H1200–H1399: *Tests of prowess: quests.*

THEBAN WARS

Cycle of legends about two related wars at Thebes, the first an unsuccessful assault on Thebes by the Seven and the second a successful campaign by their sons, the so-called Epigonoi (Successors).

The Theban Wars and the Trojan War are the two great wars of the Greek heroic age.

In outline the principal events go as follows, according to the account of the mythographer Apollodoros. When Oedipus was driven out of Thebes, he cursed his two sons, Polyneikes and Eteokles, for their disrespectful treatment of him. For their part, the brothers each claimed the Theban throne and agreed to take turns ruling in yearly intervals, but when it was time for Eteokles to relinquish the throne to his brother, he refused to give it up. Banished from Thebes, Polyneikes went to Argos, where he married Argia, daughter of King Adrastos of Argos, who undertook to restore his new son-in-law to the throne of Thebes. So King Adrastos led an army of seven leaders and their men in an at-

Duel of Polyneikes and Eteokles.

tack on Thebes. The Seven were King Adrastos, the seer Amphiaraos, Kapaneus, Hippomedon, the grievant Polyneikes, Tydeus, and Parthenopaios. Of these seven, Amphiaraos was an unwilling participant, for he foresaw that all the attackers except for Adrastos were destined to perish in the battle. The Argive army made its way to Thebes and demanded that Eteokles yield the kingdom to his brother in accordance with their agreement, but Eteokles ignored the demand. Each of the seven leaders was then stationed at one of Thebes's seven gates. Inside the city Eteokles armed the Thebans to defend the gates. In the ensuing fighting, Eteokles and Polyneikes slew each other, and as Amphiaraos had foreseen, the other attackers perished except for Adrastos, who escaped on the supernatural horse Areion. Amphiaraos himself was not actually slain, although he disappeared from the earth, for Zeus cast a thunderbolt, making a cleft in the earth, which swallowed the seer, who was then made immortal by Zeus. Since the two sons of Oedipus were dead, Kreon assumed the throne of Thebes.

Ten years later the sons of the attackers who fell at Thebes, or Epigonoi, mounted a campaign against Thebes in order to avenge the death of their fathers. When the attackers proved to have the advantage, the seer Teiresias advised the Thebans to flee, and they did so, deserting the city and relocating elsewhere. The Argives entered Thebes, pillaged it, pulled down the walls, and sent a portion of the booty to Delphi along with Teiresias's daughter Manto, for they had promised Apollon, if they should capture Thebes, to send him the fairest thing among the spoils (*Library* 3.5.9–3.7.4).

The outcomes of the two Theban Wars were quite different. The war undertaken by the Seven was an utter failure, since the grievant Polyneikes perished in the attempt and, most importantly, the attackers did not succeed in capturing the city, whereas the enterprise undertaken ten years later by the Epigonoi was a complete success (cf. Homer *Iliad* 4.365–410).

A connected account of Theban mythology from Kadmos (the founder of Thebes) to the later experiences of Alkmeon (leader of the Epigonoi) is given by the mythographer Apollodoros (*Library* 3.1.1–3.7.7). The wars at Thebes and the surrounding events were recounted in four early Greek epics belonging to the

Epic Cycle: *Oidipodeia, Thebais, Epigonoi,* and *Alkmeonis* (*Epic of Oedipus, Epic of Thebes, Successors,* and *Epic of Alkmeon*), which today survive only in fragments.

The Theban Wars slightly precede the Trojan War, and several sons of the Seven, notably Diomedes, do battle first as Epigonoi in the second Theban war and later as warriors at Troy.

> ***See also*** Trojan War
>
> ***Suggested reading:***
> Malcolm Davies. *The Greek Epic Cycle.* 2nd ed. London: Bristol Classical Press, 1989.
> Timothy Gantz. *Early Greek Myth: A Guide to Literary and Artistic Sources.* Baltimore: The Johns Hopkins University Press, 1993, 502–528.
> Gregory Nagy. *The Best of the Achaeans: Concepts of the Hero in Archaic Greek Poetry.* Baltimore: The Johns Hopkins University Press, 1979, 161–164.

THESEUS

Youth who slew the Minotaur.

According to the mythographer Apollodoros, King Aigeus of Athens consulted the Delphic oracle about his childlessness and received a cryptic response instructing him not to release the mouth of his wineskin until he reached Athens again (that is, not to have sexual intercourse until he was home). Returning to Athens by way of Troizen, he lodged there with King Pittheus, telling him of the oracular response. Although Aigeus did not perceive its meaning, his host Pittheus did, made Aigeus drunk, and put him in bed with his daughter Aithra. During the same night Poseidon also lay with Aithra. Before departing, Aigeus instructed Aithra that if she should give birth to a boy, she should raise him without naming his father; and Aigeus left a sword and sandals beneath a certain rock, telling Aithra that when their son could roll away the rock and take up these items, she should send him with them to Aigeus.

Upon his return to Athens, the king celebrated the athletic games that were part of the Panathenaic festival. Androgeos, son of King Minos of Crete, won the events, whereupon Aigeus sent the youth against the Bull of Marathon, but Androgeos was destroyed by the animal. Minos then attacked Athens with a fleet, praying to Zeus that he might punish the Athenians. A famine and pestilence came upon Athens, so that the Athenians consulted an oracle about what they should do. The response was that they should give Minos whatever satisfaction he might choose. Minos ordered the Athenians annually to send seven unarmed youths and seven unarmed maidens as food for the Minotaur, a creature with the head of a bull and the body of a man. The monster was confined in the Labyrinth, a maze in which it was impossible for a person, once he had entered it, to find the exit.

Aithra bore a son, Theseus. When he grew up, he pushed aside the rock, retrieved the sword and sandals, and set out for Athens on foot. In the course of his journey he rid the road of several evildoers. First Theseus dispatched Periphetes the Clubman, who used to kill passersby with his iron club. The youth next killed Sinis the Pine-Bender, who forced passersby to bend pine trees, which then flung them into the air, killing them. Theseus dispatched Sinis in the same way. Third, he killed the monstrous Krommyon Sow. Fourth, he slew Skeiron (Latinized form = Sciron), who used to compel passersby to wash his feet, and as they did so he kicked them into the sea to be food for a giant turtle. Theseus threw Skeiron into the sea. Fifth, he slew Kerkyon (Latinized form = Cercyon), who killed passersby after forcing them to wrestle with him. Theseus's sixth victim was Damastes, who lived beside the road and used to offer one of his two beds to passersby. He placed short men on his large bed, hammering their bodies to lengthen them, and tall men on his short bed, sawing off the parts of their body that extended beyond the bed. (Other ancient sources call this nightmarish host Prokrustes [Latinized form = Procrustes], whence our expression "Procrustean bed.")

When Theseus reached Athens, his father's wife, Medeia, was hostile to him, persuading Aigeus that the stranger was plotting against him. Aigeus sent him against the Marathonian Bull, which he succeeded in killing. Then Aigeus planned to poison Theseus, but seeing the youth's sword, he knocked the cup from his hands. Perceiving Medeia's plotting, he expelled her from Athens.

Voluntarily or by lot, Theseus was included among the annual tribute of youths and maidens to the Minotaur. Before the ship with its black sails departed, Aigeus instructed Theseus to change the sails to white if he should return alive. The ship reached Crete, where Minos's daughter Ariadnê fell in love with Theseus and offered to help him on the condition that he take her as his wife and take her away to Athens, which he agreed to do. Ariadnê learned from Daidalos, the con-

Theseus slaying the Minotaur.

structor of the Labyrinth, how a per-

son might find his way out, namely, by tying a
clew of thread to the door upon entering. So Ariadnê supplied Theseus with a ball of thread, one
end of which he tied to the door. Then he found
the Minotaur in the depths of the maze, killed
him with his fists, and followed the thread back
to the door. Theseus, Ariadnê, and the other
young persons departed by night and reached the
island of Naxos. There Dionysos, having fallen
in love with Ariadnê, carried her off.

*Theseus slaying the Minotaur,
with Ariadnê looking on.*

Pained at the loss of Ariadnê, Theseus forgot
to change the sails to white. In Athens Aigeus
stood on the Akropolis, looking for the ship, and
when he saw the ship approach with black sails, he believed that Theseus had
perished and so threw himself from the heights. Theseus succeeded his father as
ruler of Athens (*Library* 3.15.6, *Epitome* 1.11).

The legend of Theseus and Ariadnê is a Greek adaptation of an international tale in which the ogre's daughter helps a youth accomplish the tasks set
by her father and facilitates his escape.

In art, Theseus is depicted as a youth or man, and his different adventures
may be labeled if they are not sufficiently distinct. But his central accomplishment, the slaying of the Minotaur, was too distinct to require a label.

See also Biographical Pattern; Labyrinth; Monsters

Suggested reading:

Antti Aarne and Stith Thompson. *The Types of the Folktale:
    A Classification and Bibliography*, FF Communications 184.
    Helsinki: Academia Scientiarum Fennica, 1961, Type 313C:
    The Girl as Helper in the Hero's Flight + The Forgotten Fiancée.
Timothy Gantz. *Early Greek Myth: A Guide to Literary and Artistic
    Sources.* Baltimore: The Johns Hopkins University Press, 1993,
    248–270, 276–298.
William Hansen. *Ariadne's Thread:
    A Guide to International Tales Found
    in Classical Literature.* Ithaca,
    NY: Cornell University Press,
    2002, 151–166.
Jenifer Niels. *The Youthful
    Deeds of Theseus.* Rome:
    Bretschneider, 1987.
———— and Susan Woodford.
    "Theseus," in *LIMC* 7:922–951.

Ariadnê sleeping.

TITANS (GREEK TITANES)

Older family of gods who preceded the Olympians.

As a group the Titans are the older gods, the former gods, in contrast to the Olympians, who are the younger and present gods. In this opposition, the two collectivities are more important than the identities of individual deities, especially in the case of the Titans, for some of them, such as Themis, make a poor fit for the role of opposing the Olympians, not to mention being prisoners in Tartaros.

According to Hesiod's *Theogony*, the Titans are six sons and six daughters of the primordial cosmic parents Ouranos and Gaia: Okeanos (Latinized form = Oceanus), Koios (Coeus), Kreios, Hyperion, Iapetos (Iapetus), Theia, Rhea, Themis, Mnemosynê, Phoibê (Phoebe), Tethys, and Kronos (Cronus).

Hesiod recounts how Ouranos, hating his children, prevented each new child from being born, apparently by engaging in continual sexual intercourse with Gaia. In a state of permanent labor, Gaia groaned with pain. Finally she created a great, toothed sickle of adamant and conspired with her children to punish their evil father. Only the youngest of the Titans, Kronos, was willing to undertake the task. From within his mother, Kronos lopped off his father's genitals with the sickle. As a result, Ouranos nicknamed Kronos and his siblings Titans, since they strained (Greek *titaino* "strain") to do their great deed, for which they themselves would in time be punished. And indeed the twelve Titans subsequently fought a ten-year battle against the twelve Olympians, a younger family of gods who were the offspring of the Titans Kronos and Rhea. The older gods were headquartered on Mount Othrys and the younger gods on nearby Mount Olympos. Eventually the Olympians, with the help of the Hundred-Handers, overwhelmed the Titans and sent them down into Tartaros, where they remain imprisoned and under guard.

See also Olympians

Suggested reading:

Maximilian Mayer. "Titanen," in Roscher 5:987–1019.

Martin L. West, ed. and comm. *Hesiod: Theogony.* Oxford: Clarendon Press, 1966, 199–201.

TRANSFORMATION

Supernatural change of form.

Transformation, or metamorphosis, is a very frequent motif in classical mythology, appearing in hundreds of stories. The three main types of transformations, shown in boldface type, are discussed here.

Most instances are **radical transformations,** in which an entity undergoes a drastic change of form. For example, a human being is transformed into an animal, plant, or inanimate object. The maiden Arachnê ("Spider"), who boasts of her skill at weaving, is changed by Athena into a spider. The self-absorbed youth Narcissus turns into a plant of the same name. The grieving mother Niobê is transformed into a weeping stone. Or conversely something nonhuman is changed into something else. Zeus changes a colony of ants into a society of industrious human beings (Ovid *Metamorphoses* 7.614–660). Poseidon turns a ship to stone (Homer *Odyssey* 13.153–169).

Kirkê transforming a man into a swine.

Usually a feature of the original entity persists significantly in the transformed entity. A weaver transformed into a spider continues to weave webs. A busy colony of ants becomes an industrious community of humans. A ship metamorphosed to stone retains its shape. The maiden Daphnê (Laurel) escapes the erotic pursuit of Apollon by her transformation into a laurel tree, but Apollon adopts laurel as his special plant. The continuation or cessation of self-consciousness is a more complicated matter. When Arachnê becomes a spider, there is little suggestion that anything beyond a passion for weaving survives the transformation, but when the change is temporary, self-consciousness is likely to be unaffected. There may be an overt or implied aetiology, either universal (if Daphnê is the first laurel tree, then all laurel trees derive from her) or local (a particular rock is a transformed woman).

The change of form is commonly effected by a supernatural agent, who brings it about as a punishment or less often as a reward, that is, as a cosmic demotion or promotion. So Athena demotes the arrogant weaver Arachnê from human maiden to spider in punishment for her hubris. In contrast, when Jupiter and Mercury grant the wish of the loving couple Baucis and Philemon that neither outlive the other, and when instead of dying they turn simultaneously into two neighboring trees, their transformation is a reward (Ovid *Metamorphoses* 8.703–724). Or the metamorphosis just happens, as though an appropriate transformation at the appropriate moment is somehow part of the order of things. Upon the death of the youth Narcissus, his body mysteriously becomes a flower (Ovid *Metamorphoses* 3.508–510).

Temporary transformations, in which a deity temporarily adopts another form or temporarily modifies the appearance of a human being, are common. Athena takes the form of the human male, Mentor, in order to consort unrecognized with human beings. Aphroditê takes the form of a human maiden in order to seduce Anchises. Athena changes the comely looks of Odysseus into the miserable appearance of a beggar. Animal forms are also common. Poseidon once takes the form of a horse. Zeus once takes the form of an eagle. A trick that is peculiar to sea deities is a rapid series of radical transformations, even into inorganic things such as water or fire. In order for a human being to capture the sea deity, he must take hold of the deity and hang on through the frightening series of changes. Thus when Proteus, the Old Man of the Sea, is seized by Menelaos, he turns himself successively into a lion, a serpent, a leopard, a boar, some water, and a tree, and when he sees that his tricks are of no avail, he resumes his normal form and yields to his capturer (Homer *Odyssey* 4.455–461). The sea deity Poseidon granted this peculiar ability to his grandson Periklymenos, who could transform himself at will into creatures as different as an eagle, an ant, a bee, and a snake (Hesiod frag. 33 MW).

A special category of radical transformation is sexual transformation. Zeus temporarily takes the likeness of Artemis in order to gain intimate access to the maiden Kallisto. The youth Teiresias is magically transformed into a girl, lives as a woman for several years, and is once again transformed back into a man. The maiden Kainis is raped by Poseidon and, told that she may make a wish, chooses to be transformed into a man so that she cannot again be ravished.

In addition to countless instances of radical transformation, classical mythology knows cases of **aspectual transformation,** in which there is no physical change of substance or form, but rather two different things are brought into a relationship of identity by a change of viewpoint. The goddess of dawn, Aurora (Greek *Eos*), weeps for her slain son Memnon, her tears appearing on the earth as dew (Ovid *Metamorphoses* 13.621–622). From a celestial perspective, beads of moisture are the tears of Dawn, but from a terrestrial perspective they are dewdrops. The transformation lies not in the entity (tears, dew) but in the perspective of the viewer. Aspectual transformations regularly identify the body fluids (for example, tears, blood, urine) of a celestial or terrestrial being with some moist substance (for example, dew, sap, river) of the earth's surface.

Since myths and legends containing instances of transformation were very numerous, written compilations of them were made in antiquity. Two that survive are Antoninus Liberalis's *Metamorphoses* and Ovid's *Metamorphoses*.

See also Catasterism; Promotion and Demotion; Sex-Changers

Suggested reading:

P. M. C. Forbes Irving. *Metamorphosis in Greek Myths.* Oxford: Clarendon Press, 1990.

William Hansen. "Foam-Born Aphrodite and the Mythology of Transformation." *American Journal of Philology* 121 (2000): 1–19.

TRANSLATION

Supernatural transferal of a being from one place to another, usually from one cosmic realm to another.

A particular god translates (or more vaguely "the gods" translate) a particular mortal from the ordinary realm of human habitation to another place, often a distant and unusual realm such as a faraway paradise, a chamber within the earth, or a site in the heavens. Usually the relocation is permanent, in which case the mortal also escapes the normal human cycle of life and death, becoming instead immortal and ageless like the gods, although this change of status is sometimes only implied rather than expressed. The following examples illustrate the sorts of places to which characters are translated.

Earthly paradise. The hero Menelaos learned from Proteus, the Old Man of the Sea, that he was not fated to die in Argos; rather, the immortal gods would someday send him to the Elysion Field at the ends of the earth, where he would join Rhadamanthys (and other fortunates, as we learn from other sources). The living is easy in that place, for rain and snow never fall there nor do strong winds blow, but Okeanos sends the pleasant breezes from the west to refresh the inhabitants. Menelaos will go there because, as the husband of Helen, he is a son-in-law of Zeus (Homer *Odyssey* 4.561–569).

Exotic society. When the Achaeans assembled at Aulis in preparation for their campaign against Troy, Agamemnon offended the goddess Artemis, who thereupon required him to sacrifice his daughter Iphigeneia to her. Agamemnon sent for his daughter and was about to sacrifice her, but Artemis snatched her up, translated her to the Taurians, and made her immortal, substituting a doe on the altar (Proklos *Chrestomathia* p. 104 Allen).

Subterranean dwelling. In the course of the defeat of the Seven against Thebes, the seer Amphiaraos and his charioteer Baton fled the battle, pursued by the Theban combatant Periklymenos. In order that Amphiaraos not suffer the disgrace of being speared in the back, Zeus hurled down a thunderbolt that opened up a chasm in the earth, which swallowed up Amphiaraos along with his chariot and charioteer. At the same time the god made Amphiaraos immortal (Apollodoros *Library* 3.6.8). The implication is that Amphiaraos lives on in his underground dwelling.

Erebos. The Harpies, or storm winds, snatched up the daughters of Pandareos and conveyed them to Erebos, giving them to the Erinyes (Furies) to be their maidservants (Homer *Odyssey* 20.61–78).

Olympos. Tros begot three sons Ilos, Assarakos, and Ganymedes, who was the best looking of all human beings. On account of his beauty the gods snatched him up to be Zeus's cupbearer and to live among the immortals (Homer *Iliad* 20.230–235).

Sky. The Pleiades were daughters of Atlas and Pleionê. Once when Pleionê and her daughters were traveling through Boeotia, the hunter Orion became sexually aroused by Pleionê and pursued her. Although he sought her for seven years, he was unable to find her. Pitying Pleionê's daughters, Jupiter placed them among the stars (Hyginus *Poetic Astronomy* 2.21). A translation of a being or object to the sky is a catasterism.

Of course temporary relocations are also commonly found, as when Poseidon brought the handsome boy Pelops up to Olympos to be his lover and eventually returned him to his earthly family (Pindar *Olympian* 1), and a god can simply waft a mortal away from one place to another without special implication, as when Aphroditê whisked Paris away from the battlefield of Troy, wrapping him in a cloud of invisibility and depositing him safely in Helen's bedroom (Homer *Iliad* 3.380–382).

Ancient Greek had no special term for divine translation, using a variety of verbs such as *snatch up, convey, send,* and *place* to describe aspects of the process.

> **See also** Catasterism; Transformation
> **Suggested reading:**
> Erwin Rohde. *Psyche: The Cult of Souls and Belief in Immortality among the Greeks,* trans. by W. B. Hillis. London: Kegan Paul, French, Trubner; New York: Harcourt, Brace, 1925, 55–114, 581–582.

TRIADS

Structures reflecting the number three pervade Greek and Roman culture, including classical mythology.

Numbers arbitrarily favored in a particular culture are termed pattern numbers, cultural numbers, sacred numbers, or formulistic numbers. Persons whose culture predisposes them to structure their world according to a particular number typically regard such structures as inherent in nature rather than as elements of culture, but their essential arbitrariness is shown by the fact that different cultures prefer different numbers. Indo-Europeans are predisposed to triads, whereas many North American Indian societies tend to organize reality in terms of the number four, and several favor the number five.

Triadic phenomena can be divided into those that are triadic as a result of multiplication (for example, a monster having three heads) and those that are triadic as a result of division (for example, the segmentation of time into past, present, and future). Occasionally the ancient sources disagree, one author representing a particular phenomenon as a triad, another author representing it otherwise. A tension between triads and dyads is particularly evident. For Hesiod, the Graiai are two in number (Pemphredo and Enyo), whereas for Apollodoros they are three (Pephredo, Enyo, and Deino). Homer mentions two Sirens, whom he does not name, but Apollodoros lists three (Peisinoê, Aglaopê, and Thelxiepeia).

Among characters in classical mythology, the most familiar triads are the clusters of supernatural sisters of like nature and function, notably the three Graces (Aglaia, Euphrosynê, and Thalia), the three Hours (Eunomia, Dikê, and Eirenê), and the three Fates (Klotho, Lachesis, and Atropos). According to some authors, the Furies are also three in number: Alekto, Tisiphonê, and Megaira (Apollodoros *Library* 1.4.4). Triads of supernatural brothers of like nature and function are also found: the three Cyclopes (Brontes, Steropes, and Arges), who forge Zeus's thunderbolts; the three Hundred-Handers (Kottos, Briareos, Gyges), who guard the defeated Titans; the three fraternal winds (Zephyros, Boreas, and Notos); and Kronos's and Rhea's three sons (Zeus, Poseidon, and Hades), who rule the world, for which they drew lots.

Multiples of three, especially nine and twelve, are also prominent. The Muses, nine sisters of similar nature and function, are an elaboration of the triadic pattern. The earlier family of gods, the Titans, has twelve members, as does the present family of gods, the Olympians. Since, however, there really are thirteen Olympians, the ancients omitted either one sister (Hestia) or one son (Dionysos) in lists or in artwork in order to maintain the number twelve.

Triadic structures show up in other mythological features. Hades's hound Kerberos is tricephalic according to many authors, as is the serpentine being Geryoneus and the monster Cacus. Since the Aloads grew a cubit in breadth and a fathom in height each year, they were nine cubits broad and nine fathoms high when they were nine years old, at which time they decided to take on the Olympian gods (Apollodoros *Library* 1.7.4).

Actions are often trebled. According to the Succession Myth, three different gods ruled the early cosmos, one after the other: Ouranos ruled until he was overthrown by Kronos, who ruled until he was overthrown by Zeus, who now rules. In this sequence the third element receives the emphasis, like the third and youngest of three brothers in European folktales who succeeds after his two older brothers fail. The hero Bellerophon must accomplish three tasks: first he must slay the monstrous Chimaira, then he must overcome the Solymoi in bat-

Herakles and Cerberus.

tle, and third he must slay the Amazons (Homer *Iliad* 6.179–186). Three conditions must be satisfied before the Greeks can capture Troy: they must secure the assistance of Neoptolemos, obtain the bows and arrows of Herakles, and gain possession of the Palladion. More elaborately, the hero Herakles is assigned twelve labors, or tasks.

In the foregoing instances a unit is trebled, but in others an entity is viewed as consisting of three parts. The stream of time is seen as tripartite: Kalchas is a seer "who knew the present, the future, and the past" (Homer *Iliad* 1.70), that is to say, everything. Space is similarly divided into three parts, the cosmos being made up of three layered worlds: the bright sky, the earth, and the misty death realm. Or the world consists of three realms—the sky, the sea, and Erebos—for which three elder Olympians once draw lots to determine their respective provinces, Zeus getting the sky, Poseidon the sea, and Hades the death realm, while they hold Olympos and earth jointly (*Iliad* 15.187–193). In its turn, the land surface of the earth is divided into three continents: Europê, Asia, and Libya (Africa).

Trichotomy is frequently manifest in the composite creatures of heroic legend. The Chimaira (Latinized form = Chimaera) slain by Bellerophon consists of "a lion in front, a serpent in back, and a goat in the middle" (*Iliad* 6.181). The Sphinx overcome by Oedipus is part woman, part lion, and part bird. Her riddle too is tripartite: What goes on four legs in the morning, two in the afternoon, and three in the evening?

Triads have different effects in different contexts. In the case of deities such as the Graces, multiplication depersonalizes, merging individual identity into a divine committee. But multiple members such as the three heads of the infernal watchdog Kerberos serve rather to intensify, for a three-headed watchdog is more frightening than a single-headed one.

Triads did not, however, seem right for every quantifiable phenomenon. Long periods of time ending in closure are often expressed by the number ten. The Titanomachy takes ten years, the Trojan War lasts ten years, Odysseus reaches home from Troy in the tenth year, and ten years is the term of punishment for a god who breaks his or her oath (Hesiod *Theogony* 793–806). The distance between Sky and Earth and again between Earth and Tartaros is the distance that an anvil falls in ten days' time (*Theogony* 722–725). Paris is hosted by Menelaos for nine days, but on the tenth Menelaos must sail to Crete to take care of a matter, which sets up the circumstances of Helen's desertion. But even in decades there is triadic coloration, for the usual expression in Greek is that something goes on for nine days (years), and on the tenth there occurs something decisive.

> *See also* Divine Guilds; Olympians
> ***Suggested reading:***

Alan Dundes. "The Number Three in American Culture," in Alan Dundes, *Interpreting Folklore*. Bloomington: Indiana University Press, 1980, 134–159.

William Hansen. "Three a Third Time." *Classical Journal* 71 (1976): 253–254.

Stith Thompson. *A Motif-Index of Folk-Literature*, Vol. 3. Bloomington: Indiana University Press, 1955–1958, Z71.1: *Formulistic number: three.*

H. Usener. "Dreiheit." *Rheinisches Museum für Philologie* 58 (1903): 1–47, 161–208, 321–362.

TRICKSTER

Clever character whose behavior is characterized by deceit.

The term *trickster* was initially applied by scholars to Coyote, Raven, Hare, and other clever buffoons in North American Indian mythology, but similar figures are found in other narrative traditions, including those of Greece and Rome. Consequently, the term has come to be used more broadly to include any character whose dominant trait is wiliness and deceit.

Trickster tales typically feature an interaction between a deceiver and a dupe, in which the trickster figure may play now one role and now the other. Since the focus of a trickster tale may be upon the cleverness of the deceit, with little attention to its justice or morality, the trickster's behavior may be framed as amoral. He—most tricksters are male—may manifest an infantile concern only for himself in the form of gluttony, lechery, or the like, but he may also benefit humans, if only inadvertently, by playing the role of culture hero. So a trickster can combine in one character apparently contradictory traits such as cleverness and naïveté, duping others but also being easily duped.

Greek mythology features divine tricksters (notably, Prometheus and Hermes) and human tricksters (notably, Autolykos, Sisyphos, and Odysseus). Several are related to one another genealogically. Hermes, god of thieves, is father of the master thief Autolykos, and the latter, being the father of Penelopê, is in turn the maternal grandfather of the cunning Odysseus. Sisyphos may be Odysseus's father, for according to one tradition Sisyphos seduced Autolykos's daughter Antikleia, who bore Odysseus. In this case, Sisyphos is the biological father of Odysseus, and Antikleia's husband, Laertes, only his putative father.

Divine Tricksters

Hesiod relates that when gods and men gathered at Mekonê to determine how meat should be apportioned between them, Prometheus cut up an ox and distributed the meat, fat, and bones into two portions, one consisting of meat and rich entrails covered with the ox's stomach, the other made up of bones covered with fat. Zeus commented on how unjustly Prometheus had made the two portions, and Prometheus responded only that Zeus should select the one he wished. So Zeus picked the pile topped with luscious fat but was enraged to discover that it otherwise consisted of nothing but bones. (Hesiod says in defense of Zeus that he saw through the trick but selected the worse portion anyway.) For this reason, mortals burn bones on the gods' altars when they sacrifice. In retaliation for Prometheus's trick, Zeus angrily withheld fire from mankind, but Prometheus deceived Zeus once again, stealing fire from the gods in a hollow stalk of fennel and giving it to men. Twice tricked, Zeus devised a punishment for men and another for Prometheus. For mortal men, he had Hephaistos create from clay an attractive maiden, and other deities contributed other adornments and qualities. She was an irresistible deceit, and from her come mortal women, who bring misery to men but whom men also need. Zeus had Hermes bring her to Epimetheus, Prometheus's brother, and although Prometheus had warned him not to accept anything from Zeus, since it might prove to be an evil for mortal men, Epimetheus accepted the gift and only then perceived the evil that he had. For the woman, Pandora, removed the lid from a large storage jar, releasing into the world for the first time the spirits of all sorts of cares and troubles and diseases that up to that time men had lived without, and these spirits now silently roam the earth. Zeus punished Prometheus by having him bound to a column, where each day an eagle ate his liver, which grew back again during the night. Later Zeus permitted his son Herakles to kill the eagle, honoring Herakles and releasing Prometheus from his suffering (*Theogony* 519–616, *Works and Days* 42–105). In addition, Prometheus is credited with the creation of the first humans, and according to Aeschylus he subsequently enhanced human culture in many ways, teaching humans inter alia to tell time from the stars, to use numbers, to read and write, to domesticate animals, and to sail in ships (*Prometheus Bound* 436–471).

The most prodigious Greek trickster is Hermes, who practiced deceit almost from the moment of his birth. According to the anonymous *Homeric Hymn to Hermes*, the infant god secretly left his cradle on the morning he was born, came upon a tortoise, killed it, and with its shell invented a musical instrument, the lyre, upon which he proceeded to improvise a song. Feeling a longing for meat, baby Hermes ran to Pieria, where certain cattle belonging to the immortal gods had their pasture, and stole fifty cattle belonging to his older brother Apollon. Hermes drove the cattle backward to a fold in a distant cave, so that their footprints would not betray their hiding place, while he himself walked forward, having invented wicker sandals that made his own tracks hard to interpret. After rubbing two pieces of wood together, thereby inventing fire sticks, Hermes slaughtered two cows and roasted their meat. Their skins he stretched on a rock, perhaps as a trophy of his theft. Though tempted by the savor of the meat to feast upon it even though he was a god, he did not do so, but stored the meat in the cave as a sign of his theft. Then he burned up the heads and feet of the slaughtered cattle, threw his sandals into a river, put out the fire, and smoothed over the soil. By dawn of the next day, he was back at the cave on Mount Kyllenê that was his home and lay down with apparent innocence in his cradle. In the meantime, Apollon noticed that some of his cattle were missing and by inquiry and omens learned who the thief was. He confronted Hermes, threatening to hurl him into Tartaros, but Hermes denied stealing the cattle, pleading that he was a day-old baby who cared only for sleep and mother's milk. Apollon laughed at the infant's lies, declaring that Hermes would have thievery and thieves as his divine province. They took the dispute to their father. Although Zeus also found Hermes's denials amusing, he ordered him to lead the way to the cattle, which he did. Once there, the two young gods made peace. Hermes gave Apollon the lyre he had invented, adding this instrument to Apollon's repertory as god of music, and Apollon gave Hermes a whip as a token of his becoming the deity of cattle-tending. Thereupon Hermes invented a different musical instrument for himself, shepherd's pipes, and Apollon presented him in addition with a golden caduceus, or herald's staff, in acknowledgment of his new honor as messenger of the gods.

Hermes and Prometheus are similar in that both are wily characters who employ their wits to deceive their adversaries, and their actions also bring benefits to others, whether the trickster so intends it or not. The one-day-old Hermes rustles cattle successfully in order to establish his credentials as a thief and as one who knows cattle well, and along the way he amuses himself by inventing the lyre, fire sticks, and shepherd's pipes, creations that add to the pleasure and comfort of divine and human life. For his part, Prometheus outwits Zeus for the sake of humankind, gaining the advantage in sacrifice and the use of fire, and also introduces many other kinds of useful cultural knowledge to humans. So Prometheus and Hermes combine the roles of trickster and culture hero.

But they are different from each other in personality and personal style. Hermes is the brilliantly impulsive and largely amoral child who amuses himself with deceit and invention. His deceptions have no great effect on the world other than as illustrations of his talents, so that up to a point his mischief is tolerated, and ultimately he succeeds in being incorporated into the divine hierarchy and assigned provinces of his own. In contrast, Prometheus's deceptions of Zeus have permanent and far-reaching implications that are bad for gods and good for humans, so that the gods exile him from divine and human society. Hermes is naive to the extent that he is less experienced than the older gods, who are amused by his transparent attempts at lying. Prometheus is not naive or playful at all. The trait of foolishness has perhaps been assumed by Prometheus's brother Epimetheus (Afterthought), who is as stupid as Prometheus (Forethought) is clever.

Human Tricksters

Of mortal tricksters, the best known are Autolykos, Sisyphos, and Odysseus (Latinized forms = Autolycus, Sisyphus, Ulysses).

The wily thief Autolykos is a son of Hermes, the tricky god of thievery himself. According to the Roman mythographer Hyginus, when Mercury begat Autolykos by Chione, he gave his son the gift of being so masterful a thief that people could not catch him in the act, for Autolykos could transform whatever he stole into any other appearance he wished, from white to black or from a hornless animal into a horned one. For a while Autolykos rustled cattle regularly from Sisyphos, who was unable to catch him, although he perceived that Autolykos was stealing from him because his own herds were diminishing even as Autolykos's were increasing. So Sisyphos marked the hooves of his cattle. When Autolykos as usual made off with some kine, Sisyphos went to him, identified his own cattle by means of their hooves, and so retrieved them. While he was there he seduced Autolykos's daughter Anticlia, who subsequently was given in marriage to Laertes and bore Odysseus. Accordingly some authors call Odysseus a son of Sisyphos and thereby account for his shrewdness (*Fabulae* 201). What Sisyphos actually inscribed on the hooves of his cattle was: "Autolykos stole [me]" (Polyainos *Strategemata* 6.52). Homer, who says that Autolykos excelled all persons in thievery and in the use of oaths, also attributes this gift to Hermes, whom he says Autolykos had pleased with the sacrifice of many animals (*Odyssey* 19.392–398).

When it was time for Sisyphos, wily king of Corinth, to die, Thanatos (Death) came for him, but Sisyphos perceived his approach and restrained Thanatos in strong bonds, and since Death was immobilized, human beings stopped dying. But eventually Ares released Thanatos and handed the trickster over to him to carry away, and so he did. But before Sisyphos died, he told his wife, Meropê, not to make the usual funeral offerings to him upon his death.

After Sisyphos was in the death realm for a while and Meropê had not performed the customary rites, the indignant Hades permitted Sisyphos to return to Corinth to reproach his wife for her negligence, but, once there, Sisyphos did not return to Hades's realm until he died of old age. After he was securely back in Erebos, Hades assigned him the task of rolling a stone up a hill over and over in order that he might not run away again (Pherekydes *FGH* 3 F 119).

The hero Odysseus is genealogically tied to Sisyphos, his supposed biological father, and to Autolykos, his maternal grandfather, and so back to Hermes, father of Autolykos. Wishing to avoid the conscription of warriors to go to Troy, Odysseus played the fool in order to suggest that he was incompetent. He sowed his fields with salt, as if hoping to grow a crop of salt, and did other apparently foolish things. The ploy might have worked, but Palamedes, another clever man, demonstrated that his inanity was only pretense by placing Odysseus's infant son Telemachos in front of his plow. When Odysseus stopped plowing, in order not to harm his son, he betrayed his rationality. In Homer's *Odyssey*, Odysseus is the clever improviser and liar, quick to devise a strategy or to invent a story about himself. At Troy it was he who had the idea of the Wooden Horse (Apollodoros *Epitome* 5.14), the deceit that after ten years of fighting finally decided the war.

The female shape-changer Mestra must also be mentioned. The wife of Autolykos, she had once been a lover of Neptune, who granted her the power to transform herself from a woman to a man or animal and back. In order to earn money, her father, Erysichthon, repeatedly sold her as a slave or animal to this or that master, after which she would change to a different form and return home to be sold again (Ovid *Metamorphoses* 8.738–878).

See also Culture Hero; Hermes; Odysseus

Suggested reading:

Mahadev L. Apte. *Humor and Laughter: An Anthropological Approach*. Ithaca, NY: Cornell University Press, 1985, 212–236.

Barbara Babcock-Abrahams. "'A Tolerated Margin of Mess': The Trickster and His Tales Reconsidered." *Journal of the Folklore Institute* 11 (1975): 147–186.

Michael P. Carroll. "The Trickster as Selfish-Buffoon and Culture Hero." *Ethos* 12 (1984): 105–131.

Jenny Strauss Clay. *The Politics of Olympus: Form and Meaning in the Major Homeric Hymns*. Princeton, NJ: Princeton University Press, 1989, 95–151.

William Hansen. *Ariadne's Thread: A Guide to International Tales Found in Classical Literature*. Ithaca, NY: Cornell University Press, 2002, 197–201, 243–246, 405–408.

Paul Radin. *The Trickster: A Study in American Indian Mythology*. New York: Schocken Books, 1972. Originally published in 1956, Radin's classic study includes Karl Kerényi's essay, "The Trickster in Relation to Greek Mythology," 173–191.

Mac Linscott Ricketts. "The North American Trickster." *History of Religions* 5 (1966): 327–350.

Jean-Pierre Vernant. "The Myth of Prometheus in Hesiod" and "Sacrificial and Alimentary Codes in Hesiod's Myth of Prometheus," in *Myth, Religion, and Society: Structuralist Essays by M. Detienne, L. Gernet, J.-P. Vernant, and P. Vidal-Naquet,* edited by R .L. Gordon. Cambridge: Cambridge University Press, 1981, 43–79.

TROJAN WAR

Cycle of legends about the great war at Troy between the Achaeans (Greeks) and the Trojans, together with the events leading up to it and its aftermath.

The Trojan War was the longest lasting as well as the largest-scale military conflict in classical mythology. In brief outline, the chief events were as follows. When human beings became so numerous that their weight oppressed the earth, Zeus decided to bring about a great war at Ilios, or Troy, in order to reduce their numbers by means of death. So Eris (Strife) showed up at the wedding feast of Peleus and Thetis, which the gods were attending, and caused Hera, Athena, and Aphroditê to dispute among one another about which of them was the most beautiful. The question was referred to Alexander, or Paris, a Trojan shepherd and prince, who decided in favor of Aphroditê, thereby earning her favor and the hatred of the other two goddesses. Paris sailed to Greece, where he visited the palace of King Menelaos of Sparta and his beautiful wife, Helen. Seduced by Paris, Helen deserted her family and followed Paris back to Troy as his wife.

Menelaos now planned a military campaign against Troy under the leadership of his brother Agamemnon, king of Mycenae. The leaders of the Achaean forces and their men assembled from all over Greece, and after a number of delays and setbacks they reached Troy. The Trojans rejected their request for the return of Helen, and a war began. The warring went on for ten years without either the Achaeans being able to capture the city or the Trojans and their allies being able to drive away their attackers. Finally the Achaeans took Troy by the ruse of the Wooden Horse, a hollow structure filled with hidden warriors that the Trojans were induced to drag into their city. The attackers vanquished the enemy, looted the city, and retrieved Menelaos's wife Helen.

Since, however, several Achaeans had offended the gods in the course of their victory, they now experienced divine hostility. Some warriors returned quickly and safely, others perished at sea or soon upon reaching their homes, and still others arrived years later. Reaching Ithaca ten years after the conclusion of the Trojan War, Odysseus was the last hero to return home and subsequently went on to have other adventures.

The Theban Wars and the Trojan War are the two great wars of the Greek heroic age (Hesiod *Works and Days* 156–172), the one closely following the other such that several heroes (for example, Diomedes) who fought in the second war at Thebes also fought on the Achaean side at Troy. The Trojan War was the last great enterprise of the heroic age and so also of Greek mythology, and its conclusion signals the end of the era of heroes and the transition to the human era.

The rich and complex legendry relating to the Trojan War was crystallized in early times in the two Homeric epics, *Iliad* and *Odyssey*, both of which survive, and in six epics of the Epic Cycle, namely, the *Kypria, Aithiopis, Little Iliad, Sack of Troy, Returns,* and *Telegony,* which are known only from fragments and summaries.

See also Theban Wars

Suggested reading:

Michael J. Anderson. *The Fall of Troy in Early Greek Poetry and Art.* Oxford: Clarendon Press, 1997.

Norman Austin. *Helen of Troy and Her Shameless Phantom.* Ithaca, NY: Cornell University Press, 1994.

Jonathan S. Burgess. *The Tradition of the Trojan War in Homer and the Epic Cycle.* Baltimore: The Johns Hopkins University Press, 2001.

Malcolm Davies. *The Greek Epic Cycle.* 2nd ed. London: Bristol Classical Press, 1989.

Timothy Gantz. *Early Greek Myth: A Guide to Literary and Artistic Sources.* Baltimore: The Johns Hopkins University Press, 1993, 557–717.

William Hansen. *Ariadne's Thread: A Guide to International Tales Found in Classical Literature.* Ithaca, NY: Cornell University Press, 2002, 169–176.

Gregory Nagy. *The Best of the Achaeans: Concepts of the Hero in Archaic Greek Poetry.* Baltimore: The Johns Hopkins University Press, 1979.

M. Scherer. *The Legends of Troy in Art and Literature.* 2nd ed. New York: Phaidon, 1964.

Susan Woodford. *The Trojan War in Ancient Art.* Ithaca, NY: Cornell University Press, 1993.

WATERS

Seas, streams, and springs as well as their rulers.

The individual waters of the earth are divine beings belonging to a single, interconnected system of waters, whose source is Okeanos (River Ocean), or Okeanos and his wife, Tethys. Homer says that the entire sea as well as all rivers, springs, and wells issue from Okeanos (*Iliad* 21.195–197), whose waters therefore flow to every part of the earth, like blood issuing from a heart. Hesiod expresses the idea mythologically when he says that Okeanos's wife, Tethys, bore him 3,000 sons and 3,000 daughters, the former being the earth's rivers, the latter being nymphs of springs and ponds (Hesiod *Theogony* 337–370). Physically, then, Okeanos is the constant source of the earth's regional waters, just as biologically he is their father. Geographically he is a river that flows in a circle around the earth at its furthest boundaries, where unusual peoples such as Pygmies dwell, where astonishing extremes of loveliness and horror coexist, and where Eos (Dawn) has her bed, Helios (Sun) rises and sets, and constellations bathe. Since Okeanos himself is a freshwater stream, his sister and mate, Tethys, presumably incarnates the salt waters. Genealogically the two are Titans, belonging to the family of gods that was dominant before the Olympians, and so are offspring of Ouranos (Sky) and Gaia (Earth).

In the mythological present, the ruler of the waters is the Olympian god Poseidon, brother of Zeus and Hades. For after the ascendancy of the Olympians and the cosmic sovereignty of Zeus, Zeus distributed honors to the gods or confirmed those that they already had, including presumably the assignment of the waters to Poseidon (Hesiod *Theogony* 389–396, 881–885). Or, according to a different tradition, when the three brothers drew lots for the rulership of the world, Poseidon got the sea, Hades got Erebos, Zeus got the sky, and the earth and Olympos were to be held in common (Homer *Iliad* 15.187–193). Poseidon's spouse is the Nereid Amphitritê, and their son is Triton, who lives with his parents in golden homes in the depths of the sea (*Theogony* 930–933). Triton is treated by ancient authors and artists sometimes as a single sea-god and sometimes generically as multiple Tritons, or mermen.

Proteus, Nereus, Glaukos, and other male deities of the sea are subordinate to Poseidon. Proteus, known as an Old Man of the Sea, is a minor sea deity who frequents the island of Pharos, just off Egypt. Menelaos encountered him in the course of his return home from Troy (*Odyssey* 4.351–570). Nereus, a son of Gaia and Pontos (Sea), possesses a just, gentle, and truthful character. His mate is the Okeanid Doris, who bore him fifty daughters in the sea (*Theogony* 233–264). Like Proteus, Nereus is an Old Man of the Sea (Homer *Iliad* 18.141). Glaukos (Latinized form = Glaucus) had been a mortal fisherman. Noticing that fish he had caught slipped back into the sea after nibbling upon a certain grass, he too chewed some of the herb, felt an irresistible urge to trade the land for the sea, and, like the mortal woman Ino before him, was accepted by the deities of the sea (Ovid *Metamorphoses* 13.898–14.74). Another Old Man of the Sea is Phorkys (Homer *Odyssey* 13.96).

The 3,000 daughters of Okeanos and Tethys, or Okeanids (Greek *Okeanides*), and the fifty daughters of the sea-god Nereus and the Okeanid Doris, or Nereids (Greek *Nereïdes*), are the principal families of water-nymphs of Greek tradition. Like other nymphs, they are fully human in form. Nereids are strictly mermaids, living in the sea, whereas Okeanids are found in freshwa-

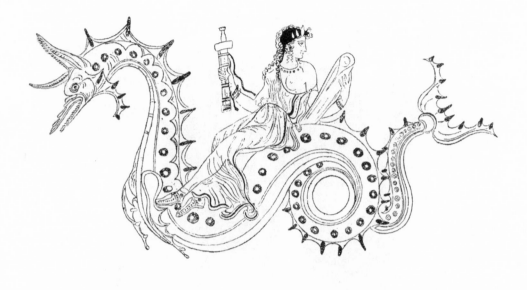

Nereid riding a sea horse (hippokampos).

ter as well as in the sea (the Okeanid Amphitritê is wed to Poseidon, lord of the sea), but a sharp distinction between them is not maintained. Indeed, the patronymic implication of the terms Okeanids and Nereids is sometimes ignored to the extent that the maidens may be assigned sires other than Okeanos and Nereus, and even the implication of sisterhood is lost when the notion of Nereids is treated as a generic term for mermaids of any origin such that the sea-goddess Leukothea, a daughter of Kadmos, can be called a Nereid (Nonnos *Dionysiaka* 40.210–211). In modern Greek tradition *neraïdes* are female beings much like the fairies of northern Europe.

Nereus riding a sea horse (hippokampos).

Although Okeanids and Nereids are usually mentioned collectively or anonymously, some are individually notable. The Okeanid Metis and the Nereid Thetis were potentially dangerous to their mates, since each was destined to bear a son who was superior to his father. Zeus swallowed Metis, his first wife, on the advice of Ouranos and Gaia, so that the son who would have overthrown him was never born (Hesiod *Theogony* 886–900). Later, when he was attracted to Thetis and discovered her quite similar destiny, he avoided her, and she was won instead by the mortal Peleus, to whom she bore the hero Achilleus (Apollodoros *Library* 3.13.5). Another pair of similar maids is the kindly goddesses Eidothea and Leukothea. Eidothea, daughter of the sea god Proteus, once appeared to the hero Menelaos when he was stranded on the island of Pharos, helping him in his distress (Homer *Odyssey* 4.351–446), and on a different occasion Leukothea (White Goddess) took pity on Odysseus, who was close to drowning, appeared suddenly to him, and saw that he reached shore safely. Leukothea had once been the mortal woman Ino, a daughter of Kadmos, but she had been transformed into a deity of the sea, and the gods had accepted her as one of them (*Odyssey* 5.333–463). Other notables are the Okeanid Styx, an important stream in Erebos, and the Nereid Amphitritê, wife of Poseidon.

Sea deities are typically knowledgeable, indeed prophetic, and capable of undergoing extraordinarily rapid transformations from one thing to another, a trick they employ mostly in order to avoid capture. If, however, a mortal seizes such a being and has the courage and persistence to hang on through all the forms the cunning deity may assume, the being will eventually resume his or her original shape and yield. Coached by Proteus's kindly daughter Eidothea, Menelaos grabbed the cunning Proteus as he napped, held on as the god metamorphosed into a lion, a snake,

Nereus and Doris.

a panther, a boar, running water, a tree, and finally back to his true form, after which the hero extracted useful information from him (*Odyssey* 4.351–570), and Peleus, advised by the wise centaur Cheiron, similarly seized the Nereid Thetis, held on while she turned into fire, water, and a wild animal, and finally made her his wife (Apollodoros *Library* 3.13.5). The river Acheloos is also a transformer, if not a rapid one. Suing for the hand of Deianeira, he approached her father in three different forms, first as a bull, next as a snake, and finally as a mix of ox and man (Sophocles *Trachiniae* 9–13). Since Hercules (Greek Herakles) also sought her hand, the two suitors fought for her. Acheloos began in human form, it seems, then changed to a snake and finally to a bull, before being overcome by Hercules (Ovid *Metamorphoses* 9.1–88). Water deities of every sort are at least binatural, being at once a kind of water and at the same time a living, anthropopathic being, and assuming watery or human form as suits the occasion. The river Alpheios (Latinized form = Alphaeus) is a stream but pursued the nymph Arethousa (Latinized form = Arethusa) as an android, and the naiad Salmakis (Latinized form = Salmacis) is a pool but assumed the form of a woman when she wished to make love to Hermaphroditos (Latinized form = Hermaphroditus), who was bathing in her waters.

In painting and sculpture, Poseidon is represented as an adult male holding a trident and sometimes in the company of his wife, Amphitritê. River gods can be shown as humanoid males beside an overturned pitcher from which water flows, symbolizing their streams, or as virile animals such as bulls. Sea deities are sometimes depicted as riding upon hippocamps (Greek *hippokampoi*), or sea horses.

A special use of mythological water is to serve as a boundary marking off the land of the dead from the land of the living and also to characterize the land of the dead as a place of misery. The stream that borders Erebos is usually Acheron (Euripides *Alkestis* 444; Plato *Phaedo* 113d), although in Homer's *Odyssey* it is the River Ocean, since in that work Erebos lies in the distant west rather than beneath the earth. In Homeric geography Pyriphlegethon (Burning), Kokytos (Wailing), Styx (Hateful), and Acheron (Grief) are all waters within Erebos, the streams Pyriphlegethon and Kokytos (Latinized form = Cocytus), a branch of the Styx, flowing together and then, as a waterfall, descending into Acheron (*Odyssey* 10.513–515), which is perhaps a lake.

The Styx, regularly called the "water of Styx" in Greek, is a major branch of Okeanos, the River Ocean, the ultimate source of all waters. Styx is exceptional in several ways, being the female spirit of a river (streams are otherwise male) and the only netherworld stream that is really personified. An Okeanid, she supported the Olympians against the Titans in the Titanomachy and was honored by being made the dread waters by which gods swear their oaths (Hesiod *Theogony* 361, 389–401, 775–806). Her waters, in later tradition at least, had the power of conferring invulnerability, for it was in the waters of the Styx that Thetis dipped the infant Achilleus in the hope of making him invulnerable, which he was, except for the heel by which she held him (Servius *Commentary on Virgil's Aeneid* 6.57).

Finally, many seas and rivers get their names from mortals who drowned in them. The Icarian Sea was named for Ikaros (Latinized form = Icarus), the unfortunate son of Daidalos (Latinized form = Daedalus), whose artificial wings failed him when, despite his father's urgings, he flew too near the sun so that the wax or glue that held the feathers together melted, and he plunged to his death in the waters below (Apollodoros *Epitome* 1.13). A maiden named Hellê gave her name to the Hellespont, or Hellê's Sea, when she was passing over it on the back of a flying ram, fell, and drowned (Apollodoros *Library* 1.9.1). The eponym of the Euenos River was a certain man named Euenos, who slaughtered his horses and cast himself into the river after he had failed to retrieve his daughter from her abductor (*Library* 1.7.8).

See also Cosmogony; Nymphs; Transformation

Suggested reading:

Harry Brewster. *The River Gods of Greece*. London: I. B. Tauris, 1997.

Ernst Buschor. "Meermanner." *Sitzungsberichte der Bayerischen Akademie der Wissenschaften*, Philosophisch-historische Abteilung, 2.1 Munich: Verlag der Bayerischen Akademie der Wissenschaften, 1941.

P. M. C. Forbes Irving. *Metamorphosis in Greek Myths.* Oxford: Clarendon Press, 1990, 171–194, 299–307.

Laura M. Slatkin. *The Power of Thetis: Allusion and Interpretation in the* Iliad. Berkeley: University of California Press, 1991.

Carina Weiss. "Fluvii," in *LIMC* 4:139–148.

WINDS

Personified or reified streams of air.

Mythological winds are treated in two principal ways: as male gods who engage anthropomorphically in humanlike activities but are also the winds themselves and as nonliving things that can be confined in a bag.

The three principal winds—Zephyros (west wind), Boreas (north wind), and Notos (south wind)—are the offspring of Eos (Dawn) and Astraios, according to Hesiod (*Theogony* 378–380). The Romans Latinized these names as Zephyrus, Boreas, and Notus. The fact that Hesiod lists three

Boreas abducting Oreithyia.

rather than four winds may reflect the Greek fondness for triads. Homer mentions an occasion on which the winds—perhaps the three brothers—were gathered for a feast at the house of Zephyros (*Iliad* 23.192–216).

Of the siblings, only Boreas plays a major role in myth. His home is in the north, in barbarous Thrace, and his character is fierce like that of the chill wind that blows down on Greece from the north. Boreas once wooed Oreithyia, lovely daughter of King Erechtheus of Athens, but his suit did not find favor with her father. So the god decided to take her by force. While the maiden was playing beside the Ilissos River, which ran through Athens, the winged Boreas suddenly appeared and like a bird of prey flew off with her to his home in the north. He had sexual intercourse with Oreithyia, who in time bore two daughters, Kleopatra and Chionê, and two sons, Zetes and Kalais. The sons, like their father, were winged (Apollodoros *Library* 3.15.2; Ovid *Metamorphoses* 6.682–721).

Although human beings run the risk of being carried off by any one of a number of deities or forces, violent winds seem to specialize in this activity. In Homer's *Iliad* (6.343–348), Helen declares that on the day on which her mother bore her, an evil storm wind (*thyella*) ought to have carried her away to a mountain or to the sea, where a wave would have swept her away before she could do what she did (namely, desert her husband for a lesser man). Similarly, the miserable Penelopê prays to Artemis to slay her with an arrow or for a storm wind to snatch her up and carry her away to the mouth of the River Ocean. She then elaborates on this thought, speaking of storm winds and Harpies (Snatchers) interchangeably (*Odyssey* 20.61–82). So the north wind's snatching Oreithyia and flying with her to a faraway place is a reflex of an established pattern in the mythology of winds.

The offspring of Boreas and Oreithyia have their own adventures. Best known is the legend told of the winged Zetes and Kalais, known as the Boreades (sons of Boreas), in the cycle of the Argonauts. In the course of their voyage in quest of the Golden Fleece, the Argonauts consulted the blind seer Phineus about their route. He agreed to help them if they would rid him of the Harpies, winged female creatures whom the gods had sent to torment him. Whenever food was placed on a table before Phineus, the Harpies would suddenly swoop down, snatch most of it away, and befoul the rest, rendering it inedible. So the table was now baited, the Harpies appeared as usual, and the sons of Boreas, swords in hand, pursued them through the air. Different authors relate different outcomes, but all agree that the Boreades freed the seer of the Harpies' scourge. Thereupon he advised the Argonauts (Apollodoros *Library* 1.9.21; Ovid *Metamorphoses* 7.1–6).

There was a widespread folk-belief in the ancient world that horses could be impregnated by the wind, producing swift offspring, and the mythological counterpart of this belief was the tradition that a personified wind impregnated a mare on a particular occasion. Homer recounts how Boreas became enamored of a particular herd of 3,000 mares, took the form of a horse, and mated with them, after which they bore twelve foals (*Iliad* 20.221–229). At another time Zephyros mated with the Harpy Podargê, west wind with storm wind, who bore the horses Xanthos and Balios. These steeds, given by Poseidon as a wedding present to Peleus and eventually owned by Peleus's son Achilleus, were the finest to be found at Troy. They were immortal and ran as fast as Zephyros, the lightest thing there is (*Iliad* 2.770, 16.145–154, 19.415–416).

A quite different conception of the winds underlies an episode in Homer's *Odyssey*. On his way home from Troy, Odysseus came to Aiolia (Latinized form = Aeolia), a floating island that was home to Aiolos (Latinized form = Aeolus) and his family. He was dear to the gods, and Zeus had made him steward of the winds. Aiolos entertained Odysseus and his companions hospitably, and when it was time for his guests to depart, he bound the raucous winds in a leather bag, tied it securely, presented it to Odysseus, and even sent a zephyr to propel Odysseus's ships. The journey went well for the Achaeans, and their homeland was in sight, but while Odysseus slept, his mistrustful companions opened the leather bag, thinking that it must contain gold or silver. The winds rushed out, a storm wind snatching the mariners and carrying them out to sea again. Returning to Aiolia, Odysseus asked once again for help, but Aiolos ordered him away, saying that it would not be right for him to give aid to someone who obviously was hateful to the blessed gods (*Odyssey* 10.1–79).

In this story, the winds are nonliving things that are subject to the will of Aiolos, a sort of king of the winds in Zeus's cosmic hierarchy. Aiolos binds up the violent winds in a sack, as though winds were so many finite objects, and dispatches a west wind to escort his guests gently home.

> ***See also*** Divine Guilds; Monsters; Triads
> ***Suggested reading:***
> William Hansen. "Homer and the Folktale," in *A New Companion to Homer,* edited by Ian Morris and Barry Powell. Leiden: Brill, 1997, 442–462, at 454–455.
> Kora Neuser. *Anemoi: Studien zur Darstellung der Winde und Windgottheiten in der Antike.* Rome: Giorgio Bretschneider Editore, 1982.
> Erika Simon. "Venti," in *LIMC* 8:186–192.
> R. Strömberg. "The Aeolus Episode and Greek Wind Magic." *Acta Universitatis Gotoburgensis* 56 (1950): 73–84.

Harpy carrying off a child.

WONDROUS ANIMALS

Animals with fabulous properties.

The quality most commonly manifested by wondrous animals is flight, and apart from birds, the animal most frequently gifted with wings is the horse. The flying horse Pegasos (Latinized form = Pegasus) was the offspring of Poseidon and the Gorgon Medusa, having sprung out of Medusa after she was decapitated by Perseus. Following his birth, Pegasos flew up to the realm of the immortal gods, where he made his home, serving as the bearer of Zeus's thunderbolts (Hesiod *Theogony* 278–286). Zeus gave Pegasos to the hero Bellerophon, who rode it when he battled the monstrous Chimaera, so that the hero was able to shoot the monster from above (Hesiod frag. 43; Pindar *Olympian* 13.60–92). Some wondrous horses were swift because they were begotten by the winds.

Bellerophon and Pegasos.

Zephyros (West Wind) mated with a Harpy, who bore the horses Xanthos and Balios, immortal steeds that were as swift as their father (Homer *Iliad* 16.145–154, 19.415–416).

Another winged mammal was the flying ram with fleece of gold that carried the siblings Phrixos and Hellê through the air away from Greece. The wondrous animal had been given to their mother by Hermes (Apollodoros *Library* 1.9.1). Like monsters, wondrous animals tend to be peculiar to a single story or adventure. It was, however, the Golden Fleece of this ram that Jason and the Argonauts subsequently undertook to obtain. A golden lamb plays a role in the legend of Atreus (Apollodoros *Epitome* 2.10–11), and golden animals also appear in other narratives.

Since horse-drawn chariots were anciently the supreme mode of transportation, chariots capable of flight were the ultimate imaginable vehicle. Helios (Sun) crossed the sky daily in his chariot with its flying steeds, and Selenê (Moon) similarly crossed the sky nightly on a wagon. Often mentioned are the winged horses that pulled the chariot of Poseidon, god of horses. When the hero Pelops asked Poseidon for the swiftest of chariots in order that he might compete for the hand of Hippodameia, Poseidon equipped him with his golden chariot and its tireless, winged horses (Pindar *Olympian* 1.75–87). Sometimes it is Poseidon's chariot that is winged (Apollodoros *Epitome* 2.2). The chariots of certain deities were pulled by animals other than horses. Hera's chariot was drawn by peacocks, Aphroditê's by swans or sparrows.

A quality not often found in wondrous animals is human speech. Achilleus's horse Xanthos was gifted by Hera with the ability not only to use human speech but also to prophesy (Homer *Iliad* 19.404–417), although only on a single occasion, when he foretold his master's death. Similarly, Phrixos's ram warned him of imminent danger (Palaiphatos 30). So the gift of monitory speech is rare and momentary.

A different sort of wondrous animal is the goat Amaltheia, which nursed the infant Zeus (Kallimachos *Hymn* 1.47–48). Nectar flowed from one of her horns, ambrosia from the other (scholiast on Kallimachos *Hymn* 1.49). In gratitude for his rearing by Amaltheia and by certain nymphs, Zeus gave one of Amaltheia's horns the power to produce whatever was asked of it, the proverbial "horn of Amaltheia," or cornucopia (*cornu copiae*), as the Romans called it (Pliny *Natural History*, preface 24; Palaiphatos 45). Or Amaltheia was a woman who possessed a bull's horn that had the power of producing an abundant supply of whatever food or drink one wanted (Pherekydes frag. 42 Fowler).

Whereas some wonder-animals manifest a trait that is proper to another animal (wings) or to no animal at all (food-producing horn, fleece made of gold), in others a trait that is proper to the animal possessing it is intensified. The many heads of the infernal watchdog Kerberos (Latinized form = Cerberus) represent a multiplication of a feature that every dog already has. If one head is a necessary and desirable trait for a watchdog, more heads must be even better. An intensifying trait can be represented as being fated and therefore as something perhaps not entirely internal, as in the case of the fox that was fated never to be caught and the dog that was fated always to catch its prey (Antoninus Liberalis 41).

> *See also* Special Rules and Properties; Wondrous Objects
> *Suggested reading:*
> F. Hannig. "Pegasos," in Roscher 3:1727–1752.
> O. Immisch. "Kerberos," in Roscher 2:1119–1135.
> H. W. Stoll. "Amaltheia," in Roscher 1:262–266.

WONDROUS OBJECTS

Tools, weapons, and the like with amazing properties.

Most of the wondrous weapons and tools found in classical mythology belong to the Olympian gods and therefore appear in divine contexts. Zeus has his thunderbolts and aegis, Poseidon his trident, Aphroditê her belt, and Hermes his caduceus.

The king of the gods wields thunderbolts because thunderbolts are the most powerful weapon in the universe. Imagined as being physical objects, they are forged for Zeus by divine smiths, the Cyclopes, and carried for his convenience by the winged horse Pegasos. Unlike some other wonder-objects, the thunderbolts are never loaned to another character, although the monster Typhon once managed to steal them, and Zeus retrieved them only with difficulty. When Zeus is engaged in combat with a supernatural being or when he is angry at the hubristic behavior of a particular mortal, he casts a thunderbolt at him;

in short, thunderbolts are Zeus's spears. He also casts a thunderbolt between adversaries whom he wishes to prevent from fighting (for example, Homer *Odyssey* 24.539–548; Apollodoros *Library* 2.5.12).

Zeus's aegis (Greek *aigis*, derived from *aix*, "goat") is, it seems, a goatskin shield or cloak, but the object is treated vaguely by ancient authorities. On one occasion, the god seems to employ it to control the weather, shrouding Mount Ida in mist (Homer *Iliad* 17.593–594), the aegis perhaps acting as a conduit of the god's powers. Physically it is a golden object with tassels that features iconic representations of frightening images and forces including the Gorgon's head (*Iliad* 5.738–742), all intended to inspire terror. Made by Hephaistos and so of divine manufacture, it is so strong that it can withstand even Zeus's thunderbolts. On occasion it is used without explanation by Zeus's daughter Athena or by his son Apollon (Homer *Iliad* 5.738–742, 15.306–311, 18.203–204, 21.400–401, 24.20–21); however, Athena's aegis may be her own, for she also is closely associated with an aegis, which in her case ancient artists represent as a cloak. Fringed with snakes, it bears the head of the Gorgon Medusa, which the goddess placed there after Perseus decapitated the monster (Herodotos 4.189; Apollodoros *Library* 2.4.3).

Iconically, Poseidon's trident (Greek *triaina*) is a three-pronged spear of the sort used by fishermen to harpoon fish. As a marine implement it is appropriate to the god of the sea, but in practice Poseidon employs it rather as a conduit of his divine power, rather like a magician's wand, stirring up the sea with it or splitting a rock apart (Homer *Odyssey* 4.505–511, 6.291–296) or striking a rock on the Athenian acropolis to produce salt water (*Library* 3.14.1). It was fashioned for him by the Telchines (Kallimachos *Hymn* 4.30–31), mythical craftsmen and sorcerers.

Aphroditê's cestus is a wondrous accessory that renders its wearer sexually irresistible, its full Greek name (*kestos himas*) indicating that it is an embroidered strap. Worn by the deity around her bosom next to her skin, the cestus is her special weapon as the goddess of love. Hera once borrowed it in order to seduce her husband, Zeus (Homer *Iliad* 14.187–223). Such straps or cords are attested in ancient erotic magic. If Aphroditê's cestus serves the cause of seduction, the arrows of Eros (Roman *Cupido*, that is, Cupid), who is often represented as her mischievous young son, serve the cause of matchmaking, since they possess the power of instilling irresistible desire in one being for another being. According to Apollonios of Rhodes, the barbarian princess Medeia fell passionately in love with the Greek hero Jason after Eros shot her with one of his invisible arrows (*Argonautika*, Book 3).

Hermes is the herald of the Olympian gods, and the golden caduceus (Greek *kerykeion* [*skeptron*], "herald's [staff]") carried by him is morphologically a herald's staff, identifying its bearer as a messenger. In form it is a short wand with two intertwined branches or serpents at the top. Apollon presented it to his younger brother, Hermes, when the infant deity acquired his divine honors, or spheres of cosmic influence (*Homeric Hymn to Hermes* 527–532), as an emblem of his new role as divine herald. But like Poseidon's trident, Hermes's caduceus is also a sort of magic wand, for with it Hermes can put human beings to sleep or rouse them from sleep (Homer *Iliad* 24.343–345). Hermes also has sandals that enable him to fly (*Odyssey* 5.43–46), as does Athena (*Odyssey* 1.96–98). The hero Perseus wore winged sandals when he slew Medusa (Hesiod *Shield of Herakles* 220).

Poseidon with trident.

The Cap, or Helmet, of Invisibility (Greek *aidos kyneê*) is a mysterious piece of headgear used by several characters in Greek mythology to make themselves unseen by others, including even by supernatural beings. It thus functions much like the more usual cloud or mist with which gods sometimes surround themselves or others to render them temporarily invisible. On one occasion during the Trojan War, Athena donned it in order to be invisible to Ares while she aided Ares's adversary Diomedes, and with her unseen help Diomedes even wounded Ares. Somehow Ares was able to identify Athena as being responsible for his wound despite her invisibility (Homer *Iliad* 5.844–909). Hermes wore the cap in his duel with a particular giant during the Gigantomachy, or battle of the gods and the giants (*Library* 1.6.2), and the hero Perseus had it when he slew the Gorgon, having gotten it from certain unnamed nymphs, to whom he returned it after the conclusion of his quest (Hesiod *Shield of Herakles* 226–227; Apollodoros *Library* 2.4.2–3). We do not know why these nymphs have custody of it, but perhaps they are merely an ad hoc narrative convenience, since they are also the unexplained source of the winged sandals and special pouch (*kibisis*) that Perseus needed for the occasion and returned afterward. Folk etymology interpreted the Cap of Invisibility, or more strictly the Cap of the Invisible One, as the Cap of Hades, leading the mythographer Apollodoros to report that during the Titanomachy the divine smiths, the Cyclopes, give the thunderbolt to Zeus, the cap to Hades, and the trident to Poseidon, and armed with these weapons, the Olympians overcome the Titans (*Library* 1.2.1). But on no other occasion is Hades said to possess or employ such a tool, not even during his abduction of Persephonê, when it would have been a useful accessory, nor are any of the employers of the cap (Athena, Hermes, Perseus) represented as borrowing it from him.

These weapons and tools lend distinction to their bearers, testifying to their importance, and except for the Cap of Invisibility, they generally externalize a quality that otherwise the deity may be thought already to have. Zeus's swallowing Metis, or Cleverness, and retaining her in his belly serves the same function, externalizing Zeus's intelligence as a thing, or in this case a being, that he possesses. In art, the gods' weapons or tools often serve as distinctive attributes that identify their bearers, Hermes being shown with his caduceus or Zeus with his thunderbolt whether he has any meaningful use for it at the moment or not.

The divine smith and craftsman Hephaistos is credited with making many wondrous objects both for others and for himself. Among the latter are different kinds of automata, including servants in the form of golden female manikins that possess intelligence and the power of speech (Homer *Iliad* 18.372–377, 417–421).

The thyrsi (Greek *thyrsoi*), or wands, carried by mythological bacchantes during the celebration of their ecstatic rites in honor of Dionysos are similarly wondrous objects, for like Poseidon's trident or Hermes's caduceus they are magical conduits. If a celebrant strikes the ground with her thyrsus, milk or wine or honey pours forth, and if she strikes a man with it, he is wounded as though by a weapon. Honey flows from them (Euripides *Bacchae* 704–713, 762–764). The magical properties of the thyrsi do not inhere in the objects themselves, but rather the thyrsi become temporarily magical channelers because of the presence of the god, whose power flows through them. As a physical object the thyrsus is a different thing at different times. In the classical period it is a stalk of fennel with ivy leaves attached at the top, but stylized representations of thyrsi by vase painters make them appear to be pine cones, which in later times they are thought by some authors to be.

Magically sticky chairs appear in Greek myth and legend. Hera bore a son Hephaistos but, ashamed of his lameness, cast him out of Olympos, but presently Hephaistos skillfully constructed a chair with invisible bonds, sending it as a gift to his mother, who happily sat down on it and then could not get up from it. Since only Hephaistos could free her, Dionysos made the god drunk and brought him back to Olympos, where he released his mother (Alcaeus frag.

349 Lobel-Page). Theseus and Peirithoos were similarly tricked by sticky chairs when they adventurously went to Erebos in the hope of securing Persephonê as a wife for Peirithoos. Hades invited them to sit down, whereupon they grew into the Chair of Forgetfulness, onto which they were held fast by coils of snakes (Apollodoros *Epitome* 1.24). Sisyphos possibly employed a sticky chair against Thanatos, or Death. Zeus once dispatched Thanatos to fetch Sisyphos, but the wily Sisyphos perceived his approach and—we are not told how—bound him in strong bonds, as a result of which mortals stopped dying and did not resume dying until Ares managed to free Thanatos (Pherekydes *FGH* 3 F 119). Since this incident—a trickster binds Death by inducing him to sit in a magic chair from which it is impossible to rise—is known from international folktales, Sisyphos likely uses the same device against the hapless Thanatos.

In human contexts the most remarkable objects with imaginary properties are ships. The world's first ship, the *Argo,* which conveys the Argonauts on their quest for the Golden Fleece, had the power of speech (Apollodoros *Library* 1.9.19). The ships of the Phaiakians, whom Odysseus visited on his way home from Troy, were even more remarkable, for they sailed as swiftly as thought, required no pilot or rudder, knew men's thoughts, were acquainted with every city and land, and were wrapped in mist, that is, were invisible to the eye (Homer *Odyssey* 7.36, 8.557–562, 13.86–87). After passengers or crew members embarked, the wondrous ship itself did the rest, since it knew where one wanted to go and how to get there and accomplished the journey swiftly and invisibly.

Many wondrous objects are unnaturally golden, such as the golden apples of the gods, which are guarded by the Hesperides and the dragon Ladon; the single golden apple that Eris (Strife) tossed before the goddesses Hera, Athena, and Aphroditê as a beauty prize; the Golden Fleece sought by Jason and the Argonauts; and the golden chariots in which gods travel. The shower of gold into which Zeus metamorphosed himself when he impregnated the maiden Danaê is another instance. Virtually any object owned by a god is likely to be golden except for a weapon, for which the material of divine choice is adamant, a fabulous metal of extreme hardness.

Some objects possess a marvelously desirable property, such as the spear of the hunter Kephalos that never missed its mark. Peleus owned a similarly marvelous spear with which he was always successful in battle and in the hunt; it was fashioned by Hephaistos and bestowed upon the virtuous hero by the gods (Zenobios *Centuriae* 5.20). The blind seer Teiresias possessed a magical wooden staff, a gift from Athena that permitted him to walk like a person with sight (Apollodoros *Library* 3.6.7). Amaltheia had a bull's horn that had the power of producing an abundant supply of whatever food or drink one wanted (Pherekydes frag. 42 Fowler).

See also Special Rules and Properties; Wondrous Animals

Suggested reading:

Christopher Blinkenberg. *The Thunderweapon in Religion and Folklore: A Study in Comparative Archaeology.* Cambridge: Cambridge University Press, 1911.

E. R. Dodds, comm. *Euripides: Bacchae.* 2nd ed. Oxford: Clarendon Press, 1960, 82.

Christopher A. Faraone. *Ancient Greek Love Magic.* Cambridge, MA: Harvard University Press, 1999, 97–110.

Monique Halm-Tisserant and Gérard Siebert. "Kerykeion," in *LIMC* 8:728–730.

William Hansen. *Ariadne's Thread: A Guide to International Tales Found in Classical Literature.* Ithaca, NY: Cornell University Press, 2002, 405–408.

————. "The Theft of the Thunderweapon: A Greek Myth in Its International Context." *Classica et Mediaevalia* 46 (1995): 5–24.

Josef Roeger. *Aidos Kyneê: Das Märchen von der Unsichtbarkeit in den homerischen Gedichten.* Graz, Austria: Leuschner and Lubensky, 1924.

W. H. Roscher. "Aigis," in Roscher 1:149–151.

K. Seelinger. "Argo," in Roscher 1:502–503.

F. J. M. de Waele. *The Magic Staff or Rod in Greco-Italian Antiquity.* Nimeguen, Holland: Privately published, 1927.

ZEUS (ROMAN JUPITER, ALSO JOVE)

God of the sky.

Zeus's parents are the Titans Kronos and Rhea. Having learned from Gaia and Ouranos that a son would overthrow him, Kronos swallowed his children by Rhea as each was born. When the grieving mother was about to bear Zeus, she consulted Gaia and Ouranos and upon their instructions hid her newborn son in a cave on Crete, giving her husband instead a stone wrapped in swaddling clothes, which he swallowed. A year later Zeus was fully grown, and Kronos was tricked into vomiting up the stone and his children. Presently Zeus led a war of the younger gods, the Olympians, against the older gods, the Titans. He and his supporters were ranged on Mount Olympos, and the Titans on Mount Othrys. After ten years of battle, the Olympians and their allies overcame the Titans. Their allies included the Cyclopes, who gave Zeus the thunderbolt as his weapon, and the Hundred-Handers, immensely powerful warriors. Another threat arose, for Gaia (Earth) and Tartaros mated and produced a new monster, Typhon, but Zeus overcame him, also after a battle of cosmic proportion. The other Olympians now urged Zeus to be their ruler, and as king of the gods he distributed to them their honors or in some cases confirmed honors that they already possessed (Hesiod *Theogony*).

According to a different myth, Zeus acquired his honor, or sphere of influence, by chance rather than as a consequence of his prowess in combat. The three brothers Zeus, Poseidon, and Hades drew lots to determine what honor each should have in the cosmos. To Zeus fell the sky, to Poseidon the sea, and to Hades Erebos. Earth and Olympos were to be held by them in common (Homer *Iliad* 15.187–193). Although the myth presents the three brothers as equals, the mythological tradition otherwise represents Zeus's brothers deferring to him as ruler of the gods.

As ruler of the Olympian gods, Zeus is king of gods and humans, maintaining his authority by means of his great physical strength, which he once declared exceeds that of all other male deities combined (Homer *Iliad* 8.1–27); by his cosmic spear, the thunderbolt (Hesiod *Theogony* 501–506), the world's most powerful weapon, which is carried for him by the winged horse Pegasos (Hesiod *Theogony* 278–286); by his mental alertness, the result of his retaining Metis (Cleverness) in his belly as his adviser (*Theogony* 899–900); and by his numerous offspring. As king he presides over the celestial council on Olympos and generally manages matters on Olympos and earth. As the source of earthly sovereignty, he chooses and oversees mortal kings, rewarding good rulers with prosperity and punishing others.

In addition, as deity of the sky, Zeus controls weather phenomena such as storms and thunder. When Odysseus's companions offended Helios (Sun) by slaughtering his cattle, Helios threatened to shine in the realm of the dead if the offenders did not pay for their deed, and Zeus quickly promised to strike the ship with a bolt of lightning. After the vessel put out to sea, Zeus made a cloud hover over the vessel, sent a hurricane-like wind against the ship, snapping its mast, and finally struck the boat with lightning (Homer *Odyssey* 12.376–419). The thunderbolt is the god's all-purpose tool. He employs it as a weapon in combat against gods and monsters, as he did in the war against the Titans, or Titanomachy. He uses it to annihilate individual mortals who offend him by their presumption or other hubristic behavior, as did the mortal physician Asklepios, who dared to raise the dead (Apollodoros *Library* 3.10.4), and King Salmoneus, who, driving around in a chariot and throwing into the air torches that he said were thunderbolts, declared he was Zeus himself (*Library* 1.9.7). But Zeus also employs his lightning as a tool for the purification and sanctification of mortals, conveying them by fire from earth to Olympos and promoting them from mortal to immortal, as he did his lover, Semelê (Pindar *Olympian* 2.27), and his son, Herakles (Diodorus of Sicily 4.38.4–5). Accordingly, just as Artemis can use an arrow to execute an offensive mortal or to bring a gentle, nonlingering death to a deserving person, so also Zeus can employ a thunderbolt to destroy an opponent on one occasion and to promote a mortal to godhead on a different occasion.

Another of the god's provinces of mythological importance is hospitality, the relationship of host and guest. Zeus sometimes travels the earth in disguise, observing the behavior of humans, by himself or in the company of Hermes or other gods. Ovid recounts how Jupiter, Neptune, and Mercury (Greek Zeus, Poseidon, and Hermes) were traveling and came in disguise to the hut of a poor Boeotian farmer, Hyrieus. After the man treated the strangers kindly, the visitors revealed that they were divinities and offered to grant him any wish. He wanted a son. So the three gods urinated onto an oxhide, buried it in the ground, and ten months later a boy was born, Urion (*Fasti* 5.493–544). The narrative builds upon a folk etymology that connects the proper name Urion (Greek *Orion*) with the common noun *urine* (Greek *ouron*). On another occasion Zeus, in the guise of a day-laborer, visited Lykaon, king of the Arcadians, and his fifty arrogant sons, wishing to test their impiety. They mixed the entrails of a slaughtered human child with the sacrificial victim and served this to their guest. In revulsion, Zeus killed Lykaon and most of his family with thunderbolts (Apollodoros *Library* 3.8.1). Zeus's disgust with human behavior eventually led him to destroy most of humanity by means of a great flood.

Many myths focus upon Zeus's sexual relations with different beings divine or mortal, female or male, willing or unwilling. According to Hesiod, Zeus has had seven wives. The first was the Okeanid Metis (Cleverness). When he learned that she was fated to bear first a daughter, Athena, and then a son who would displace him, Zeus swallowed her, keeping her in his belly in order that she might advise him. In time he gave birth to Athena, who emerged fully grown and armed from his head, but no other child was born, since he had forestalled its conception. Second, he wed Themis, who bore the three Hours (Greek *Horai*) and the three Fates (Greek *Moirai*). His third wife was the Okeanid Eurynomê, who gave birth to the three Graces (Greek *Charites*). His sister Demeter was his next spouse, and their daughter was Persephonê. Then he loved Mnemosynê (Memory), who bore him the nine Muses. Sixth, he wed Leto, and their offspring were Apollon and Artemis. His seventh and present wife is Hera, who gave birth to Hebê (Youth), Ares, and Eileithyia (*Theogony* 886–929).

Just as Zeus gave birth to his daughter Athena from his head, so also he later gave birth to his son Dionysos from his thigh. Zeus once carried on an affair with a Theban woman, Semelê. When he agreed to grant her a wish, she bade him appear to her in the form in which he appeared to his divine spouse, Hera. Zeus did so, but the power of his divinity destroyed Semelê. He rescued from her body the fetus that she was carrying, placed it in his thigh, and in time untied the stitches, delivering the infant Dionysos (Apollodoros *Library* 3.4.3). So Athena and Dionysos can be said to be twice-born, just as were the children of Kronos and Rhea, whom Kronos swallowed and later spewed up. Male pregnancy and parturition pervades the early doings of the Titans and the Olympians.

Among Zeus's male loves is the handsome Trojan prince Ganymedes (traditionally anglicized as Ganymede), whom he seized and carried off to Olympos, where the youth became cupbearer for the gods (*Homeric Hymn to Aphrodite* 202–217). In many myths, Zeus gains an advantage by approaching his love (or lust) interest in a transformed state. So he took the form of Artemis in order to gain access to Kallisto, a huntress and companion of Artemis. Their son was Arkas,

Kallisto and Artemis (Zeus), with Eros looking on.

Eagle (Zeus) abducting Ganymedes.

Europê and the bull (Zeus).

eponymous ancestor of the Arcadians (Apollodoros *Library* 3.8.2). Attracted to
the mortal maiden Europê (Latinized form = Europa), he initially assumed the
form of a tame white bull. When she was induced to sit on the animal's back, it
leaped into the sea and swam to Crete, carrying Europê on its back. There Zeus
mated with her, and she bore the sons Minos, Rhadamanthys, and Sarpedon (*Library* 3.1.1). Zeus similarly gained access to Danaê in the form of a golden
shower, to Leda in the form of a swan, to Antiopê in the form of a satyr, and to
Alkmenê in the guise of her husband Amphitryon (cf. Homer *Iliad* 14.317–327).
Many of these myths feature Zeus's wife, Hera, as persecutor of the female with
whom Zeus had sexual relations, whether they were consensual or coerced,
and/or of the offspring. Thus Hera engineered the destruction of the mortal

Semelê, who was having an affair with Zeus, and for a while Hera was hostile to their son, Dionysos.

Zeus's many epithets include Cloud-Gatherer, Delighting-in-Thunder, and Far-Seeing. The Romans identified him with their deity Jupiter (commonly spelled *Juppiter* in Latin) or Jove (Latin *Jovis*). Jupiter is a compound of *dieu* + *pater* (Jove Father).

The god's principal attribute in ancient art is the thunderbolt, which he holds in his right hand like a spear or wand. The weapon is often stylized as a symmetrical object having multiple prongs at

Leda and the swan (Zeus).

each end, like a double-ended lily. Other attributes include a scepter and his regal bird, the eagle. Favorite scenes with artists include the birth of Athena from Zeus's head, the birth of Dionysos from his thigh, and his unusual erotic encounters, such as Europê carried over the sea on the back of a bull and Leda mating with a swan.

See also Hera; Olympians

Suggested reading:

Fulvio Canciani et al. "Iuppiter," in *LIMC* 8:421–470.

Arthur B. Cook. *Zeus: A Study in Ancient Religion.* 3 vols. in 5. Cambridge: Cambridge University Press, 1914–1940.

Timothy Gantz. *Early Greek Myth: A Guide to Literary and Artistic Sources.* Baltimore: The Johns Hopkins University Press, 1993, 57–61.

Erwin Rohde. *Psyche: The Cult of Souls and Belief in Immortality among the Greeks,* trans. by W. B. Hillis. London: Kegan Paul, French, Trubner; New York: Harcourt, Brace, 1925, Appendix 1: "Consecration of Persons Struck by Lightning," 581–582.

Michalis Tiverios et al. "Zeus," in *LIMC* 8:310–374.

4

ANNOTATED PRINT AND NONPRINT RESOURCES

PRINT RESOURCES

Ancient Sources

The most important primary sources of classical mythology available in English translation, arranged in approximately chronological order.

Homer. *The Iliad.*
> Many excellent translations are available of Homer's epic about an incident in the Trojan War, such as those by Lattimore, Fitzgerald, and Fagles. The most extensive scholarly commentary on the poem in English is that edited by G. S. Kirk, *The Iliad: A Commentary*, 6 vols. (Cambridge: Cambridge University Press, 1985–1993).

Homer. *The Odyssey.*
> Again, there are many fine translations of Homer's epic about the return of the hero Odysseus from the Trojan War. The most extensive scholarly commentary on the poem in English is that edited by Alfred Heubeck et al., *A Commentary on Homer's Odyssey*, 3 vols. (Oxford: Clarendon Press, 1988–1992).

Hesiod. *Hesiod's Theogony* [and *Works and Days*]. Translated, with Introduction, Commentary, and Interpretive Essay, by Richard S. Caldwell. Cambridge, MA: Focus, 1987.
> Good rendering into English of the *Theogony* and initial part of the *Works and Days* by the Greek poet Hesiod, with very useful commentary. Outstanding scholarly commentaries on the poems can be found in *Hesiod: Theogony*, edited with Prolegomena and Commentary by M. L. West (Ox-

ford: Clarendon Press, 1966), and *Hesiod: Works and Days*, edited with Prolegomena and Commentary by M. L. West (Oxford: Clarendon Press, 1978).

The Homeric Hymns. Translated, with Notes, by Susan C. Shelmerdine. Newburyport, MA: Focus Books, 1995.

One of several good English renderings of these thirty-three early Greek hymns addressed to different deities. For an excellent exegesis of the longer hymns, see Jenny Strauss Clay, *The Politics of Olympus: Form and Meaning in the Major Homeric Hymns* (Princeton, NJ: Princeton University Press, 1989).

Greek Epic Fragments from the Seventh to the Fifth Centuries B.C. Edited and translated by Martin L. West. Cambridge, MA: Harvard University Press, 2003.

Greek text and facing translation of the fragments of the Epic Cycle and other early Greek epics. Malcolm Davies, *The Greek Epic Cycle,* 2nd ed. (London: Bristol Classical Press, 1989), gives a succinct survey of the cycle.

Pindar. *The Odes and Selected Fragments.* Translated by G. S. Conway and Richard Stoneman; edited by Richard Stoneman. The Everyman Library. London: J. M. Dent; Rutland, VT: Charles E. Tuttle, 1997.

Translation, with brief notes, of the Greek lyric poet Pindar.

Aeschylus, Sophocles, and Euripides.

Many fine translations are available of the Greek tragedians, who set most of their dramas in the heroic period.

Palaephatus [Palaiphatos]. *On Unbelievable Tales.* Translation, Introduction, and Commentary by Jacob Stern. Wauconda, IL: Bolchazy-Carducci, 1996.

Greek text, translation, and brief commentary upon the fifty-two mythological narratives and interpretations by the Greek mythographer and theorist.

Apollonius of Rhodes. *The Voyage of Argo: The Argonautica.* Translation and Introduction by E. V. Rieu. Harmondsworth, UK: Penguin, 1959.

English rending of a literary epic on the voyage of Jason and the Argonauts.

Star Myths of the Greeks and Romans: A Sourcebook Containing The Constellations *of Pseudo-Erastosthenes and the* Poetic Astronomy *of Hyginus.* Translation and Commentary by Theony Condos. Grand Rapids, MI: Phanes Press, 1977.

English translation of, and commentary for the general reader upon, two ancient Greek treatises on catasterisms, or mythological accounts of the origins of the constellations.

Diodorus of Sicily. With an English Translation by C. H. Oldfather. Volumes 1–3. Cambridge, MA: Harvard University Press, 1933–1939.
    Greek text and facing English translation of the mythological portion of *The Library of History* by the Greek historian Diodorus Siculus.

Erotika Pathemata: The Love Stories of Parthenius. Translated, with Notes and an Afterword, by Jacob Stern. New York: Garland, 1992.
    Thirty-six romantic legends compiled by the Greek mythographer Parthenios. For a scholarly edition with Greek text, English translation, and commentary, see *Parthenius of Nicaea: The Poetical Fragments and the Erotika Pathemata*, edited with introduction and commentaries by J. L. Lightfoot (Oxford: Clarendon Press, 1999).

The Narratives *of Konon*. Text, Translation, and Commentary of the *Diegeseis* by Malcolm Kenneth Brown. Munich: K. G. Saur, 2002.
    Greek text, translation, and scholarly commentary upon the fifty mythological narratives compiled by the mythographer Konon and preserved in an abridgement.

Virgil. *Aeneid*.
    Many excellent translations are available of this Roman literary epic recounting the escape of a band of Trojans from the fallen city of Troy and their resettlement in Italy.

Ovid. *Metamorphoses*. Translated by Rolfe Humphries. Bloomington: Indiana University Press, 1955.
    One of several pleasant renderings into English of the Roman poet's charming mythological epic, consisting of hundreds of Greek and Roman myths and legends thematically linked by the motif of transformation.

Ovid. *Ovid's Fasti: Roman Holidays*. Translated and edited by Betty Rose Nagle. Bloomington: Indiana University Press, 1995.
    Fine English rendering of another important mythological poem by Ovid. For a scholarly commentary, see *The Fasti of Ovid*, edited with translation and commentary by James G. Frazer, 5 vols. (London: Macmillan, 1929).

Apollodorus. *The Library of Greek Mythology.* Translated, with an Introduction
and Notes, by Robin Hard. Oxford: Oxford University Press, 1997.
> Translation, with notes for the general reader, of the work of the important
> Greek mythographer Apollodoros (Latinized = Apollodorus), who recounts
> Greek traditions as a continuous narrative from the beginning of the cos-
> mos to the end of the heroic age. For an earlier translation with Greek text
> and outstanding scholarly notes, see *Apollodorus: The Library,* with an
> English translation by Sir James George Frazer, 2 vols. (London: William
> Heinemann; Cambridge, MA: Harvard University Press, 1921).

Hyginus. *The Myths of Hyginus [Fabulae; Poetic Astronomy].* Translated and
edited by Mary Grant. Lawrence: University of Kansas Press, 1960.
> Translation of and scholarly notes on two mythological works in Latin
> that have come down under the name of Hyginus: *Genealogies* (called usu-
> ally *Fabulae,* or *Tales*), a mythological dictionary of some 277 entries; and
> Book Two of *Poetic Astronomy,* a compilation of forty-three catasterisms.

Pausanias. *Guide to Greece.* Translated, with an Introduction, by Peter Levi, S.J.
2 vols. Harmondsworth, UK: Penguin, 1971.
> Translation, with brief notes for the general reader, of the report by the
> Greek writer Pausanias of his travels around Greece, in which he describes
> sites and records regional traditions. For an extensive scholarly commen-
> tary with illustrations, see *Pausanias's Description of Greece,* translated
> with a commentary by J. G. Frazer, 6 vols. (London: Macmillan, 1898).

Antoninus Liberalis. *The Metamorphoses of Antoninus Liberalis: A Translation
with a Commentary.* Translated by Francis Celoria. London: Routledge, 1992.
> English translation, with a commentary for the general reader, of a Greek
> compilation of forty-one myths and legends featuring transformations.

Quintus of Smyrna. *The War at Troy: What Homer Didn't Tell.* Translated, and
with an Introduction and Notes, by Frederick M. Combellack. Norman:
University of Oklahoma Press, 1968.
> English rendering of Quintus Smyrnaeus's *Posthomerica.*

Fabius Fulgentius. *Fulgentius the Mythographer.* Translated from the Latin,
with Introductions, by Leslie G. Whitehead. Columbus: Ohio State University
Press, 1971.

English translation of the *Mythologiae,* or *Mythologies,* a handbook by the fifth-century Christian mythographer Fulgentius, a retelling of pagan myths and legends with allegorical interpretations.

Nevio Zorzetti, ed., and Jacques Berlioz, trans. *Le Premier Mythographe du Vatican.* Paris: Belles Lettres, 1995.

Latin text and French translation of the so-called First Vatican Mythographer, anonymous Latin author of a late handbook of classical mythology, organized as a lexicon.

Reference Works (Excluding the Visual Arts)

Bonnefoy, Yves, compiler. *Mythologies.* Translated under the direction of Wendy Doniger. 2 vols. Chicago: University of Chicago Press, 1991.

Translation from the French of the monumental *Dictionnaire des mythologies et des religions des sociétés traditionnelles et du monde antique* (1981). Of particular interest are Part 2 (The Ancient Near East), Part 4 (Greece), Part 5 (Rome), and Part 6 (Western Civilization in the Christian Era). The lexical entries deal generously with both themes and characters.

Brazouski, Antoinette, and Mary J. Klatt. *Children's Books on Ancient Greek and Roman Mythology: An Annotated Bibliography.* Westport, CT: Greenwood Press, 1994.

History of classical mythology in children's literature in the United States, together with an annotated list of children's books treating classical mythology.

Carnoy, Albert. 1957. *Dictionnaire étymologique de la mythologie gréco-romaine.* Louvain, Belgium: Éditions Universitas.

Etymological dictionary of the principal characters of classical mythology and/or of Greek and Roman cult. Some toponyms and objects are also included.

Gantz, Timothy. *Early Greek Myth: A Guide to Literary and Artistic Sources.* Baltimore: The Johns Hopkins University Press, 1993.

Outstanding narrative survey of the texts and illustrations of early Greek myth and heroic legend.

Grant, Michael, and John Hazel. *Who's Who in Classical Mythology*. London: Weidenfeld and Nicolson, 1973.
> Reliable dictionary of classical mythology.

Grimal, Pierre. *The Penguin Dictionary of Classical Mythology*. Edited by Stephen Kershaw from the translation of A. R. Maxwell-Hyslop. London: Penguin Books, 1991.
> Concise edition and translation of Pierre Grimal's *Dictionnaire de la mythologie grecque et romaine* (1951), the standard lexicon of classical mythology in French.

Hansen, William. *Ariadne's Thread: A Guide to International Tales Found in Classical Literature*. Ithaca, NY: Cornell University Press, 2002
> Mini-encyclopedia of classical myths and legends that are international stories.

Mayor, Adrienne. "Bibliography of Classical Folklore Scholarship: Myths, Legends, and Popular Beliefs of Ancient Greece and Rome." *Folklore* 111 (2000): 123–138.
> Annotated compilation of books and articles that bridge the disciplines of classics and folklore.

Murr, Josef. *Die Pflanzenwelt in der Griechischen Mythologie*. Groningen, Netherlands: Verlag Bouma's Boekhuis, 1969 [1890].
> Lexicon of the trees, shrubs, herbs, and flowers that appear in Greek mythology.

Preller, Ludwig. *Griechische Mythologie*, revised by Carl Robert. 4th ed. 3 vols. Berlin: Weidmannsche Buchhandlung, 1894–1926.
> Survey of Greek myth and heroic legend, with scholarly commentary. An old standard.

Roscher, W. H., ed. *Ausführliches Lexikon der griechischen und römischen Mythologie*. 7 vols. Leipzig: B. G. Teubner, 1884–1937.
> The most extensive dictionary of classical mythology ever published. Richly illustrated.

Thompson, Stith. *A Motif-Index of Folk-Literature: A Classification of Narrative Elements in Folktales, Ballads, Myths, Fables, Mediaeval Romances,*

Exempla, Fabliaux, Jest-Books and Local Legends. Rev. ed. 6 vols.
Bloomington: Indiana University Press, 1955–1958.

> Folkloric classification of recurrent narrative motifs in traditional litera-
> ture from all parts of the world, with bibliography of sources and scholar-
> ship.

Tripp, Edward. *The Meridian Handbook of Classical Mythology.* New York:
New American Library, 1974.

> A reprint of *Crowell's Handbook of Classical Mythology* (1970), an espe-
> cially useful and trustworthy dictionary of classical mythology. The en-
> tries include references to the principal ancient sources.

Vernant, Jean-Pierre. *The Universe, the Gods, and Men: Ancient Greek Myths,*
translated by Linda Asher. New York: HarperCollins, 2001.

> Charming retelling and personal exegesis of Greek mythology from the
> birth of the universe to the era of the heroes, by a prominent French
> mythologist.

Classical Mythology and the Arts

Agard, Walter R. *Classical Myths in Sculpture.* Madison: University of
Wisconsin Press, 1951.

> Sculpture inspired by classical mythology, from antiquity to the present
> day.

Carpenter, T. H. *Art and Myth in Ancient Greece: A Handbook.* London:
Thames and Hudson, 1991.

> Surveys the treatment of Greek myth and legend by Greek visual artists.

De Carolis, Ernesto. *Gods and Heroes in Pompeii.* Translated by Lori-Ann
Touchette. Los Angeles: The J. Paul Getty Museum, 2001.

> Popular survey of Pompeiian frescoes with mythological subjects. Richly
> illustrated.

Fabre-Serris, Jacqueline. *Mythologie et littérature à Rome: La réécriture des
myths aux 1ers siècles avant et après J.-C.* Lausanne: Editions Payot, 1998.

> Roman rewriting and reinterpretation of Italian legends and Greek
> mythology.

Henle, Jane. *Greek Myths: A Vase Painter's Notebook.* Bloomington: Indiana University Press, 1973.
> Traces the modes of mythological illustration on Greek vases from the eighth to the fourth century B.C., concluding with a useful index of iconographic types.

Impelluso, Lucia. *Gods and Heroes in Art.* Edited by Stefano Zuffi; translated by Thomas Michael Hartmann. Los Angeles: The J. Paul Getty Museum, 2002.
> Richly illustrated dictionary of classical deities, heroes, and heroines in Renaissance, Baroque, and Neoclassical art, with helpful explanations of the iconographical conventions.

Keuren, Frances van. *Guide to Research in Classical Art and Mythology.* Chicago: American Library Association, 1991.
> Helpful guide to the use of reference tools for research in ancient iconography and mythology.

Koortbojian, Michael. *Myth, Meaning, and Memory on Roman Sarcophagi.* Berkeley: University of California Press, 1995.
> Roman transformation of Greek myths and legends on sarcophagi.

Leach, Eleanor W. "Imitation or Reconstruction: How Did Roman Viewers Experience Mythological Painting?" In *Myth: A New Symposium,* edited by Gregory Schrempp and William Hansen, 183–202. Bloomington and Indianapolis: Indiana University Press, 2002.
> Exploration of how Romans responded to and evaluated wall-paintings of mythological scenes.

Lexicon Iconographicum Mythologiae Classicae (LIMC), edited by Hans Christoph Ackermann and Jean-Robert Gisler. 8 vols. Zurich: Artemis Verlag, 1981–1997.
> The most extensive resource available for the investigation of classical mythology in ancient art. Four volumes consist of text, with alphabetically arranged entries; the remaining four contain black-and-white illustrations keyed to the entries in the text volumes. Entries are written in English, German, French, or Italian, depending upon the nationality of the author of each entry.

March, Jennifer R. *The Creative Poet: Studies on the Treatment of Myths in Greek Poetry.* London: University of London, Institute of Classical Studies, 1987.
> Chronological study of five legends set in the heroic period, those concerning Peleus and Achilleus, Meleager, Deianeira and Herakles, Klytaimnestra and Orestes, and Oedipus, with close attention to the original texts.

McDonald, Marianne. *Sing Sorrow: Classics, History, and Heroines in Opera.* Westport, CT: Greenwood Press, 2001.
> Influence of classical culture, including mythology, on opera.

Poduska, D. M. "Classical Myth in Music: A Selective List." *Classical World* 92 (1999): 195–276.
> List of characters from classical mythology given musical treatment, with references to compact discs. Supplements the list by Reid and Rohmann (see following).

Reid, Jane Davidson, with Chris Rohmann. *The Oxford Guide to Classical Mythology in the Arts, 1300–1990s.* 2 vols. Oxford: Oxford University Press, 1993.
> Extensive lexicon of classical mythology in literature, music, and the visual arts from the medieval period to modern times. Volume 2 contains a rich bibliography.

Rochelle, Mercedes. *Mythological and Classical World Art Index: A Locator of Paintings, Sculptures, Frescoes, Manuscript Illuminations, Sketches, Woodcuts and Engravings Executed 1200 B.C. to A.D. 1900, with a Directory of the Institutions Holding Them.* Jefferson, NC: McFarland, 1991.
> Lists of artistic treatments of elements of the classical world, including mythological characters, organized as a lexicon.

Schefold, Karl. *Myth and Legend in Early Greek Art.* Translated by Audrey Hicks. London: Thames and Hudson, 1966.
> Surveys Greek mythological art from the eighth century to 560 B.C.

———, with the assistance of Luca Giuliani. *Gods and Heroes in Late Archaic Greek Art.* Translated by Alan Griffiths. Cambridge: Cambridge University Press, 1992.
> Sequel to the foregoing, tracing Greek mythological illustration in the second half of the sixth century B.C.

Shapiro, H. A. *Myth into Art: Poet and Painter in Classical Greece.* London: Routledge, 1994.
>   Compares treatments of the same myths and legends by Greek poets and by Greek vase-painters.

Solomon, Jon. *The Ancient World in the Cinema.* Revised and expanded edition. New Haven: Yale University Press, 2001.
>   Includes a discussion of filmic treatments of classical mythology.

van der Meer, L .B. *Interpretatio Etrusca: Greek Myths on Etruscan Mirrors.* Amsterdam: J. C. Gieben, 1995.
>   Classical mythology etched on bronze mirrors from Etruria.

Weitzmann, Kurt. *Greek Mythology in Byzantine Art.* Princeton, NJ: Princeton University Press, 1984.
>   Greek mythology in Byzantine ivories and illuminated books.

Winkler, Martin M., ed. *Classical Myth and Culture in the Cinema.* Oxford: Oxford University Press, 2001.
>   Fifteen essays by different scholars on classical culture, including mythology, in modern film.

Woodford, Susan. *Images of Myths in Classical Antiquity.* Cambridge: Cambridge University Press, 2003.
>   Richly illustrated discussion of how Greek and Roman artists conveyed mythological narrative in static form, including the development of formulas for depicting particular stories, events, and characters.

Surveys and Studies on Particular Subjects

Blundell, Sue. *The Origins of Civilization in Greek and Roman Thought.* London: Croom Helm, 1986.
>   Discussion of ancient texts concerning the origin of the human race and of the elements of human culture.

Bremmer, Jan, ed. *Interpretations of Greek Mythology.* London: Routledge, 1988.
>   Twelve essays by different scholars on mythological topics.

Brewster, Harry. *The River Gods of Greece: Myths and Mountain Waters in the Hellenic World.* London: I. B. Tauris, 1997.
> Illustrated survey of ancient Greek rivers that were regarded as deities.

Burkert, Walter. *Structure and History in Greek Mythology and Ritual.* Berkeley: University of California Press, 1979.
> Highly original investigation of Greek mythology and ritual.

———. *Greek Religion.* Trans. John Raffan. Cambridge: Harvard University Press, 1985.
> Outstanding survey of ancient Greek religion.

Buxton, Richard. *Imaginary Greece: The Contexts of Mythology.* Cambridge: Cambridge University Press, 1994.
> Study of Greek mythology in its original contexts, both narrative and cultural.

Caldwell, Richard. *The Origin of the Gods: A Psychoanalytic Study of Greek Theogonic Myth.* Oxford: Oxford University Press, 1989.
> Sets forth aspects of psychoanalytic theory and interprets Greek mythology accordingly.

Chance, Jane. *Medieval Mythography.* 2 vols. Gainesville: University Press of Florida, 2000.
> First two of three planned volumes tracing and interpreting the interest in and use of classical mythology by European authors from the fifth to the fifteenth century. Black-and-white illustrations and extensive documentation.

Clay, Jenny Strauss. *The Wrath of Athena: Gods and Men in the* Odyssey. Princeton, NJ: Princeton University Press, 1983.
> Includes discussions of the nature of gods and humans in Greek mythology.

———. *The Politics of Olympus: Form and Meaning in the Major Homeric Hymns.* Princeton, NJ: Princeton University Press, 1989.
> Exegesis of the four longest *Homeric Hymns*, those to Apollon, Hermes, Aphroditê, and Demeter.

Detienne, Marcel. *The Creation of Mythology.* Translated from the French by Margaret Cook. Chicago: University of Chicago Press, 1986.
> Examination of Greek mythology as concept and construct.

———. *The Gardens of Adonis: Spices in Greek Mythology.* Translated from the French by Janet Lloyd. Princeton, NJ: Princeton University Press, 1994.
> Interpretation of the myth and festival of Adonis.

———. *The Writing of Orpheus: Greek Myth in Cultural Context,* translated by Janet Lloyd. Baltimore: The Johns Hopkins University Press, 2003.
> Interpretive essays, several dealing with Greek myth, mythology, and mythography.

Detienne, Marcel, and Jean-Pierre Vernant. *The Cuisine of Sacrifice among the Greeks.* Translated by Paula Wissing. Chicago: University of Chicago Press, 1989.
> Essays by different scholars on Greek sacrifice, including its associated mythology.

Doherty, Lillian E. *Gender and the Interpretation of Classical Myth.* London: Duckworth, 2001.
> Different theoretical approaches to classical mythology viewed by a feminist through the lens of gender studies.

Dougherty, Carol. *The Poetics of Colonization: From City to Text in Archaic Greece.* Oxford: Oxford University Press, 1993
> Study of the mythology of the founding of colonies.

Dowden, Ken. *The Uses of Greek Mythology.* London: Routledge, 1992.
> Introduction to the problems of and scholarly approaches to Greek mythology.

DuBois, Page. *Centaurs and Amazons: Women and the Pre-History of the Great Chain of Being.* Ann Arbor: University of Michigan Press, 1982.
> The mythology of centaurs and Amazons in Greek culture.

Edmunds, Lowell, ed. *Approaches to Greek Myth.* Baltimore: The Johns Hopkins University Press, 1990.
> Eight essays by different scholars, each illustrating a different interpretive approach.

Eisner, Robert. *The Road to Daulus: Psychoanalysis, Psychology, and Classical Mythology.* Syracuse, NY: Syracuse University Press, 1987.
　　Critique of psychoanalytic interpretations of classical mythology.

Foley, Helene, ed. *The Homeric Hymn to Demeter: Translation, Commentary, and Interpretive Essays.* Princeton, NJ: Princeton University Press, 1994.
　　Greek text, English translation, and commentary by Foley, supplemented by essays on the hymn by other scholars.

Fontenrose, Joseph. *Python: A Study of Delphic Myth and Its Origins.* Berkeley: University of California Press, 1959.
　　Comparative study of the Combat Myth in Greece and other societies, beginning with the combat of Apollon and Python.

———. *The Ritual Theory of Myth.* Folklore Studies, 18. Berkeley: University of California Press, 1966.
　　Critique of the ritual theory of myth.

———. *Orion: The Myth of the Hunter and the Huntress.* University of California Publications: Classical Studies, 23. Berkeley: University of California Press, 1981.
　　Study of the mythology of hunting in Greek tradition, with special attention to the hunter Orion.

Forbes Irving, P. M. C. *Metamorphosis in Greek Myths.* Oxford: Clarendon Press, 1990.
　　Excellent survey and interpretation of myths of transformation.

Gentile, Bruno, and Giuseppe Paione, eds. *Il Mito Greco: Atti del Convegno Internazionale (Urbino 7–12 maggio 1973).* Rome: Edizioni dell' Ateneo and Bizzari, 1977.
　　Essays by many scholars, mostly European, on Greek myth and legend.

Gordon, R. L., ed. 1981. *Myth, Religion and Society: Structuralist Essays by M. Detienne, L. Gernet, J.-P. Vernant, and P. Vidal-Naquet.* Cambridge: Cambridge University Press; Paris: Editions de la Maison des Sciences de l'Homme, 1981.
　　Twelve essays on Greek myth by members of the Paris school.

Graf, Fritz. *Greek Mythology: An Introduction*. Translated by Thomas Marier. Baltimore: The Johns Hopkins University Press, 1993.
    Greek mythology in its relationship to festival, history, and literature.

Grant, Michael. *Roman Myths*. New York: Charles Scribner's Sons, 1971.
    Study of Roman legends about Italy and Rome from the arrival of Aeneas to the Roman Republic.

Larson, Jennifer. *Greek Nymphs: Myth, Cult, Lore*. Oxford: Oxford University Press, 2001.
    Study of nymphs in Greek tradition, including mythology.

Lefkowitz, Mary. *Women in Greek Myth*. London: Duckworth, 1986.
    Nonfeminist view of how the Greeks portrayed the female experience in mythology.

Littleton, C. Scott. *The New Comparative Mythology: An Anthropological Assessment of the Theories of Georges Dumézil*. Revised edition. Berkeley: University of California Press, 1973.
    Traces the thought of this prolific and influential scholar of Indo-European comparative mythology.

Mayor, Adrienne. *The First Fossil Hunters: Paleontology in Greek and Roman Times*. Princeton, NJ: Princeton University Press, 2000.
    Argues for a genetic connection between ancient finds of giant bones and fabulous animals in Greek mythology.

Nagy, Gregory. *Greek Mythology and Poetics*. Ithaca, NY: Cornell University Press, 1990.
    Thirteen essays dealing with archaic Greek mythology, ritual, and poetics, with frequent reference to the Indo-European background.

Nilsson, Martin P. *The Mycenaean Origin of Greek Mythology*. New York: W. W. Norton, 1965.
    Argues for the formative influence of the Mycenaean, or Late Bronze, Age upon Greek mythology, showing that most places that are prominent in Greek mythology were important sites in the Mycenaean Age.

Penglase, Charles. *Greek Myths and Mesopotamia: Parallels and Influence in the Homeric Hymns and Hesiod.* London: Routledge, 1994.
> Investigates the extent of Mesopotamian influence on Greek mythology, as seen in early Greek literature.

Puhvel, Jaan. *Comparative Mythology.* Baltimore: The Johns Hopkins University Press, 1987.
> Survey of Indo-European comparative mythology, organized by country (for example, Vedic India, Ancient Rome) and theme (for example, God and Warrior, Twin and Brother).

Romm, James S. *Edges of the Earth in Ancient Thought: Geography, Exploration, and Fiction.* Princeton, NJ: Princeton University Press. 1992.
> Study of the distant regions of the earth and their inhabitants in Greek and Roman tradition.

Saïd, Suzanne. *Approches de la mythologie grecque.* Paris: Nathan, 1993.
> Introduction to the themes, sources, and interpretation of Greek mythology.

Segal, Robert, introducer. *In Quest of the Hero: Otto Rank, Lord Raglan, and Alan Dundes.* Princeton, NJ: Princeton University Press, 1990.
> Reprints of two classic pattern-studies of traditional hero narratives (Rank, Raglan), along with an essay by folklorist Alan Dundes applying the technique to the life of Jesus.

Seznec, Jean. *The Survival of the Pagan Gods: The Mythological Tradition and Its Place in Renaissance Humanism and Art.* Translated by Barbara Sessions. New York: Harper and Brothers, 1961.
> Outstanding study of the transmission and interpretation of classical mythology in the Middle Ages and Renaissance.

Sissa, Giulia, and Marcel Detienne. *The Daily Life of the Greek Gods.* Translated by Janet Lloyd. Stanford, CA: Stanford University Press, 2000.
> Ethnography of the Greek gods as they appear in early Greek epics.

Slater, Philip E. *The Glory of Hera: Greek Mythology and the Greek Family.* Boston: Beacon Press, 1968.
> Psychoanalytic interpretation of Greek myth and legend in relation to the dynamics of the ancient Greek family.

Stafford, Emma. *Worshipping Virtues: Personification and the Divine in Ancient Greece.* London: Duckworth and the Classical Press of Wales, 2000.
    Study of personified abstractions such as Themis (Order) in Greek mythology, cult, and art.

Tyrrell, Wm. Blake. *Amazons: A Study in Athenian Mythmaking.* Baltimore: The Johns Hopkins University Press, 1984.
    Investigation of the legends concerning Amazons in relation to ancient Athenian culture.

Tyrell, Wm. Blake, and Frieda Brown. *Athenian Myths and Institutions: Words in Action.* New York: Oxford University Press, 1991.
    Athenian mythology in its relation to Athenian culture.

Vernant, Jean Pierre. *Myth and Thought among the Greeks.* London: Routledge and Kegan Paul, 1983.
    Fifteen essays on different aspects of Greek mythology and mentality by an influential French scholar.

———. *Myth and Society in Ancient Greece.* Translated by Janet Lloyd. New York: Zone Books, 1988.
    Nine essays on Greek mythology and culture.

Veyne, Paul. *Did the Greeks Believe in Their Myths? An Essay on the Constitutive Imagination.* Translated by Paula Wissing. Chicago: University of Chicago Press, 1988.
    Asks whether the Greeks held their mythological narratives to be true and explores the nature of truth.

Vidal-Naquet, Pierre. *The Black Hunter: Forms of Thought and Forms of Society in the Greek World.* Translated by Andrew Szegedy-Maszak. Baltimore: The Johns Hopkins University Press, 1986.
    Sixteen essays on Greek mythology in its relation to Greek culture.

Von Hendy, Andrew. *The Modern Construction of Myth.* Bloomington: Indiana University Press, 2002.
    Includes a chapter on recent approaches to mythology by classical scholars.

West, M. L. *The Hesiodic Catalogue of Women: Its Nature, Structure, and Origins.* Oxford: Clarendon Press, 1985.

> Study of a mythologically important work by the poet Hesiod that survives only in fragments.

————. *The East Face of Helicon: West Asiatic Elements in Greek Poetry and Myth.* Oxford: Clarendon Press, 1997.

> Study of the extensive parallelism between Greek mythology and the mythological traditions of Anatolia and the ancient Near East.

Wiseman, T. P. *Remus: A Roman Myth.* Cambridge: Cambridge University Press, 1995.

> Examines the development of the Roman legend of Romulus and Remus and its relation to Roman ideology.

NONPRINT RESOURCES

A small selection of the many nonprint resources for classical mythology, excluding videotapes and personal web sites.

The Beazley Archive (http://www.beazley.ox.ac.uk).

> Electronic archive of the Beazley Archive, a research unit of the Faculty of Classics at the Ashmolean Museum, Oxford University, focusing upon Athenian figure-decorated pottery and engraved gems. Accessible materials include images, dictionary, and bibliographies.

Mythology in Classical Art. Sets I–III, each set containing 100 35 mm color slides. Dayton Lab, 3235 Dayton Ave., Lorain, OH 44055. E-mail: dayton@erienet.net. Telephone and fax: (449) 246–1397.

> Vendor: "paintings (not sculpture) depicting scenes from Greek and Roman myth."

The Perseus Project Digital Library. Gregory Crane, editor-in-chief. Tufts University (http://www.perseus.tufts.edu).

> Interactive, multimedia library of textual and visual resources for the study of archaic and classical Greek civilization. Continually being expanded, Perseus now includes also some Latin texts and Renaissance materials.

Jocelyn Penny Small. *Sibyl: The Database of Classical Iconography.* CD-ROM (Windows). University of Pennsylvania Museum of Archaeology and Anthropology, 1999. ISBN 1-931707-10-3.

Database of information about classical mythology and its representation in classical art, providing data on individual objects, by the director of the U.S. Center of the Lexicon Iconographicum Mythologiae Classicae.

Jon Solomon, ed. *Accessing Antiquity: The Computerization of Classical Studies.* Tucson: University of Arizona Press, 1993.

Essays by several scholars on different computer-related projects in classical studies, including several of mythological interest such as Perseus and the Lexicon Iconographicum Mythologiae Classicae.

ABBREVIATIONS AND SELECTED REFERENCE LIST

ABBREVIATIONS

Allen = Allen, Thomas W., ed. 1946. *Homeri Opera.* Vol. 5. Oxford: Clarendon Press.

FGH = Jacoby, Felix, ed. 1926–1958. *Die Fragmente der griechischen Historiker.* 3 vols. in 15. Leiden: Brill (reprint 1954–1960).

Fowler = Fowler, Robert L. 2000. *Early Greek Mythography.* Vol. 1: Texts. Oxford: Oxford University Press.

LIMC = Ackermann, Hans Christoph, and Jean-Robert Gisler. 1981–1997. *Lexicon Iconographicum Mythologiae Classicae.* 8 vols. Zurich: Artemis.

Lobel-Page = Lobel, Edgar, and Denys Page, eds. 1963. *Poetarum Lesbiorum Fragmenta.* Oxford: Clarendon Press.

MW = Merkelbach, R., and Martin L. West, eds. 1967. *Fragmenta Hesiodea.* Oxford: Clarendon Press.

Perry = Perry, Ben E., ed. 1952. *Aesopica: A Series of Texts Relating to Aesop or Ascribed to Him or Closely Connected with the Literary Tradition that Bears His Name.* Urbana: University of Illinois Press.

Roscher = Roscher, W. H., ed. 1884–1937. *Ausführliches Lexikon der griechischen und römischen Mythologie.* 7 vols. Leipzig: B. G. Teubner.

REFERENCES

Conventionally Cited Ancient Texts

Apollodoros *Library* (includes Apollodoros *Epitome,* an ancient summary of a portion of the *Library* that is otherwise lost)

Apuleius *Metamorphoses*

Aristophanes *Birds*

Aristotle *Politics*

Arnobius *Adversus Gentes*

Arrian *Cynegetica (On Hunting)*

Athenaios *Deipnosophistai*

Babrios *Fabulae (Fables)*

Dionysios of Halikarnassos *Roman Antiquities*

Herodotos *Histories*

Hesiod *Theogony, Works and Days, Shield of Herakles*

Isokrates *Panathenaikos*

Kallimachos *Hymns* (sometimes Latinized as Callimachus)

Longos *Daphnis and Chloe* (author's name is sometimes Latinized as Longus)

Lucian *Hermotimos, Lover of Lies, Zeuxis*

Musaios *Hero and Leander*

Nonnos *Dionysiaka* (author's name is sometimes Latinized as Nonnus)

Oppian *Cynegetica (On Hunting)*

Parthenios *Love Stories* (author's name is sometimes Latinized as Parthenius)

Petronius *Satyrica (Satiricon)*

Pindar *Odes* (includes the *Isthmian, Nemean, Olympian,* and *Pythian Odes*) *Paians* (these latter are, strictly speaking, not part of the *Odes;* they survive only in fragments, but translators often include some of them in translations of Pindar's *Odes*)

Plato *Cratylus, Critias, Menexenus, Phaedo, Phaedrus, Politics, Republic, Timaeus*

Pliny *Natural History*

Plutarch *On the Obsolescence of Oracles*

Polyainos *Strategemata*

Pseudo-Eratosthenes *Catasterisms*

Servius *Commentary on Virgil's Aeneid*

Sophocles *Oedipus the King, Trachiniae*

Virgil *Aeneid, Georgics*

Vitruvius *On Architecture*

Xenophon *Anabasis, On Hunting*

Zenobios *Centuriae*

Books and Articles

Allen, Don Cameron. 1963. *The Legend of Noah: Renaissance Rationalism in Art, Science, and Letters.* Urbana: University of Illinois Press.

Bascom, William. 1965. "The Forms of Folklore: Prose Narratives." *Journal of American Folklore* 78, 3–20.

Bauman, Richard. 1984. *Verbal Art as Performance.* Prospect Heights, IL: Waveland Press.

Berger, E. H. 1904. "Mythische Kosmographie des Griechen." In Roscher 7.

Bonnefoy, Yves, comp. 1991. *Mythologies.* Trans. under the direction of Wendy Doniger. 2 vols. Chicago: University of Chicago Press.

Bowra, Cecil M. 1964. "The Meaning of a Heroic Age." In *The Language and Background of Homer,* edited by Geoffrey S. Kirk, 22–47. Cambridge: Heffer; New York: Barnes and Noble.

Bremmer, Jan, ed. 1988. *Interpretations of Greek Mythology.* London: Routledge.

Bremmer, Jan, and N. M. Horsfall. 1987. *Roman Myth and Mythography.* Bulletin Supplement 52. London: Institute of Classical Studies, University of London.

Brown, John. 1968. "Cosmological Myth and the Tuna of Gibraltar." *Transactions of the American Philological Association* 99, 37–62.

Burkert, Walter. 1960–1961. "Elysion." *Glotta* 39, 208–213.

———. 1979. *Structure and History in Greek Mythology and Ritual.* Berkeley: University of California Press.

————. 1985. *Greek Religion.* Trans. John Ruffan. Cambridge, MA: Harvard University Press.

Chance, Jane. 2000. *Medieval Mythography.* 2 vols. Gainesville: University Press of Florida.

Clay, Jenny Strauss. 1983. *The Wrath of Athena: Gods and Men in the* Odyssey. Princeton, NJ: Princeton University Press.

————. 1989. *The Politics of Olympus: Form and Meaning in the Major Homeric Hymns.* Princeton, NJ: Princeton University Press.

Cox, George W. 1883. *An Introduction to the Science of Comparative Mythology and Folklore.* 2nd ed. London: Kegan Paul, Trench.

de Vries, Jan. 1961. *Forschungsgeschichte der Mythologie.* Freiburg, Germany: Karl Alber.

Dilke, Oswald AshtonWentworth. 1998 [1985]. *Greek and Roman Maps.* Baltimore: The Johns Hopkins University Press.

Dover, Kenneth J. 1994. *Greek Popular Morality in the Time of Plato and Aristotle.* Indianapolis, IN: Hackett.

duBois, Page. 1982. *Centaurs and Amazons: Women and the Pre-History of the Great Chain of Being.* Ann Arbor: University of Michigan Press.

Dundes, Alan. 1980. "The Number Three in American Culture." In *Interpreting Folklore,* 134–159. Bloomington: Indiana University Press.

Edmunds, Lowell, ed. 1990. *Approaches to Greek Myth.* Baltimore: The Johns Hopkins University Press.

Edsman, Carl-Martin. 1949. *Ignis Divinus. Le Feu comme Moyen de Rajeunissement et d'Immortalité: Contes Légendes Mythes et Rites.* Lund, Sweden: C. W. K. Gleerup.

Feeney, Denis. 1998. *Roman Literature and Its Contexts.* Cambridge: Cambridge University Press.

Feldman, Burton, and Robert D. Richardson. 1972. *The Rise of Modern Mythology 1680–1860.* Bloomington: Indiana University Press.

Fontenrose, Joseph. 1959. *Python: A Study of Delphic Myth and Its Origins.* Berkeley: University of California Press.

————. 1981. *Orion: The Myth of the Hunter and the Huntress.* University of California Publications: Classical Studies, 23. Berkeley: University of California Press.

Forbes Irving, Paul M. C. 1990. *Metamorphosis in Greek Myths.* Oxford: Clarendon Press.

Fowler, Robert L., ed. 2000. *Early Greek Mythography.* Vol. 1: *Text and Introduction.* Oxford: Oxford University Press.

Frazer, James G. 1898. *Pausanias's Description of Greece.* 6 vols. London: Macmillan.

Gerber, Douglas E., ed. and trans. 1999. *Greek Iambic Poetry.* Cambridge: Harvard University Press, 1999.

Graf, Fritz. 1984. "Women, War, and Warlike Divinities." *Zeitschrift für Papyrologie und Epigraphik* 55, 245–254.

———, ed. 1993. *Mythos in mythenloser Gesellschaft: Das Paradigma Roms.* Stuttgart: B. G. Teubner.

Grant, Michael. 1971. *Roman Myths.* New York: Charles Scribner.

Griffin, Jasper. 1980. *Homer on Life and Death.* Oxford: Clarendon Press.

Gruppe, Otto. 1921. *Geschichte der klassischen Mythologie und Religionsgeschichte während des Mittelalters im Abendland und während der Neuzeit.* Leipzig: B. G. Teubner.

Guthrie, William K. C. 1950. *The Greeks and Their Gods.* Boston: Beacon Press.

———. 1957. *In the Beginning: Some Greek Views on the Origins of Life and the Early State of Man.* Ithaca, NY: Cornell University Press.

Hansen, William. 1996. *Phlegon of Tralles' Book of Marvels.* Exeter: University of Exeter Press.

———. 2002. *Ariadne's Thread: A Guide to International Tales Found in Classical Literature.* Ithaca, NY: Cornell University Press.

Havelok, Erik A. 1987. "The Cosmic Myths of Homer and Hesiod." *Oral Tradition* 2, 31–53.

Heubeck, Alfred, et al. 1988–1992. *A Commentary on Homer's Odyssey.* 3 vols. Oxford: Clarendon Press.

Kellehear, Allan. 1996. *Experiences Near Death: Beyond Medicine and Religion.* Oxford: Oxford University Press.

Kirk, Geoffrey S., ed. 1985–1993. *The Iliad: A Commentary.* 6 vols. Cambridge: Cambridge University Press.

Kirk, Geoffrey S., and J. E. Raven. 1962. *The Presocratic Philosophers.* Cambridge: Cambridge University Press.

Kleingünther, Adolf 1933. *Protos Heuretes: Untersuchungen zur Geschichte einer Fragestellung.* Philologus Suppl. 26. Leipzig: Dieterich'sche Verlagsbuchhandlung.

Larson, Jennifer. 2001. *Greek Nymphs: Myth, Cult, Lore.* Oxford: Oxford University Press.

Lévi-Strauss, Claude. 1979. *Myth and Meaning.* New York: Schocken Books.

Littleton, C. Scott. 1973. *The New Comparative Mythology: An Anthropological Assessment of the Theories of Georges Dumézil.* Rev. ed. Berkeley: University of California Press.

Lovejoy, Arthur O., and George Boas. 1997 [1935]. *Primitivism and Related Ideas in Antiquity.* Baltimore: The Johns Hopkins University Press.

McDowell, John. 1998. "What Is Myth?" *Folklore Forum* 29, no. 2:79–81.

Nagy, Gregory. 1990. *Pindar's Homer: The Lyric Possession of an Epic Past.* Baltimore: The Johns Hopkins University Press.

Nilsson, Martin P. 1965 [1932]. *The Mycenaean Origin of Greek Mythology.* New York: W. W. Norton.

Olrik, Axel. 1992. *Principles for Oral Narrative Research.* Trans. Kirsten Wolf and Jody Jensen. Bloomington: Indiana University Press.

Palaephatus. 1996. *On Unbelievable Tales.* Translation, Introduction, and Commentary by Jacob Stern. Wauconda, IL: Bolchazy-Carducci.

Panofsky, Dora and Erwin. 1965. *Pandora's Box: The Changing Aspects of a Mythical Symbol.* 2nd ed. revised. New York: Harper and Row.

Philippson, Paula. 1936. *Genealogie als mythische Form: Studien zur Theogonie des Hesiod.* Oslo: A. W. Brøgger.

Puhvel, Jaan. 1987. *Comparative Mythology.* Baltimore: The Johns Hopkins University Press.

Richlin, Amy. 1992. "Reading Ovid's Rapes." In *Pornography and Representation in Greece and Rome,* edited by Amy Richlin, 158–179. Oxford: Oxford University Press.

Robertson, Donald S. 1951. "Prometheus and Chiron." *Journal of Hellenic Studies* 71, 150–155.

Rohde, Erwin. 1925. *Psyche: The Cult of Souls and Belief in Immortality among the Greeks.* Trans. W. B. Hillis. London: Kegan Paul, Trench, Trubner; New York: Harcourt, Brace.

Romm, James S. 1992. *The Edges of the Earth in Ancient Thought: Geography, Exploration, and Fiction.* Princeton, NJ: Princeton University Press.

Schrempp, Gregory, and William Hansen, eds. 2002. *Myth: A New Symposium.* Bloomington: Indiana University Press.

Sebeok, Thomas A., ed. 1965. *Myth: A Symposium.* Bloomington: Indiana University Press.

Seznec, Jean. 1961. *The Survival of the Pagan Gods: The Mythological Tradition and Its Place in Renaissance Humanism and Art.* Trans. Barbara Sessions. New York: Harper and Brothers.

Sissa, Giulia, and Marcel Detienne. 2000. *Daily Life of the Greek Gods.* Trans. Janet Lloyd. Stanford, CA: Stanford University Press.

Snowden, Frank M., Jr. 1970. *Blacks in Antiquity: Ethiopians in the Greco-Roman Experience.* Cambridge, MA: Harvard University Press.

———. 1983. *Before Color Prejudice: The Ancient View of Blacks.* Cambridge, MA: Harvard University Press.

Strutynski, Udo. 1975. "Germanic Divinities in Weekday Names." *Journal of Indo-European Studies* 3, 368–384.

Tester, Jim. 1987. *A History of Western Astrology.* New York: Ballantine.

Thalmann, William G. 1984. *Conventions of Form and Thought in Early Greek Poetry.* Baltimore: The Johns Hopkins University Press.

Thieme, Paul. 1968. "Hades." In *Indogermanische Dichtersprache,* edited by Rüdiger Schmitt, 133–153. Darmstadt: Wissenschaftliche Buchgesellschaft.

Thompson, Stith. 1955–1958. *A Motif-Index of Folk-Literature: A Classification of Narrative Elements in Folktales, Ballads, Myths, Fables, Mediaeval Romances, Exempla, Fabliaux, Jest-Books and Local Legends.* Rev. ed. 6 vols. Bloomington: Indiana University Press.

Thomson, George. 1972. *The Greek Language.* Cambridge: W. Heffer and Sons.

Turnbull, Colin M. 1961. *The Forest People: A Study of the Pygmies of the Congo.* New York: Simon and Schuster.

Tyrrell, Wm. Blake. 1984. *Amazons: A Study in Athenian Mythmaking.* Baltimore: The Johns Hopkins University Press.

Veyne, Paul. 1988. *Did the Greeks Believe in Their Myths? An Essay on the Constitutive Imagination.* Trans. Paula Wissing. Chicago: University of Chicago Press.

Vidal-Naquet, Pierre. 1986. "Divine Time and Human Time." In *The Black Hunter: Forms of Thought and Forms of Society in the Greek World,* trans. Andrew Szegedy-Maszak, 39–60. Baltimore: The Johns Hopkins University Press.

Von Hendy, Andrew. 2002. *The Modern Construction of Myth.* Bloomington: Indiana University Press.

Watkins, Calvert. 1970. "Language of Gods and Language of Men: Remarks on Some Indo-European Metalinguistic Traditions." In *Myth and Law among the Indo-Europeans: Studies in Indo-European Comparative Mythology,* edited by Jaan Puhvel, 1–17. Berkeley: University of California Press.

West, Martin L., ed. and comm. 1966. *Hesiod: Theogony.* Oxford: Clarendon Press.

———. 1978. *Hesiod: Works and Days.* Oxford: Clarendon Press.

Wiseman, Timothy P. 1994. *Historiography and Imagination.* Exeter: University of Exeter Press.

———. 1995. *Remus: A Roman Myth.* Cambridge: University Press.

Woodford, Susan. 2003. *Images of Myths in Classical Antiquity.* Cambridge: Cambridge University Press.

Zaleski, Carol. 1987. *Otherworld Journeys: Accounts of Near-Death Experience in Medieval and Modern Times.* Oxford: Oxford University Press.

Zerubavel, Eviatar. 1985. *The Seven Day Circle: The History and Meaning of the Week.* New York: Free Press; London: Collier Macmillan.

———. 2003. *Time Maps: Collective Memory and the Social Shape of the Past.* Chicago: University of Chicago Press.

GLOSSARY

Aition Cause of something (Greek *aition* = cause), the key element in an aetiological narrative. Thus Athena transformed the boastful weaver Arachnê into a spider, and for this reason spiders weave webs.

Allegory, or **allegorism** A particular strategy for the interpretation of mythological narratives. It makes the assumption that the composer of the story deliberately intended two levels of meaning, a surface level that should be accessible to everyone and a hidden or subtextual level that should be accessible only to a few; the latter was the truer and more important message of the narrative. The earliest Greek terms for this notion were *hyponoia* "underthought" and *allegoria* "other-say."

Anthropomorphism Attribution of human characteristics, especially human form, to nonhuman entities. For example, Ouranos (Sky) thinks, feels, and behaves much like a human male.

Apotheosis Conversion into a god. The mortal woman Ino leaped into the sea and became Leukothea, the White Goddess.

Apotreptic narrative Cautionary story. My term for a correlative to protreptic narrative.

Attribute Feature such as an object that is associated with and serves to identify a mythological being in verbal narrative and/or visual art. For example, the trident is an attribute of Poseidon (Neptune).

Autochthonous Indigenous to a place. The Athenians claimed that their ancestors emerged from the earth in the region later known as Attica, where they dwelled.

Binatural being Term I have devised to denote a being who fully combines two different natures. A nonanthropomorphic thing is treated as fully having both its own proper characteristics and also those proper to human beings. For example, Gaia is both the physical earth and also a living anthropomorphic female being capable of thoughts, emotions, and sexual reproduction. Compare **composite being**.

Cautionary story Narrative that links a particular behavior with a negative outcome, as though to illustrate the harmful consequences of a form of ac-

363

tion. Such a story can be employed by a narrator as a warning against adopting such behavior. See also **apotreptic narrative**.

Centauromachy   Battle with centaurs, usually referring to the battle of the centaurs and the Lapiths, a human group.

Chaos   Originally: a chasm; that is, bounded space. Later the word came to signify a state of utter disorder and confusion. Mythologists use the word generically to denote the initial state or being in a mythic cosmogony.

Composite being   Term I have devised to denote a fabulous being consisting of parts of two or more naturally occurring creatures in a complementary relationship. For example, a centaur is an incomplete man and an incomplete horse, having the head and upper body of a man joined to the trunk and legs of a horse. Similarly, a sphinx combines parts of a human being (head), a lion (body), and sometimes a bird (wings). Compare **binatural being**.

Cosmogony   Birth or coming into being of the world, or cosmos. A cosmogonic myth recounts how the world came into being and acquired its present nature.

Cosmology   Structure and nature of the world. Mythological cosmology refers to the physical world as it is represented in mythological narrative.

Cosmos   Physical world viewed as an integrated, orderly system.

Epiphany   Appearance of a deity to one or more human beings. The deity manifests himself or herself in some form and makes his or her identity known. Thus Aphroditê, after taking the form of a maiden and seducing the mortal Anchises, appears to him again in a form that he immediately recognizes as that of the goddess Aphroditê, and she addresses him in the person of the goddess.

Euhemerism   Term for a particular interpretive strategy for understanding religion and mythology. It assumes that gods (or particular gods) are deified human beings and that the stories told of them are therefore exaggerated accounts of actual deeds. Euhemerism is a form of rationalism, like palaephatism. The term comes from the ancient Greek author Euhemeros, author of a novel entitled *Sacred Scripture*, which is no longer extant.

Folktale   Traditional story that, because it makes no earnest claim to historicity, is told typically of unnamed characters and set in the timeless past. Folktales are recounted primarily to entertain or to point a moral.

Genre   One of several principal classes of traditional narrative. Some scholars, including myself, distinguish three broad classes: myth, legend, and folktale, with subdivisions in each class (for example, heroic legend). Others distinguish only two categories: myth and folktale.

Gigantomachy   Battle with the Giants (Greek *Gigantes*), referring to the battle of the Giants and the Olympian gods.

Heroic legend   Subset of legend dealing with the heroes, or demigods, of the heroic age and their contemporaries, such as the legend of Perseus.

Internalization/externalization of properties   Terms I have used to denote a quality (usually a power) of a character as being an inherent property or as being something external to which the personage has access. For example, Aphroditê is irresistibly seductive because she is beautiful and sensuous (internalized quality) or because she possesses a wondrous garment, the cestus (externalized quality). Once they mature, the Olympian gods do not age because that is the nature of gods (internalized) or because they consume the wonder-foods nectar and ambrosia (externalized).

Katabasis   Descent. In mythological contexts, a katabasis refers to a journey undertaken by a hero to Erebos, the realm of the death, in quest of someone or something, as when Orpheus attempted to retrieve his deceased wife, Eurydikê, from among the dead.

Legend   Traditional story that typically is set in the relatively recent past, is recounted of named characters, and makes a claim to historicity. A subset of legend is *heroic legend,* a story set in the age of heroes, or demigods.

Myth   Traditional story that typically is set in the relatively distant past, is told of named characters such as gods and monsters, and makes a claim to historicity. Frequently it is not only primordial in its setting but also foundational in that it may recount how something came to be established as a feature of the world order. Some stories of the gods, however, are set in the recent past.

Mythographer   Person who records mythological narratives in writing. The ancient mythographer Apollodoros composed the *Library,* a synthetic account of Greek mythology in the form of a continuous narrative. The mythographer Hyginus compiled the *Fabulae,* or *Tales,* a lexicon of classical mythology.

Mythologist   Scholar of mythology as an object of study.

Mythology   Traditional prehistory of a people in narrative form. Also, the study of such narratives.

Once-and-always (or *semel ac semper*) **principle**   My term for a compositional pattern in myths according to which a particular action on a particular occasion establishes a principle that cannot be changed or a precedent that cannot be broken. Usually no explanation is given for the rule, which is implicit. For example, once the gods induce Epimetheus (a member of the community of men) to accept Pandora (the first human woman), women must hereafter always be part of the community of men, for a principle is established that is somehow irreversible.

Palaephatism   Rationalist strategy for the interpretation of mythology. It assumes that fabulous narrative elements arose through human misunderstanding of external phenomena and of the usage of language. For example, male warriors wearing long robes gave rise to the idea of a nation of female warriors, the Amazons. The term derives from Palaephatus (Greek Palaiphatos), author of a work *On Incredible Stories,* who explains the fabulous elements in Greek legends by this method; however, he himself did not invent rationalist explanations, which can be found in earlier authors. Palaephatism is the ancestor of mythological interpretations such as euhemerism that explain myths and legends as distorted history.

Parthenogenesis   Production of offspring by a being without sexual intercourse with another being. Parthenogenesis is characteristic of myths set in the early days of the cosmos, before the availability of sexual partners for the first beings or before the establishment of the present order with current rules of sexuality.

Pattern number (also called cultural number, formulistic number, and sacred number)   Culturally preferred number. For example, like other Indo-Europeans, the Greeks and Romans make a frequent use of three and its multiples, and triads are very common in mythology (three Graces, three Fates, three Hundred-Handers, and so on).

Protreptic narrative   My term for a narrative that links a particular behavior with a positive outcome, as though to illustrate the beneficial consequence of a particular form of action. The opposite is a cautionary, or apotreptic, story.

Quest-object   Rare and/or desirable object, difficult to obtain, that a hero undertakes to acquire. For example, Jason and the Argonauts sailed to Colchis in quest of the Golden Fleece.

Reification   Treatment of a nonphysical thing such as an abstraction as having material existence. When the god Zeus became angry at mankind, he concealed fire from them, but Prometheus stole it and made it available to the human community. Here fire is treated as an object that can be hidden and stolen.

Scholiast   Ancient commentator who has annotated an author's work by writing notes, known as scholia, in the margin or between the lines of a manuscript. Although scholia are usually anonymous and undatable, they sometimes contain valuable information such as summaries of myths and legends that are otherwise unknown to us.

Theogony   Birth or coming into being of the gods.

Titanomachy   Battle with the Titans, referring to the ten-year battle of the Titans and the Olympian gods.

Type   Traditional plot realized in different texts. For example, the sequence of action in the deluge myths of the Mesopotamians, Hebrews, and Greeks is so similar that the myths of a great flood in these societies must be regarded as different forms of the same migratory story; that is, they are variants of a single myth-type.

Page numbers for main entries in 'Deities, Thems and Concepts' or 'Glossary' are in bold.

ABOUT THE AUTHOR

William Hansen is professor of Classical Studies and Folklore and co-director of the program in Mythology Studies at Indiana University, Bloomington. He is the author of *Ariadne's Thread: A Guide to International Tales Found in Classical Literature* (2002), *Anthology of Ancient Greek Popular Literature* (1998), *Phlegon of Tralles' Book of Marvels* (1996), *Saxo Grammaticus and the Life of Hamlet: History, Translation, and Commentary* (1983), and (with Gregory Schrempp) *Myth: A New Symposium* (2002), as well as other works.